IDEAL AND REALITY

IDEAL AND REALITY

SOCIAL AND POLITICAL CHANGE IN MODERN CHINA

1860-1949

Edited by

David Pong

and

Edmund S.K. Fung

UNIVERSITY
PRESS OF
AMERICA

LANHAM • NEW YORK • LONDON

Copyright © 1985 by

University Press of America,® Inc.

4720 Boston Way
Lanham, MD 20706

3 Henrietta Street
London WC2E 8LU England

All rights reserved

Printed in the United States of America

Library of Congress Cataloging in Publication Data
Main entry under title:

Ideal and reality.

   Bibliography: p.
   Includes index.
   1. China—Politics and government—1644-1912.
2. China—Politics and government—1912-1949. 3. China
—Social conditions—1644-1912. 4. China—Social
conditions—1912-1949. I. Pong, David, 1939-
II. Fung, Edmund S. K.
DS754.17.I34   1985   951   85-22785
ISBN 0-8191-4918-7 (alk. paper)
ISBN 0-8191-4919-5 (pbk. : alk. paper)

For Barbara and Lucia

CONTENTS

Foreword	*Wang Gungwu*	ix
Preface		xi
1	Social and Political Change in Modern China: Framework, Themes and Highlights *David Pong and Edmund S.K. Fung*	1

Part 1: Reformist Ideas, Changing Concepts and Foreign Models

2	The Vocabulary of Change: Reformist Ideas of the 1860s and 1870s *David Pong*	25
3	Changing Concepts of the Role of Women from the Late Qing to the May Fourth Period *Sally Borthwick*	63
4	Lessons from an Italian Connection *Michael R. Godley*	93

Part 2: The State and Policy Implementation

5	The Nationalist State and the Regulation of the Chinese Industry during the Nanjing Decade: Competition and Control in Coal Mining *Tim Wright*	127

CONTENTS

6	Education in the Guomindang Period, 1928-1949 *Colin Mackerras*	153
7	Nationalist Foreign Policy, 1928-1937 *Edmund S.K. Fung*	185

Part 3: Socio-Political Groups and Competition for Power

8	The Treaty Port Commercial Community and the Diplomacy of Chinese Nationalism, 1900-1911 *Louis T. Sigel*	221
9	Some Reflections on Political Change, 1895-1916 *K.S. Liew*	251
10	The Hakka Chinese of Lingnan: Ethnicity and Social Change in Modern Times *S.T. Leong*	287
11	The Chinese Communist Party's Strategy for Galvanising Popular Support, 1930-1945 *K.K. Shum*	327
12	Conclusions *David Pong and Edmund S.K. Fung*	355
Suggested Readings		365
Notes on the Contributors		373
Index		375

FOREWORD

Australian scholarship on modern China did not receive serious support until the arrival of Professor C.P. FitzGerald to the Australian National University and the creation of the Department of Far Eastern History in 1954. The first doctoral candidates were admitted in the 1960s and on graduation several of them began to staff the history departments of various universities around the country. This in turn was supported by new recruitments from abroad, including new appointments to the Department of Far Eastern History both on a permanent and a temporary basis. During the 1970s, this work began to bear fruit and a number of books and monographs were published which reflected the work of the previous decade. The work has continued into the 1980s and this volume of research papers is a fine example of the continued co-operation and support of our colleagues all over Australia which made the 1981 workshop at the ANU such a successful one.

I am particularly grateful to the two editors, Dr. Pong and Dr. Fung, who not only planned and organised the workshop and brought the team of authors together, but also inspired them to turn their original research into thoughtful studies on a common theme. Even more remarkable is their ability to get their colleagues to hold to one theme and distinguish between the ideals which the Chinese elites were able to project and the reality which historical sources reveal. There are many fresh insights here that fellow historians of modern China would greatly appreciate and the overall picture of intelligent and vigorous Chinese leaders of one kind or another struggling to change, or preserve against change, will add considerably to our

FOREWORD

understanding of modern Chinese history. But, most of all, I believe that the ten authors of this volume have also succeeded in producing a book which is valuable for undergraduate classes everywhere. They have avoided both the generalisations of the survey textbooks of modern China and the overwhelming details of large compendia of documents and specialised essays. Their offer of a select number of topics moulded to bring out the theme of contrasting ideal and reality seems to strike a good balance, providing both enough detail to stimulate undergraduate interest and a controlling framework to aid comprehension. This attempt to teach through a skilful and expert use of a wide range of specific examples of Chinese exhortation and endeavour deserves to succeed.

Finally, I must thank the two editors for drawing attention to the way seven universities in Australia have collaborated on this volume: Griffith, Murdoch, New South Wales, Melbourne, Tasmania, Monash and the ANU. There are, of course, several other universities in Australia with much to offer in modern Chinese studies and there will be opportunities in the future for other co-operative efforts to show the direction of teaching and research going on in the country. Ultimately, of course, it must be remembered that the best in scholarship knows no national boundaries. The proof may be found in this volume itself. One of the editors, Dr. Pong, is British-trained and teaches in the United States and came to collaborate on the workshop that produced the volume because he spent three years at the ANU. Several others were also trained in the United States, Britain and Hong Kong before their association with the ANU. And no one can deny the crucial importance to their training of the Chinese collections and archives and the work of Chinese scholars whether in China, Taiwan or Hong Kong. Without the latter, all our work in Australia will remain impoverished. So although we have emphasised that this volume is largely an Australian enterprise, we must also acknowledge its deep and extensive connections with the finest traditions of Chinese scholarship.

Wang Gungwu
Department of Far Eastern History
Australian National University
March 1985

PREFACE

The year 1949 was truly a major, if not the most important, watershed in modern Chinese history. With the founding of the People's Republic of China that year, the Chinese have, for the first time in the modern era, a strong and effective government. To be sure, there have been abrupt changes in public policy and violent shifts in the direction of the nation's development. In spite of that, China still emerges as a power to be reckoned with. Further, with the formal launching of the Four Modernisations (industry, agriculture, science and technology, and defence) in 1978, it would also appear that she is finally and firmly set on a path to wealth and power.

In essence, the search for wealth and power is an expression of Chinese nationalistic consciousness. As such, it has long roots even though the efforts made since 1949 represent a sharp break in both methods and policies from the past. It is therefore no surprise that the present surge towards the Four Modernisations is accompanied by a revived interest among Chinese historians in the achievement and failure of the 'self-strengthening movement'—China's first serious attempt at progress and military might from the 1860s to the 1890s.

Our interest, by contrast, is not tied to political trends. Without exception, all contributors to this volume have developed for over a decade an interest in China's checkered path to wealth and power. Directly or indirectly, we are all searching for an answer to the question why China developed the way it did. Our interest arises also from the belief that what one finds in China today is in many ways related to past efforts. We simply cannot understand contemporary China without a greater appreciation of where the components of its present-day socio-political system came from, even though some of these components may have been the products of lessons learned from past errors and failures. This is the rationale behind our present undertaking.

To gain an insight into the processes of change, we have chosen as our vehicle the relationship between the ideals and aspirations of those Chinese who were concerned about the fate of their country and their attempts to translate their ideas into reality. To illustrate the dynamics of this relationship, we examine the lives of specific groups—government leaders, reformers, elites, women, peasants, and ethnic minorities—and the manner in which they impinged upon the socio-political environment, especially in the areas of public administration, foreign affairs, economy, and social justice.

Despite their importance, many of these topics receive passing mention in general works on modern Chinese history. Their significance is often lost in the course of chronological narrative. In fact, a good number of the topics in this volume have never been dealt with before by Chinese, Japanese or Western scholars. By focusing on the various groups and their struggle to promote change, we hope to provide a fresh perspective on the dynamics of modern Chinese history, to shed new light on some of the protagonists, and to provoke thought and inquiries.

The second, though no less important, reason for our putting this volume together has to do with the fact that all of the contributors are university teachers. We have long felt the gap between scholarship and teaching and lament the years or even decades before the scholar's research finds its way into university text books. We intend to bridge that gap by presenting ten original scholarly studies to the academic community and to the classroom of upper-level undergraduates. For this dual purpose, topics were chosen in terms of historical significance, breadth, and general interest, and the contributors were selected for the strength of their scholarship. Last but not least, we also strove for readability.

Great care was taken in preparing this volume. To ensure that all the above-mentioned objectives were met, a weekend workshop was held in October 1981 at the Australian National University in Canberra to go over the first drafts intensively.

PREFACE

Non-contributing scholars and students were also invited to comment on all the individual contributions. Substantial revisions followed, and some papers were practically rewritten afresh. No effort had been spared.

This volume, however, could not have been completed without the help of a number of people. Our thanks go first of all to Professor Wang Gungwu, who, as a teacher, has a lifelong influence on many of the contributors to the book. His trenchant remarks at the October 1981 workshop had spurred many of us to months of additional research and revision. Subsequently, he graciously wrote the Foreword to the book. We are also deeply indebted to the non-contributing participants at the workshop. In particular, we wish to thank Professor Liu Ts'un-yan for his rich and encyclopaedic mind, Dr Colin Jeffcott for his sharp criticism, and Mr (now Dr) John Fitzgerald for both his critical attitude and his constant reminder of the student's needs. Because so much of the content of this volume was shaped during the workshop, it would be fair to say that we are deeply indebted to one another. In hindsight, that weekend workshop emerges as even more instrumental than we realised at the time. We therefore wish to extend our thanks specially to Professor Sydney Crawcour for his moral support and to the Department of Far Eastern History of the Australian National University for generous financial assistance.

While most of the original manuscripts were typed by the professional staff at the various institutions where we worked, three chapters and the bulk of the duplicating were done in Canberra. We are particularly indebted to Mrs Marion Saville, Mrs Sally Demets and Mrs Marie Short.

The camera-ready manuscript was produced in the School of Modern Asian Studies, Griffith University. Special thanks must go to Mrs Kerrie Gibbon for her excellent typing, and to Mr Jeffrey Russell for his assistance in the computing process and in the preparation of the Index. We are especially grateful to the School of Modern Asian Studies, Griffith University, and the University of Delaware, for their generous financial contributions towards the production of the manuscript.

David Pong	E.S.K. Fung
University of Delaware	Griffith University

May 1985

1

SOCIAL AND POLITICAL CHANGE IN MODERN CHINA FRAMEWORK, THEMES, AND HIGHLIGHTS
David Pong and Edmund S.K. Fung

This volume, comprising ten chapters of original scholarship, aims at providing a fresh perspective on modern Chinese history. In general terms, it focuses on the ideals and aspirations of people in and out of government and on how these people tried to further their objectives. By studying the interplay between ideal and reality in each case, the chapters collectively shed new light on the period 1860-1949 and contribute to a better understanding of the forces that subsequently helped shape China.

In this introductory chapter, we shall first explain why we select the period between 1860 and 1949 for analysis and then explain the dynamics between ideals and aspirations on the one hand and the struggle to realise them on the other. Finally, we shall highlight the findings of each chapter, put them in a broader context, and weave them into a coherent whole.

Framework and Themes

There has been considerable debate among historians as to when modern China began. Some prefer the founding of the Qing dynasty in 1644 on account of the great political changes it introduced which, naturally, had also an important impact on the social structure. Others insist that it began with the Opium War (1839-1842), that first violent encounter between China and the West which symbolises the beginnings of Western domination of the Middle Kingdom and the initial, though limited, Chinese push for the adoption of Western military technology and international law to defend the empire and its civilisation.[1] In the most recent work on the modernisation of China, Gilbert Rozman and his co-authors argue in favour of the eighteenth century, a survey of which allows them to determine China's capacity for change.[2] We certainly benefit from their findings though we may differ in interpretation. But because our concern is with the processes of socio-political change that had a direct impact on developments in the modern era, because these processes did not begin in a more-or-less sustained manner until the early 1860s, and because these changes took place in a much weakened China, not at the height of Qing power in the eighteenth century, we have chosen 1860 as our point of departure, though not necessarily as the 'beginning' of modern China.

Nevertheless, the choice of 1860 has its problems, for the first signs of a political awareness, which led to a growing demand for change, had already appeared in the opening decades of the nineteenth century. These signs were a response to the early omens of dynastic decline. Thus, in contrast to the efforts of the 1860s and after, they represented a purely *indigenous* reformist force. Further, the early proponents of change had a direct influence on the reformist thinking of the post-1860 era. We certainly acknowledge the importance of these early influences. The intellectual and, to a lesser extent, personal linkages between the two eras of reformist thought are therefore highlighted in Chapter 2. As we emphasise the reformers' ties with the past, we also underscore the fact that both the ideas and actions for change after 1860 were a combined response to two very powerful forces: dynastic decline or, after 1911, political and social disintegration, and foreign threats. Since it was this combined response that gave substance to change during and beyond the late Qing, the choice of 1860 as the point of departure is not misplaced.

China's response to foreign threats during and after the Opium War was rather haphazard and limited to isolated individuals. Several factors contributed to this. First, wartime hostilities were restricted mainly to the Guangzhou (Canton) and the Nanjing areas, still far from the imperial capital at Beijing. Second, from the Chinese viewpoint, the war was fought over opium, an issue on which they felt that they had justice on their side. Why, indeed, should one change when one was right? Third, extraterritorial privileges, the most-favoured-nation treatment, and the five ports opened to foreign trade by the Treaty of Nanjing (1842)—the beginnings of the unequal treaties and the treaty port system—could easily be and were actually rationalised in terms of the traditional tributary system. This system, founded on the belief that Chinese civilisation was both superior and universal, justified the management of their affairs with neighbouring states on the basis of paternalism. When foreign demands for greater commercial concessions continued after 1842, thereby exposing the fallacy of that rationalisation, the Beijing court encouraged obstructionism. As the country plunged into chaos as a result of large-scale uprisings in the fifties, foreign affairs received little attention. The throne, in any case, had become vehemently anti-foreign under the Xianfeng emperor (r. 1851-1861).

The impact of the Second Sino-foreign War (1856-1860), the so-called *Arrow* War, was much greater; it lasted longer and wrought greater destruction. The city of Guangzhou was bombarded and captured, as were Tianjin and Beijing. The emperor was forced to flee (he died a broken man in 1861), and his government to make vast concessions. In addition to the five southern ports, eleven others on the Yangzi (Yangtze), on Taiwan, and in the north were opened, including Tianjin, the port city of the imperial capital. Foreigners with passports were permitted to travel and missionaries to own property anywhere in China. The opium trade was legalised. Foreign warships were given the right to visit treaty ports. Further, representatives of the treaty powers were granted the right to reside in Beijing.

Given the fact that China was still deeply troubled by rebellions, especially the Taipings who wrought havoc in the central and the richest provinces of the empire, Chinese official reactions to both the internal and foreign threats in the 1860s were much stronger than those of the preceding decades. This set the stage for the more intense and sustained efforts at dynastic regeneration after 1860.

This volume ends with the founding of the People's Republic in 1949. To go beyond that date will require a much larger effort and probably double the space. This, however, is only a practical consideration.

The promulgation of a New China and new, socialist ideals in 1949 certainly marks the beginning of a new era. Of course, the divorce from the past was not total; many of the forces at work in the last thirty-odd years still have their roots in the past. Thus, we find many end-products of the processes of change from the pre-1949 era are still presenting difficulties for the new government. While mass campaigns were employed to correct or eradicate old injustices, values and vested interests, the state could not do without the expertise and capital acquired by individuals and groups before 1949. The continued employment of these pre-Communist material and human assets has been a matter of some controversy and contributes in no small degree to the frequent policy changes under the Beijing government. Many of these changes were themselves a reflection of old political practices. One of the more noticeable examples is the reliance on personal leadership rather than on law, though, hopefully, the incorporation of the Four Modernisations in the state's constitution (March 1978) would presage a period of steady development.

In a larger sense, efforts at national reconstruction after 1949 can be subsumed under the quest for wealth and power and for reducing the gap between ideal and reality to a tolerable level—goals pursued by successive governments since 1860. There is certainly continuity. Nevertheless, post-1949 China is qualitatively different. Its government is the most powerful one China has ever seen. It is able to assert the nation's sovereignty, avoid defeat, wipe out the grossest forms of socio-economic inequalities, and mobilise human and material resources on a large scale—problems that had been the curse of earlier regimes. And despite the vestigial existence of some old forces, they have not been given the free play that they used to enjoy.

In examining the socio-political changes of the period under review, we focus on the relationship between reality and stated ideals. It is our belief that the gap between the two holds one of the keys to understanding the broad sweep of modern Chinese history. Without pre-empting what is to come, we suggest here that a large gap between ideal and reality would sooner or later generate discontent or even alienation. A situation would then develop in which disaffected groups would claim a larger political say in order to close the gap either through reform or revolution. In this interplay between the power-holders and the disaffected groups, socio-political changes occurred. Any concession by the government of the day was bound to alter the balance of power between itself and the interest groups and, often times, among the interests groups as well. This was exactly what happened throughout much of the late Qing as a result of its limited programme for defence modernisation and industrialisation, and during much of the Republican era as a consequence of the government's support for carefully defined political and economic transformation. An intransigent government, on the other hand, was likely to intensify the strife over the long haul, as was the case with the last decade or so of the Qing over sweeping institutional reforms and the National Government (1928-1949) over socio-political issues as well as over its stance towards Japanese imperialism. Though it is beyond the scope of our investigation, we should note that the gap between ideal and reality continued to create tensions in post-1949 China even if the disaffected groups, by and large, belong to a relatively small (but by no means insignificant) minority.

In the course of our study, a number of questions arise. What were the ideals the Chinese set for themselves and what were the sources of these ideals? Although successive governments subscribed to wealth and power as an ideal, in what ways did their perceptions of it change over time? To what extent were the ideals as defined by the government in power shared by the various components of China's political entity? What exactly was the nature of the discrepancy between ideal and reality in a given period, and to what extent did it affect the course of China's modern history? Finally, what was the environmental context in which changes in both ideal and reality took place? By scrutinising China's recent past in the light of these questions, we hope to contribute to our understanding not only of the history itself but also of the forces that continued to plague or shape China today.

In broad terms, the theme of this volume is to spell out the goals and aspirations of both the state and the socio-political groups within it, and contrast them with the efforts made to realise them. The gap between stated ideals and actual achievements is then explained, first, in terms of strengths and shortcomings inherent in those goals and efforts, and then in terms of the forces and larger environment which impinged upon them. The impact of the gap on future policies and actions will also be discussed. It behooves us to bear in mind that both ideal and reality were changing variables.

Since ideal and reality, like *yin* and *yang*, act upon each other and since an ideal, even if vastly divorced from reality, could provoke reaction, none of the studies in this volume deals exclusively with one or the other. Nevertheless, to underscore the theme, the chapters are divided into three groups. The three chapters following this one, grouped under Part 1, focus on ideals, especially those espoused by the state, tracing some of the important changes from the 1860s to the 1930s (the 1930s was the last time a national government was in any position to set long-term goals). The three chapters in Part 2 deal with the government's attempts to realise its goals. To gain some depth and insight into this problem, we concentrate on the National Government, particularly in the Nanjing decade (1928-1937), that period when pre-1949 China had the greatest chance of success in effecting socio-political change. The final group of four chapters (Part 3) is concerned with the socio-political groups that gained varying degrees of political awareness in the modern era. Here, we examine their ideals and their efforts, culminating in the study on the rise and success of the Chinese Communist Party and the socio-political groups that gave it their support.

This arrangement, clearly, is not chronological. The theme of the book, and the diversity of the topics covered, preclude a strictly chronological approach. In fact, it is not at all our intention to present another chronological survey of modern Chinese history. Rather, as we move away from this conventional approach, we try to provide a new angle in which to interpret and understand modern China.

Highlights of this Volume

The purpose of this section is to bring out the key points of each chapter and to provide the links between the chapters. Further, because the topics dealt with are necessarily selective, editorial remarks have been inserted here and there to put them in a broader perspective. The brief comments are offered here with the full knowledge that they cannot by any means do justice to the richness of each of the studies.

In Chapter 2 David Pong examines intensively the ideas of the reforming officials of the 1860s and 1870s. By tracing the provenance of their ideas, he demonstrates how the officials, by drawing on China's reformist tradition, were able to overcome the narrow confines of Qing orthodoxy and come up with new policy proposals. The constant fear of greater foreign encroachments further increased their efforts at digging deeper into China's past for inspiration and justification for change. In the process, traditional ideas were given new meanings, old precepts for personal cultivation became new concepts for collective regeneration. While groping for methods for collective self-strengthening, they were forced by circumstances to lay down guidelines for practical and long-term planning to identify and remedy China's ills. The willingness to modify established institutions and practices or to create new ones is particularly noteworthy. With rare clarity, this chapter shows the breadth of vision of these men, whose ideas contributed to the evolution of a fundamental and comprehensive 'programme' for change. But for the lack of a strong, steadfast imperial commitment to reform, this 'programme' would have drastically transformed the organisational structure and the administration of the Qing state. Though largely rejected at the time, it foreshadowed many of the later attempts to build a stronger China. These attempts are studied mainly in Chapters 4 to 8, and partially in the other chapters.

Some of the reformers' proposals could well have been voiced to bolster their own interests. Whether such interests were identical to those of the state can be questioned. A number of modern scholars have argued that personal, gentry, or regional power was the main motive behind these reform proposals. Pong agrees that, if implemented, these proposals would have undermined the authority of the Qing court under the Empress-Dowager but contends that they, instead, would have strengthened a reconstituted Manchu dynasty.

The plan for change was based on a composite picture of the reformers' ideas culled from vast amounts of their writings. Could one therefore regard these ideas as a coherent plan? The chapter itself reveals that none of the reformers, with the possible exception of Feng Guifen, was a theorist; they addressed themselves to specific issues. Whether their ideas could be so put together to represent a coherent programme is a matter of historical judgment. It can certainly be argued that had the throne adopted and carried out a substantial portion of their ideas, they would have had the impact of a coherent reform programme.

The throne's partial support for self-strengthening did result in change. Throughout the last half century of the Qing, arsenals and shipyards were built, a government-sponsored merchant shipping company was founded, students were sent abroad and, eventually, Chinese officials also branched out into textile and other commercial enterprises, though still on a small scale. Meanwhile, Western influence centred around the treaty ports increased. At the same time, however, imperialist inroads also intensified. Under these circumstances, marginal as well as established social and political groups began to acquire measures of political awareness. In their eyes, Qing objectives were either inadequate or hollow. They started to search for their own fulfilment. Among them were the treaty-port community and the 'new' gentry (see Chapters 8 and 9). It was in this context, too, that we find the roots of the movement for the emancipation of women.

In Chapter 3, Sally Borthwick analyses the concepts relative to the role of women in traditional times and the changes from the 1890s to the mid-1920s. In her deft examination of traditional literature, history and popular culture, she demonstrates that the requirements of the Confucian family system, though oppressive, were not as rigid and demeaning as missionary and Chinese debunkers of Confucianism at the turn of the century would have us believe. Just as Pong stresses how traditional ideas facilitated the formulation of reformist thought, so Borthwick underscores the readily available indigenous models for change. This applies especially to the issues of foot-binding and female education. It was the failure to curb foot-binding and to channel female education in a direction amenable to Christian influence that made them the foci of missionary activities. But missionary ideas, centred as they were on turning out better wives and mothers, were as narrow as they were conservative. Neither the traditional models nor missionary ideals had much impact on the Chinese thinking until after 1895.

It was the defeat by Japan that year that led some Chinese leaders to recognise the contribution women could make to building a stronger China. Given this concern, it was to be expected that the first reformers, practically all men, called for an improvement in the conditions of women as part of the larger programme to eradicate the ills of China. Foot-binding was attacked along with opium-smoking and beggars. Concern with China's plight and the conditions of upper-class women blinded their vision for change. Better wives and mothers were still their theme. The 'emancipation' of lower-class women was regarded as useful only because they could then be released from traditional obligations to work in factories. Only a bare handful would consider the plight of the masses of working, peasant women and argue for fundamental reforms. Such ideas did not gain currency until the beginning of the May Fourth era (from 1916) when the new political environment and industrialisation demanded broader changes. The atmosphere of the era, particularly in the urban areas, was electrifying, as Borthwick's survey of contemporary publications shows. Be that as it may, old ideas of limited reforms for upper-class women through education and the like, and the use of 'emancipated' women as a work force to strengthen the nation, remained the preoccupation of those who led China into the late 1920s and after. The ideal, new woman as conceived by the state was thus left farther and farther behind by those who wanted a greater degree of liberty and equality. Consequently, an increasing number of women intellectuals and activists began to turn to the political left for leadership.

In 1911 the old imperial order was destroyed, but the search for wealth and power continued, even as Republican China plunged deeper and deeper into warlordism and the Japanese increased their hold on the country. New hopes came with the establishment of the Guomindang (GMD, Nationalist) government in Nanjing in 1928. By the 1920s and 1930s, however, new forces had emerged: communism from within and intensified Japanese aggression from without. Chinese society in general had also become more complex and diversified. Consequently, as Chapter 4 by Michael Godley shows, the Nanjing government had also to find an ideological undergarment for unity and harmony to combat class struggle and for national reconstruction to curb foreign incursions.

The government under Chiang Kai-shek (Jiang Jieshi) found a solution in Mussolini's Italy, which, in GMD eyes, showed the way to new national strength through the revitalisation of a past great civilisation. It was a model China, itself once a great civilisation, could emulate. For some time the GMD leadership, too, had been insisting that a new China could only be built on old values.[3] Be that as it may, the Italian model had several other important features to offer. First, there were the techniques for generating a spirit of dedication and self-sacrifice among the people. Second, it provided the methods for building a highly disciplined and regimented party machinery, one that was almost military in character. Third, it would give this new political system, now espoused by the GMD leadership, an image of a modern and even 'revolutionary' government. And because that system presaged the eventual triumph of the new morality over materialism, it had a role to play in the future of human civilisation. Besides ideology and techniques, there were real material interests in the Italian connection as well—the acquisition of war material, especially planes. Frantic efforts were thus made to cement Sino-Italian relations. Thanks to the Italian desire to increase their international stature in East Asia to demonstrate the universality of their new-found model, the initial results were promising. Deterioration in the international scene eventually brought incompatible national interests to a head. As Mussolini abandoned China for Japan, Italy could no longer serve officially as a model for the Nanjing government.

The search for a strong and united China had its beginnings in the 1860s. The exigencies of the 1930s made it all the more urgent to find the means to realise those aims. In this first concise study of Sino-Italian relationship, Godley has successfully portrayed a main thrust of the GMD's search for an overall ideological basis for this purpose. One may indeed detect from the author's analysis that, so strong was the appeal of a resolute leader and an effective government, a great deal more people were attracted to the Italian model than just those who would reap immediate benefits from such a system. Further, when seen against the fact that there had never been much substance in Sino-Italian relations before the Nanjing decade, the frantic efforts to shore up that friendship also underscore the desperation of the Nationalist government. Nanjing's failure in this attempt brutally exposed the limitations of a weak state.

The special concern of the three chapters in Part 2 is with the implementation of goals that had been formulated and refined since 1860. The chapters deal specifically with the Nanjing government's attempts to promote and regulate the economy, to expand modern education, and to regain full sovereignty as well as to enhance China's international standing. Together, they constitute a study of the ways in which the government tried to mobilise the nation's resources to achieve wealth and power.

With the passage of Confucianism as the state orthodoxy, the Nanjing decade was arguably China's 'last chance' to transform itself without a total destruction of its traditional components. A deeper understanding of the achievements of this period may well hold the key to a balanced view of what went wrong in modern China. To what extent, then, was the Nationalist government able to reduce the gap between ideal and reality to a tolerable level?

To a large extent, modern China's failure to keep abreast with a country like Japan can be attributed to its material backwardness and its inability to generate wealth or mobilise its limited resources to bring about necessary changes. In Chapter 5 Tim Wright looks into this problem by analysing the role of the state in economic development. The GMD came to power in 1928 committed to a programme of reconstruction and economic change. As envisioned by Sun Yat-sen, this entailed state-initiated and -controlled industrialisation. The weakness of the state, however, forced the government to a less direct form of involvement: the *regulation* of private industries through cartelisation.

During the Nanjing decade, cartels were introduced for a number of industries. By and large, as Wright's study shows, the government, through its control over foreign trade licences, procedures and tariff, was more able to influence industries which relied mainly on imported materials and exported finished products than those on domestic resources and markets. The coal industry, which fell into the latter category, illustrates the point. Despite the generally favourable political milieu, the drop in imported coal (brought about by raising tariff) and improved conditions within the coal industry itself, the government's attempt to work with private enterprises to regulate the industry failed. The inability to control entry or expansion of smaller mines—a sure sign of a weak central authority—prevented any nation-wide effort at cartelisation, as did the opposition of the Japanese who controlled much of the Shandong mines. The government was also helpless in pressuring the provinces to fall in line; some even established regional cartels in direct conflict with Nanjing's interests. Together with intra-governmental rivalry, corruption and a weak economy (which resulted in limited demands and insufficient capital), these efforts led to the collapse of Nanjing's efforts. Though the state's power over the economy increased during and after the war against Japan (1937-1945), its control in the preceding decade was extremely weak. Whatever development took place in that period owed little to government action.

The fact that the GMD could not even regulate the modern industrial sector with which it shared many common interests boded ill for its endeavours elsewhere. The failure to harness effectively the resources from that sector and to increase its economic base had a direct and adverse effect on other government measures as well, as the next two chapters will show.

Chapter 6 by Colin Mackerras makes available in English for the first time the history of education in the Republican period. Focusing especially on the government-regulated educational system under the GMD, it addresses the role of that system in shaping Chinese society and political culture.

Educational aims had been spelled out by successive governments since 1911, stressing either the moral, technical and military dimensions of education, as in the early republic, or the cultivation of individualism and democracy, as during the May Fourth era. Under the GMD, the promotion of democracy was mentioned, but the stress was on cultivating a social-minded and nationalistic citizenry. Nationalism, however, was interpreted to mean both love of one's country and loyalty to the party. In real terms, this entailed accepting the GMD's presupposition that the interests of the nation and the party were identical. As Edmund Fung's chapter will show, this also meant the adoption of the official view that support for the government's domestic policies should take precedence over grass-root, violent anti-imperialism.

The Nanjing government aimed at universal primary education, equally accessible to boys and girls, and laid out plans for secondary and tertiary education. The system provided for a large measure of government control down to the county and district levels, including the power to appoint education directors and the use of text books. If successfully implemented, it would have raised the educational level of the Chinese people as never before and could well have contributed to the consolidation of GMD power.

Actual achievements fell far short of the government's goals. Inadequate funding undermined the already weak central authority. But the worst predator of central fiat was the government itself: the small budget was biased in favour of university education, which benefited the urban-based ruling elite at the expense of lower-level schools outside the metropolises. The system was also plagued by corruption and excessive political interference. Consequently, universal primary education remained a myth. The expansion of women's education was even less successful in primary and vocation schools.

Under these circumstances, private schools continued to flourish, but neither the rural-based traditional schools (*sishu*), which fostered the old culturalism, nor the missionary schools, which spread Western ideas, contributed much to promoting modern nationalism or loyalty to the party. Though missionary schools did enroll a high proportion of females, they, especially the Protestant ones, tended to exacerbate the elitism of the government's educational system.

Ironically, it was the Japanese war that brought greater changes and progress to education. The government's withdrawal into the interior brought education to the countryside and exposed Chinese intellectuals to the realities of life in rural areas. Patriotism also led more to seek a means of national salvation through education under a revised, more practical curriculum. But heightened nationalism only increased the disillusionment with the government's role in the War of Resistance. Many felt that nationalism and loyalty to the GMD were simply not coterminous.

The fact that the GMD debacle on the mainland in 1949 was due in large measure to its failure to deal with the fundamental questions of rural reforms is an issue not directly discussed in this chapter. A serious shortcoming of the Nationalist educational system was its irrelevance to the needs of the rural masses. The number of agricultural colleges was infinitesimal. Without government encouragement, the students, given their elitist and urban background, tended to pursue studies leading to careers in the modern sector. The attitude and training of the professors, who hailed from the same social group, also alienated them from China's hinterland. Education never fulfilled that social-harmonising function assigned it by the Nationalist government. Nevertheless, Mackerras concludes that for all its shortcomings education was probably among the GMD's better achievements. Since the implementation of the educational system, unlike the attempt to regulate the coal industry, was generally free from persistent foreign interference, this assessment reflects poorly on the government of the day.

In its handling of foreign relations, the GMD was equally, if not more, helpless. The problem, of which we have already had a foretaste in Godley's chapter, is tellingly illustrated in Chapter 7 by Edmund Fung. The GMD's conduct of foreign affairs was characterised by the absence of a long-term policy. Fung therefore focuses on the short-to-medium-term objectives and their implementation. In general terms, the goal was to secure national independence and international equality which, in short, amounted to the removal of the unequal treaties. The question was essentially one of strategy. While in opposition, when the first united front with the Communists was still in force, the GMD had used mass movements and, at times, mob violence to attain its goals. From 1928 the party leadership, now in government and committed to anti-Communism, concerned itself first and foremost with national reconstruction aided by foreign co-operation. Earlier anti-imperialist aims were kept alive, but they were now to be achieved by negotiation, even though this involved a considerable amount of time.

The new strategy, much criticised by the party's left as betraying the spirit of the Nationalist revolution, involved tortuous negotiations, the success of which depended on the goodwill of the powers. In Fung's description, it was a diplomacy of weakness, one that had precluded the formulation of any long-term policy in the first place. Fortunately, after the Nationalists broke with the Communists and the Soviet Union, the powers, notably Britain and the United States, were prepared to come to terms with Chinese nationalism and the GMD. As a result, Nanjing was able to make significant gains in retrieving tariff autonomy and recovering a number of treaty-port concessions. Negotiations for the abolition of extraterritoriality, though complicated and difficult, were well under way until the Manchurian incident of 1931.

The goodwill of the powers, however, was always subordinated to their self-interests. Whenever the GMD government, under pressure from its left-wing elements and popular nationalistic outcries, was forced to depart from its conciliatory approach, the powers closed ranks. Thus Britain and the United States, their anti-Communism notwithstanding, supported the Soviet Union when the Chinese unilaterally attempted to gain control over the Chinese Eastern Railway in 1929.

Japan was Nanjing's greatest obstacle; its interests and ambitions on mainland Asia were too great to accommodate Chinese nationalist aspirations. The invasion of Manchuria halted Nanjing's drive for treaty revision. Caught between foreign aggression and internal demands for resistance, the GMD, not wishing to fight, drifted from concession to concession. Its repeated call for unity, reconstruction and Communist suppression before resistance sounded increasingly hollow. Ironically, then, the war with Japan, which brought the government closer to its goals in education and economic control, as demonstrated by Mackerras and Wright, also forced the GMD to choose between party interests and national defence and, ultimately, hastened its demise.

Theoretically, one cannot fault the GMD's emphasis on national reconstruction. After all the Japanese had been able to negotiate the abolition of the unequal treaties once the country had put its own house in order. But it had probably escaped the GMD that the case of Japan was different, since Japan had never been exposed to the high level of imperialist encroachment that China experienced. The intensity of Japanese imperialism in China renders the comparison even less tenable. Nevertheless, the GMD's priority on national reconstruction was clear, enjoying the support of the Western powers, whose interests were best served by a stable yet modernising China. And since national reconstruction also depended on Western co-operation, treaty revision through negotiations, not militant anti-imperialism, was the only option available to the GMD, but it was an approach that would eventually cost it considerable political support.

Interestingly, although the Ministry of Foreign Affairs had the best trained staff within the Nanjing administration, it was unable to escape the vices of bureaucratism, corruption and factionalism that permeated every level of government. When further compounded by the GMD's inability to combine party loyalty with nationalism and by an increasingly hostile international environment, the ministry became demoralised.[4]

Chinese Nationalist foreign policy has received relatively little scholarly attention to date. Fung's general account should stimulate further research on the subject using Chinese rather than the more familiar Western or Japanese sources. The view that a weak nation is deprived of effective diplomacy had been expressed by despondent Chinese patriots of the 1930s.[5] Fung's research leads to a similar conclusion. It implies a materialistic view of history which may not be shared by other students of international relations but which will further stimulate scholarly interest.

Part 3 deals with a number of socio-political groups that worked either in tandem or at cross purposes with the government of the day. Contacts with the outside world and the 'self-strengthening movement', despite its limited success, had led to a partial transformation of old social classes and the emergence of new groups, whose interests and aspirations were not necessarily those of the government. The four chapters in this part underscore the chronological development most clearly, beginning with a study of those who supported the government and ending with those who either remained ambivalent or were bent on overthrowing it. Despite changes over time, it is worth noting that the goals, broadly defined, remained consistent: to build a strong China and to rid it of foreign domination. Naturally, the perceptions of the overall problem and the methods with which to resolve it varied from group to group and from one period to another.

In Chapter 8, Louis Sigel examines the rise of a new corps of diplomat-officials in 1900 and their aggressive assertion of China's sovereign rights in both the political and economic spheres. Coming from the treaty-port mercantile community, this new breed of bureaucrats differed in background and outlook from the self-strengthening leaders of the 1860-1895 period. Up to the end of that period, the latter, steadfast in their belief in China's cultural superiority, had relied on the treaty system as 'a bulwark of Chinese territorial integrity and administrative autonomy'. In contrast, the treaty-port elites, far more receptive to Western ideas, had called for far-reaching reforms well before 1895 in order to assert China's national rights. Their programme included the abolition of extraterritoriality, the recovery of tariff autonomy and the suppression of the opium trade. To develop China's commerce and industry, they urged the government to grant greater freedom to private entrepreneurs, although they equally recognised the importance of state protection and patronage. To prepare their community for a greater role in all these undertakings, they sent their younger members to study in the United States on a government-sponsored education mission. It was from these returned students that the bulk of the new leadership came.

The rise of this new breed of diplomat-officials, often dubbed 'the Young China', was helped by the changing international environment at the turn of the century. The decline in British trade, the rise of Japanese imperialism and the acceleration of foreign intervention in China had all contributed to the growing influence of Yuan Shikai. An advocate of reforms at that time, Yuan surrounded himself with many young talents with nationalistic aspirations. The way was thus paved for the assertion of a second generation of treaty-port community leaders in the movement for rights protection and recovery.

Until 1909, these modern diplomat-officials, equipped with Western diplomatic skills, pursued a vigorous and aggressive course to thwart imperialist designs, to reassert China's sovereignty over hitherto neglected border regions and to recover lost economic and political rights. Despite a hostile external environment, notable achievements were made, especially in Shandong, Zhili and the North-east. Yuan's fall in 1908 and the accompanying purge of his associates ended this period of what Sigel calls the diplomacy of nationalism. Sigel is convinced that the removal of this dynamic group 'left the Qing bureaucracy tangibly less able to counter foreign pressures, and the anti-imperialist effort lost ground in many areas'. Consequently, the provincial gentry and merchant elites lost their confidence in the government and eventually deserted the Manchu ruling house and rejected the monarchy in 1911.

Sigel's characterisation of the self-strengtheners differs from Pong's. The difference, however, is more apparent than real. Whereas the former focuses on the actual strategy of the modernising officials, the latter deals largely with their ideas. The contrast between reformist thought and its implementation drives home once again the importance of making a distinction between ideal and reality.

Sigel is certainly correct in pointing to the advanced ideas of the treaty-port community in the last decades of the nineteenth century and to the fact that their scions were able to put them into practice in the opening years of the present century. But perhaps it is equally important to note that their rise to positions of influence and responsibility was due no less to the support of

Yuan Shikai, a second-generation self-strengthener. It may seem trite to stress that the self-strengtheners were not a homogeneous group and that their policies changed over time, but the alliance between the treaty-port leaders and Yuan was possible precisely because of the latter's response to the new international environment which brought him closer to the views of the Young China group, at least in the area of foreign policy.

Earlier in this volume, Fung has argued that weak nations are deprived of effective diplomacy. Sigel's findings give a different impression. It would appear, however, that the diplomacy of nationalism, for all its vigour, was effective only when the powers, like Germany or Britain, were prepared to come to terms. Present scholarship indicates that Young China's performance in relation to the North-east was less impressive because Russia and Japan, both having vital interests in the region, remained intransigent. Only further research on the history of the region can validate or otherwise Sigel's claim that the Young China group was able 'to prevent Japan and Russia from consolidating their spheres of influence' there.

In any event, the immediate fate of China was determined by larger and more powerful groups which were either emerging or undergoing changes in the period, 1895-1916. Reviewing the literature on the political development of this period, K.S. Liew discusses in Chapter 9 the character and composition of each group and their bid for power. As well, he assesses their different roles in the Revolution of 1911 and the collapse of the first republic in 1916.

There exists a large body of literature on the 1911 Revolution, including works by Chinese, Japanese and Western scholars. Interpretations abound, and many questions remained unanswered. In this bibliographical essay, Liew ably summarises and synthesises a large number of major studies available to date and, in the course of doing so, raises some interesting questions and suggests areas for further research.

The socio-political groups active in the late Qing and early Republican periods make for an interesting but extremely complex landscape. In Liew's opinion, none of the groups, not even the army or the gentry, was in a position strong enough to topple the Manchu dynasty. The army, potentially the most powerful, was as a whole without a vision of its own for which to fight; nor was it given one by its leaders. The gentry, on the other hand, had by this time split into several interest groups, some of which were stronger than others. In Liew's opinion, it was the timely desertion of the constitutionalists, made up largely of the upper gentry, that tipped the balance in favour of the revolutionaries. The new republic was thus founded on the basis of a precarious 'alliance' of numerous and divergent interest groups. It was the delicate balance of power within this alliance that contributed to the rise of Yuan Shikai and the eventual destruction of the republic. Despite the early collapse of the republic, however, Liew maintains that it was still 'a genuine democratic revolution...the first and the last chance of Western liberalism in China'. He thus disagrees with those who argue that the 1911 Revolution was not a revolution and those who insist that liberalism remained an important force in China's political life long after 1913. The question, then, is: In what way was the abortion of liberalism related to the rivalry among leading interest groups of the era?

In Chapter 10, S.T. Leong studies a different form of competition for power by a different type of interest group, the Hakka Chinese of south China, in terms of their aspirations and efforts at socio-economic and, at times, political advancement from the nineteenth century to the 1930s. He begins by tracing their migration to the south and then examines their position within the wide cultural and ethnic context of the Lingnan region. Using socio-anthropological concepts, he differentiates between cultural and ethnic groups and explains how a cultural entity such as the Hakkas could become an ethnic group through conscious self-identification and attempts to promote its communal well-being. In addition, following William Skinner's model, he demonstrates how Hakka ethnic assertiveness increased with the decline of a region's economy after a period of expansion between the late seventeenth and the eighteenth centuries. But because the Hakkas straddled three separate macro-regions, each having a distinct developmental cycle, ethnic assertiveness reached a peak at different times in each of the major communities. Thus no real, long-term ethnic solidarity emerged.

Nevertheless, owing to successive and increasingly intense conflicts between Hakka and Punti ('native' Cantonese), the gentry on both sides found themselves more deeply drawn into communal affairs. Hakka leaders engaged themselves actively in myth-making and in articulating a particularistic ethos to bolster ethnic pride and cohesion. As leaders of a sizable minority, Hakka gentry were keen to take advantage of available opportunities and were more receptive to new ideas. Under the Qing, they sought and largely succeeded in advancing their own position and that of their community through the imperial civil service examinations. As they obtained office, many became reformers. With the progressive breakdown of the socio-political order towards the end of the nineteenth century, they availed themselves of the new opportunities for advancing their communal interests. Embracing new political ideas, many Hakkas joined the revolutionaries in 1911. The political movements of the 1920s and 1930s saw active Hakka participation in both the Nationalist and the Communist camps in numbers out of proportion to the size of the community they represented.

Thus, from a position where their primary concern had been socio-economic advancement, the Hakkas had, by the early decades of the present century, made significant inroads into the political arena as well. They must be considered one of the very few social groups in modern China whose aspirations were largely met.

The final chapter by K.K. Shum examines the most important struggle for power in modern China which resulted in the establishment of a Communist government in 1949. In this significant revisionist essay, Shum challenges the popular view that peasant support was by far the most important cause of Communist victory. That support, however powerful, would still have not been enough without the Chinese Communist Party's (CCP) successful bid for support from substantial segments of the landlord-capitalist classes which had hitherto sided with the GMD.

Contrary to popular belief and latter-day Maoist assertions, Shum maintains that during the Jiangxi Soviet period (1930-1934) Mao Zedong was in basic agreement with the then dominant Russian Returned Student group (RRS) in pursuing a radical land redistribution programme. While the land policy succeeded in galvanising peasant support, it failed to strengthen the Communist forces to the extent that they could hold their base areas against the superior military might of Chiang Kai-shek. Towards the second half of 1935, during and immediately after the Long March, both the RRS and Mao, in reviewing the causes of defeat, decided to abandon the strategy of a 'united front from below'. This strategy, which condemned all elements opposed to the CCP's social programme, had severely hurt the party and restricted its ability to exploit the strong popular anti-Japanese sentiments after the loss of Manchuria in 1931. A 'united front from above' was thus adopted in December, opening the party to an alliance of all social classes and political elements in a national revolutionary struggle against both Japan and the Nationalists. Class struggle was now subordinated to the War of Resistance, and land confiscation gave way to the more moderate policy of rent and interest reduction. In short, policy of unification before resistance against Japanese imperialism, similar to the GMD's 'internal pacification before external resistance', was abandoned.

With the adoption of the new strategy, Mao and Wang Ming, already in deep disagreement over the latter's military strategy which had cost them the Jiangxi base areas, drifted further apart, culminating in a split in July 1937. While still relying firmly on the proletariat and the peasantry, Mao wanted to enlist the active support of the intermediate classes (rich peasants, small landlords and the national and petty bourgeoisie) and isolate the ultra-rightists (big landlords and big capitalists) who were thought to have capitulationist tendencies. Wang, on the other hand, wanted the united front to be all-inclusive so as to facilitate Communist expansion in urban areas. The two strategies co-existed until August 1938 when the GMD's successful suppression of Wang's mass organisations in Wuhan led to the triumph of the Mao line. Emphasis thereafter was placed on expansion in the countryside, while not neglecting the need to attract the co-operation of patriotic elements in the landlord-capitalist classes. To this end, Mao instituted in 1940 the 'three-thirds' system of administration which, by its inclusion of elements from the intermediate classes and the progressive left, had great appeal to non-Communist patriots.

This united front strategy, Shum stresses, was not just a bipartisan, CCP-GMD alliance, which came to an abrupt end in January 1941, but a broadly-based, multi-class policy which continued, though with modifications, well beyond 1941. During the civil war period (1945-1949), a new democratic united front was inaugurated to include workers, peasants, petty bourgeoisie, national bourgeoisie and the 'enlightened gentry' in a common struggle against Chiang Kai-shek and American imperialism. Although land confiscation and redistribution were reintroduced in some areas, CCP leaders cautioned against a relapse into the excesses of the Jiangxi period. This still moderate policy, combined with the increasing disillusionment with the Nationalist government on the part of the national bourgeoisie, intellectuals and 'enlightened gentry', contributed significantly to the Communist success.

Shum's essay questions many old assumptions about peasant support, the united front strategy and the support from other socio-political groups, and the nature as well as the timing of the Mao-Wang split. It adds a great deal to our understanding of the pre-1949 Communist movement and is likely to provoke debates among historians and political scientists.

NOTES

1. Immanuel C.Y. Hsü, *The Rise of Modern China*, 3rd ed. (New York and Oxford, 1983), pp. 4-7.

2. Gilbert Rozman, ed., *The Modernization of China* (New York, 1981).

3. Mary C. Wright, *The Last Stand of Chinese Conservatism: The T'ung-chih Restoration, 1862-1874*, 2nd printing (Stanford, 1962), pp. 300-312.

4. David Pong, 'The Ministry of Foreign Affairs during the Republican Period, 1912 to 1949', in *The Times Survey of Foreign Ministries of the World*, selected and edited by Zara Steiner (London, 1982), pp. 135-152.

5. Chen Tiqiang, *Zhongguo waijiao xingzheng* [China's administration of foreign affairs] (Chongqing, 1945).

PART 1

REFORMIST IDEAS, CHANGING CONCEPTS AND FOREIGN MODELS

2

THE VOCABULARY OF CHANGE: REFORMIST IDEAS OF THE 1860s AND 1870s
David Pong

From the early 1860s to the present, successive governments have adopted 'self-strengthening' (*ziqiang*) as the catchword to galvanise official and popular support for building a richer and stronger China.[1] The continued use of this slogan bespeaks the failure of that attempt. Explanations for the Qing dynasty's failure in its last fifty years of existence have largely centred around the adequacy of Confucianism or the Confucian order as a basis for transforming China into a modern state.[2] The discussion, embracing some very impressive scholarly works, nevertheless fails to draw a sharp distinction between Confucianism, as a body of socio-political ideas, and the Confucian order which, historically, had never been totally derived from Confucianism. But because of the tendency to equate the Qing socio-political system with the Confucian order, and the latter with Confucianism, the discussion also fails to underline sufficiently that the sources of strength and weakness of the Qing state were not all Confucian in origin.

For the above reasons, it has often been overlooked that the reforming officials of the late Qing, despite their predominantly Confucian upbringing, could and did avail themselves of a much richer reformist tradition than the confines of Confucianism. Neither their contribution to China's reformist tradition nor their failure to conceive of greater changes can be attributed to Confucianism alone. By the same token, many of the socio-political forces impinging on their efforts at reform were also non-Confucian in character. More importantly, even if one accepts that the Qing order was largely Confucian, one should note that it was not the only possible expression of Confucian ideals. It was quite possible for the Qing officials to seek other alternatives. Therefore, to understand the provenance and nature of the reform efforts of this period and the reasons for their failure, it is necessary to analyse both the Confucian and the non-Confucian forces at work.

In this chapter, the evolution of reformist ideas and the vocabulary used in the 1860s and 1870s will be examined to demonstrate the following points. Firstly, these ideas, though largely rooted in Confucianism, were drawn from a much broader and richer reformist tradition dating back to at least the beginning of the Chinese empire (third century BC), but particularly from the ideas of the school of 'practical statecraft' (*jingshi*) formulated earlier in the nineteenth century, before the impact of the West was felt. Secondly, some of these traditionally-derived concepts also acquired new meanings as they were adopted to meet new exigencies. Lastly, these ideas were deliberately revived to form a coherent programme for change, and, if implemented, this programme would form an adequate basis for transforming the country into a state that was modern and yet still Chinese.

What was adequate, of course, is debatable. Catching up with the Western powers would have been impossible, but if the Chinese could make sufficient progress to keep abreast of the Japanese and check their aggression, then China's international standing would have been significantly improved. As the Chinese themselves recognised, a well-governed China would greatly reduce the sources of Sino-foreign conflict and a visibly stronger China would deter any aggressive posture against it.[3]

What changes, then, were necessary for China to become adequately wealthy and strong? First, it would require a strong imperial leadership, backed up by a centralised government. The latter would in turn necessitate a far more hierarchically structured administrative system and a bureaucracy organised on the principle of specialisation and well-defined responsibilities. The entire government would then need to establish specific objectives for achieving wealth and power, including the reordering of spending priorities, rationalisation of the tax system, development of new industries and communication facilities, modernisation of military training and equipment, and means of mobilising the country's human as well as material resources.

In the following analysis, it will become evident that the reforming officials of the sixties and seventies were thinking along very similar lines, though not in exactly the same terms. With one exception (Feng Guifen), however, none of these officials was a political theorist. Their ideas usually appeared in official discussions of specific issues; they therefore rarely dealt comprehensively with the problems of China's search for wealth and power (*fuqiang*). But by looking at their proposals collectively, one can certainly see a coherent programme emerging. Nevertheless, many ideas remained only partially developed. This, to some extent, can be attributed to the fact that the rejection of their initial proposals had discouraged or even stifled further elaborations. Had there been greater successes, more advanced ideas and actions would have been generated. This is not to deny, however, that the reformers were sometimes reluctant to develop certain ideas to their logical conclusions because of political considerations or vested interests.

Many of the terms appearing in official documents fall easily into the category of clichés. That they were often used by officials to gloss over difficult problems or avoid committing themselves to a particular policy is obvious; they were often condemned by the court or fellow officials as 'empty words' (*kongyan*).[4] On the other hand, this same vocabulary was employed by officials to justify or introduce concrete proposals, many of which were subsequently adopted and implemented. Its existence naturally invited its use, and familiarity could also help minimise the shock of some of the drastic reforms that were proffered. To avoid confusion, only those terms used in support of *concrete* reform proposals will be considered. In addition, to maintain our focus sharply on the reform efforts themselves, we shall concentrate on the writings of those who had a direct input into the policy making process at the time. The writings of Zheng Guanying and Wang Tao, interesting though they may be, will be excluded since their influence was felt later.

The Awakening

Although minor reforms, or more precisely, adjustments and modifications of existing administrative mechanisms were to be found throughout much of Chinese history, the broad reformist ideas of the 1860s and 1870s could not have come about without some significant degree of political awakening. In this, the work of the reformers was made easier by earlier warnings of dynastic decline. As early as 1815-1816, the scholar-official Gong Zizhen (1792-1841) observed that government was deteriorating and called for reform (*gaige*).[5] Gong's view was soon shared by a small coterie of scholar-officials of the 'practical statecraft' persuasion, notable among whom were Wei Yuan (1794-1856) and Lin Zexu (1785-1850). They saw in reforming the administrative system a means of arresting the decline.[6] Their call was echoed in the 1840s and 1850s by Zeng Guofan (1811-1872), then an emerging scholar and official, who lamented that 'today, everything is in ruins' and the officialdom had been nothing but lethargic and apathetic since the beginning of the century.[7] Zeng, of course, was later to become a leading reform figure in the post-1860 era. He was a vital personal link between the two phases of political awakening.

A key approach to government in traditional China was 'to examine the time and assess the situation' (*shenshi duoshi*) or *kuishi duoshi* in managing the affairs of the day.[8] Following the crushing defeat by the Anglo-French forces in 1860 and after a decade of domestic upheavals, many more officials recognised the imminence of dynastic decline. By assessing China's position in the new international environment in January 1861, Prince Gong (1833-1898), Guiliang (1785-1862) and Wenxiang (1818-1876), the new power holders at Beijing, observed, though cautiously, that 'the present situation is somewhat different from that of the past' and proposed a new administrative system for the management of 'barbarian' affairs. On the strength of their recommendation, the Zongli Yamen (a proto-foreign office), two high offices for overseeing the administration of the northern and the southern treaty ports, and a language school (Tongwen guan) were instituted to improve foreign affairs management and intelligence gathering.[9]

The realisation that the advent of the West had created 'a changed situation' (*bianju*) first occurred in 1844 in the personal jottings of Huang Junzai, a scholar-gentry, who came to this conclusion after having surveyed the history of the Western presence and the recent carving up of concession areas in the treaty ports.[10] Uttered in a period of increasing conservatism and apathy, Huang's observation aroused little official interest. The humiliation of 1860 and the rise of new leaders like Prince Gong in the capital and Zeng Guofan in the provinces, however, changed the political climate. In no small measure, the warning by Prince Gong and others and their new approach to foreign affairs set the tone for a new era. They gave the more progressive officials hope for further changes. Then, with the quelling of the Taiping Rebellion in 1864, the central government also regained confidence and became more receptive to reformist proposals. So, in 1865 and 1866, when Robert Hart and Thomas Wade presented their constructive, though sharply critical, memoranda for the dynasty's regeneration, the Qing court felt confident and open-minded enough to circulate them to high-ranking officials for discussion.[11] Nevertheless, the possibility of restoring order and sound government did not blunt the Chinese awareness that the problems brought about by the Western presence still remained. These problems, as the Zongli Yamen described them in 1867, involved not only the protection of Chinese sovereignty and interests under the extremely unfavourable terms of the unequal treaties but also the physical danger of further imperialist inroads along the land frontier from Tibet, Annam and Central Asia. 'This', the Yamen warned, 'is indeed an unprecedented situation (*chuangju*)',[12] a much stronger term than 'a somewhat different situation' used in 1861.

By calling the situation 'unprecedented', the Yamen conveyed a sense of urgency. While maintaining that solutions should and could be found to bring the situation under control, it also recognised that, given the existing conditions in China, the problems were serious. In the first half of the nineteenth century, reformers had tended to express, often obliquely, their concern for the empire's deterioration in treatises and private writings. To be sure, the problems at the time were not as grave, but because the court at Beijing refused to recognise publicly many of the empire's troubles, the few lone voices for reform failed to gain support among official circles. By contrast, in the 1860s, the leading figures at the capital were prepared to assess the problems publicly and, by and large, candidly. In 1866, for example, the Zongli Yamen specifically reminded the officials concerned that the memoranda from Hart and Wade did contain useful proposals for improving the management of both internal and foreign affairs. And in 1867, by proclaiming that the present situation was unprecedented, it also opened the way for the officials to deal with the situation as it really was. Ruilin, the governor-general at Guangzhou (Canton), immediately adopted the term and proposed defence modernisation. Ding Richang (1823-1882), Jiangsu's provincial treasurer, went a step further, calling the situation unprecedented since ancient times (*qiangu wei chuang zhi ju*) and submitted a sweeping programme for reform.[13]

In the context of post-1860 China, an 'unprecedented situation' was not one laden with golden opportunities; it portented serious adversities ahead. Because of this negative connotation, the terms 'changed' or 'unprecedented situation' were not to be bandied about lightly. In treatises and private writings, they were used to express lament, and in public documents, mostly to lend weight to important reform proposals or to argue for the continuation or expansion of existing undertakings. Thus by arguing that China was confronted with the greatest change in more than three thousand years, Li Hongzhang (1823-1901), the powerful governor-general of Zhili and superintendent of trade for the northern ports, defended the country's nascent modern shipbuilding efforts in 1872 and, two years later, proposed a broad programme for defence modernisation and various forms of industrialisation.[14]

Although the expressions 'changed' or 'unprecedented situation' were mostly employed to describe the predicament introduced by the aggressive West, there was a strong current of thought among the reformers that China's difficulties were really the combined product of foreign aggression and internal decline; to blame the foreigners for all of China's ills was to sidestep the issue. The development of modern defence, industrial and commercial enterprises (*yangwu*, literally, foreign matters) was therefore only a partial solution (see section on self-strengthening).

What then was to be done? Earlier in the century, when faced only with the problem of internal decline, the 'practical statecraft' reformers saw the restoration of a sense of shame (*chi*) among the scholars as a first step towards dynastic revival. 'If the scholars possess a sense of shame', Gong Zizhen wrote in 1814, 'then the country will never have anything to be ashamed of. If they have no sense of shame, then it is a disgrace for the whole country'.[15] In the thinking of Confucius and his followers, the ultimate purpose in man's cultivation through education was service to society. The failure of education, which accounted for the blatant lack of a sense of shame, was therefore at the core of China's social and bureaucratic ills.[16] In the opinion of the scholar-reformers of the 'practical statecraft' persuasion, the abstract theories and speculations of the Song school and the trivia into which the textual research of the Han school had degenerated had obfuscated true learning. They called for a return to the study of the Confucian and Mencian classics, the histories, as well as works outside the narrow confines of Qing orthodoxy. Once the scholars were exposed to the true principles of moral cultivation and government service, and thus made aware of their own shortcomings, they would acquire a sense of shame and strive for regeneration (*zizhen*). When this was done, they contended, a regeneration of the empire would follow.[17] In the 1860s and 1870s, this line of reasoning continued to occupy an important place in the scholar-officials' thinking,[18] but because of the new situation with which they were confronted, the more reform-minded officials used these traditional notions to convey other ideas as well.

In 1860-1861 Feng Guifen asked the question why China, 'the largest of all nations' and 'the most richly endowed with natural resources', was so weak. The answer, he said, lay in the inferiority of the Chinese. Had the Chinese been born inferior, there was nothing they could do about it even though they should still feel ashamed of it. But if the inferiority was due to man-made causes, then they should really be ashamed of it.[19] In 1862, Li Hongzhang admitted that he felt ashamed of the inferiority of Chinese arms.[20] Then, in 1866, Liu Kunyi (1830-1902), Jiangxi's governor, spoke of avenging China's humiliation (also *chi*, shame).[21] Thus, as used by the reforming officials of the sixties, the traditional 'sense of shame' had acquired three additional meanings. First, it had nothing to do with the falling short of lofty Confucian ideals, although that remained an important consideration in official and day-to-day behaviour. Rather, as used by Feng and Li, it originated from a comparison with the West and was at this stage largely measured in terms of material culture. Second, explicit in Feng's and Liu's statements and implicit in Li's, it was a collective shame arising out of collective, not just individual failings. Finally, when used in the context of Liu's memorial, the shame was the result of a lost war and its attendant consequences. As such, it represented a revival of the ancient term *guochi* (literally, national shame or national disgrace), which at times referred to an internally-caused disgrace and at other times to a foreign-inflicted condition. This ambivalence is also evident when Wei Yuan quoted it from the *Book of Rites* (*Liji*) in 1842.[22] Though *guochi* as a foreign-inflicted disgrace was not used in the public documents of the sixties and seventies, the above examples show that this notion was very much present at the time, foreshadowing the widespread currency of the term a generation or so later.

To forestall further foreign aggression (*waiwu*, literally, foreign insult), the source of China's collective disgrace, Prince Gong, Guiliang and Wenxiang insisted in January 1861 that the Chinese government must 'stir itself up' (*zizhen*), so that the country could become strong by its own efforts (*ziqiang*, literally, self-strengthened).[23]

The concept of self-strengthening goes back a long way in Chinese history. Originally, it was used to describe efforts at character building.[24] Later, it was also used for referring to a country's attempt to build up its strength against foreign enemies. For example, in the middle of the thirteenth century, when asked by the Southern Song emperor (Lizong) about border affairs, the minister Dong Huai replied, 'When a country is faced with an enemy, the best strategy is self-strengthening. The reason is that if we are self-strengthened, then the others will fear us and we will not be overawed by them'.[25] What exactly Dong meant by 'self-strengthening' is not clear. Available sources indicate that he devoted himself to restoring sound government and training troops.

In modern times, the term 'self-strengthening' was used for the first time, as far as can be ascertained, by Xu Jiyu in 1848 while relating how the tiny island kingdom of Sulu (modern Sulu archipelago) fought off the Spanish by dogged resistance.[26] But here too, the meaning is obscure; it seems to suggest little more than a combination of the kingdom's military tradition and the tenacity of its people to maintain its independence. For the Chinese in the 1860s, that in itself was lesson enough. Nevertheless, the first use of the term in the sense of a conscious and sustained effort at reform in building up the country's strength did not occur until 1860 when such a proposal was presented to the throne by Zhao Shuji, a Hanlin compiler.[27] He was soon followed by Feng Guifen, whose plan for self-strengthening was much more comprehensive and far-reaching.[28] By this time, however, Prince Gong, Guiliang and Wenxiang had already issued their call for self-strengthening in their memorial of 24 January 1861:

> Regarding the six-item proposal presented by your humble ministers [in connection with the founding of the Zongli Yamen], the main purpose is to scrutinise the enemies and protect our borders so as to allay future troubles. But this is treating only the symptoms, not the basic problems. The strategy for dealing with the latter rests with self-strengthening.[29]

What remained to be done was to establish some sort of guidelines and determine the contents of the self-strengthening effort.

The 'Guiding Principles' for Self-Strengthening

To be sure, the Chinese did not consciously try to establish a set of guidelines, but over time a number of principles emerged by which reform proposals were justified or judged. Two such 'guiding principles' were already present in the memorials of 13 and 14 July 1861 by the Prince Gong triumvirate.[30] Firstly, since the purpose of self-strengthening was to prevent future troubles, pre-crisis preparation was considered most important. Subsequently, the reformers adopted the traditional expression *weiyu choumou* (literally, taking precautions before the rain) to convey this idea. The phrase studded the public documents of the time.[31]

Closely associated with this idea of preparation was long-term planning, for which a number of phrases were used but none seemed to have been favoured.[32] Initially, the idea was used to promote such basic defence efforts as modern shipbuilding and arms production, and to defend them against hostile criticism. To emphasise that the success of these projects must depend on sustained government support, Ding Richang, when he was serving as Jiangsu's provincial treasurer, cited the *Analects* of Confucius to warn the critics that in government, 'those who desire to have things done quickly will never attain their objectives, and those who see only the small advantages will never accomplish great things'.[33] By the late 1860s, the idea of long-term planning and investment had also led the Chinese to develop new economic resources and to send students abroad for advanced studies.

The second 'guideline', calling for overall planning, was often expressed in the traditional phrases *tongji quanju* and *tongchou quanju* (literally, taking the whole situation into consideration). Depending on the subject matter under discussion, the 'overall situation' might refer to either the entire government or only a sector of it.[34] Although there is no doubt that in most cases the officials' pleas for overall planning were sincere, scarcity in resources meant that such appeals necessarily demanded a reordering of priorities and became an instrument for power struggles.

The third 'guiding principle', concerned with the protection of Chinese administrative integrity, appeared in 1860 when Zeng Guofan considered the possibility of foreign military help and foreign merchants shipping rice to supply Beijing's needs. Zeng was not enthusiastic about the former but saw no objection to the latter if detailed agreements were drawn up to protect China's authority over the matter. Prince Gong, Guiliang and Wenxiang agreed and said that if done in this way, 'the ultimate authority will rest with us' (*qi quan zai wo*).[35]

As the foreign presence grew, and especially when that was accompanied by persistent requests for further commercial privileges and permission to set up telegraphs, railways and mechanised mines, a number of Chinese officials began to think of *quan* as inherent rights. Though the term 'sovereign rights' (*zizhu zhi quan*) did not appear in public documents until perhaps the mid-1870s,[36] the idea was already present in 1867 when the Chinese, in preparation for the coming negotiations on treaty revision, discussed means of halting further Western encroachments. Of the seventeen officials involved in the deliberation, five used the term *quan*, and of the latter group, three did so to mean preserving China's authority or control over specific matters, while Chonghou and Li Hongzhang used it to convey the notion of inherent rights as well. Li was particularly explicit about what he meant when he said that the foreigners' demands amounted 'to encroaching upon our country's economic rights (*liquan*) and seizing our merchants' means of livelihood... The right to protect its people and to exercise autonomy over its own financial affairs belongs to every country'. Li, in effect, was providing his colleagues with a definition of China's sovereign rights. But because of the specific circumstances under which the discussion took place, he focused mainly on the question of economic rights. He then suggested that his government should employ foreign engineers to develop China's coal, iron and copper resources in order to 'supply our military needs and retain our right to the benefits (*shou liquan*)'.[37]

Thus from its original meaning of China having the ultimate say in protecting its traditional socio-political order from foreign encroachment—a defensive position—the concept of *quan*, and especially its derivation, *liquan*, had come to connote as well China's right to pursue its own course of development. From this position—a more aggressive one—the Chinese were only a short step away from the idea of competing with the West for economic benefits and retrieve lost economic rights (*shouhui liquan*), a subject to which we shall return.

The fourth and final 'guiding principle' called for a practical and pragmatic approach. Its immediate antecedent can be found in the writings and deeds of the scholar-reformers of the 'practical statecraft' persuasion in the pre-Opium War era who dedicated their energy to reforming the education of the scholar-officials and mending the dynasty's crumbling institutions. Regarding the former, they advocated a back-to-basics curriculum, involving the study of the classics (both Confucian and non-Confucian) and the histories, and a restructuring of the civil service examination system to encourage these pursuits.[38] This was precisely the kind of reform Liu Kunyi had in mind when he suggested in 1866 that the examination system be modified to promote 'substantial learning' (*shixue*).[39] By this time, however, the more progressive reformers like Ding Richang and Shen Baozhen were already demanding sweeping changes, including the study of specialised and technical subjects for scholars and on-the-job training as well as retraining for incumbent officials. As Ding claimed in 1867, this was the way to cultivate useful talents (*shiyong zhi cai*). Usefulness had to be the criterion for training and educating China's bureaucrats.[40]

In dealing with the empire's ailing institutions, too, the reformers of the post-1860 era went beyond the ideas of their *jingshi* predecessors. As we shall see momentarily, not only did they call for reforming existing institutions, but also for replacing antiquated ones with new administrative or military organs and practices. This, they insisted, was 'turning the useless into something useful' (*hua wuyong wei youyong*).[41]

Self-Strengthening

Begun in January 1861 with the founding of the Zongli Yamen, the Beijing Language School (Tongwen guan) and related reforms, the 'self-strengthening movement' was from the very outset inseparable from the management of foreign affairs (*yangwu*). Even the upgrading of the military for keeping internal peace and order was viewed as having a role in solving foreign affairs problems. If the Chinese could improve their military training and weaponry, reasoned Prince Gong and his colleagues, then they could suppress the rebels 'and, as a result, foreign aggression would disappear'.[42] It was the naivety of this argument that set the goal of military modernisation at a low level, at least at this stage.

By the mid-sixties (roughly 1866-1867), the 'movement' had begun to change and take a fuller shape. With the experience learned from military co-operation with foreign officers at several treaty ports and from the small arsenals founded by Zeng Guofan and Li Hongzhang, it was realised that the gap between Chinese and Western military technology was much greater and therefore the Chinese had to reach for higher goals. With the foreigners willing to help in establishing and operating the larger and more advanced Jiangnan Arsenal (established in 1865) and Fuzhou Navy Yard (established in 1866), new possibilities also opened up. Wei Yuan's dictum of 'learning the superior techniques of the barbarians in order to control them' appeared an attainable objective; China would soon be able to back up its diplomacy by power.[43] It was this type of optimism that enabled some reluctant *yangwu* supporters to see self-strengthening as desirable.[44]

To equate military reform and defence modernisation with self-strengthening was superficial, as some Chinese were beginning to see. Unfortunately, most modern historians of China also tend to regard self-strengthening as military or foreign affairs related. In traditional Chinese thinking, however, external threats were always associated with internal disorder—the one invited or caused the other—as epitomised in the old saw *neiluan waihuan* (literally, internal disorder and external disaster).[45] To forestall either catastrophe, the reforming officials called for a harder look at *all* of China's domestic ills.

In a diary entry of 1862, Zeng Guofan explained that 'the way of self-strengthening' (*ziqiang zhi dao*) was made up of two components: the restoration of sound government and the learning to manufacture modern arms and warships.[46] But it was the Hart-Wade memoranda that first spelled out in detail the mutuality between the internal and the external forces in self-strengthening. The matter then became a subject of public discussion when the Zongli Yamen circulated them for deliberation. Of the seven officials who responded, five agreed that internal administration was an important aspect of self-strengthening. Partly because the memoranda had come from foreigners, most officials denied the need for the 'new methods' (*xinfa*) proposed; they opted for rectifying the existing system rather than reforming it. Only Liu Kunyi saw the need to restructure the examination system and encourage the scholars to engage in 'substantial learning', while Zuo Zongtang recommended a more careful way of appointing governors-general and governors and, at the same time, giving them greater power in appointing their subordinates. The two also advocated the adoption of certain types of Western technology.[47]

The most thorough exposition by a Chinese official on the mutual dependence of internal and external forces came from Shen Baozhen in 1867. Arguing that the real foundation of self-strengthening was sound government (*zizhi*, literally, self-government), he proposed reforms that ranged from the education of the emperor and scholars to the restructuring of the government down to the sub-village levels. These measures were then to be buttressed by such *yangwu* undertakings as mechanised mining and defence modernisation. Only then could China become truly self-strengthened.[48]

Ding Richang, too, saw self-strengthening in much the same light and proposed broad changes. He was, however, more progressive and visionary on *yangwu* modernisation, including the creation of a modern navy and other defence projects, the exploitation of mineral resources, the expansion of overseas trade, the large-scale recruitment of Chinese and Overseas Chinese experts on foreign affairs and technology, and the founding of newspapers to whip up patriotism. In addition, he advocated an aggressive diplomacy, mobilising Overseas Chinese and forming alliances with Japan and China's tributary states, especially Korea and countries in Southeast Asia, so that in a few decades or a century China would be in a position to bring the five continents under its control.[49]

In the mid-sixties, although Shen and Ding were not the only ones prepared to admit publicly that China's survival in a menacing international environment depended on success in domestic reforms, they were alone in proposing sweeping changes. This calls for little surprise, for they were the only high-ranking officials with personal experience in running *yangwu* enterprises in a conservative socio-political environment: Shen was the director-general of the Fuzhou Navy Yard while Ding had spent years managing the Jiangnan Arsenal. This experience had sensitised them to the urgency of internal reform. Yet, as they sought new solutions, they drew heavily on China's own tradition. They were both radical and revisionist: radical in that they attempted to return to the roots of China's socio-political ideas; revisionist because they tried to give new meanings to established concepts and behaviour. Neither became less Confucian as they turned reformers.

Self-strengthening, then, required major and fundamental reforms (*bianfa*, literally, to change methods). Unlike the term 'self-strengthening', which even conservatives would use (though to mean little more than revitalising the traditional order by adhering to orthodoxy),[50] the term *bianfa* was inherently controversial. In China, as in other traditional societies, administrative methods were closely identified with the institutions that carried them out. They were part of the established order and could not be easily changed. If the methods had been introduced by an early and revered dynast, changes could be regarded as iconoclastic although imperial approval could remove that stigma. Furthermore, the concept of *bianfa* was indisputably Legalist in origin and, after the bitter struggle during and subsequent to the reforms of Wang Anshi (1021-1086) in the Song dynasty, it became a dirty word.[51] Though not totally tabooed, it was not to be used liberally.

So, despite a revived interest in *bianfa* among the reformers of the 'practical statecraft' persuasion in the pre-Opium War era, the term was not used in public documents unless in connection with *minor adjustments* of administrative methods.[52] During the Taiping period, Zeng Guofan also expressed privately a desire to see *bianfa* implemented in some areas but avoided using the term.[53] The credit for reintroducing the term to the reformers' vocabulary to propose broad and fundamental changes goes to Li Hongzhang, whose plea for *bianfa* was presented to the throne by the Zongli Yamen in 1864. His example was soon followed by Ding Richang in 1867 and 1868. Then, in 1874, Li again called for *bianfa* for self-strengthening and to improve maritime defence.[54] The term's appearance in the memorials of the sixties and seventies thus marked a turning point in reformism in Qing history.

Nevertheless, to protect themselves from undue criticism and to broaden their appeal, the reformers preferred a milder phraseology or to appeal to the authority of the classics even when proposing changes that were no less sweeping. Li, Ding, and others frequently described their reforms as 'adjustments' (*biantong*).[55] At other times, they would also justify their *bianfa* proposals by citing in part or in full the following passage from the *Book of Change* (*Yijing*, a Confucian classic): 'When a system is exhausted, it must be modified; that modified, it will work; and that working, it will endure'.[56]

The reformers' next question was what could and should be changed. In 1874, after the Japanese invasion of Taiwan had revealed how far the reality of self-strengthening had fallen short of its goals, Shen Baozhen had this to say:

> There is something that should remain unchanged in order for it to endure, and that is the will to become self-strengthened which must remain firm even in the face of a hundred adversities... [On the other hand,] there is something that needs to be changed in order that it may last, and that is the method for self-strengthening which requires us to change for the better when we learn of something good.[57]

The scope for change, then, was limited only by the goals of self-strengthening.

Our understanding of the 'self-strengthening movement' has largely been shaped by the prevailing interpretation of Zhang Zhidong's maxim: 'Chinese learning for the essential principles,

Western learning for the practical applications' (*Zhongxue wei ti, Xixue wei yong*), which was sloganised as either *Zhongti Xiyong* or simply *ti-yong* (substance-application). According to this view, Zhang's position was to graft certain elements of Western civilisation, particularly its science and technology, onto Chinese culture. Since in traditional Chinese thinking *ti* and *yong* were correlatives in a unifying whole whereas Chinese and Western civilisations were fundamentally incompatible, Zhang's formula is untenable conceptually and impossible practically. By tracing the root of Zhang's formula to Feng Guifen, whose thinking is generally regarded as the most advanced in the post-1860 era, we are led to believe that the less enlightened reformers, like Zhang, were locked in an intellectual cul-de-sac and a reformist dead end.[58] The argument certainly holds if the Chinese *ti* (substance or principles) remained unchanged or changed in the 'wrong' direction. Was this the case?

If Feng's writings are considered in their entirety, it is clear that his intent was to return to the teachings of the sages and use them, not the Ming-Qing orthodoxy, as guiding princples for a selective revival of past social and political institutions (legendary or otherwise), adapting them to the conditions of his time and make them more effective by incorporating Western institutions. For example, to strengthen local government and social organisation, he would revive, with appropriate modifications, the Han system of local administration and the clan organisation of the Song, and then reinforce them by incorporating the Western practice of election (complete with the ballot) and the institutions for poor relief and compulsory education. Feng's borrowings from the West therefore included not only science and technology, but also governmental and social institutions. More importantly, the borrowings were feasible because, as his line of argument implies, the Chinese socio-political system had the capacity to accommodate and take advantage of them. If that capacity was found wanting, he would modify the indigenous institutions first, in the manner just described. His *ti-yong* formula was not as forced or contrived as we are led to believe.[59]

Feng, however, had no political power to speak of and his influence in the sixties and seventies was limited to only a few persons. Nevertheless, the Chinese did frequently think in *ti-yong* terms,[60] and ideas similar to his did appear in memorials by those who actually enjoyed power. In 1867, Ding Richang declared that the *ti* and *yong* of self-strengthening lay respectively in improving the well-being of the people and proper intra-bureaucratic management on the one hand, and in enriching the state and increasing its military power on the other. In the same year, Shen Baozhen, while engaging in a massive introduction of Western science and technology at Fuzhou, insisted that the Chinese should use their intelligence (based on the teachings of the sages) to study Western technology and, at the same time, avoid the undesirable influences of the West.[61] It was this *ti-yong* mode of thinking which enabled Ding and Shen to press for reviving and adapting traditional institutions to increase the capacity of the Qing system for coping with the demands of self-strengthening.

Goals and Obstacles

After a few years' experience in self-strengthening, the reformers identified a number of serious obstacles, notably the lack of funds, shortage of qualified personnel, intra-bureaucratic opposition and inadequate imperial leadership. Similar problems had already been noted by Feng Guifen in 1860-1861, though not as obstacles, but as weaknesses to be overcome in the quest for wealth and power (*fuqiang*).[62] The correlation between the goals and the obstacles suggests the correctness of the reformers' diagnosis and their readiness to take the path of greatest resistance.

The reformers attributed the lack of funds to three main causes: the small tax base, corruption and inadequate planning. Little could be done to expand the tax base, however, as the land tax, the largest single item of revenue, had been frozen at the 1723 level. Though it was possible to increase surcharges, the traditional way to cope with rising expenditure (and to line the officials' pockets), the reformers' policy was to reduce them—to minimise popular discontent and facilitate post-Taiping reconstruction.[63] A national cadastral survey to tax unregistered land was also ruled out partly because of a century-old imperial decree against it and partly because the reformers feared a landlord 'rebellion' and exploitation by the as yet unreformed bureaucracy.[64] There were of course two new and substantial sources of revenue—the excise duty on goods (*lijin*) and customs duties on foreign trade—but both soon proved inadequate for rebel-suppression purposes (against the Nian and the Moslems) and the few modern defence establishments. So, to increase the government's tax receipts, the reformers tried to eliminate corruption and wastefulness.

To combat corruption and improve official performance, the reformers adopted both a personal approach, by enforcing the traditional method of punishment and reward, and a novel institutional scheme, by suggesting increases in salary and a higher status for yamen underlings to enhance their self-esteem and promotion opportunities.[65] Most reformers were vigorous in applying disciplinary measures and enjoyed temporary successes, but their across-the-board proposals to upgrade the bureaucracy were ignored since the central government feared that such changes would threaten too much vested interests.

The attack on administrative wastefulness was intended to increase efficiency, cut costs, and reduce impositions on the people. It had been a preoccupation of the 'practical statecraft' scholar-officials. In the 1860-1880 period, there were additional reasons for this type of reform: to release funds for defence modernisation and to assist merchant and joint government-merchant efforts to move into modern profit-making ventures. Here again, vested interests blocked the reformers' attempts. Moves to cut or abolish the vast, decrepit but expensive traditional armed forces produced little result. Nevertheless, they did succeed in undermining the less powerful, outmoded tribute grain transport system on the Grand Canal by directing more grain for sea transport and for the vessels of the China Merchants' Steam Navigation Company (CMSN Co., established in 1872).[66]

To augment government revenue, the reformers also probed new sources of income (*kai liyuan*, literally, to open new sources of profit). In the sixties, this referred mainly to mining, especially coal mining, with a view to supplying the needs of defence industries. The first government mine, however, was not set up until 1875. By then, ideas on *kai liyuan* had been broadened to include the exploitation of such other resources as petroleum, sulphur and camphor, not only to supply government needs but also to increase revenue and improve the people's livelihood (*guoji minsheng*), which was both a self-strengthening and a traditional goal.[67] Although little was actually achieved before 1880, these modest beginnings do underscore the fact that the reformers, in trying to increase revenue from a small and inflexible base, were prepared to modify established practices and institutions (*ti*) to accommodate borrowings from the West and to meet the requirements of self-strengthening (*yong*).

The most exciting idea on economic development to appear in this period was that of *shangzhan* (commercial warfare), first advanced by Zeng Guofan in 1862 and revived by Li Fan, a censor, in 1878. Zeng's idea, as he admitted, was inspired by the Legalist concept of 'agricultural warfare' (*gengzhan*), first introduced by Shang Yang in the fourth century BC.[68] As such, it meant little more than taxing commerce to support the country's war effort while allowing greater freedom to the merchants. By 1867, Zeng's view began to change: he now regarded international trade as an instrument for undermining the wealth of an enemy state prior to military conquest. But as he looked at the international environment in the mid-1860s, he could only see China as the victim of a Western-initiated commercial offensive.[69] At the time Li Fan spoke of 'commercial warfare', however, the term was given a completely different connotation. It had the twin objective of developing China's industry and commerce to curb and eventually to drive out foreign economic interests (*shouhui liquan*), already a current idea, and competing for markets abroad.[70]

Though Li must be credited with giving the idea a thorough exposition and popularising it, the notion was already evident in the proposal made in 1864 by Ding Richang and others to promote modern shipping to rival foreign firms.[71] Ten years later, Li Hongzhang also toyed with the idea of developing manufacturing industries to compete with imports.[72] Then, in 1876, Zhen Lanbin, minister-designate to the United States, urged the CMSN Co. to buy up its American rival and expand its services abroad to undermine foreign shipping interests. The purchase materialised in 1877 and, by 1880, the company had extended its routes to Honolulu, the United States and Southeast Asia.[73] China's new potentials, then, had created a climate in which a reintroduction and fresh interpretation of 'commercial warfare' could be meaningfully made. And so, in less than two decades, Zeng's crude and sometimes pessimistic conception had developed into a sophisticated, aggressive one and, in the case of the CMSN Co., put into practice.

Of all the immediate financial difficulties, the lack of

centralised accounting and budgeting was the most serious, especially when the country was confronted with a shrinking revenue or a sudden increase in expenditure, or a combination thereof. It was an old problem which, apart from making planning impossible, also caused unnecessary political disputes. From the 1860s on, it was also a source of frustration for the reformers.[74] Correcting this administrative defect required restructuring the government at Beijing and the willingness on the part of the provinces to surrender their control over local resources; both amounted to a head-on clash with vested interests. So, while most officials complained and pleaded that their resources be not committed to additional expenditures, few were prepared to demand the necessary changes. Among the few was Shen Baozhen, who had proposed as early as 1867 that the government be reorganised more hierarchically and that members of the central agencies be given specialised responsibilities. In 1874 and 1876, he also called for the provinces to submit financial reports to the Board of Revenue and for the latter to reset spending priorities and work closely with the Zongli Yamen when planning for the entire self-strengthening effort (*tongpan chouhua*).[75] Once again, the demands of self-strengthening had led to a plea for transforming the existing governmental structure.

The second goal of the reforming officials was to transform the bureaucracy into one capable of handling traditional administrative problems as well as modernising enterprises. As the officials concerned were well aware, these were sensitive issues questioning the importance of the generalist, moral man (the ideal Confucian administrator) as opposed to the specialist or institutional devices. The reformers of course were not inimical to institutional change but, being Confucian scholars themselves, they also accepted in varying degrees the importance of having 'good men' (in the Confucian sense) in government. So, in order to create a new generation of efficient and practical-minded bureaucrats who would still cherish Confucian ethical standards, they proposed adding such practical subjects as administration, military affairs and topography to the civil service examinations. They hoped thereby the literati would be induced to pursue these studies and abandon their obsession with stylistic refinements. In addition, incumbent officials were to be retrained. Shen Baozhen, for instance, wanted to see Hanlin scholars, the cream of the traditional education system, sent to the Grand Council and the Zongli Yamen for practical training, so that these men of exceptional intelligence would be exposed to real administrative experience, acquire special skills and become useful.[76]

In their attempt to produce an increasing number of officials who could man and manage modernising enterprises, the reformers could find little support from the Confucian classics other than general statements approving change. Such statements, however, could not be reconciled with the strong Confucian preference for men of high principles. The reformers were thus compelled to turn to examples from earlier dynasties when special devices, including the examination system, were employed to seek out men with special skills. They also argued (by stating the obvious) that it was necessary to engage in self-strengthening and to have a pragmatic and utilitarian approach to government.[77]

As a way out of this dilemma, they tried to combine the best of two worlds: to provide specialised training for youths in their teens after they had been adequately tutored in Confucian values. This was the principle on which students were recruited and trained in such new government institutions as the Beijing Language School and the Fuzhou Navy Yard School.[78]

In the mind of the reformers, such a combination was feasible because, as Li Hongzhang asserted in 1865, science and technology were universal; the West had learned from China in the past, therefore there was nothing wrong with reversing the process now, even if it meant sending Chinese to study abroad. Later, he and Li Shoutong, a probationary magistrate, argued that, to produce this new type of 'human talents' effectively and in sufficient numbers, there must be a broad base from which talents were to come. The Chinese should therefore emulate the Westerners, making books on science and technology widely available so that the people could regard them as part of their daily reading. This was the secret of the Westerners' success.[79] In 1874 Shen Baozhen also drew the government's attention to the Prussian system of compulsory and specialised education and called upon the literati to study science. To provide incentive, he and Ding Richang urged the incorporation of mathematics, science, foreign affairs and languages in the examination system.[80] Though unable to change this sytem, these reformers, along with Zeng Guofan, succeeded in sending over a hundred and sixty students and a small number of army officers to study in the United States and Europe in the seventies.[81]

But the most sweeping proposal for educational reform came from Luo Yingliu, an expectant daotai, who in 1879 suggested that the Imperial Academy and the provincial academies—seats of traditional learning—be converted into 'practical statecraft schools' (*jingshi shuyuan*) to educate young scholars in both Confucian values and Western learning. Though Li and Shen favoured an expansion of this type of education from its small base, neither was prepared to see the whole old system swept away[82] —it would have turned reform into revolution.

For analytical purposes, the last two areas of reformist concern—divisiveness within the government and weak imperial leadership—are best discussed together in the context of the larger problem of unity, including the government's relationship with the common people. The idea that government was established for the benefit of the people was a cardinal principle of Confucian thinking. The separation and alienation between the rulers and the ruled under the Qing therefore came under periodic attack.[83]

In the 1860s and 1870s, the reformers found weaknesses at every level of government a real hindrance to vertical communication and mobilisation of the empire's human resources. These weaknesses also allowed free play to all sorts of bureaucratic resistance to reform. The reformers' exasperation was reflected in their constant call for 'unity between the capital and the provinces' (*zhongwai yixin*) and 'unity among officials high and low' (*shangxia yixin*). But their promotion of modernising enterprises—an important part of the quest for a stronger China—only drove the opposing parties further apart. Nevertheless, they recognised that such a schism could only work to their disadvantage. They therefore sought reconciliation by appealing to the traditional ideal of harmony, urging those involved in self-strengthening and those outside it to be at one with each other (*juzhong juwai yixin*).[84] Shen Baozhen also attempted to enhance solidarity and sensitise the Chinese to the need of self-strengthening by appealing to their patriotism:

> If everyone, in and out of government, at the capital and in the provinces, will always place before him the

[catastrophic and humiliating] events of 1860, then who can for a moment put aside the thought of self-strengthening?[85]

It was a novel idea, but how was patriotism to be aroused?

One of Ding Richang's solutions was to found Chinese-owned newspapers to expose the foreigners' oppression of the Chinese people.[86] But in a more general and substantial way, the reformers called for changing the existing administrative structure and practices, arguing that a more hierarchical and specialised system of government would be more effective and responsive to people's needs. Starting from the top, they remonstrated with the emperor to alter his approach to government. The idea of the ruler setting an example and thereby rectifying the thought and behaviour of the people came of course from Confucius;[87] it had been the ideal of government since Han times. During the 1860s and 1870s the throne, constituted of a boy emperor and two empresses-dowager, was weak and, after 1874, because of a controversial succession problem, lacking in legitimacy. Its policy wavered, much to the chagrin of reformers and conservatives alike. All called upon the throne to be firm.[88]

Throughout this period, the reformers realised that whenever the throne lent a policy its support, that policy stood a great chance of success.[89] So, some reformers tried to change the attitude of the emperor himself. In the sixties, Shen Baozhen was probably alone in adopting this approach. By first pointing out that there was a distinction between the learning of the scholar and that for the sage (implying the emperor), he implored the emporer to avoid pendantic pursuits and learn the moral principles of government from the interpretative histories of Confucius, Zuo Qiuming, and of the Song Neo-Confucianists, Sima Guang and Zhu Xi. In addition, the emperor should discuss his studies with the ministers around him on a daily basis, and examine them in the light of real political situations. In this way, he averred, a new trend would be set and the officials would follow.[90] Pursuing this idea further, Li Shoutong pleaded with the throne in 1879 to modify its administrative method for the sake of self-strengthening and unity. The throne, for example, should emulate the Yongzheng emperor (r. 1723-1735) and pass judgment on official proposals and reports promptly and decisively. While some matters might require deliberation by the several government organs, clear-cut issues, especially those affecting the livelihood of the people, should be dealt with expeditiously. Moreover, a time limit should be set for implementing policies and officials judged solely by results, thus curbing bureaucratic procrastination and waywardness. Clearly, Li was trying to transform the government in a Legalist direction.

To make the government more efficient and benevolent, Shen proposed that such experienced civilian commanders and administrators as Zeng Guofan and Zuo Zongtang (both with strong *jingshi* leanings) be appointed to the Grand Council, which made all the important decisions. Whereas Ding Richang pressed for the abolition of sinecures, Shen called for the merger or retrenchment of offices with overlapping responsibilities and for the streamlining of the internal organisation of the six boards, charging each of the high officials with specialised duties. Li Shoutong also added that there should be a large-scale collection of all types of data for central and local planning. These measures, of course, were to be buttressed by new methods of recruiting and training officials.

To strengthen provincial and local government, the reformers suggested the removal of either the governor-general or the governor whenever the two existed side by side in the same province in order to prevent rivalry or shunning of responsibility. For better control over local government, Zuo Zongtang also pleaded for greater power for these high officials in appointing their subordinates,[91] whereas Shen asked for the removal of the daotais who constituted an unnecessary barrier between provincial and local governments. Concern for efficient local government also led Ding to counsel longer terms of office and lifting the rule of avoidance, thus allowing the officials to gain knowledge of and feel a special sense of responsibility for the areas they administered. To extend government effectively to the people, the reformers joined Feng Guifen in suggesting the establishment of smaller administrative units. Following the Han model, Shen insisted that such units should reach the sub-village levels, with officials partly appointed by the government and partly elected by the people. And to ensure that local conditions were properly represented, he also suggested that only magistrates with a good record be made censors. In this way, he believed, people's affairs would be attended to and the rulers and the ruled would share common interests and become one.

Perhaps, the most noteworthy attempt at improving intra-governmental co-operation and co-ordination in this period was the Zongli Yamen's vigorous revival of the consultative process. In line with the reformers' concern with practicality and thorough assessment of the situation, the Yamen tried hard to ascertain facts and solicit opinions so that it would be in a position to formulate policies that were relevant and enforceable. This approach of 'pooling intellectual resources and physical energy' (*qunce qunli*) was particularly important since the Yamen had neither the experience in defence and foreign relations at the local level nor the desired degree of control over the provinces. A policy originating from or supported by the provinces could therefore be more realistic and widely acceptable; it stood a better chance of successful execution.[92] The approach could also effectively curb deviation from stated policies and neutralise opposition.

As an administrative practice, policy discussions held conjointly by the court and provincial officials were as old as the imperial system itself.[93] It was a practice that reflected the Confucian spirit. In Qing history, what was new in this period was the frequency and intensity of policy consultation. In the decade beginning in 1866, three major policy discussions were initiated by the Zongli Yamen. In 1866, eleven governors-general and governors of the Yangzi and coastal provinces were ordered to deliberate on the Hart-Wade memoranda. Because of the controversial issues raised and perhaps the officials were uncertain of the Yamen's intention, only seven officials replied, tardily and in some cases perfunctorily.[94] Learning from this experience, the Yamen, when planning the discussion on treaty revision in 1867, drew up a detailed six-point agenda and set a time limit for the officials' replies. All but one of the eighteen officials consulted responded promptly; the one who did not was on a leave of absence. Some even discussed the matter with their local experts and forwarded their proposals verbatim.[95]

The third policy discussion, launched in November 1874, was the most important and comprehensive. Following hard on the Japanese invasion of Taiwan, its purpose was to formulate an effective policy for the whole self-strengthening effort. As the Yamen took stock of past failings, it also made some very bold proposals for the officials to consider, thus inviting similarly daring discussions and proposals. Relevant ideas on issues not covered by the agenda were also eagerly sought. To emphasise the urgency and seriousness of the exercise, the Yamen instructed the fifteen high provincial officials to discuss its proposals in detail, item by item, always bearing in mind that their recommendations were to be realistic and have long-term value. Also, for the first time, it informed the officials the exact procedure to be followed: the officials were to respond within a month; their proposals were then to be discussed in a court conference; and finally, the decision reached was to be submitted to the throne for consideration, approval and then handed down for implementation. So, in contrast to the earlier policy discussions, the one in 1874 was designed to have all the proposals discussed together in a court conference. Subsequently, after the first round of provincial replies were received, the conferees, including the powerful imperial princes, the grand councillors and board presidents, met in camera for several days.[96]

The entire deliberation took nearly eight months during which over fifty memorials were submitted and three additional proposals from the provinces were also circulated for discussion. It was truly an effort to pool the intellectual and human resources of the upper strata of the imperial government. At this juncture, unfortunately, the throne felt most insecure—Empress-Dowager Cixi had just violated dynastic law by installing her three-year-old nephew as emperor in order to prolong her own rule. She badly needed support from the conservative majority. Leading proponents of Qing orthodoxy—imperial princes and all—as well as defendants of vested interests were thus given free rein to indulge in vitriolic attacks on the reformers. A severely trimmed programme then emerged, providing for the creation of two modern fleets with a four-million-tael budget, two modern coal mines, increased power for the northern and the southern imperial commissioners, and minor reorganisation of the traditional armed forces. Though still the most comprehensive programme for self-strengthening up to the mid-1880s, it was a far cry from what the reformers had wanted. Worse still, since none of the institutional changes regarding overall planning, budgeting and governmental restructure was accepted, the programme stood little chance of success.[97]

Lack of imperial commitment to reform also hindered the reformers' attempt at mobilising the people, especially the scholar-gentry and merchants, in their struggle for self-strengthening. The merchants, of course, could be a source of capital and entrepreneurial skill for government-sponsored enterprises but for the mutual distrust between them and the government.[98] And despite Li Hongzhang's success in launching his shipping company with both government and merchant capital, the problem remained. In the mid-1870s, more positive measures were considered. If the government could be prevailed upon to provide protection for the merchants and help them with low-interest or interest-free loans, reasoned the reformers, then the twin goal of retrieving economic interests lost to foreigners and of promoting government-merchant solidarity (*guanshang yiti*) could be achieved.[99] In the last analysis, few reformers were prepared to grant the merchants the freedom needed for rapid economic growth. The fear of a rival merchant class was overwhelming.[100] Thus, although Ding Richang had private enterprise in mind when he first broached the idea of modern shipping in 1864, by the time the matter was seriously considered, increased government intervention was favoured. The result was the CMSN Co, a *guandu shangban* (official supervision and merchant management) enterprise.[101]

Yet, as the Japanese experience shows, the absence of a strong merchant class was not critical in the initial stages of the struggle for wealth and power if only the state would promote modern enterprises and transform the outlook of the old elite.[102] In China, the reformers recognised the need to change the attitude (*kai fengqi*, literally, to inaugurate a new socio-political climate) of the gentry and commoners to accept and eventually to contribute to modern enterprises.[103] Their attempt at changing scholar-gentry outlook has been studied. They also hoped that the advantages of modern enterprises would convince the people to abandon their traditional occupation.[104] But the people, when left to themselves, changed only slowly, and the reformers, fearful of social disorder which might jeopardise their restoration achievements, could not afford to push their modern enterprises too far.[105] Once again, they looked to the throne for leadership. As Li Hongzhang cried out in exasperation, 'The reason why the people do not learn is because those who have the authority do not instruct'.[106]

Conclusion

All the reforming officials examined above were brought up in the traditional education system. Though influenced by the 'practical statecraft' reformers, none was in any significant way exposed to Western ideas until the 1860s. Consequently, they tended to draw their ideas from China's past, revamping them to meet the demands of a new age. Even the introduction of Western institutions and science was justified in terms of traditional goals. Naturally, they turned first to Confucianism and traditional administrative practices for inspiration, but when these were found wanting, they looked to other schools of thought as well, notably the Legalist. The outcome was a 'blueprint' for change that was essentially Chinese, though not necessarily Confucian or Qing (as it then existed).

Regarding China's long-term development, this was a wise approach to take, since using the West as a model at this early stage could only have invited greater opposition. Already, Li Hongzhang and Ding Richang had been accused by conservative die-hards of trying to transform China with barbarian ways. It should be noted, however, that these attacks were largely politically motivated and did not in any way reflect the truth since such other reformers as Zuo Zongtang and Shen Baozhen were not similarly vilified.[107] By and large, these conservative objections to change, though dressed in Confucian garb, were no more Confucian or Chinese than the reformers they attacked.

There were flaws, of course, in the reformist thought of this period. The reformers, living in an age of internal upheaval and mounting imperialist threats, were too worried about social disturbances, gentry opposition and diminution of state control to grant enough freedom to the merchants to develop modernising enterprises. To be sure, the state could perform the role of industrialist, capitalist and entrepreneur, as the reformers suggested, but the officials, themselves products of the traditional order, lacked the skills to play that role. Further, as beneficiaries of the existing socio-political order and subjected to its dictates, most would not see themselves losing status and power by engaging *personally* in modernising ventures. Men like Ding Richang and Shen Baozhen were rare. Even though they were doing no more than directing the government's defence industries, their career had suffered enormously.[108] To overcome all these inhibiting factors, structural changes were needed. Hence the reformers' demand for overhauling the administrative system. It was in this context that imperial leadership became critical. But the throne, dependent as it was on the support of both the conservatives and the self-strengtheners, was unwilling to commit itself to change on a large scale.[109]

Another flaw in the reformist thinking of this period was the ambiguous role assigned to the new, modernising man. In part, this can be explained, as we have just done, in terms of the reformers' jealousy of their own power for they, too, had their vested interests. There is no doubt, however, that they also genuinely believed in the Confucian dogma that insisted on putting government in the hands of men of high ethical principles. A number of them (Zuo Zongtang, Shen Baozhen and Ding Richang, for example) had led an impeccable life both in public and in private. Here, Confucian principles and the scholar-officials' group interests became one. So, despite their call for sweeping institutional change and their willingness to re-educate the literati for handling *yangwu* projects, they were not prepared to see a new generation of Sino-Western specialists rising from these establishments and making an inroad into the civil bureaucracy. Of the major reformers, only Ding Richang seems to have been groping for true integration between the two sectors when he suggested that those in charge of making modern farming implements today should be the civil servants of tomorrow.[110] But the ability to see the importance of such an integration was still some years away. Although a scholar-gentry, Zhen Zuolin of Nanjing, began to think of *yangwu* as *shiwu* (current affairs) in 1876, it was not until perhaps 1898 that *yangwu* was officially described as current affairs, thus giving it recognition as an integral part of civil administration.[111]

Nevertheless, when considered in its totality, the reformers' programme was both fundamental and comprehensive. Many of their proposals assumed prominence in later reform movements: those on 'commercial warfare', abolition of sinecures and offices with overlapping functions, changes in the education and examination system, and much more. But by far the most important feature of their programme was the search, perhaps a half-conscious one, for a new political form. It envisaged a government structure with a strong imperial leadership, a powerful central bureaucracy with greater access to information and control over the provinces, a provincial government with effective control over its officials, and a more penetrating and representative local administration that would be more responsive to the wishes of the people, or at least the local elite (which encompassed a larger group than the gentry). In short, although the reformers' programme would undermine the throne's capacity to exercise patronage and manipulate the provincial authorities, it would also greatly strengthen its authority over a more specialised and efficient bureaucracy. More importantly, it would have transformed a pyramidal administrative structure to a hierarchical one—the type that is more suited to directing and integrating reformist efforts.[112]

To conclude, it can be said that the reformers' programme, if implemented, would have been adequate to propel China along the road of self-strengthening. Although greater initial success would probably have led the reformers to delve deeper and wider into China's tradition to justify further changes, it would also have made later reform efforts appear less drastic, and therefore more acceptable. But the forces opposing change were great, and continued to be so well into the present century, quite independent of the fate of Confucianism or the 'Confucian order'. In hindsight, therefore, the Qing government's failure in the 1860s and 1870s to deal with its internal problems along the lines the reformers suggested proved doubly costly.

NOTES

I would like to thank members of the workshop on 'China in Transformation' and particularly Dr Tim Wright and Dr Edmund Fung for their helpful comments. Since parts of this chapter have been drawn from a paper I presented at the XCI Annual Meeting of the American Historical Association, Washington, DC, in December 1976, I am also grateful to Professor K.C. Liu for his comments on that paper. Above all, I am indebted to the early publications of Mr Wang Ermin for arousing my interest in this topic and to his recent writings for inspiration and bibliographical information. Despite overlapping interests, our approaches to the subject are quite different.

ABBREVIATIONS

DXTG: Dao Xian Tong Guang si chao zouyi [Memorials from the Daoguang (1821-1850), Xianfeng (1851-1861), Tongzhi (1862-1874) and Guangxu (1875-1908) reigns], Wang Yunwu, *et al*, comps. (Taibei, 1970).

YWSM: Chouban yiwu shimo [The complete account of our management of barbarian affairs] (Beiping, 1930). -*DG* (Daoguang reign), -*XF* (Xianfeng reign) and -*TZ* (Tongzhi reign).

1. For example, the year 1980 was called the 'Self-strengthening Year' in Taiwan. *Taiwan xinsheng bao* [The New Life Daily of Taiwan], 1 January 1980.

2. Since the appearance of Mary Wright's magisterial study on the Tongzhi Restoration, there has been much discussion on the subject. Wright contended that the claims of the Confucian order and those of the modern state were basically incompatible. On the other hand, Wang Ermin and others have argued that Confucian values were not in themselves inimical to change and, in some cases, were an adequate basis for formulating new and modern concepts. Mary C. Wright, *The Last Stand of Chinese Conservatism: the T'ung-chih Restoration, 1862-1874*, 2nd printing (Stanford, 1962), pp. 196-221, and esp. p.312; Wang Ermin, 'Rujia chuantong yu jindai Zhong-Xi sichao zhi huitong' [The Confucian tradition and the understanding of Western ideas in modern times], *Xinya xueshu jikan* [New Asia quarterly], 2 (1979), 163-178; Lu Shiqiang, 'Feng Guifen di zhengzhi sixiang' [The political ideas of Feng Guifen], *Zhonghua wenhua fuxing yuekan* [Chinese cultural revival monthly], IV:2 (February 1971), 1-8; Liu Kwang-ching, 'Nineteenth-century China: the Disintegration of the Old Order and the Impact of the West', in Ping-ti Ho and Tang Tsou, eds., *China in Crisis*, Vol.1, Book 1 (Chicago, 1968), p. 142; Albert Feuerwerker, 'Economic Aspects of Reform', and Saundra Sturdevant, 'Imperialism, Sovereignty, and Self-Strengthening: a Reassessment of the 1870s', in Paul A. Cohen and John E. Schrecker, eds., *Reform in Nineteenth-Century China* (Cambridge, Mass., 1976), pp. 36 and 67; Shannon R. Brown, 'The Ewo Filature: A Study in the Transfer of Technology to China in the 19th Century', *Technology and Culture*, XX:3 (July 1979), 550-568.

3. *YWSM-TZ*, 40:10b-13b.

4. *Ibid.*, 50:28b.

5. Shi Jun, comp., *Zhongguo jindai sixiang shi cankao ziliao jianbian* [Selected sources on the modern history of Chinese thought] (Beijing, 1957), pp. 8-10.

6. Judith Whitbeck, 'Three Images of the Cultural Hero in the Thought of Kung Tzu-chen,' in Cohen and Schrecker, pp. 26-30; Arthur W. Hummel, ed., *Eminent Chinese of the Ch'ing Period* (Washington, DC, 1943), I, 431-432 and II, 850-851; Hu Bin, *Zhongguo jindai gailiang zhuyi sixiang* [Reformist thought in modern China] (Beijing, 1964), pp. 7-23; Shen Chen Han-yin, 'Tseng Kuo-fan in Peking, 1840-1852: His Ideas on Statecraft and Reform', *Journal of Asian Studies*, XXVII:1 (November 1967), 62, 67-69.

7. Qian Mu, *Zhongguo jin sanbai nian xueshu shi* [A history of Chinese learning in the last three hundred years] (Shanghai, 1937), pp. 580-581.

8. *YWSM-XF*, 71:17b; -*DG*, 54:1. Guo Songdao used a variation of the term in discussing the handling of foreign affairs: *shenshi duoqing* (to scrutinise the matter and ascertain the facts). Guo, *Yangzhi shuwu wenji* [Collected literary writings of Guo Songdao] (1892), 11:11-13.

9. *YWSM-XF*, 71:17-28.

10. Huang Junzai, *Jinhu qi mo* [Huang's jottings] (1929), 'Langmo', 4:3.

11. On the spirit of the time, see Wright, pp. 48-49. On the Hart-Wade memoranda, see *ibid.*, pp. 263-268 and *YWSM-TZ*, 40:10b-36.

12. Prince Gong, Guiliang and Wenxiang had alluded to the danger of Western threats from various directions as early as 1861, but the Yamen's analysis of 1867 was much more detailed and precise. *YWSM-XF*, 71:17b; -*TZ*, 50:24-30b. In 1865, Huang Entong, former governor of Guangdong, described the changed situation as one greater than any in hundreds of years. Huang's remark was made in the preface of the account of his management of foreign affairs at Guangzhou (Canton). Its influence at the time was probably limited.

For later appearances of the terms *bianju* and *chuangju*, see *The Cambridge History of China, Volume 11, Late Ch'ing, 1800-1911, Part 2*, John K. Fairbank and Kwang-ching Liu, eds. (Cambridge, 1980), pp. 156-157; Wang Ermin, *Wan-Qing zhengzhi sixiang shi lun* [Articles on late Qing political thought] (Taibei, 1969), pp. 8, 192-193.

13. *YWSM-TZ*, 52:16-18; 55:17-26.

14. Li Hongzhang, *Li Wenzhong gong chuanji* [The complete works of Li Hongzhang] (Shanghai, 1921), 'Memorials', 19:44-50b; *YWSM-TZ*, 99:12b-32. For the terms and their variations used by other officials in 1874, see *ibid.*, 99: 34b, 52; 100:10.

15. Qian Mu, II, p. 533.

16. Confucius, *Lunyu* [The Analects], Book II, Chapters 1 and 3; and his *Daxue* [Great Learning].

17. Qian Mu, II, 523-568 (especially p. 566). For a brief description of the major schools, see Shen Chen Han-yin, pp. 62-69.

18. See for example the ideas of Zeng Jize in Li Enhan, *Zeng Jize de waijiao* [The diplomacy of Zeng Jize] (Taibei, 1966), p. 38.

19. Feng Guifen, *Jiaobinlu kangyi* [Straightforward words from the Lodge of Early Zhou Studies] (1897), ff. 70b-71.

20. Li Hongzhang, 'Letters', 2:47.

21. *YWSM-TZ*, 41:49b.

22. Shi Jun, p. 60. For the early appearance of *guochi*, see Morohashi Tetsuji, *Dai Kan-Wa jiten* [Chinese-Japanese dictionary] (Tokyo, 1955), III, 82.

23. *YWSM-XF*, 71:18 and 72:11a-b. For another example of this thought process, see Feng Guifen, ff. 70b-71.

24. The term *ziqiang* came from the texts of the Spring and Autumn as well as the Warring States periods (722-481 and 403-221 BC, respectively). Morohashi, IX, 406; *Cihai* [Dictionary of phrases in the Chinese language] (Shanghai, 1948), p. 1108.

25. *Songshi* [Dynastic history of the Song], Tuotuo, *et al*, comps., Zhonghua shuju edition (Beijing, 1977), XVIII, 12428-12432 (*juan* 414); *Zhongguo renming dai cidian* [Biographical dictionary of China] (Hong Kong, 1931), p. 1317.

26. Xu Jiyu, *Ying huan zhilue* [A brief survey of the maritime circuit] (Fuzhou, 1850; author's preface, 1848), 2:9-10.

27. Wang Ermin, *Qingji binggongye di xingqi* [The rise of the armament industry in the late Qing period] (Taibei, 1963), pp. 39-40.

28. Feng Guifen, *passim*, especially ff. 70b-71.

29. *YWSM-XF*, 72:11.

30. *Ibid.*, 71:17b-19; 72:11-13.

31. For example, see *ibid.*, 50:27b, 35; 54:14; 98:42; *Yangwu yundong* [The Westernisation movement], Zhongguo kexue yuan jindaishi yanjiusuo, *et al*, comps. (Shanghai, 1961), I, 160.

32. Phrases used include *jiuyuan zhi tu* (lasting plans) and *jingjiu zhi dao* (the principle of planning for long-term effects). *Ibid.*, p. 27; *YWSM-TZ*, 99:24a-b.

33. *YWSM-TZ*, 55:22b. This passage, quoted from the *Lunyu*, Book XIII, Chap. 17, was also cited by Yang Changjun in *ibid.*, 99:36.

34. *YWSM-XF*, 71:17-28; *YWSM-TZ*, 99:23b.

35. *YWSM-XT*, 71:9b-12; 72:3-8b.

36. For example, see the Chinese text of the Sino-British agreement on the sale of the Woosung Railway, 24 October 1876. The term *zizhu zhi quan* appeared twice in this document. Great Britain, Foreign Office Archives, FO 682/123(13). For the English text, see FO 228/577, pp. 401-402. For a discussion of the Chinese perception of sovereignty, see Sturdevant, pp. 63-70, and David

Pong, 'Confucian Patriotism and the Destruction of the Woosung Railway, 1877', *Modern Asian Studies*, VII, 4 (1973), 647-676.

37. *YWSM-TZ*, 55:9. For references to *quan* in the 1867 discussion, see *ibid.*, 53:2, 6b; 54:3, 19, 22b; 55:4b, 14, 15b-16.

38. Peter M. Mitchell, 'The Limits of Reformism: Wei Yuan's Reaction to Western Intrusion', *Modern Asian Studies*, VI:2 (April 1972), 195; Feng Youlan, 'Wei Yuan di sixiang', in *Zhongguo jindai sixiang lunwen chi* [Essays on modern Chinese thought], Shanghai renmin chubanshe, ed. (Shanghai, 1958), pp. 20-25; Qian Mu, II, 529-530, 532-536.

39. *YWSM-TZ*, 41:45b. Feng Guifen also used the term *shixue*, but he meant by it the study of Western science, technology, government and social institutions. Wong Young-tsu, 'Feng Kuei-fen's perception of reform', *Monumenta Serica*, XXXI (1974-1975), 140.

40. *YWSM-TZ*, 53:26-29; 55:10a-b, 17-20; Ge Shijun, comp., *Huangchao jingshi wen xubian* [Collection of Qing dynasty writings on statecraft, continued] (Shanghai, 1888), 101:11.

41. *Haifang dang* [Facsimile of the maritime defence file], Zhongyang yanjiu yuan jindai shi yanjiu suo, comp. (Taibei, 1957), II, 367-372; *YWSM-TZ*, 99:12, 15b-17, 23, 45b, 54-56b; 100:14a-b, 21, 27; Ge Shijun, 101:8b-9. The other officials were Yinghan, Yulu, Wang Kaitai, Wang Wenshao, Li Hanzhang, Li Henian and Liu Kunyi.

42. *YWSM-XF*, 72:11.

43. *YWSM-TZ*, 41:30, 48; 42:45b-48b; 45:53b-54; 53:1, 31b; Lu Shiqiang, *Ding Richang yu ziqiang yundong* [Ding Richang and the self-strengthening movement] (Taibei, 1972), p. 215.

44. For example, see the memorials of Ding Baozhen, Jiang Yili and Yinggui. *YWSM-TZ*, 52:28; 53:32a-b; 54:12b.

45. The origin of this idea comes from the *Liji* (The Book of Rites) of the Han period. *Cihai*, p. 143. For an early exigesis by Zhongchang Tong, see Xiao Gongquan, *A History of Chinese Political Thought*, Frederic W. Mote, trans. (Princeton, 1979) I, 545-546.

46. Cited by Li Enhan, p. 40.

47. The officials who responded were Chonghou, Guanwen, Liu Kunyi, Zuo Zongtang, Ruilin and Jiang Yili (joint memorial), and Ma Xinyi. *YWSM-TZ*, 41: 26b-30, 40b-43, 43-50; 42:45b-48b, 58b-65b and 45:44b-54.

48. *Ibid.*, 53:1-7b, 26-29b.

49. *Ibid.*, 55:17-26.

50. For example, see *DXTG*, VIII, 3421.

51. J.J.L. Duyvendak, *The Book of Lord Shang* (London, 1963), pp. vii-ix; James T.C. Liu, *Reform in Sung China, Wang An-shih (1021-1086) and His New Policies* (Cambridge, Mass., 1959), pp. 22-30, 35-37.

52. Thomas Metzger, *The Internal Organization of Ch'ing Bureaucracy* (Cambridge, Mass., 1973), p. 53. Gong Zizhen, for instance, did not use the term *bianfa*, but all the ingredients of that concept were present in his treatises. Shi Jun, p. 6.

53. Zeng's letter to Liu Yong, 'The reason why we treasure the virtuous and able men is that they do not adhere rigidly to the written statutes. Instead, they can take into consideration the conditions of their time and create new regulations. And while making these considered changes, they do not lose sight of the principles embodied in the system and rites of the three ancient dynasties (*sandai*)'. Cited by Qian Mu, II, 588.

54. Lü, *Ding Richang*, pp. 202-203; *YWSM-TZ*, 25:10; 55:25b-26; 99:15 and 29.

55. *YWSM-TZ*, 55:10a-b, 17b, 19b, 20b, 34.

56. For example, see *ibid.*, 55:13b; 99:12, 14b-15; Lü, *Ding Richang*, pp.

195, 203.
57. Ge Shijun, 101:10b.
58. Wright, pp. 64-66; Joseph R. Levenson, *Confucian China and Its Modern Fate: A Trilogy* (Berkeley, 1968), I, 59-78.
59. Feng Guifen, ff. 69a-b, 71. My analysis here draws heavily on the following works: Lu, 'Feng Guifen'; Wong, 'Feng Kuei-fen's perception'; Frank A. Lojewski, 'Reform Within Tradition: Feng Kuei-fen's Proposals for Local Administration', *Qinghua xuebao* ['The Tsing Hua Journal of Chinese Studies'], n.s., XI:1 and 2 (December 1975), 147-161.
60. Wang, *Wan-Qing zhengzhi sixiang*, pp. 51-67.
61. Lü, *Ding Richang*, p. 215; *Haifang dang*, II, 81.
62. These obstacles were frequently referred to separately. The first three were listed in Zongli Yamen's memorial of 5 November 1874 and all four in Li Hongzhang's of 7 January 1880. *DXTG*, VI, 2610-2614; Li Hongzhang, 'Memorials', 35:45-48; Feng Guifen, f. 71.
63. Xia Nai, 'Taiping tianguo qianhou Changjiang gesheng zhi tianfu wenti' [The land tax problem in the Yangzi provinces before and after the Taiping rebellion], *Qinghua xuebao*, X:2 (1935), 429-474.
64. Wright, p. 166; Wang Yeh-chien, *Land Taxation in Imperial China, 1750-1911* (Cambridge, Mass., 1973), pp. 28-29; Ge Shijun, 101:8b-11.
65. *YWSM-TZ*, 55:17-18b, 25b-26; Lü, *Ding Richang*, pp. 112-118, 150-156, 278-280; Wright, pp. 87-90.
66. Li Hongzhang, 'Memorials', 30:29-32b, 33a-b; *Haifang dang*, I, 976-979.
67. *Yangwu yundong*, I, 150-151; Sun Yutang, *Zhongguo jindai shi gongye shi ziliao* [Sources on modern Chinese industrial history] (Beijing, 1957), II, 581-585; Ge Shijun, 101:10.
68. *Shangzhan* was used by Zeng to justify the *lijin*. Tang Qingzeng, 'Zeng Guofan zhi jingji sixiang' [Zeng Guofan's economic thought], *Jingjixue jikan* [Economics quarterly], V:4 (March 1935), 57. The term used by Shang Yang was not *gengzhan* but *nongzhan*, both meaning the same. Shang Yang, however, did not intend the character *nong* (agriculture) to be used adjectivally. Rather, *nong* and *zhan* (warfare) were two separate activities, the former supporting the latter. Duyvendak, pp. 31, 185-196.
69. *YWSM-TZ*, 54:1b.
70. *Yangwu yundong*, I, 165-168.
71. Lü, *Ding Richang*, p. 62.
72. *YWSM-TZ*, 99:25b-26.
73. *DXTG*, VII, 3079-3081; Zhang Sijun, 'Benju biannian jishi' [A chronological account of our Company], in Shen Zhongyi, *et al*, eds., *Guoying zhaoshangju qishiwu zhounian jiniankan* [Commemorative volume on the 75th anniversary of the state enterprise, the China Merchants' Steam Navigation Company] (Shanghai, 1947), p. 49.
74. David Pong, 'The Income and Military Expenditure of Kiangsi Province in the Last Years (1860-1864) of the Taiping Rebellion', *Journal of Asian Studies*, XXVI:1 (November 1966), 49-65; Immanual C.Y. Hsu, 'The Great Policy Debate in China, 1874: Maritime Defence vs Frontier Defence', *Harvard Journal of Asiatic Studies*, XXV(1964-1965), 212-228.
75. Ge Shijun, 101:10; Shen Baozhen, *Shen wensu gong zhengshu* [The memorials of Shen Baozhen] (Suzhou, 1880), 6:9-13b, 33-36.
76. *YWSM-TZ*, 53:26-27b; 55:19a-b.
77. *Ibid.*, 99:10, 30; *Yangwu yudong*, I, 116; Ge Shijun, 101:11; Zhu Shoupeng, comp., *Guangxu chao Donghua lu* [The Donghua records of the Guangxu reign] (Beijing, 1958), pp. 74-75.
78. Knight Biggerstaff, *The Earliest Modern Government Schools in China*

(Ithaca, 1961), pp. 127, 170-172, 209.

79. *Haifang dang*, II, 16; III, 13-21; *DXTG*, IX, 3690-3691.

80. Shen Ke, comp., 'Xian Wensu Gong zhengshu xubian' [The memorials of Shen Baozhen, continued] (hand copied in 1889). Manuscript in the possession of Mr Shen Zuxing of Taibei, to whom I am grateful for its use. The manuscript is used here because Shen's memorial of 23 December 1874 differs from the text printed in Ge Shijun, 101:8b-11. On Ding's proposal, see *YWSM-TZ*, 55:19a-b.

81. *The Cambridge History of China, Volume 10: Late Ch'ing, 1800-1911, Part I*, John K. Fairbank, ed. (Cambridge, 1978), pp. 537-542.

82. *Yangwu yundong*, I, 170-184; Li Hongzhang, 'Memorials', 35:46b. Shen was opposed to the idea, saying that the existing programmes, if expanded, would be adequate. Li, on the other hand, was non-committal.

83. Hu Bin, pp. 9-10; Shi Jun, pp. 3-5; Feng Guifen, f.47.

84. *DXTG*, VI, 2611; *YWSM-TZ*, 100:17b.

85. Ge Shijun, 101:10b-11.

86. *YWSM-TZ*, 55:23b.

87. *Lunyu*, Book XIII, Chap. 4.

88. *DXTG*, VII, 2742-2744, 2764-2765.

89. For examples, see Kwang-ching Liu, 'Politics, Intellectual Outlook, and Reform: The T'ung-wen Kuan Controversy of 1867', in Cohen and Schrecker, pp.92-98; Thomas L. Kennedy, *The Arms of Kiangnan: Modernization in the Chinese Ordnance Industry, 1860-1895* (Boulder, 1978), p. 84.

90. The works listed were the *Chunqiu* [The spring and autumn annals], the *Zuozhuan* [The commentary of Zuo], the *Zizhi tongjian* [General mirror for the aid of government] and the *Tongjian gangmu* [Outline and digest of the general mirror]. Unless outherwise stated, sources for this and the next two paragraphs come from the memorials of Shen, Ding and Li in *YWSM-TZ*, 53:26-29b; 55:17-26; and *DXTG*, IX, 3681-3692.

91. *YWSM-TZ*, 42:48b.

92. *Ibid.*, 50:24b, 26-27, 30a-b.

93. Wang Yu-ch'uan, 'An Outline of the Central Government of the Former Han Dynasty', *Harvard Journal of Asiatic Studies*, XII (1949), 134-187. For the use of the deliberative process in early Qing, see Silas H.L. Wu, *Communication and Imperial Control in China: Evolution of the Palace Memorial System, 1693-1735* (Cambridge, Mass., 1970), pp. 9-19.

94. *YWSM-TZ*, 40:10b-36; 41:26b-30, 40b-43, 43-50; 42:45b-48b, 58b-65b; 45:44b-54. For a brief analysis of this discussion, see Wright, pp. 263-268.

95. The subject has been discussed by Knight Biggerstaff and Mary Wright. Biggerstaff, 'The Secret Correspondence of 1867-1868: Views of Leading Chinese Statesmen Regarding the Further Opening of China to Western Influence', *Journal of Modern History*, XXII:2 (June 1950), 122-136; Wright, pp 271-277. For a complete list of memorials, see *ibid.*, pp. 385-386, n.84.

96. Wade to Earl of Derby, 3 May 1875. Great Britain, Foreign Office Archives, FO 17/698, no. 71.

97. *DXTG*, VI, 2610-2614; *Yangwu yundong*, I,26-165; Ge Shijun, 101:8b-11.

98. *YWSM-TZ*, 55:13b-14.

99. *Haifang dang*, I, 948-951.

100. Wright, p. 149.

101. Lü, *Ding Richang*, pp. 56-63, 197-207.

102. Charles D. Sheldon, *The Rise of the Merchant Class in Tokugawa Japan, 1600-1868* (New York, 1958), p. 175; Thomas C. Smith, *Political Change and Industrial Development in Japan: Government Enterprise, 1868-1880* (Stanford, 1955).

103. For example, see Ge Shijun, 101:10; Li Hongzhang, 'Memorials', 35: 43b.

104. Lü, *Ding Richang*, p. 201.
105. Pong, 'Confucian Patriotism', 647-676; Guo Songdao, 11:17b.
106. *YWSM-TZ*, 99:29b-31.
107. *Yangwu yundong*, I, 120-136, especially 121, 129-130. See also note 110.
108. Prosper Giquel, *The Foochow Arsenal and its Results* (Shanghai, 1874), p. 10.
109. Lloyd E. Eastman, *Throne and Mandarins: China's Search for a Policy During the Sino-French Controversy, 1880-1885* (Cambridge, Mass., 1967).
110. Lü, *Ding Richang*, p. 195. It was this sort of idea, taken out of context of the overall thrust of Ding's proposals, that was seized by the conservatives to attack him for trying to change China with barbarian ways.
111. Zhen Zuo-lin, *Yelu shanfang congshu* [The collected works of Zhen Zuo-lin] (Taibei, 1976), VII, 138, see also p. 342 for a later reference; Mai Zhonghua, comp., *Huangchao jingshi wen xinbian* [Collection of statecraft writings, new compilation] (Shanghai, 1902), see Preface (dated 1898):1b.
112. David E. Apter, *The Politics of Modernization* (Chicago, 1965), pp. 85-93.

THE VOCABULARY OF CHANGE

GLOSSARY

bianfa 變法
bianju 變局
chi 恥
chuangju 創局
fuqiang 富強
gaige 改革
gengzhan 耕戰
guanshang yiti 官商一體
guochi 國恥
guoji minsheng 國計民生
hua wuyong wei youyong 化無用為有用
jingjiu zhi dao 經久之道
jingshi 經世
jingshi shuyuan 經世書院
jiuyuan zhi tu 久遠之圖
juzhong juwai yixin 局中局外一心
kai fengqi 開風氣
kai liyuan 開利源
kongyan 空言
kuishi duoshi 揆時度勢
lijin 釐金
liquan 利權
neiluan waihuan 內亂外患
nongzhan 農戰
qi quan zai wo 其權在我

qiangu wei chuang zhi ju 千古未創之局
quan 權
qunce qunli 群策群力
sandai 三代
shangxia yixin 上下一心
shangzhan 商戰
shenshi duoshi 審時度勢
shiwu 時務
shixue 實學
shiyong zhi cai 實用之才
shouhui liquan 收回利權
shou liquan 收利權
ti-yong 體用
tong chou chuanju 通籌全局
tong ji chuangju 統計全局
tongpan chouhua 通盤籌劃
waiwu 外侮
weiyu choumou 未雨綢繆
yangwu 洋務
Zhongti Xiyong 中體西用
zhongwai yixin 中外一心
Zhongxue wei ti, Xixue wei yong 中學為體、西學為用
ziqiang 自強
zizhen 自振
zizhi 自治

3

CHANGING CONCEPTS OF THE ROLE OF WOMEN FROM THE LATE QING TO THE MAY FOURTH PERIOD
Sally Borthwick

This chapter looks at changing concepts of women's role in the decades between the Sino-Japanese War and the May Fourth period. The varying strands making up traditional expectations of women's role are first examined: woman as a productive or parasitic member of the family unit, woman as a vital link in the chain of family continuity, and finally woman as death-welcoming or death-dealing heroine. These are contrasted with the ideas of women's role imported into China in the last years of the Qing: on the one hand, woman as good wife and mother, her nurturant and compassionate disposition complementing the active striving of the male; on the other, woman as independent actor, mistress of her own fate, demanding to do whatever men did. The interaction of these concepts and their effect on women's position over the following decades is discussed. Finally, the chapter looks at the broadening of the women's movement from an initially narrow base among the educated and well-to-do to include those for whom the goals of bourgeois emancipation—rights of inheritance, university education, and suffrage—and those of feminine moderation—woman as mother of the race and conscience of the nation—were equally unreal.

Old Beliefs and Old Forces

In 1907 a radical Chinese women's magazine published in Tokyo declared that 'for the past several thousand years, women's position has been of the lowliest, declining continuously, like living in the darkest hell... In our view, this is because women have been harmed by the old beliefs of former days. So if we want to create a new womanhood, we must first thoroughly and completely overthrow these old beliefs, so that they are no longer a force in society...and with banners raised and drums beating, in bold array, discover from new knowledge and new ideals the brightest, most upright, newest theories about women'.[1] What were these harmful old beliefs, and what forces, after thousands of years of quiescence, made their overthrow urgent? The first part of this paper addresses itself to these questions. Confucianism was a male-centred philosophy which allocated to women a dependent and subordinate role. From the Master himself came the contemptuous observation, 'Only women and small-minded people are hard to rear'. The *Book of Poetry* defines women's position in the lines 'When a boy is born, he is placed on the bed and given a piece of jade to play with; when a girl is born, she is laid on the ground and given a piece of tile to play with'. Other classical works are the source for the 'Three Submissions'—a woman submits to her father before she marries, her husband after, and her son during widowhood—and the assertion that 'Men deal with the outside world, women with inside [household] matters'. This last statement was buttressed by the ancient etymology for the pictograph for 'woman' (*fu*)—a female figure holding a broom.[2]

Woman's role was conceived of in terms of her place in the family line. She was on loan, so to speak, in her family of origin, merely awaiting the time when she would go to produce sons and serve in-laws in her husband's family. For the latter, she was indispensable but at the same time threatening, an unknown outsider. Hence, works of feminine instruction laid great stress on the virtues of accommodation: dutiful service to the elderly, unselfish affability to those of the same generation, lack of jealousy if a second wife were taken, willingness to treat a first wife's children as one's own and so on. In return for these tasks, her husband's family had to support her; she could not be sent home simply at her husband's whim. Obligations were thus reciprocal, as in the other relationships in the Confucian code.

To the original limitations of women's role, scholarly morality added a host of tortuous refinements to be observed by gentlewomen. As early as the *Lienü zhuan* (Biographies of outstanding women), compiled in the first century BC, an elderly widow had been praised for refusing to leave a burning house without the proper attendants. Her fiery death established the principle that a woman of good family did not appear outside the women's apartments. Song Confucianism reinforced the segregation of the sexes, assisted by the newly popular custom of foot-binding; this so crippled its victim that it was difficult for her to walk far, thus making confinement to the home a necessity as well as a virtue. It was neo-Confucianism, too, which established chaste widowhood (preferably accompanied by suicide) as an ideal. As a man should not serve two masters, neither should a woman serve two husbands. (Men, of course, could take as many wives as they wished, either sequentially or simultaneously.) This trend continued in the Qing. Young widows who did not remarry were honoured by the court with commendations and memorial plaques and arches—honours which raised the status of the whole family unit. Such cases established the principle of family dominance over individual satisfaction.

A less restrictive way of earning social commendation was to be a sage mother—a position of some importance when one's son was emperor or high official. While there was little formal role for women in government, and influence exerted informally through feminine wiles was severely condemned, the propriety of maternal counsel in affairs of state had been recognised since the compilation of the *Lienü zhuan*. Respect for the mother-son bond was institutionalised in the custom of granting officials leave to mourn their mothers' deaths, and in the assumption that the unfilial son was at fault in any charges brought against him by a dissatisfied mother. A missionary who generally concurred with the dark assessment of woman's position made by Westerners sojourning in China was forced to admit that 'the quality of her slavery is...much tempered by the great veneration which Confucian principles require sons to pay both parents'.[3]

Ever since Mencius' mother taught her truant son the value of study, the mother-as-teacher had been a model held up for emulation. The chastisement of the idle and encouragement of the persevering appear to have been regarded as the woman's preserve, with fathers abdicating their responsibilities in this field to their wives. Memoirs of those educated in the late Qing frequently pay tribute to maternal influence, rarely to paternal; it is women who beat, plead and remonstrate with their sons, who fight for the money to send them to school and hear their lessons in the evening lamplight.[4] In this area at least the stereotype of appropriate feminine behaviour appears to have influenced conduct.

Anti-Confucian feminists frequently quote the saying that 'lack of talent is a virtue in a woman' as evidence that Confucianism frowned on the education of women. This saying, however, is not a summation of Confucian thought on the subject but merely a slogan used by one side in a debate on female literacy which began in the Ming. As Jennifer Holmgren has recently pointed out, the Confucian identification of moral and intellectual cultivation meant that there was little of the Western tendency to allocate reason to men and emotion or intuition to women.[5] Confucian orthodoxy held in general that women, like men, could best come to an understanding of their duties by acquaintance with the classical precepts defining them; education was valued, theoretically at least, insofar as it made a woman a better daughter, wife, and mother.

Confucianism offered active and constructive images of womanhood as well as negative and passive ones. All these exemplary roles, however, were familial, and within the family vertical relationships (daughter-in-law, other-in-law, motheron) took precedence over the cross-generational one of husband and wife. Even continued widowhood was made praiseworthy not simply by fidelity to the dead husband but by dutiful service to his aged parents or devoted care of his young sons. The *Book of Rites* summed up the purpose of marriage succinctly: 'Above, to serve the ancestral temple, below, to continue the line of descent'.[6]

Popular culture took a more generous view of women's place in the world. Women warriors were the stuff of legend as virtuous suicides were not. Children were reared on stories of Hua Mulan, who took her father's place in the army and fought as a man for twelve years, and Meng Jiang Nü, whose tears brought down the Great Wall of China as she searched for her lost husband. The opera *Yangmen nü jiang* (Women generals of the Yang family) depicts its heroines going into battle against the invading barbarians, an example followed in real life by the Ming loyalist Qin Liangyu.[7] One of the most striking portrayals of female gallantry occurs in Wen Kang's *Ernü yingxiong zhuan* (The Gallant Maid, c. 1840), in which a namby-pamby hero is first discomfited by the novel's roving heroine, whom he meets alone in an inn-yard and takes for a robbers' lookout, and then rescued by her from the simultaneous attack of ten armed monks whom she slaughters one by one. Throughout, her shrewdness, frankness, dexterity and courage are contrasted with his timidity, foolishness, and equivocation—to the evident delight of audiences, for 'Thirteenth Sister's' prowess in the inn-yard and the monastery became a popular item in the repertoire of storytellers and opera companies. Female revolutionaries of the late Qing did not have to look far for models if they wished to advance 'with flags flying and drums beating'.

Literary as well as martial distinction lay within the reach of China's fictive heroines. In *Liang Shanbo and Zhu Yingtai* the heroine studies, in male disguise, alongside the slow-witted object of her affections; and one Ming dramatist so far set aside probability as to compose a play in which a woman (again in disguise) wins first place in the empire in the state examinations. The pinnacle of imaginary emancipation is reached in Li Ruzhen's *Jinghua yuan* (Flowers in the Mirror) which depicts a country of women and the holding of imperial examinations for women.

All the works mentioned above give their heroines a sphere of action considerably larger than the women's apartments. In each, however, the potential threat of unfettered womanhood is neutralised first by the temporary nature of the release—heroines in disguise resume their feminine garb; Thirteenth Sister settles down in the lowly position of second wife; the Empress Wu, patron of women's examinations, is overthrown by the candidates' husbands and brothers—and second by the fact that all the heroines are not merely gifted but virtuous, that is, their sorties into a male world are actuated not by the desire for liberty but by filial or wifely duty. This is most notable in *Jinghua yuan*, in which many of the women end as widow-suicides after their husbands are killed in battle. Even the more trenchant critics of Confucianism would only pick on its inconsistencies — polygamy for men, monogamy for women; remarriage for men, widowhood for women—without ever contemplating the extension of men's prerogatives to women or women's departure from the domestic sphere.[8]

Most of the conditions of women's life in nineteenth-century China—arranged marriage, limited opportunities for education, lack of independent occupation—derived from their subordination to the family unit as a whole and from the necessity of its perpetuation. With variations, this mode of social organisation had held sway for over two thousand years. What were the forces which discredited 'the old beliefs' at the turn of the century?

There was little impetus for change within the Chinese heritage. Can the alterations, then, be attributed to the success of missionary work, as the Chinese came into contact with Western mores for the first time in the latter part of the nineteenth century? To answer these questions one will have to look at the targets of criticism and the model of reform put forward by Westerners in China.

Criticisms and Reform Proposals

Nineteenth century Western writers present a bleak picture of the lives of Chinese women. Most accord with the fiery editorialists of *Zhongguo xin nü jie* (China's New Women), in ascribing to women at best a servile status, at worst a life in hell. They were not so much hostile to the Chinese norms for feminine behaviour as oblivious to them; instead of filial duty, fidelity, and obedience they saw infanticide, foot-binding, and the selling of girl children. That is, it was the 'cruel and unnatural' practices of Chinese family life which first caught Western attention, presumably both as being sensational in themselves and as offering the widest scope for missionary amelioration. As early as 1858, the Reverend William C. Milne felt constrained to disabuse his countrymen of the notion that foot-binding caused agonising pain and sometimes death and that female infanticide was so common that special carts were provided to pick up dead girl babies each morning.[9] Missionary rescue of girl children sold into slavery by impoverished parents likewise attacked a social evil while simultaneously providing heart-rending stories to unloose the purse-strings of the home mission.

Two areas in which missionaries were particularly active were the abolition of foot-binding and the promotion of female education. The Kangxi emperor had issued a short-lived edict proscribing foot-binding in 1662,[10] and the practice was criticised by non-conformist scholars of the early nineteenth century. None of these attacks, however, had succeeded in shaking Chinese attachment to a practice which was a mark both of racial distinction (Manchu women did not bind their feet) and social status. Tightly bound feet ('three-inch golden lotuses') ensured a girl's eligibility for marriage: the saying ran 'Buying an ox, one buys a pair of horns; marrying a wife, one marries a pair of feet'. In these circumstances, there was some justification in the missionary claim that 'the only impulse towards reform of this useless and cruel custom originated with foreigners in China'.[11] The first anti-foot-binding society was set up in a Protestant congregation in Xiamen in 1875; its appeals were publicised in Young J. Allen's *Wan'guo gongbao* ('Review of the Times'), a long-lived periodical whose tactful advocacy of Western practices won it a wide audience in the 1890s. The same journal announced the establishment in Shanghai in 1895 of the Tianzu hui (Natural Feet Society) by one Mrs Little, a British entrepreneur's wife who sought out high government officials to present her case.[12]

The Chinese had no objection in principle to women receiving an education, but since daughters left the family their education was not as pressing a matter as that of sons. Furthermore, a woman, no matter how talented, could never have an official career. The education of girls therefore tended to be an occasional indulgence rather than a serious family investment for most households. Another obstacle to women's education was that girls were not supposed to gad about outside the home; boys might get cheap or even free schooling at a village or lineage school, but girls were usually confined to more expensive home tuition.[13] These prejudices meant that the early mission schools had trouble attracting pupils. Like the early anti-foot-binding societies, they ministered almost entirely to the faithful or at most to potential converts, usually from the lower ranks of society. The McTyeire School, set up at Young J. Allen's instigation in the treaty port of Shanghai in 1892, was one of the first to aim at 'pupils from the higher class families who have hitherto refused to send their daughters to an ordinary mission school', as did the hopefully named 'Upper-class Anglo-Chinese Girls' School' in Fuzhou.[14]

Missionaries hoped that their societies, tracts, and schools, together with their personal and national examples of equality in domestic life, education, and the work force, would lead Chinese women to the enjoyment of 'that elevation of the sex which we now witness in full development [in Christian countries]'.[15] Unaided, however, they would never have been able to persuade the Chinese to turn black into white and white into black; to give up models of behaviour which went back thousands of years in favour of those of barbarians, whose social life was popularly thought to be more animal than human. What aided the missionaries in their struggle was China's political weakness and military defeat in the latter half of the nineteenth century. Missionary writings provided much of the information on which Chinese reformers based their arguments, but Chinese receptivity to this information and the impulse to reshape Chinese society in accordance with it depended less on the intrinsic merits of the Western model than on China's precarious international position. The editorialists of *Zhongguo xin nü jie* put the reasons for the crisis of confidence succinctly:

> If there is nothing wrong with the old virtues, how does it happen that the Chinese race has been getting steadily weaker for several thousand years? Leaving aside the dreary existence of our two hundred million crippled and imprisoned women, even our country's men are listless and apathetic, only interested in themselves and their families, and allowing foreigners to humiliate them at will. They can't form patriotic organisations that strengthen the race, and yet surely the Chinese are not slaves by nature?[16]

The self-strengthening movement discussed by David Pong in the preceding chapter had been prepared to adopt schemes for administrative reform and defence modernisation which had a solid basis in Chinese culture. Following China's defeat by Japan in 1894-1895, however, the feeling grew that Chinese culture was in itself defective. In this climate politically alert Chinese—especially those who had not been involved in formulating or executing government policy—were ready to accept the foreign estimate that 'the position of women [was] one of the dark blemishes in the...social life of the Chinese'[17] and to devote considerable effort to its reform.

Kang Youwei petitioned the throne for the abolition of footbinding in 1898 in terms which indicated that the Chinese had internalised the shock felt by Westerners over Chinese 'backwardness':

> In our country, houses are shacks and clothes are rags. In

addition, our air is polluted by the smoke of opium and our streets are lined with beggars. For some time now, foreigners have taken photographs to circulate among themselves and to laugh at our barbaric ways. But the most appalling and the most humiliating is the binding of women's feet. For that, your servant feels deeply ashamed.[18]

In the same year, Kang's daughter expressed the admiration of foreign institutions which was the corollary of shame over China's weakness.

The power of Europe and America is unprecedented. If we examine the excellence of their institutions, the profusion of their human talents, the flourishing of intelligence and wisdom, the sincerity and honesty of their customs, and their overwhelming superiority over the myriad nations, all are due to their schools.[19]

The arguments of the reformers were expressed most ably by Liang Qichao in a formulation which dominated discussion of women's issues for the next ten or fifteen years. Liang went so far as to say that the key to *all* reforms was to be found in women's education. For this startling assertion he adduced four reasons. Firstly, education would make women economically independent and reduce the burden on their menfolk. China's population of four hundred million already contained too many unproductive men; even worse was the fact that

Out of two hundred million women, every one is a consumer, and not one is a producer. Because they cannot support themselves, but depend on others for their support, men keep them like dogs and horses or slaves, to their great misery; and because they depend on men for support, but the men are unable to support them, a man's laboriously earned income is not enough to look after his wife and children, to his great misery.[20]

A second reason—a good Confucian one—was that education could reduce the trouble which women could make in the household. A knowledge of human relations and outside events would take their minds off the petty struggles and recriminations, the sighing and discontents, which otherwise were endemic among the sisterhood. The third reason was the importance of maternal education for sons:

> The governance of the world rests on two principles; one is the rectification of men's hearts, the other the expansion of their talents. These two must begin in a child's early upbringing, and his early upbringing depends on maternal instruction. The basis of maternal instruction is women's education, and this is why education for women is truly the root cause of national survival or disappearance, national strength or weakness.[21]

Finally, women's education was urged on eugenic grounds. Physical education in particular would contribute to that strengthening of the race which had led mankind upward from the apes and produced civilised races from barbarous tribespeole.[22] Liang's views were summed up in his announcement of the foundation of the first Chinese-run girls' school in Shanghai: the new woman 'above, will be a helpmeet to her husband, below, a source of instruction for her sons; in her immediate surroundings, she will give ease to the family, and in a wider sphere, she will improve the race'.[23]

The themes of economic wastage and genetic deterioration were repeated in the preface to the regulations of Shanghai's Chinese Anti-foot-binding Society written by the elder statesman Zhang Zhidong. Zhang claimed that throughout the empire, all but the poorest families bound their daughters' feet, with the result that women sat idle or wasted their time on trifles like embroidery. Even if they worked they could not achieve one fifth of what a woman with unbound feet could do. Unlike Liang, Zhang had some concrete proposals for the employment of the two hundred million: unbound feet were a necessity for operatives in mechanised silk filatures and textile mills.[24]

The arguments of the reformers of the late nineteenth century show several traits which remained characteristic of the movement for the emancipation of women into the May Fourth period. Firstly, foreign example was used as a justification for reform. Most writers still buttressed their proposals with quotations from the classics, but these were increasingly prefaced by the assertion that such-and-such was the practice in the 'civilised' countries of the West. Europe and America provided models as authoritative as any furnished by the Three Dynasties, the golden age of Confucian antiquity.

Secondly, the subjects of discussion were upper-class women. This was not evident to the writers themselves: Liang includes a moving passage about poor families forced to suffer cold and starvation by the necessity of feeding unproductive members. In actuality, however, Chinese women in working-class households were not unproductive. It is true that the main extra-familial occupations open to women were disreputable or menial—singing girl, prostitute, household servant. Within the family, however, women not only cooked and minded children but often spun, wove, and sewed—shoes as well as clothes—and made soap and candles. In many parts of the country women worked outdoors too, weeding, gleaning, transplanting rice, picking cotton or collecting firewood. In more commercialised areas, their labour might even produce a cash return for the household. It was only well-to-do families which could afford to support women who had nothing to do but embroider, write poetry, quarrel with their sisters-in-law and complain to their husbands. The empty minds and idle hands pictured by Liang form a description of the women of a gentry household, and a fairly stereotyped description at that.

Finally, the remedy for all ills of the sex and the nation was education. The predilection for education as a means of producing talent, and talent as the base for strengthening the nation, came naturally to talented and well-educated men steeped in Confucian tradition and familiar with the expansion of public and professional education in the West. Germany's strength and Japan's rise were held to be primarily due to their system of public schools. Modernisation, to most scholars of Liang's generation, meant education; industrialisation was very much an afterthought.

All three traits are evident in a 1904 article entitled 'Women's Work'. Despite its name, it made no mention of the work currently performed by women in the home, the fields, or the growing textile industry; rather, it was a reiteration (often in the same words) of Liang's contention that two hundred million women were idle, and that this was the cause of poverty in China. The author cited Britain and America as examples, and concluded that the solution 'lies in the promotion of women's education'. Reluctantly leaving aside for the time being the provision of a full Western-style education—reading, writing and arithmetic, sewing and embroidery, letter-writing, knitting, drawing, making artificial flowers, health and hygiene, music, religious principles, physical education and geography—he proposed instead that Chinese women learn to spin, weave, reel silk, twist hemp, sew, or make shoes or straw hats, with literature as a spare-time occupation.[25] All these appear to have been conceived of as handicrafts—Zhang Zhidong is unique in spelling out women's place as factory operatives.

The proposals of Liang and his followers tended to have a patronising tone. 'Rights' were to be generously bestowed by men on their womenfolk, to make them more tolerable to live with and less of a burden to support. It was indeed Liang who popularised the concept of 'sage mother and good wife'.[26] He did not rule out a public role for women—his missionary mentors Young J. Allen and Timothy Richard had repeatedly pointed out that women could make a major contribution to society as doctors, nurses, and educators of the young. But the jobs which women were to take up were extensions of their nurturing role within the family. 'The equality of men and women' meant not that women could do whatever men could, but that the different endowments of the sexes—modesty, gentleness, tenacity and patience on the part of women; boldness, strength, and grasp of general principles on the part of men—were to be equally respected, and made an equally important contribution to society.[27] Fundamental social change—the dissolution of the Confucian family—was not envisaged as a prerequisite to or a consequence of the new education.

Alongside these conciliatory proposals for gradual reform a more radical critique of current morality was taking shape, foreshadowing the anti-Confucian movement of the May Fourth Period. Tan Sitong, executed for his heretical writings in 1898, wrote:

> Whenever you have categorical obligations, not only are the mouths of the people sealed so that they are afraid to speak up, but their minds are also shackled so that they are afraid to think... On what basis does the husband extend his

power and oppress [his wife]? Again it is the [Confucian] theory of the three bonds [between ruler and subject, father and son, and husband and wife] which is the source of the trouble. When the husband considers himself the master, he will not treat his wife as an equal human being. In ancient China the wife could ask for a divorce, and she therefore did not lose the right to be her own master... People in China and abroad are now talking of reforms, but no fundamental principles and systems can be introduced if the five relationships remain unchanged, let alone the three bonds.[28]

An equally drastic reinterpretation of Confucianism was offered in Kang Youwei's *Datong shu* (The Universal Commonwealth). Kang envisaged a utopia in which all divisions between people would be dissolved. Property would be held in common, children reared communally, and public dormitories and dining halls would replace home and family. The work was finished in 1902, but Kang judged that the world was not yet ready for his ideas; the full *Datong shu* was not published until 1935.[29]

Kang Youwei and Tan Sitong were in advance of their time when they formulated their iconoclastic theories in the 1890s; it was Liang Qichao's advocacy of the 'good wife and mother' which held the field. In the first decade of the twentieth century, however, there was a growing number of educated women, familiar with Western ideas, for whom Liang's presentation of feminism as an end to nationalism was not enough. Women's rights to political, financial, and familial independence began to be raised as a separate issue, albeit usually in the context of national regeneration. The discontents and aspirations of such women were articulated in *Nü jie zhong* (A Clarion Call to Women), published in 1903. Like the editorialists of *Zhongguo xin nü jie*, its author, the anarchist Jin Yi, was hostile to old beliefs but had unbounded trust in 'new morality and civilised thought'. He declared that women should struggle to regain their right to study, to make friends with the opposite sex, to marry as they wished, to pursue a career and to own property. He also raised the question of women's participation in politics.[30] In short, *Nü jie zhong* presented an agenda for women's economic, social and political liberation which was to be worked through by the women's movement over the next two decades.

The Women's Movement in the Late Qing

The ideal woman, according to *Nü jie zhong*, would be compassionate, strong, and free, a revolutionary foreknower possessed of a masculine breadth of vision and a commitment to the public welfare. This definition might have been made for the revolutionary heroine Qiu Jin (c. 1879-1907), whose unconventional life and tragic death made a deep impression on her contemporaries.[31] Qiu Jin had been given a good deal of freedom in her own home, where she learnt to ride and use a sword as well as more feminine accomplishments. Arranged marriage to a minor official she found less satisfactory, and accordingly she separated from her husband and in 1904 left for study in Tokyo—one of the first unaccompanied women to do so, for her few predecessors had travelled mainly with family members. Tokyo offered a heady atmosphere: students were not only removed from the constraints and expectations of their homes, but were also effectively beyond the jurisdiction of the Qing government. In 1903, student activism had crystallised around the 'Resist Russia' movement aimed at frustrating Russian designs on Manchuria. Women in Tokyo had played their part by organising a band of nurses to travel north with their brother students of the Volunteer Corps to Resist Russia, while their counterparts in Shanghai organised a Women's Society of Comrades to Resist Russia. In this environment Qiu Jin had little difficulty in making the revolutionary contacts which were to lead her to insurrection and a martyr's death in Shaoxing three years later.

What led a Qing gentlewoman to such a career so far removed from the 'Three Submissions' supposed to characterise the old society? External political pressures were certainly one factor. The Manchu government appeared incapable of resisting the imperialist powers, and young revolutionaries felt that the fate of the nation rested in their hands. Political crisis created an atmosphere in which the traditional occasions for female heroism—self-mutilation or suicide to avoid rape, or daring gallantry like Thirteenth Sister's—were transformed into self-sacrifice on behalf of the nation, in the manner of Madame Roland or Sophia Perovskaya. Wealth and a sympathetic family also played a part: both Qiu Jin and her fellow revolutionary,

Chen Bijun, could rely on their mothers for financial support.[32]

Few women possessed Qiu Jin's spiritual and financial resources, and her dramatic solution to the problems of marriage, motherhood, education and career attracted few followers. Although female students in Japan, contemplating the difference between the sexes, might propose that women were especially fitted for the task of destruction of the social fabric, most women were concerned simply with raising their own standing within existing social forms. In this task the radicalism of student feminists may in the short term have been a hindrance rather than a help.

In so far as the Qing government was concerned, the goal was to improve China's women within the framework of traditional virtues in the home. Thus on his return from Tokyo 1902, Wu Rulun, the dean of Beijing University, expressed a desire to adopt the Japanese approach to women's education which insisted that 'a good family atmosphere depends on maternal instruction, and maternal instruction depends on the education of our women'.[33] Wu's opinion notwithstanding, the regulations for China's modern school system, promulgated in 1904, specifically excluded schools for girls. Zhang Zhidong, the system's main architect, feared that 'in China's present circumstances, the setting up of girls' schools would give rise to numerous evils'—chief among them the desire to choose one's own mate.[34] Education for girls was fine as long as it was carried out in the privacy of the home. It seems reasonable to suppose that Zhang, who seven years earlier had inveighed against the restrictions placed on women by foot-binding, had been frightened out of his previous tolerance by the spectre of the 'new woman' demanding the right to control her own destiny.

When the regulations for girls' schools were finally promulgated in 1907, they erred on the side of caution. In keeping with the view that women's place was in the home, no high schools or tertiary education for women were provided: girls could attend only primary schools or lower level normal schools.[35] The latter were designed to provide teachers for the former, since to avoid suspicion of sexual misconduct girls' schools were supposed to employ women teachers only. Administrative staff, if male, had to be over fifty, and students were to wear Chinese dress (though most boys' schools had adopted the semi-military Western-style school uniform worn in

Japan). The curriculum was geared to the production of 'virtuous wives and mothers'; sexual radicalism was to be kept at bay by stories of exemplary women from the Zhou dynasty on, and the higher classes were to take domestic science, sewing, and handicrafts. Dissolute theories on breaking down the barriers between the sexes and choosing one's own mate were to be firmly repudiated, as were political gatherings and speeches.[36] Overall, the wording of the regulations suggests a reluctant blend of Confucian conservatism and timid modernism, united in defence against the twin bogeys of sexual and political radicalism.

In actuality girls' schools reflected the shifting battleground between conflicting interpretations of women's role. The Ministry of Education's black-and-white prohibitions were hard to enforce in the real world: the shortage of women teachers meant that men often had to be employed, and in the treaty ports wealthy private individuals and foreign missions set up technical and secondary schools for girls. From 1908, the North China Union College for Women, a missionary college, offered a few courses above high school. The failure of the Ministry of Education to produce usable textbooks meant that private publishing houses took up the task. A Commercial Press reader for girls' higher primary schools compares favourably, in the non-sexist content of most lessons, with many primers recently in use in the West. Most lessons are about the natural world: watermelons, snails, mulberry trees, mice—or other items of general knowledge—paper-making, pickling, accounts. Girls are presented as active, helpful, and intelligent, and the first chapter of the fifth book gives a spirited defence of their right to education, contrasted with the ignorance in which they were formerly kept.[37]

Girls' schools attempted to stress conservative values in the social realm: regulations forbad visits from non-family members and correspondence from unauthorised persons, and students were warned that 'equal rights' meant simply 'an educated woman, able to manage her own household and tasks, and thus the same as a man', while freedom was the self-regulation which ensured that every act accorded with what was right.[38] Even so, a salacious public assumed the worst. Pupils dressed up in Shanghai styles and leather shoes incurred the suspicion of disreputable conduct, and might be mocked in the streets which they traversed with indecent freedom.[39]

What effects did the women's movement have in the late Qing? First, one must realise the limitations of its influence even in the comparatively non-controversial areas of women's education and the abolition of foot-binding. A Western observer commented in the last year of the dynasty:

> The reform [of foot-binding] has not reached farther than the cities and the higher classes. Much of the open country is not yet aware there is such a movement. The poor fear ridicule and, besides, they hope to get a better bride-price for their girls... Chinese from the big coast ports, where Western influence is ascendant, will tell you in good faith that foot-binding has nearly died out. The fact is the release of the overwhelming majority of its victims is yet to come.

Between 75 and 95 per cent of Chinese women were estimated still to have bound feet.[40]

Women's education reached an even more minuscule proportion of the population. There were 13,489 girls at Chinese-run girls' schools in 1909; several thousand more attended missionary schools, and an unknown number studied alongside boys in the earliest grades of primary school. Fewer than 0.1 per cent of school-age girls attended school, and girl students formed only 2 per cent of the total number of students in Chinese-run schools. Schools for girls tended to be concentrated in the treaty ports; many of the inland provinces mustered fewer than a thousand girl students.[41] A disproportionate number of those who attended school came from wealthy and enlightened households where home tuition had often preceded schooling. The better schools charged fees, and even where tuition costs were low the twenty or thirty yuan charged each term for board put these schools beyond the reach of wage-earners. Mission schools which hoped to use education as a means of conversion offered cheaper schooling, and there were some philanthropic Chinese enterprises aimed at the poorer classes of society. As a whole, however, Chinese women were at best observers of this new phenomenon, at worst totally ignorant of its existence. The same could be said of attempts to raise the level of women through journals published for their benefit. Papers for women had been published since 1898, one short-lived periodical succeeding another, but it was not until the end of the 1900s that women's journalism was set on a firm commercial foundation. Even then, its price and content show that it was aimed firmly at women of the middle classes and above.[42]

If reform measures tangential to Confucian familism had only limited success, those which ran counter to it had even less. The freedom to refuse or leave an arranged marriage, demands to own property, study abroad, or participate in electing or overthrowing a government, were largely confined to those with privileged access to wealth and Westernisation and exceptionally indulgent families. All the women stalwarts of the early Tongmeng hui (Revolutionary Alliance)—Qiu Jin, Chen Bijun, and He Xiangning—came from well-to-do families. Chen and He, moreover, grew up outside the Chinese mainland, Chen in Malaya and He in the colony of Hong Kong. All studied in Japan on money provided by their families, which enabled Qiu Jin to leave her marriage and Chen Bijun to contract hers—to the dashing young revolutionary Wang Jingwei.[43] (The opportunity for further study was also a factor enabling Chen Hengzhe, China's first woman professor, and Yang Buwei, the future wife of the linguist Zhao Yuanren (Chao Yuenren), to break off arranged marriages).[44]

If wealth produced one kind of revolt, poverty brought about another. The experience of working outside the home, so eagerly sought by a handful of upper-class women, was forced on many from poorer households. As Zhang Zhidong had foreseen, the modernising textile industry required a growing number of female operatives. In the treaty port of Shanghai in particular women formed a significant proportion of the factory workforce. Forced to work for low wages and in poor conditions, several hundred of them went on strike for a one cent rise in pay in 1911. The women's movement, however, did not take cognizance of their problems: it continued to treat the plight of the upper-class woman—confined to her own apartments, maids and servant-girls her only confidants, the applying of makeup her chief occupation—as the predicament of all women. It was not until the 1920s that elite radicalism and working-class protest united under the Communists and the left wing of the Guomindang.

The Women's Movement in the Early Republic

Feminists greeted the birth of the Republic in 1911 with high hopes; here at last was an opportunity for the dedication, public spirit, and revolutionary intensity recommended in *Nü jie zhong*. In the first days of the fighting around Wuhan, when the Republican side was short of troops, a Miss Wu Qingshu organised a women's army of several hundred volunteers who were said to have performed well in the fighting around Hankou and Nanjing. 'Amazons' also fought alongside men in the Republican army.[45] More in line with the nurturant role of women envisaged by Young J. Allen was the contribution of Zhang Zhujun, a missionary-educated woman doctor who raised money and volunteers for a Red Cross team to go to the battlefront. (The exploits of both are celebrated in *Shenzhou nü zi xinshi* [A new history of China's women, 1913] alongside those of traditionally virtuous faithful wives,[46] suggesting that the categories of Confucian conservatism, moderate reform, and feminist radicalism are more clearly distinct to the historian than they were to contemporaries).

The new government speedily rebuffed hopes for equality. One of the first acts of the new Army Ministry was to disband women's troops and forbid the raising of any more such armies; women were henceforth to be confined to nursing. Nor was women's contribution to the revolutionary movement recognised in the new constitution. Militant women lobbyists demanded that the Nanjing parliament expand the definition of 'citizen' to include the words 'without distinction of sex', but were given an unsympathetic hearing. To press their demands, Tang Qunying and other members of the Society for Women's Participation in Government stormed a parliamentary session, breaking windows, attacking guards, and threatening the members. The fracas attracted much notice but achieved nothing; laws on voting and election rights passed in 1912 confirmed that 'citizen' meant 'man'.[47]

The éclat with which the women's movement burst on the Republican era was not sustained. Under the conservative rule of Yuan Shikai and his warlord successors, a woman's position remained at best that of 'good wife and mother'. Even there, the concept of equality within different spheres sought by reformers of the late Qing was not recognised. Under the revised Qing criminal code (valid until 1929-1930), a wife was legally subordinate to her husband, who controlled her actions and her money. Her adultery or failure to serve his parents were grounds for divorce, but the reverse did not apply. Concubinage was implicitly recognised, and a daughter inherited only if the deceased had no other immediate family members. A contemporary critic observed that the new laws were simply the Qing code under another name and that China was unique among modern nations in continuing to base her laws on familism.[48]

Even more striking evidence of the survival of the 'old beliefs' against which *Zhongguo xin nü jie* had crusaded ten years earlier were the 1917 regulations governing the award of honours to women. A woman could receive presidential commendation for being a good wife and mother, for twenty years of virtuous widowhood, for not remarrying after her fiance's death, and for resisting or atoning for rape by suicide.[49]

Moderate reforms which had a measure of traditional sanction continued to be implemented under Yuan and conscientious warlords such as Yan Xishan and Feng Yuxiang. The anti-foot-binding movement spread, and the number of girls in Chinese-run schools rose to 172,000 by 1917—a twelve-fold increase in the space of eight years. These figures, however, still represented less than one-twentieth of the total enrolment. Conservative older people thought that the new schools gave girls ideas above their station: they came home wayward and idle, not content with their old clothes and food, and were perpetually gadding about.[50] Even if parental permission could be obtained, fees were a problem: as late as 1918-1919, 532 county-level units out of 1819 had no girls' schools,[51] leaving boarding as the only alternative for many. Co-education (in the same school but in separate classes after the first two grades) was permitted up to higher primary level, but many schools did not take advantage of this provision.

Since a woman's education was simply a preliminary to marriage (or at best to a kindred career in caring for the sick or teaching young children), higher education for women was not a priority. China's first four-year college for women, the missionary-run Jinling in Nanjing, opened its doors only in 1916;[52] Chinese-run institutions did not follow until 1918, when the Beijing Women's Normal School was upgraded to the tertiary level. Contrary to the expectations of the early reformers, most women were entering the workforce without any education at all: there were some 620,000 women in industry by 1915, working a twelve- or fourteen-hour day for twenty or thirty cents.[53]

The media which shaped public opinion were no more daring than their masters in government. Early issues of *Funü zazhi* (Women's Journal), a periodical founded in Shanghai in 1915, steered clear of the controversial, concentrating instead on such acceptable subjects as women's education or the improvement of family life. Articles covered age of marriage, family size, child care, hygiene, and home nursing, but rarely touched on such contentious subjects as the arranged marriage. *Dongfang zazhi* (The Eastern Miscellany) mentioned 'free marriage' in a 1917 article only to dismiss it: the pursuit of love would waste young people's energies on pretence, jealousy, and decadence. Even if they were allowed to mix more freely, they should strive to keep love at bay through judicious observance of Confucian morality.[54]

The reign of Confucian morality was, however, coming to an end. *Xin qingnian* (New Youth), founded at the end of 1916, challenged the repressive conservatism which had marked Yuan's rule. Confucianism was identified with the preservation of despotic authority in the family and the state, and its treasured virtues of filial piety and brotherly behaviour became 'the mainstay of two thousand years of the family system and its despotic politics'.[55] As a representative of 'modern, rational man', Chen Duxiu attacked the blind veneration of chaste widowhood, the segregation of the sexes, and the power of parents to interfere in their children's lives, and asserted in their place the enlightened customs of Western society, in which 'women run their own lives in every capacity from lawyer and doctor to salesgirl and factory worker' and men and women could even dance together without being accused of dissipation.[56]

Contributors' views covered a wide range, but all agreed on the necessity for reform if not revolution in family relations. Initially, contributors were content with rescuing woman from the Confucian dungeon and placing her on the pedestal prepared by Liang Qichao and Young J. Allen: woman's importance was still that of mother of the race, and although she should receive higher education it should be of a kind befitting her different endowments and purpose in life.[57] By 1919, however, the reshaping of family life foreseen in Kang Youwei's *Datong shu* was again being considered, as earnest visionaries laboured on ways of freeing womankind through communal kitchens and creches.[58] Marriage itself was challenged: if a monarchy could become a republic and a dictatorship a democracy, why could the equally ancient, corrupt, and despotic institution of marriage not be overthrown?[59] By 1920, almost every issue of the *Funü zazhi* ran a discussion on women's emancipation, social intercourse between men and women, or love and marriage. Love, in the sense of romance, had been chastely eschewed in the 1910s, but along with sex—another previous unmentionable—it dominated the *Funü zazhi* of the mid-1920s. The first issue of 1925 was dedicated to 'the new sexual morality' and typical articles published during the year covered 'Love Matches and Eugenics', 'Male and Female Sex Life and Creativity', and 'Sex and Society'.

Yet brave words were not necessarily followed by brave acts when the student reader returned to the bosom of his family. Even on such basic matters as the refusal of an arranged marriage, he had—being financially dependent on his parents—no recourse but to 'urge', 'remonstrate' and 'persuade' them against it. One article suggested that the future bride first be given an education; if she turned out well, the match could go ahead.[60] As late as the 1930s, nearly half of a sample of 194 married college students had not seen their brides before marriage and less than a quarter had chosen their own partner.[61]

Although writers for the early *Xin qingnian* and kindred periodicals thought of themselves as pathbreakers, they had much in common with reformers of the late Qing. The chief difference was that whereas Tan Sitong, Kang Youwei and Liang Qichao were interested in clearing away later accretions and restoring the purity of Confucius' teachings, Chen Duxiu and his fellow contributors considered Confucianism itself outmoded, and felt that Kang's teachings were as passé as those of his conservative opponents.[62] This break obscured other fundamental continuities. Writers still used foreign examples—Europe and America—as a clinching argument, showing their erudition (or lack of it) with references in English to 'Ionian lyric poets', 'freedomism', or 'sexual impulse'.[63] American women, in particular, were favourite models.[64] Again, the subject of discussion purported to be China's two hundred million, but in reality was still only a tiny fraction of that two hundred million—those to whom inheritance of property or suffrage or university education were significant issues. Finally, education for women was still thought of as a panacea. Writer after writer acknowledged it as the key to women's emancipation. It was no longer possible, with nearly 200,000 in school, to say that Chinese women received no education; the question therefore became one of giving them more education (to university level instead of secondary) or a different kind of education (the same as that which men received).[65] Education was a slogan which confirmed young people's superiority to their elders, for the young had received a better, more up-to-date education than their parents' generation; if they could only transfer their own experiences and attitudes to the rest of the population, China's problems would be solved.

The May Fourth movement was a testing ground for students' ideas about their virtue and their power. Originating in a protest by Beijing tertiary students against China's poor treatment at the Versailles conference, the movement soon spread throughout the country. Girl students, initially more restricted than men—those at Beijing Higher Normal School for Women did not join the first wave of strikes because their parents would have taken them home at the first sign of trouble[66] —were radicalised by the experience. Chow Tse-tsung summarised their achievements in the political area:

> [Like] the boys, the Chinese girl students developed a great interest in political affairs during the latter stages of the May Fourth Movement. The women's suffrage movement made great advances. In 1920 a number of women in Changsha joined the citizens' demonstration, asking for marriage freedom and personal freedom. In February of the following year the Women's Association of Hunan...was established, and proposed the realization of five rights for women, i.e. equal right of property inheritance, right to vote and be elected to office, equal rights of education, equal rights to work, and the right of self-determination in marriage... It succeeded in December 1921 in obtaining provision for suffrage and women's personal freedom in the Hunan provincial constitution, and in electing a woman to the provincial legislature. Similar movements took place in Chekiang and Kwangtung

provinces.[67]

In Beijing, too, girl students set up groups to demand the vote and equal rights for women.[68]

Despite this access of vigour, the women's movement had obtained only limited success in the struggle for equal rights by the mid-1920s. In education, women were admitted to university along with men, but few took up this opportunity and some of those who did so were suspected of simply trying to improve their marriage prospects. In careers, women had won entry to a small corner of man's world: there were in 1924 women bank clerks, salesgirls, and company employees, and even a few university lecturers and civil servants.[69] Politically, women had won some rights at the provincial level, but had no place at the national level. In law, the delayed revision of the civil code meant that women were still unequal to men in regard to divorce provisions, inheritance, and control of property.

Faced with these obstacles, some women retreated from the fray to re-emphasise the complementary role of woman as wife and mother, while others girded themselves for a renewed attack on male strongholds. A contemporary analyst divided the two types as follows:

> The first type believes that men and women are basically equal psychologically, so that all men's work will eventually be performed by women too, and all men's rights will eventually be enjoyed by women too. From this basic principle flow the following actions: 1) they seek political equality, and raise the cry for women's suffrage; 2) they seek economic equality, and agitate for careers to be opened to women; 3) they seek intellectual equality, and have the prohibition on co-education lifted; 4) they seek liberation in the sphere of morality, and promote theories of free marriage and free divorce.

In contrast to this group stands the second type, who believe

> that men and women are different in nature and are differently endowed. They think that taking a job is contrary to women's nature. As for politics, that dirty world is already a blot on male civilisation, and is something that women in particular should keep away from

at present. They say that the best use of women's talents...is for women to develop their natural gentleness and compassion to the full through motherhood.[70]

Conclusion

In short, the different conceptions of women's role which had intermingled and contended over the past thirty years—woman as obedient daughter-in-law and heir-provider; woman as wife and mother; and woman as independent agent—continued to be rehearsed in the 1920s. At the same time, a new element had entered into the equation. The growing pains of industrialisation, the political activism of the May Fourth movement, and the propagation of Marxism meant that the figure of 'two hundred million women', bandied about by reformers and radicals since Liang Qichao, was no longer simply a shorthand for the wives and daughters of the gentry and their modern equivalents. The movement for women's equality was coming from two directions: at the top intellectual middle-class women tried to carry out the slogans of equality raised in the French Revolution; at the bottom, women workers stood side by side with their male comrades fighting for the realisation of the new world. Both were affected by the industrialisation which was driving women into factories and offices on the one hand, and on the other breaking down the family and dissolving the old morality.[71] In even more outspoken terms, the Communist labour organiser, Xiang Jingyu, contrasted the half-measures of the educated middle class with the struggles and sacrifices of women workers: 30,000 had participated in strikes in 1922.[72] Proletarian feminism, however, had no better fortune than its elite counterpart. The vicissitudes of political change meant that theoretical equality with men was not achieved for some decades; and even today in China, equality in practice is still in the process of development.

NOTES

1. Lian Shi, 'Benbao wu da zhuyi yanshuo' [An address on the five major principles of our journal], in Li Youning and Zhang Yufa, eds., *Jindai Zhongguo nüquan yundong shiliao* [Source materials on the feminist movement in modern China] (hereafter cited as *Shiliao*) (Taibei, 1975), p. 775.
2. For the customary critical appraisal of Confucian concepts of women's

role, see Chen Dongyuan, *Zhongguo funu shenghuo shi* [History of the life of Chinese women] (first ed., Shanghai, 1928; repr. Taibei, 1975), passim, and Vermier Y. Chiu, *Marriage Laws and Customs of China* (Hong Kong, 1966), pp. 17-18. For a dissenting view of women's status in traditional China, see J. Holmgren, 'Myths and Fantasies about Women in Traditional China', *Australian Journal of Chinese Affairs*, 6 (1981), 147-170.

3. T.T. Meadows, *The Chinese and Their Rebellions* (London, 1856), quoted in Lien-sheng Yang, *Excursions in Sinology* (Cambridge, Mass., 1969), p. 27.

4. Sally Borthwick, *Education and Social Change in China: The Beginnings of the Modern Era* (Stanford, 1983), pp. 26-27.

5. Holmgren, p. 155.

6. Qing Ru, 'Lun nü xue' [On women's education], *Shiliao*, p. 558.

7. Mary Backus Rankin, 'The Emergence of Women at the End of the Ch'ing: The Case of Ch'iu Chin', in Margery Wolf and Roxane Witke, eds, *Women in Chinese Society* (Stanford, 1975), p. 40. Roxane Witke discusses the legacy of these warlike popular heroines in her thesis, Transformation of Attitudes Towards Women During the May Fourth Era of Modern China (University of California, Berkeley, 1970), pp. 45-49, 334.

8. *Ibid.*, p. 43; Chen Dongyuan, pp. 249-251.

9. William C. Milne, *Life in China* (London, 1858), pp. 38-46.

10. 'Jindai Zhongguo nüquan yundong dashi ji' [A record of major events in the women's movement in modern China], *Shiliao*, p. 1514.

11. A.H. Smith, *Village Life in China: a Study in Sociology* (New York, 1899), p. 261.

12. 'Xiamen jiechanzuhui' [The Xiamen Anti-Footbinding Society], 'Tianzu hui zhengwen qi' [Notice soliciting contributions for the Natural Feet Society], *Shiliao*, pp. 837-841; A. Little, *Gleanings from Fifty Years in China* (London, 1910), p. xiii.

13. A partial exception occurred in South China, especially in and around Guangzhou. See Mary Raleigh Anderson, *Protestant Mission Schools for Girls in South China (1827 to the Japanese Invasion)*. (Mobile, Alabama, 1943), pp. 27, 52-53.

14. See *The China Mission Handbook*, First Issue (Shanghai, 1896), p. 232; *Mission Educational Directory for China* (Shanghai, 1910), pp. 23, 58.

15. Smith, p. 306.

16. Lian Shi, in *Shiliao*, p. 783.

17. Thomas G. Selby, *Chinamen at Home* (London, 1900), p. 179.

18. Quoted in Jerome Ch'en, *China and the West: Society and Culture, 1815-1937* (London, 1979), p. 381.

19. Kang Tongwei, 'On the Advantages and Disadvantages of Educating Women' (1898), in J. Mason Gentzler, ed., *Changing China: Readings in the History of China from the Opium War to the Present* (New York, 1977), p. 97.

20. Liang Qichao, 'Lun nuxue' [Women's education], *Shiliao*, p. 550.

21. *Ibid.*, p. 552.

22. *Ibid*.

23. Liang Qichao, 'Changshe nü xuetang qi' [Promoting the establishment of women's schools], *Shiliao*, p. 561.

24. 'Zhang Shangshu buchanzu hui xu' [Governor-general Zhang's preface to the Anti-foot-binding Society], *Shiliao*, pp. 847-849.

25. 'Lun nü gong' [Women's work], *Dongfang zazhi*, I:8 (October 1904), 108-112.

26. See Chen Dongyuan, p. 323.

27. Young J. Allen, 'Lun nannu zhi fenbie jiqi guanxi' [The differences between men and women and their relationship], *Shiliao*, pp. 382-388; and 'Lun

Zhongguo bianfa zhi benwu' [The basic tasks of Chinese reform], *ibid.*, pp. 388-390; Timothy Richard, 'Xinu you gong Zhongguo shuo' [Western women's contribution to China], *ibid.*, pp. 764-766.

28. Tan Sitong, *Renxue* [The study of humanity], in Gentzler, p. 96.

29. See Kung-chuan Hsiao, *A Modern China and a New World: K'ang Yu-wei, Reformer and Utopian, 1858-1927* (Seattle, 1975), pp. 411, 442-478.

30. Chen Dongyuan, p. 337.

31. See Rankin, pp. 62-63.

32. *Ibid.*, pp. 49, 51; Howard L. Boorman, ed., *Biographical Dictionary of Republican China* (New York, 1967-1979) I, 219.

33. Wu Rulun, *Dongyou conglu* [Records of a journey in the east], quoted in Huang Fuqing, *Qingmo liu-Ri xuesheng* [Chinese students in Japan at the end of the Qing] (Taibei, 1975), pp. 57-58.

34. Taga Akigoro, ed., *Kindai Chugoku kyoiku shiryō* (*Shinmatsuhen*) [Source materials on the history of modern Chinese education] (late Qing) (Tokyo, 1972), pp. 309-312 (hereafter cited as *Shiryo*).

35. See Yu Qingshang, 'Sanshiwu nian lai Zhongguo zhi nü zi jiaoyu' [Women's education in China over the past thirty-five years], in Cai Yuanpei, *et al*, *Zuijin sanshiwu nian lai zhi Zhongguo jiaoyu* [Chinese education over the past thirty-five years] (Shanghai, 1931), p. 177.

36. *Shiryō*, p. 460.

37. *Dingzheng nü zi guowen jiaokeshu* [National language textbook for girls, revised edition], vols. 4-8 (Shanghai, 1912). The revised version was issued after the establishment of the Republic, but the publishers state that few changes were made in the text.

38. *Xingqi huabao* [Illustrated Weekly], 22 (1907).

39. 'Xuejie yi su shefa yi baoquan nü xue zhi mingyu' [Educated circles should hasten to find a way of preserving the reputation of women's education], *Shiliao*, pp. 1163-1165.

40. Edward Alsworth Ross, *The Changing Chinese: the Conflict of Oriental and Western Cultures in China* (New York, 1911), pp. 181-182.

41. China, Xue Bu [Ministry of Education], *Xuantong yuannian: disanci tongji tubiao* [The first year of Xuantong: the third statistical compilation] (Beijing, 1911), Gesheng, p. 9, and provincial entries.

42. See *Shiliao*, pp. 800 and 1523-1535, for listing of periodicals from 1898 to 1911.

43. See Boorman, I, 218; II, 67; Liao Mengxing, *Wode muqin He Xiangning* [My mother He Xiangning] (Hong Kong, 1973), pp. 2-3.

44. See Boorman, pp. 184-185; Chen Hengzhe, 'Wo younian qiuxue de jingguo' [My youthful search for education] in Tao Kangde, ed., *Zizhuan zhi yizhang* [Chapters of autobiography] (Guangzhou, 1938), pp. 70-83; Buwei Yang Chao, *Autobiography of a Chinese Woman* (first ed., 1947; repr. Westport, Conn., 1970), pp. 76-81.

45. Xu Tianxiao, *Shenzhou nuzi xinshi (xubian)* [A new history of China's women (continuation)] (first ed., Shanghai, 1913; repr. Taibei, 1978), pp. 71-75; Edmund S.K. Fung, *The Military Dimension of the Chinese Revolution: The New Army and its Role in the Revolution of 1911* (Vancouver, 1980), p. 233.

46. Xu Tianxiao, *passim*.

47. *Ibid.*, pp. 98-100; Chen Dongyuan, pp. 359-360.

48. Zhu Hong, 'Nüquan yu falü ' [Women's rights and the law], in Mei Sheng ed., *Zhongguo nuxing wenti taolunji* [Collected essays on Chinese women's questions], (3rd edition, Shanghai, 1934; hereafter *Taolunji*) II, 66-73. *Taolunji* consists of articles reprinted from journals and the press from the May Fourth Period.

49. Zhao Fengjie, *Zhongguo funü zai falü shang de diwei* [The legal

position of Chinese women] (Taibei, 1973), p. 124.

50. Ji Tao, 'Nuzî jiefang cong nali zuo qi? Qi liu' [Where do we start with women's liberation? VI], *Taolunji*, I, 102.

51. Shu Xincheng, ed., *Jindai Zhongguo jiaoyushi ziliao* [Source materials for the history of modern Chinese education] (Beijing, 1961), p. 382.

52. See Holly Ellen Newcomb, 'Western Influence and the Transition of Chinese Upper Class Women, 1830s-1930s', Master's thesis, University of Washington, 1967, p. 104.

53. Bo Xi, 'Funü laodongzhe de gongzi wenti' [The question of the wages of women workers], *Taolunji*, II, 56-58; Mary Ninde Gamewell, *The Gateway to China: Pictures of Shanghai (1916)*, quoted in Genzler, pp. 162-163.

54. Cang Fu, 'Ziyou jiehun' [Free marriage], *Dongfang zazhi*, XIV:5 (May 1917), 7-12.

55. Wu Yu, 'Jiazu zhidu wei zhuanzhi zhuyi zhi genju lun' [The family system as the basis of dictatorship], *Xin qingnian*, II:6 (February 1917), 3. The early issues of *Xin qingnian* are not continuously paginated.

56. Chen Duxiu, 'Kongzi zhi dao yu xiandai shenghuo' [Confucianism and modern life], *Xin qingnian*, II:4 (December 1916), 4-5. Those interested in a more detailed treatment of such iconoclastic ideas should consult Witke, pp. 77-83 *et passim*.

57. See Chen Qian Aichen, 'Xianmushi yu Zhongguo qiantu zhi guanxi' [The relevance of 'good mothers' to China's future], Nü zi wenti, *Xin qingnian*, II:6 (February 1917), 2-4; Liang Hualan, 'Nuzi jiaoyu' [Women's education], Nü zi wenti, *Xin qingnian*, III:1 (March 1917), 1.

58. Da Bai, 'Nü zi jiefang cong nali zuo qi? Qi wu' [Where do we start with women's liberation? V], *Taolunji*, I, 96-97; Shen Jianshi, 'Ertong gongyu' [Communal upbringing of children], *Xin qingnian*, VI:6 (November 1919), 563-567. For reprint of Shen's article and ensuing debate, see *Taolunji*, VI, 1-74.

59. Zhang Songnian, 'Nannü wenti' [The question of relations between men and women], *Xin qingnian*, VI:3 (March 1919), 320.

60. Lu Qiuxin, 'Hunyin wenti de san xiao shiqi' [Three subdivisions in the history of the marriage question], *Taolunji*, IV, 108-109.

61. Olga Lang, *Chinese Family and Society* (first ed., New Haven, 1946; repr. Archon Books, 1968), p. 122.

62. Chen Duxiu, 'Kongzi zhi dao yu xiandai shenghuo' [Confucianism and modern life], p. 1.

63. For examples see Chen Dezheng, 'Xing'ai de jiazhi' [The value of sexual love], *Taolunji*, IV, 32-46; Li Sanwu, 'Xiandai jiehun jichu de quexian he jinhou ying qu de fangzhen' [Shortcomings in the foundations of modern marriage and the direction to be taken from now on], *Taolunji*, IV, 168-176.

64. See Hu Shi, 'Meiguo de furen' [American women], *Xin qingnian*, V:3 (September 1918), 213-224.

65. See Hu Shi, 'Nü zi jiefang cong nali zuo qi? Qi yi' [Where do we start with women's liberation? I], *Taolunji*, I, 90; Han Min, 'Nü zi jiefang cong nali zuo qi? Qi er' [Where do we start with women's liberation? II], *ibid.*, 92; Tang Gongxian, 'Woguo nü zi de shixue ji qi jiuji' [Lack of schooling among Chinese women and its remedy], *ibid.*, 175; Tao Yi, 'Funü jiaoyu de yongjiu jihua' [A lasting plan for women's education], *Funü zazhi*, X:1 (1924), 42-50.

66. Li Shuangqing, *Wusi yundong zhengshi* [What really happened in the May Fourth Movement] (Taibei, 1968), p. 27.

67. Chow Tse-tsung, *The May Fourth Movement: Intellectual Revolution in Modern China* (Cambridge, Mass., 1960), pp. 258-259. For the Hunan Constitution, see Wu Xiangxiang, *Zhongguo xiandaishi congkan* [Collected articles on modern Chinese history] I (Taibei, 1960), 272-296.

68. See Chow Tse-tsung, p. 259; Gao Yihan, 'Nü zi canzheng wenti' [The

question of women's suffrage], *Taolunji*, II, 126. For an overview of the women's suffrage movement in the 1920s, see Roxane Witke, 'Woman as Politician in China of the 1920s', in Marilyn B. Young, ed., *Women in China: Studies in Social Change and Feminism* (Ann Arbor, 1973), pp. 33-45.

69. Se Lu, 'Zuijin shiniannei funü jie de huigu' [An overview of women over the past ten years], *Funü zazhi*, X:1 (1924), 21.

70. Ji Sheng, 'Funü yundong de jinglu' [The path of the women's movement], *Taolunji*, I, 110-111.

71. *Ibid.*

72. Suzette Leith, 'Chinese Women in the Early Communist Movement', in Young, p. 51.

4

LESSONS FROM AN ITALIAN CONNECTION
Michael R. Godley

On 25 October 1937, surrounded by the splendour of the Palazzio Venezia, Benito Mussolini awaited the arrival of a Nationalist Chinese representative. At 6.00 p.m., dressed in his general's uniform, Jiang Baili stood before Il Duce and Foreign Minister Galeazzo Ciano with a secret message from Chiang Kai-shek. There was little suspense for this was one of the final scenes in a drama that had already climaxed with Rome's decision to join the Anti-Comintern Pact. General Jiang had, in fact, been in Italy for two weeks, arranging his contacts and waiting for this moment. Everyone knew that he was there to ask for a continuation of arms sales to China and to make a bid for Italian mediation in the escalating Sino-Japanese dispute. The Chinese Ambassador, Liu Wendao, who was Jiang's protege, had done his best to keep a sputtering romance alive after events at the ironically-named Marco Polo Bridge caught Italy with friends on both sides. It was hoped, nonetheless, that the general might use his friendsp with the early fascist finance minister, Alberto de Stefani, to renew a broken courtship. Moreover, with considerable diplomatic experience in China and a gallery of wellwishers there, Ciano was still believed to retain warm feelings for that country. A historian with any curiosity will want to know what fate brought this cast together.[1]

China and the 'New' Rome

The Nanjing decade (1928-1937) had proved to be a frustrating one for the Guomindang. Hoped for national unity never fully materialised. Beset by civil war, Japanese aggression, factionalism and corruption, the Nationalist government was never able to bring off the promised revolution. A new approach was needed to revive the spirit of dedication, to win the ideological battle with the communists and to fend off further foreign encroachment. Given the domestic and international context it is not difficult to understand how some Chinese, in a quest for political stability, external respect, and a compromise for a philosophical undergarment, took a closer look at Italy and Germany.

It must not be forgotten that this was a time when fascism still possessed an attraction and competed openly in Chinese political and intellectual circles. If fascism represented the latest stage in Western development, many individuals were naturally interested. All the more so if fascism, as the wave of the future, was about to restructure the global situation. For a while, the notion that Italy had found a way to avoid class conflict and carry out revolutionary changes at the same time she revived traditional virtues also struck a responsive chord. Even after fascism lost some of its glamour as an alternative to capitalism and a rebuilder of ancient Empire, Rome and Berlin held out promise as middlemen in critical negotiations with the Japanese invader.

Scholars have already shown a good deal of interest in the paradoxical conservatism of the Nanjing regime. In the mid-1950s, Mary Wright proposed that Guomindang China had tried to revive the traditional policies and attitudes of the earlier Tongzhi Restoration (1862-1874) and failed, not only because the party elders lacked the positive attributes of the late Qing self-strengtheners but also because the precedent had been inconsistent with the requirements for modernity. More recent writers have acknowledged that the era was a time of conservative revival but suggest that the goals were not necessarily anti-modern. Rather, as Lloyd E. Eastman has argued, it was the methods that were traditional.[2] In either case, there were Chinese who firmly believed that modernisation could only be successful if rooted in tradition, a perspective that may well have seemed reactionary in effect but which had much in common with the progressive-sounding policies then being followed by Italy and, nearer to home, Japan.

Rome was General Jiang Baili's favourite city. That great metropolis, as he told Chinese military cadets in 1936, was a 'sea of culture' with 'human history everywhere'. Yet, under Mussolini, Rome was also 'Europe's newest place'. Jiang was convinced that fascism was not the shooting star portrayed by some. Italy was a real success in her ideology which had stopped class conflict and produced a spirit of co-operation and self-sacrifice. She had managed to revive the very spirit of the Roman Empire.[3] When he returned to Europe on his special mission, he told Ciano: 'All roads lead to Rome...this was an ancient saying but it is current in the twentieth century'. In *The History of the Former Han Dynasty*, Jiang continued, 'Rome was called the Great Qin' and, moreover, 'Rome produced the spirit of the Occident in the same way that China was the cultural centre of the Orient'. The very future of East-West intercourse now rested in their hands.[4]

By more objective standards, Sino-Italian relations were never very important. Contact with Italy was not nearly as significant as Nanjing's better-known and far more extensive commercial and military ties to Nazi Germany. In all truth, there were never many Italians in China. At one stage there were a few hundred Chinese in Italy, mostly students or military cadets along with a small diplomatic community. In turn, Rome dispatched to China an aviation mission, and some advisers and journalists in addition to the expected missionary population. But statistics can be misleading. Despite the frailty of the material bonds, there was an Italian connection in modern Chinese history. When analysed against the backdrop provided by the 1930s, the relationship with Italy reveals several important factors in the transformation of China. Among these are: a confusion of conservative with revolutionary rhetoric, the initial attractiveness and ultimate failure of a foreign political model, and the nation's preoccupation with the problems posed by disunity, military weakness and inadequate leadership.

Modern Rome never took much interest in developments in Asia until after Mussolini's rise to power. Then, largely through the work of Ciano, who was secretary to the legation and, thereafter, minister resident at Shanghai, the fascist image rapidly gained stature.[5] As Mussolini's son-in-law after 1930, he was more than a diplomat. He and his wife were among the most-widely followed members of the foreign community. The 'Young Marshal', Zhang Xueliang, was only one of those who joined in their circle. Indeed, his frequent association with

Ciano's wife, Edda, was a matter for gossip.[6] As she later recalled: 'The Chinese mentality and the division of power were such that only personal relations with the different provincial governors...could allow Italy to hold its own with the great powers.' She also remembered when the Chinese foreign minister was shaving in Ciano's bathroom.[7]

It is now known that while Zhang Xueliang earned his playboy reputation, the Japanese were making preparations for the occupation of his Manchurian homeland. The Sino-Japanese conflict, in January 1932, spread to Shanghai, where the Western powers quickly arranged an armistice. With perhaps the least national interest involved and cordial relations with both combatants, Ciano played an active role in the mediation effort which brought about a new appreciation of Italy in the region.[8]

When, in early May 1932, Foreign Minister Dino Grandi commented on his nation's new interest in China, the door was already open for a spectacular improvement in relations. In fact, he noted with some pride the establishment of a direct steamer link between Shanghai and Naples.[9] The Lloyd-Triestino Line was the most tangible connection of all. Italy could boast of the fastest time to Europe (23 days), the largest ship on the route (*Conte Biancamano*) and, possibly, the most luxurious accommodations on the *Conte Rosso*. As a result, the line carried a high proportion of the diplomatic traffic which ensured that important Chinese who might not otherwise have done so were frequent visitors in Rome. Mrs Wellington Koo, for example, recalled being seen off to Paris by the Cianos.[10] Important functions were held on board in Shanghai and, when Count Ciano departed China to begin his rapid rise in 1933, he travelled on the *Conte Verde* accompanied by his friend Zhang Xueliang.[11]

There is little question that Italian fascists, on their own terms, saw themselves as revolutionaries. The fact that they may well have ended up as precisely the opposite must not totally discredit the significance of self-assessment. Italo Balbo, the aviator close to Mussolini, consistently spoke of revolution which he linked to technological advancement. It was the Italian air force, as much as the trains keeping to schedule, that typified the attitude. Fascists believed that they were the cutting edge to the modern era. Just as they pioneered in the air, Italians would create a new civilisation upon the terra firma of ancient Rome.

It is therefore most significant that the high mark of Sino-Italian relations was achieved in the summer of 1935 when Mussolini, in an obvious display of friendship, sent his personal airplane—a luxurious and fast Savoia-Marchetti trimotor—as a gift to Chiang Kai-shek. When it flew into Shanghai on 5 August, it was escorted by two Brenda aircraft already belonging to the Chinese air force and piloted by a Chinese officer and an Italian instructor. After landing, the crew of the trimotor was welcomed by consulate officials, important Guomindang members, and a conspicuous party of Italian Black Shirts.[12]

Back in the spring of 1932, Chiang Kai-shek had sent Kong Xiangxi (H.H. Kung) on a special mission to study industrial and defence developments in the West and to procure German and Italian armaments. Early the next year, after seeing Hitler and the Krupps, he visited Mussolini in Rome. As he remembered the somewhat ironic conversation, his host advised: 'Italy has no navy; Japan has a great navy'. The punch line, of course, was that aircraft could be built in less time and with much less expense than a great armada.[13] Upon returning to China with a promise of Italian assistance, he was offered a position to supervise a national aviation development programme but declined to take up an appointment with the Bank of China. In the years thereafter, particularly when, as Minister of Finance, Kong would make use of Italian advisers in the area of fiscal and monetary reform. Of present interest is the fact that Chiang Kai-shek also offered him an opportunity to return to Rome as Chinese minister. On 10 April, he told the press that he really preferred the diplomatic post because of his great admiration for Mussolini.[14]

Edda Mussolini Ciano tells a different version which credits her relationship with Zhang Xueliang for the beginning of the Chinese air force. Zhang, whom she described as 'a most powerful person whose friendship was greatly in demand', is said to have passed her a note at dinner suggesting that they might visit the summer palace the next day. As Mrs Ciano observed in her memoirs: 'I accepted, and for several hours one of the most important men in China acted as my guide and kept ministers and other important persons waiting while he walked with me'. Although Zhang was not particularly known for his statecraft in those days, Edda does claim to have convinced her friend to purchase Italian aircraft. To keep the record straight, the most consistent advocate of Chinese air power was General Jiang Baili whose articles on the pioneering Italian aviator Giulio Douhet, who had recommended strategic bombing and 'the command of the air', widely circulated in China as early as 1921.[15]

In any event, the *Conte Rosso* delivered the first Fiat pursuit plane in June 1933. The deal apparently included its pilot who was the first of the promised aviation advisers to arrive in China.[16] Towards the end of the year, Colonel Roberto Lordi became the head of a growing air mission. When the same ship docked the following year bringing home Zhang Xueliang, she carried two more planes in her hold.[17] In February 1934, the Italians even took part in a stunt show in the sky over Shanghai. But one scholar's trivia is another's treasure. Below in the reviewing stand were Zhang Xueliang, Kong Xiangxi, Song Ziwen (T.V. Soong) and Commander Raffaele Boscarelli, Ciano's replacement as Italian minister.[18]

The Kong visit with Mussolini in 1933, followed closely by one from Song Ziwen, also resulted in the cancellation of the major portion of the outstanding Boxer indemnity. By closing this account, Italy hoped to encourage even better relations while freeing foreign reserves for the purchase of planes and equipment.[19] Subsequently, on 29 September 1934, Liu Wendao and the Italian minister at Nanjing announced that their respective legations would be raised to embassies.[20] In the middle of the following month, the Chinese approved the appointment of Vincento Lojacono as Rome's first ambassador to China.[21] This move was more than symbolic in importance for, until this time, only the Soviet Union had granted China this level of recognition. Once Liu and his counterpart were exchanged, a great obstacle had been removed in the way of legitimising the Nationalist Revolution. Japan, Germany, Great Britain, the United States and France soon opened embassies of their own.

Liu Wendao's choice as ambassador further demonstrated the growing importance to Sino-Italian relations. He had served as minister to Berlin from September 1931 until the same month in 1933 when he was transferred to the identical post in Rome.[22] In Germany, Liu had witnessed the rise of Hitler's regime and arranged, on orders from Nanjing, the invitation which brought General von Seeckt to China. He was, in fact, helping Song Ziwen negotiate 10,000,000 marks worth of machine guns when he was reassigned to Italy.[23] Initially as minister, and then as

China's first true ambassador to the West, Liu continued his quest for up-to-date weapons. It was he who arranged for the Italian advisers, helped Chinese students who passed through the embassy on Via Asmara, and played host to one visitor from the homeland after another. Kong Xiangxi and Song Ziwen would come again. Yang Jie, in charge of the Army Staff College, came through in 1933-1934 and General Jiang Baili visited in 1936 a year before his fateful meeting with Mussolini.[24]

For his part, however, Il Duce had already begun to display a degree of uncertainty about China's future. As early as 1934, in an article first published in America, he expressed his concern over the rise of Japanese militarism. Taking notice of Japan's military heritage and industrial might, he showed a grudging admiration for the manner in which those sons of the Orient, through sacrifice and martial virtues, were assembling a formidable war machine. But at this stage, his loyalty—reinforced by that of the Cianos—was with Nanjing. 'Now the future of civilisation and of the white race in the Far East, the destiny of the Pacific', he wrote, 'depends on the mission that China takes upon herself in the course of this century'.[25]

Fascism and Chinese Nationalism

To speak only of diplomatic history, however, is to miss the deeper significance of the Italian connection. Ciano, for one, was convinced that Italy enjoyed great prestige in China. And, for a time, there were a number of important individuals who spoke as if the destinies of China and Italy were intertwined, that the two nations shared something fundamental. Song Ziwen was greeted by a Mussolini who talked in mid-1933 about the profound historical similarities between China and Italy. By emulating the Italian example, China could also regain her rightful place in the world.[26] Ciano's replacement as Italian minister, Boscarelli, observed in November of the same year that 'the glorious past of China has been and still is the object of study and admiration on the part of the whole civilised world'. Events in China, he went on, 'would be followed with keen interest and meet the heartfelt sympathy of the Italian national government'.[27] When Ambassador Lojacono presented his credentials to the Nanjing regime in January 1935, he commented that Italy, through Marco Polo, had been the first Western nation to make contact with the great Chinese civilisation and that both were now reviving their cultures.[28] Likewise, Mussolini advised Liu Wendao that it was natural for the two countries to become close friends since they represented the historical civilisations for their respective parts of the globe.[29]

In the summer of 1937, even as the relationship was about to be destroyed by unforeseen events, Cesare Galimberti of the Stefani News Agency wrote about the bright future still ahead for Sino-Italian relations. 'A more fruitful collaboration between China and Italy', he observed, 'should be founded on the relations of the present, and on the marked existing similarity between the two peoples and their two revolutions.'[30]

Liu Wendao wrote extensively about his own experiences in Italy and has admitted how he, and other Chinese, were attracted by the concept of cultural revival.[31] But it was the man who served as Jiang Baili's interpreter in Rome, the late Nationalist scholar, Paul Sih (Xue Guangqian), who had recently received his doctorate in Italy where he worked under de Stefani, that extended the 1930s analogy to its limits: 'The fundamental motive of the National Revolution in China is similar to that of the Fascist Revolution in Italy' because both had discarded materialism in order to establish 'a new moral standard to meet the national need'. China's own National Economic Reconstruction and the New Life Movement coincided with 'the ideas of Mussolini, who intends to promote the welfare of his people by reviving the old Roman spirit and power'. 'Since Revolutionary China and Fascist Italy have similar ideas and purposes', Sih concluded, 'their future co-operation will not only benefit the peoples of these two nations but those of other countries as well.'[32]

The entire issue of fascist ideological penetration into China is unquestionably controversial as is the general applicability of the term 'fascism'.[33] The further history moves from the special circumstances that brought Mussolini to power, the easier it seems to be to spot sympathisers in every corner of the world. Perhaps, as some scholars have suggested, it would be best to confine discussion to a single country and time period.[34] Nevertheless, the very fact that Mussolini and many of his supporters believed in the universality of at least some of their values and that non-Italians drew upon the experiment must not be overlooked. In any case, the issue is not fascism but what the belief in a special relationship with Italy can tell us about the transformation of China.

J.S. Barnes wrote in *The Universal Aspects of Fascism* in 1929, a book that was widely cited in China, that: 'Fascists in each country must make Fascism their own national movement, adopting symbols and tactics which conform to the traditions, psychology and tastes of their own land.' In the preface, written by his hero, fascism was praised as 'a purely Italian phenomenon in its historical expression but its doctrinal postulates have a universal character.' As Mussolini also claimed: 'Fascism sets and solves problems which are common to many peoples who have experienced and tired of Demo-Liberal rule and of the conventional lies attached thereto'. 'It is our proud prohecy that fascism will come to fill the present century with itself even as liberalism filled the nineteenth century'.[35] When still in China, Ciano advised a class studying the principles of fascist law at Suzhou University that the applications of fascism were universal for only it could combine the ideals of motherland and social justice.[36]

While time would spot the flaws in this idealism, fascism did appear as a workable and even progressive system to observers all over the world. Although he would later write that the Italians had misinterpreted Machiavelli in their search for historical relevance, when he returned to China for consultation in the autumn of 1934, Liu Wendao favourably compared Mussolini to Zhuge Liang, who had once helped rebuild the country in the chaos following the collapse of the Han Dynasty, rival to ancient Rome. 'If China is to lift herself from the present status of internal instability and external encroachments', he continued, 'she must have a Mussolini and all those at the helm of state must copy Mussolini'.[37] Not surprisingly, Zhang Xueliang, who had just received a high decoration from the Italian ruler, had much the same to say when he came home from Rome. Praising both Hitler and Mussolini, he made his personal preference quite clear: 'The greatest and most picturesque statesman in Europe today is Mussolini of Italy'. Reportedly with his own son dressed as a Black Shirt, Zhang asked: 'Cannot China produce another Mussolini?'[38]

Much attention has naturally centred on Chiang Kai-shek since he, as the dominant political personality at the time, was the most likely to become China's Mussolini. Numerous critics noticed a trend toward dictatorship in the clandestine Chinese

Blue Shirts and in the slogans of the New Life Movement.[39] In the summer of 1933, Chiang observed how everyone was talking about 'the revived states of Italy, Germany and Turkey'. Just as the Italians and Germans had built themselves back up through personal sacrifice so might the Chinese.[40] And, he frequently referred to Germany as the primary example of national revival through military strength. Indeed, his youngest son, Jiang Weiguo, was in Berlin as a cadet in 1937 when General Jiang Baili arrived in that city.

In public Chiang denied that he aspired to become China's dictator and even went so far as to deny the applicability of fascism. On 1 March 1934, for example, shortly after Zhang Xueliang's enthusiastic endorsement of Mussolini, he called a press conference to allay widespread reports that he was about to assume dictatorial powers.[41] While Hu Shi and other liberals cautioned against authoritarian solutions, a Wang Jingwei who was in opposition to Chiang Kai-shek's rising star was the principal champion of democracy. He warned against the imitation of foreign political systems and argued in 1933 that fascism in China could only lead to the establishment of a military dictatorship.[42] The same thought no doubt struck another critic but he christened Chiang 'the little Napoleon from Ningbo'.[43] The fact that both Wang and the German-educated Tang Liangli, who was editor of the increasingly right-wing newspaper, *The People's Tribune*, came to embrace the Axis powers themselves near the end of the decade, directs us towards the emerging theme. Fascism, like any other foreign example, came to mean different things to different Chinese depending on their political standing and intellectual perspective.

Zhang Xueliang noted that the greatness of Mussolini 'lies in non-compromise and in allowing no opportunity to escape to get greater power in his hands'.[44] No doubt the road to power interested some of his contemporaries. Others saw the apparent success of fascism as exoneration for the teachings of Sun Yat-sen or, in direct contrast, as a more practical prescription for the ills plaguing Chinese society. A few were attracted to the 'corporate state' and the promise of an economic system that seemed to offer some of the advantages of capitalism and socialism without their well-known drawbacks. There were also those who used the Italian example to launch a somewhat paradoxical attack on the West and its bourgeois-democratic values. Even while opposing Chiang Kai-shek, Tang Liangli still editoralised: 'That there should be in China a feeling that some form of fascism would be infinitely more satisfactory than the present political regime is not surprising'.[45]

Cheng Tianfang, Nanjing's envoy in Berlin after 1933, has told of the almost magnetic appeal of Nazi Germany with its sense of obedience, responsibility and optimism. He remembered the excitement at the great Nuremberg rally and Hitler's triumphant entry into the Olympic Games, where one could clearly see 'the spirit of the Germanic race'.[46] Only a matter of weeks before he set off for his ambassadorial post, Cheng added his contribution to a spreading academic debate on the applicability of authoritarianism to China with the opinion that 'dictatorship is better than democracy...because given the realities of China, dictatorship stands a better chance of success'.[47]

The general discussion has already received scholarly attention. Debate had been initiated by the American-educated Jiang Tingfu, who, after all was said and done, was the most perceptive when he wrote in December 1933: 'China now seems to have reached a point at which there is no way out except revolution while revolution itself is no way out'. His recommendation was the establishment of a strong central authority that would enable the country to avoid civil war. Others, after surveying the regimes in Turkey, Germany, Italy and Russia, concluded that the specific political system was only a creature of the times. The successful 'new' states all had a party and leader who could correlate economic and military development so that even an oppressed or backward land might still produce a strong nation. The geologist, Ding Wenjiang, suggested that China should find her own 'ideal dictator' in the shortest possible time.[48]

It was Zhang Xueliang who observed in 1934 that 'too many self-seekers stand between China and unity today; it is time they placed the good of the nation before their own purposes and desires'.[49] 'The rejuvenation of Italy and Germany', he wrote in a letter, 'is due chiefly to their peoples' wholehearted support of their leaders who, therefore, have sufficient strength to overcome the obstacles on the way to national rejuvenation'. 'It is not the case with China. When a leader has shown his ability to lead the people, there spring up jealous people to engineer his downfall.

This has been responsible for the civil wars and foreign aggression.'[50] Although there were the expected reports that Zhang saw himself in the role of Mussolini, circumstantial evidence suggests that he was actually signalling his willingness to follow Chiang Kai-shek.[51] As the academic Jiang Tingfu put it, Chiang's new historical mission was 'to sweep away with a big broom the provincial feudalisms and create a central power that can at least keep the peace'. 'With peace, the efforts towards modernisation, both governmental and popular, can fructify'.[52]

There can be no question that twentieth-century China, with its multiple problems, demanded solutions. When an editorialist, most likely a Blue Shirt, wrote that 'fascism is the only tool of self-salvation for nations on the brink of destruction',[53] he was not necessarily advocating a strictly ideological remedy. The need for a stronger state was self-evident to most Chinese and had been since the final decades of the Qing. At least one scholar has fervently argued that admirers of Italian fascism, including the Blue Shirts, were really only interested in finding the *means* to implement Sun Yat-sen's Three Principles of the People (*sanmin zhuyi*).[54] The Chinese political scene had, of course, inherited more than a touch of elitism from the Confucian tradition. With the help of Bolshevik rather than fascist advisers, Sun Yat-sen had tried to reshape the Guomindang along the lines of a tightly-disciplined vanguard in the early 1920s. His 'General Theory of Knowledge and Action' first presented in 1919, with its emphasis on the need for an elite group of thinkers and a mass of followers, also foreshadowed developments in the Nanjing period.[55] Thus, there was nothing particularly novel when Zhang Xueliang, for example, remembered a conversation he had with Mussolini during which the Italian drew a triangle to illustrate an important point. At the base he wrote: 'Work should be done by all'. 'At a little higher and narrower', according to his Chinese guest, 'he wrote, talking shall be done by the minority', and at the top of the triangle he wrote, 'the decision should rest with one man'.[56]

A high ranking official in the Ministry of Foreign Affairs compared the ideas found in the Three Principles of the People with those of fascism and noted that they had many points in common: nationalism, racial solidarity, spiritual revival, class co-operation and the people's livelihood'.[57] Indeed, the head of the Suzhou University programme who introduced Ciano to his students observed that while not a fascist himself, he believed that fascism corresponded to the writings of Sun Yat-sen.[58] This analogy seems to have been most actively pursued by the C.C. Clique, perhaps in part, to undercut the movement by the rival Blue Shirts to propagate a nation-wide cult of the state and its leader. Ju Jiahua, who was a chief functionary behind the New Life Movement, glorified Sun while at the same time boosting Chiang's status as heir-apparent with statements such as 'the immortal words and deeds of a national leader are the crystalisation of his precious life-blood and the great heritage of a nation'.[59]

A general mixing of metaphors had, however, been characteristic of Guomindang ideology from the very beginning. Consequently, there will always be argument over what the 'fascist' model meant to the man usually thought of as China's 'leader'. Although Eastman has convincingly shown that Chiang Kai-shek admired the success of the fascist powers and secretly encouraged Blue Shirt activities which included an attack on democracy, the advocacy of one-man rule and the often violent removal of his political enemies, these ingredients do not of themselves make a fascist state.

Fascism may never have meant much more than a militaristic leadership technique to Chiang Kai-shek. The central core of the Blue Shirts was composed largely of graduates of the Huangpu (Whampoa) Military Academy who owed their careers to the patronage of its former director and rallied to his side when, ironically, his prestige as a 'leader' was at an all time low in the early 1930s. Thus, he was probably reacting in an instinctive way when he reportedly told a Blue Shirt gathering in September 1933 that the key element in fascism was trust in a sagely leader and that there could be no national reconstruction until Chinese believed in just such a person.[60]

At one stage he seems to have visualised China as a gigantic military academy. He spoke proudly of the training he had received as a cadet in Japan and, on another occasion, denounced the traditional Chinese aversion to a career as a soldier and, instead, held up army virtues as a model for the entire society.[61] There was, of course, nothing exclusively fascist about these notions as the 'learn from the PLA (People's Liberation Army)' campaign of more recent vintage illustrates. The warlord, Yen Xishan, had long advocated similar values, a fact which, no doubt, prompted his own admiration for Mussolini and Hitler.[62] Always the most romantic of our examples, General Jiang Baili also stressed martial values as the key to national salvation. For him, the nation could never really be saved until there was a fusion of culture with at least the capacity for war.[63] Indeed, it is this area of Guomindang cultural policy that raises the most interesting parallels with Italy.

This is not the place to discuss the ideology or victories of the right wing in Europe except to note three areas of striking similarity with trends developing independently in China. In both Italy and in the Far East, a preoccupation with political unity, a demand for the revival of past greatness, and a discovery of the necessity of military strength, began to shape the national destiny. After the defeat at Andowa in 1896, a new wave of nationalism—not unlike that first produced in China in the aftermath of the first Sino-Japanese War—swept the country. There was a disillusionment with institutions and leadership as well as a longing for lost heroes. In much the same way that Mazzini revived interest in the Renaissance, a later generation of twentieth-century men also believed it incumbent to fulfil an earlier potential. For those like Gioacchino Volpe, fascism was a vindication of discarded Risorgimento ideals and the last stage in a national revival begun with the Renaissance. By the end of the first world war, the youth of Italy, disheartened by the Communist International's inability to prevent the great conflict and also motivated by their nation's own shabby treatment at Versailles, were ready for another effort at rousing national consciousness. But the Italians held no monopoly on ideas. China's exposure to the West would start her off towards the same crossroads.

Appropriately, the trial of the Italian connection can be picked up in Rome in the year 1919. A younger Jiang Baili, Carson Chang (Zhang Jiasen) and Liang Qichao, who had all been part of an unofficial delegation to the Versailles peace talks, left France in February to tour the rest of Europe. Liang, the elder statesman of China's reforming tradition going back to before 1898, hoped to make up for the gaps in his personal knowledge of the West. Undoubtedly he was also looking for confirmation of his emerging syncretist leanings. As early as 1902, he had suggested that the intellectual pattern of the Qing Dynasty was similar to that of the European Renaissance.[64] But it took the collaboration of the scholar-general, Jiange Baili, to develop the argument.

Largely researched on the continent and published in China in 1920, Jiang's short volume, *Ouzhou wenyi fuxing shi* (The history of the European Renaissance) appeared just as the student protest of the May Fourth Movement was generating radical consequences. Sinologists will know that the long forword Liang wrote for this work eventually stood alone as the famous *Qingdai xueshu gailun* (Intellectual trends of the Qing period) and that Jiang more properly confined his prefatory words to just a few basic remarks. At essence was the belief shared by Liang that 'the spirit of Qing learning was virtually in harmony with the European Renaissance'. If such were the case, China would soon experience her own Reformation.[65]

For a majority of participants, the May Fourth Movement was the Chinese Renaissance—an exciting time to write in the vernacular and to glorify humanity. It was a time of individual freedom, of reason against authority. A few thinkers spied obvious confusion: for them the events promised 'China's Enlightenment'. The real point was that in China's search for a significant past and a viable political form for the future, the whole of Western history was fair game. Individuals of differing but rarely pure persuasions shared the same presupposition: the nation's dark ages had passed. In the most general sense they all wanted to remember Italy.

Had Chinese continued to turn the page of history, they would have discovered the toll taken by the Counter-Reformation and the length of Spanish hegemony. A more meaningful comparison would have been the Risorgimento, that gradual intellectual reawakening of interest in letters, science and national feeling which began in the eighteenth century and gathered force in the wake of the French Revolution until the nation had its independence to go with the extraordinarily rich cultural legacy from an earlier time. But few Chinese in the 1920s talked about Mazzini, Cavour and Garibaldi. Certainly not as many as would soon write of Mussolini.

Ironically, Liang Qichao had discussed the Italian revival movement near the turn of the century. In one of the stranger works of the period, he produced the sketch for a traditional-style Chinese opera entitled 'The Story of the New Rome' (*Xin Luoma zhuanqi*). It featured the soul of Dante, Mazzini, Cavour and Garibaldi, the last three as young men. All sing about the destiny of Italy while keeping faithful to standard Beijing tunes. Dressed in a sailor suit, a youthful Garibaldi recalls how Rome was once the most famous and beautiful capital in Western history and then laments: 'Roma, Roma, how can thou be dead and unloved?' Predictably, soon inspired by nationalism, he reaches a decisive moment: 'We must bring you back to life again.' Earlier in the script, Mazzini sings his own impassioned plea only to return in another scene to stir fellow students to action.[66]

How tempting it is to believe that Liang Qichao saw himself as China's Mazzini and Jiang Baili as another Garibaldi. Perhaps Zhang Jiasen, the influential intellectual, might have become another Cavour? But to make such an argument would be to miss the moral of the Italian connection: the universal misplacing of analogies is itself subject for analogy.

A June 1934 issue of *Rassengna di politica internazionale* noted that Italy was developing an active interest in 'all fields (navigation, Chinese fascism, Catholic missions)'. In January 1937, the Italian fascist organ *Gerarchia* took notice of political and cultural trends within China and concluded that the Asian nation had now found its own 'dictator, who while not of the same calibre as Mussolini, met the needs of the Chinese race.'[67] China's head of state, Lin Sen, must have agreed for he had said much the same: 'Today our countries under the direction of enlightened leaders are experiencing the same spirit of revolution and revival'. 'The co-operation of China and Italy will assure their glorious success'.[68] The journalist Galimberti had pushed an identical point when he wrote that both countries had their 'enlightened leader of genius who is therefore loved and respected and who has set himself as a living example of the will of the people to renew itself'.[69]

At about the same time, the perhaps exaggerated story of a Chinese Catholic who had walked all the way from China to Rome to see the pope was also reported in the press. It is therefore prudent to caution that there were always more Catholics than proto-fascists in Guomindang China. Although there is a pressing need for a comprehensive study of the overall influence of European developments on educational and cultural policies during the Nanjing period, as well as in the more obvious areas of government and economics, little will be achieved by name calling. The challenge is not to prove 'conversion' but 'convergence'—to illustrate how disparate environments continue to produce analogous-appearing circumstances.

In 1907, Liang Qichao paid homage to the Risorgimento and to Mazzini in particular. An even stronger link to Italy was forged in a widely-read essay first published in 1911. In *Yidali jianguo sangjie zhuan* (Biographies of the three nation-building heroes of Italy), he introduced the very same themes which were to reappear in the 1930s: China and Italy had experienced parallel histories. Once they were the supreme countries in their part of the planet, the oldest and most honoured. They had decayed, come under foreign domination and cruel autocrats and lost all sense of unity. 'There is mutual sympathy in the same illness', Liang wrote. 'China should take the three heroes as the starting point in the building of a new China'. 'Everyone should aspire to be one of the three heroes'.[70]

In the 1930s, a right-wing Chinese periodical in Shanghai, after giving extensive coverage to fascist Europe, announced that Mussolini and Hitler were 'contemporary heroes'. What China required was a leader to be the heart of the Guomindang in order to revitalise the Chinese people. In its hour of need, the nation required her own Mussolini or Hitler.[71] Just as had Liang before them, more and more individuals came to believe that China desperately needed heroic personalities who could revive the glory of the past while, at the same time, instilling a nationalistic, and essentially modern, perspective. This was, of course, also Jiange Baili's point of view. Whereas the Chinese had admired dead men, Westerners had come to adore living ones. While China's heroes had been idealistic archetypes in the past, those in the West were admired on the basis of real political success. The secret to the glory of both ancient and modern Rome was the way in which the entire population appreciated, encouraged and worshipped heroic qualities.[72]

It is always easy to overstate a case. Those familiar with Liang Qichao will know that he also wrote a biographical treatment of Kossuth, the Hungarian patriot, and often glorified Napolean and other Western figures—especially militarists and statesmen—for their determination and nationalism. Nevertheless, Italy was important to him. In his autobiography, he identified the date of his birth as 'ten years after the Taiping regime perished at Nanjing, one year after the Grand Secretary Zeng Guofan died, three years after the Franco-Prussian War, and the year in which Italy rounded out its independence with the acquisition of Rome'.[73]

Liang's protégé within the Political Studies Clique, Jiang Baili, had likewise praised the careers of great men in the West when, for example, he translated the famous Victorian book *Duty* by the Scottish moralist Samuel Smiles in 1917. But Jiang wrote that he found his deepest inspiration in Rome. Long impressed by ancient Roman culture, its laws, fine arts and Christian religion which had made that city 'the capital of the world', he was almost instinctively drawn to its twentieth-century revival. Just as the earlier legions had practised and the later Church taught, individualism needed to be sacrificed for the good of the group. The spirit of the 'New Rome' now inspired the people to discard self-interest and the class conflict that characterised the contemporary world culture. Fascism, which has arisen out of the need to find some way out of the dead end faced by Western civilisation, had discovered a 'new frontier'. By restoring the values of ancient Rome, it had opened a path into the future.[74]

At the heart of any argument over 'Chinese fascism' is the difficulty separating an interest in methods from a deeper commitment to ideology. Neither Mussolini nor, for that matter, Chiang Kai-shek ever claimed to be a great or original thinker. For the Italian, fascism was always more of a 'state of mind' rather than a theory. If anything, Gentile's task as theorist was to justify a regime already in existence. His notion that fascism was both practice and thought with doctrine somehow inherent in historical experience and brought to reality by men of action was in no way original. It was old hat to European Marxists, common sense to Confucianists and not unknown to American pragmatists.

A number of years before Mao Zedong's famous essays 'On Theory' and 'On Practice', General Jiang Baili argued that there was a distinction between 'knowledge' and 'ability' (*shi yu neng*). He proposed that the critical talent was ability.[75] Thus, when he wrote the foreword to Paul Sih's decidedly pro-fascist book, *Yidali fuxing zhi dao* (The road to Italian revival), which went into considerable detail about Italian political theory, Jiang noted not only the importance of cultural revival but proposed that Chinese readers learn from the success the fascists had enjoyed when they drew their theory out of reality and, through action, changed reality. Mussolini had said: 'Originally I did not have a theory; all I have to make a decision on was reality. In solving the real, contemporary questions one after another came fascist theory'. 'The Banner of Theory; the Truth of Reality'.[76] Citing Goethe, Jiang also wrote that 'only the real is true'.[77] In retrospection, the utility of this sort of advice, as was the case with the communist effort to create a theory out of circumstances, rested on the ability of the Guomindang leadership to identify the fundamental problems and come to grips with them.

Zou Rong, the anti-Manchu polemicist had recognised the difficulties which would be faced as the twentieth century matured. He once wrote: 'The Revolution we are carrying out today is a revolution which will destroy in order to construct. However, if you wish to destroy you must first possess the means to construct'.[78] From its inception, Republican China had been searching for those means of national reconstruction.

When Zhang Xueliang came home from Italy in 1934, he excitedly announced that he knew the secret to fascist success: Mussolini had realised the importance of education along the lines of least resistance'.[79] While Eastman has argued outright that Chiang Kai-shek was quite clear in his own mind about the correspondence between fascism and the New Life Movement,[80] it is important to note that the Chinese leader himself once advised a mass meeting at Nanchang that the new mass movement marked the inauguration of 'China's Renaissance'.[81] It now seems quite likely that he believed that faith in the leader and militarisation would not in themselves be enough to mobilise a nation. The people also needed to have faith in their own inherent greatness. Although it has always been tempting to view the exhumation of Confucian maxims in the Nanjing decade as proof that the Guomindang had lost its revolutionary zeal, to do so is to miss the largest strand to the Italian connection.

In a major New Life Movement speech, Chiang Kai-shek remarked: 'The Chinese people used to set great store on traditional virtues, the revival of which is imperative and essential to the welding of China into a modern nation'.[82] A people who used to be 'well organised in all the essentials of life' had become 'disorganised, cowardly and torn between conflicting perverse teachings'. 'The life of a people must accord with the time and environment in which it lives'. 'A new life', Chiang continued, 'is possible only when there is a complete break with the old modes of living'. Yet, 'if during the transition from an old order to a new one nothing is done to assist the introduction of new customs and usages, such new institutions are liable to be stultified in their development'. Later, in one paradoxical sweep, he concluded that the introduction of modern values which were in accord with 'the spirit of the age in which we live' depended on the revival of old virtues.[83]

With the help of Liang Qichao's classical Chinese restatement, Mazzini had offered his own assessment back in the year 1911: 'If you seek revolution, sow the seeds of revolution. If you seek culture, build up an earthen terrace. Tend to it and restore the national spirit'.[84] To coax a new nation out of culture took more love and patience than anyone expected.

For many years it has been assumed that the May Fourth era constituted a watershed, a time when the values of science and democracy triumphed during an iconoclastic assault on the old order. At best the proposition is only half true for there was also an important backlash. Zhang Jiasen, who spent the period 1919 to 1922 in Germany, launched an attack on the new faith that science could solve the world's problems. Joined by Liang Qichao, he argued that the modern preoccupation with the material universe was leading mankind into moral degeneracy. Their message, echoed by a number of prominent Western thinkers, was that civilisation could only be saved by a resort to more intuitive, largely moral, ideas. For a few, 'spirituality' may well have been euphemistic for a return to nineteenth-century conservatism with its total rejection of Western culture. For many others in the 1920s and 1930s, however, a renewed interest in the importance of national spirit had little in common with the old *ti-yong* dichotomy. Modern culture was no longer bifurcated into East and West, substance and technique. Neither had a monopoly on truth. The future demanded a synthesis, a higher level of civilisation, that combined the best of both.

Jiang Baili believed that Mussolini's strength came, in part, because of his revival of the traditional Italian family structure as well as the ideals of ancient Rome.[85] Chen Lifu argued that there was no reason for Chinese to feel inferior to the West. If anything the path to national regeneration could be found in the regeneration of older moral values. He did not think of himself as a reactionary for culture was no longer an end in itself but a means.[86] Chen, Zhang Jiasen and the aging Liang Qichao all thought that they saw Chinese traditions that would ease the pangs of modernisation. The two militarists, Jiang Baili and Chiang Kai-shek, proposed that spiritual weapons were as important as technological ones, a notion that seems far from reactionary when placed beside the radical slogans of the Great Proletarian Cultural Revolution with its emphasis on faith in the great helmsman. Even the rhetoric of the New Life Movement was no more comical than some of the clichés of the 1960s. In the context of the 1930s, it sounded decidedly modern.

A number of scholars have suggested that one of the appeals of Marxism in China was the fact that it was extremely critical of Western society. With the Leninist anti-imperialist additions it was possible to believe in modernisation without giving up a basic distrust of the West. The same can be said for the Italian fascist example. In activities that would be duplicated by Red Guards, Blue Shirts frequently attacked foreign influences in China. Thus, China could join the West in a new synthesis by first condemning the Occident and its apostles in Asia.

It has been said that Chiang Kai-shek once told a group of his close supporters that the basic principles of fascism were: 'militarisation, devotion to the leader and a belief in natural superiority'.[87] A possibly more savvy and definitely pro-Italian political commentator was more specific in the fascist-inspired elements he wanted to introduce into China: spirit of the race, elimination of class struggle, opposition to both capitalism and communism, centralisation of power and dictatorial government.[88] While it is not fantasy to see all of these things to varying degrees in China under Nanjing rule, Chinese fascism (if it is permissible to use the term) did not provide a short-cut to the future.

The Failed Analogy

If in 1934 Mussolini was far from certain that Japan would make an ally and was unwilling to sacrifice a developing friendship with China, the Rome-Tokyo courtship was under way by 1936 even while the overall attractiveness of the fascist model was on the ascendancy in Nanjing. Lojacono tried to assure the Chinese government that nothing had changed. All the same, sharply critical comments about Italian 'imperialism' gradually began to replace earlier enthusiastic discussion of the 'New Roman Empire' in the popular press.[89]

Liu Wendao did his best in Rome. But when the Nanjing regime appeared willing to go along with economic sanctions in the League of Nations, Mussolini was livid. He warned Liu that the international organisation had already sold out China and would never apply the same strict standards to Japan. He was even more upset that, given the hand of friendship, China dared to turn her back on Rome. Ciano, all along saying, 'I am a friend of China', tried to tempt Chiang Kai-shek with a deal. Italy would again be a pioneer and renounce extraterritoriality and concessions in exchange for Chinese support. Apparently after lengthy communication, Liu passed on a negative reply from China. The Nanjing government, Chiang had written, would follow the League because Sino-Japanese relations, obviously unlike those with Italy, were a matter of life and death for his country.[90]

At the end of 1936, Rome recalled Lojacono and replaced him with Julio Cora, formerly ambassador to Brazil. Although the Chinese press was indignant when it learned that he had once been consul-general in Tokyo, he was not necessarily a bad appointment to the strategic geo-political post. Moreover, when he presented his credentials to Lin Sen in April 1937, he observed that 'the amity between Italy and China cannot but increase in the future'.[91] While the words of diplomats should always be taken with a grain of skepticism, Kong Xiangxi was welcomed in Rome less than one month later as if he were visiting his oldest friends. He was decorated by Victor Emanuel, met with Ciano, and took pains to remark how much he admired Mussolini. By the time he passed through in October it would be too late to save the friendship. Even as late as May of the fateful year, Ciano was encouraging the expansion of Sino-Italian relations. He praised the fact that his government had sent legal, financial and military advisers.[92]

Nothing better illustrates the strength that the personal touch gave to China's relations with Italy than the arrival of Alberto de Stefani on an Italian liner in late February 1937. The visit of the sixty-year old, often given credit for rebuilding the Italian economy, was a final accomplishment for the Chinese embassy in Rome. It was arranged with Mussolini's approval through the efforts of Liu Wendao and Jiang Baili who was in Europe in 1936 to study the military mobilisation under way in Germany and Italy. Not surprisingly, Jiang reported favourably on the importance of air power but, in stressing the critical need for a solid economic infrastructure, was instrumental in getting de Stefani to come to China. As might also be expected, the foreign expert assisted in fiscal reforms but it was his collaboration with General Jiang that was most important. The two travelled about the country together, looking at industrial and transport facilities in anticipation of war. His role as adviser to Chiang Kai-shek was just beginning when the outbreak of Sino-Japanese hostilities placed Mussolini's fascist state in an increasingly awkward position.[93] Within twelve days, the Japanese ambassador, Sugimura, called on Ciano to ask about the Italians in the Chinese air force. Ciano lied and said that the group was commercial rather than military. But, by late August, when Liu Wendao asked for more planes to use in the defence of Shanghai, Ciano took a firm stand bluntly noting in his diary that Nanjing could not expect Italian sympathy.[94] He told the American ambassador that he had advised a Chinese friend, most probably Kong, that China would have to seek the best terms she could get from Japan. Far better 'to lose a leg', he said, 'than the more vital parts of the body'.[95] Nevertheless, de Stefani managed to stay on until September when Jiang Baili, fresh from emergency meetings with the Generalissimo, joined him in the first-class cabins of the *Conte Rosso* for the three-week voyage to Italy.

Not to be deterred, Chiang Kai-shek asked the German ambassador, Oskar Trautman, if Berlin could exert influence on Mussolini. He suggested that he was willing to offer Italy a favourable barter trade agreement similar to the one existing with Germany.[96] Chiang was aware, of course, that his representative, armed with the latest secret code books and with de Stefani by his side, was now in Rome. While Jiang Baili's party was still at sea, however, Mussolini and Hitler met to consummate the new Rome-Berlin alliance which would bring Italy all that closer to Tokyo.

General Jiang told Ciano, who passed the message on to his leader, that while the Japanese reported that he was in Rome to procure arms (which happens to be true), he was really in Italy to secure 'invisible weapons', ones that were more 'spiritual' than physical. When speaking later to Mussolini, he reiterated Chiang Kai-shek's warm feelings for Italy and how Chinese could understand the desire to restore the glory of the Roman Empire. He also stressed Chiang's fundamental opposition to communism, a point which reportedly brought Mussolini's assurance that the Anti-Comintern Pact was not directed against China. In a final plea at a reception hosted by Gentile at the Far Eastern Cultural Association, he again stressed the historical analogy: Roman and Chinese civilisations were like 'older and younger brothers'. But the most symbolic moment came when he presented Mussolini with a gift of the Chinese classics.[97]

International relations are, of course, a two-way street and there were events in China which also spelled the end of the analogy. The Blue Shirts had long been actively anti-Japanese, a factor of little importance until Rome began her courtship of Tokyo. Had Chiang Kai-shek and others remained anti-communist in practice there might have been more hope for Italian or German mediation. In December 1936, due to increased domestic pressure to end the civil war, Zhang Xueliang refused to fight the communists. Chiang, arriving in Xi'an, was kidnapped. The negotiations have never been revealed but Chiang was freed, civil war abated, the Blue Shirts gradually disbanded and preparations began under the direction of Jiang Baili for what now seemed the inevitable war with Japan.[98]

Count Ciano was apparently distressed by the possibility of co-operation with the communists and warned Nanjing of the risks involved. He is said to have cabled Zhang Xueliang, warning: 'You are my friend. If you join the communists you will be my enemy. China cannot exist without General Chiang Kai-shek'.[99] If the story is true, his words are ironic. Eleven months later, Ciano would write: 'Peace with the government of Chiang Kai-shek is impossible. It is therefore necessary to establish a new government in Nanking'.[100]

On 6 November 1937, Ciano, Ribbentrop and the Japanese representative, Hotta, signed the tripartite agreement in the Palazzio Venezia. By this time, Jiang Baili was already in Berlin. It was now the Germans, more than the Italians, that kept the fascist aura alive. Of course, now that the diplomatic record is open, we know that Ciano and the German ambassador in Rome met on 27 July and concluded that their governments favoured Japan.[101] Be that as it may, Nanjing dispatched a goodwill mission to Italy and Germany led by Chen Gongbo, then propaganda minister. Chen allegedly requested a large amount of cash so that he could take along an unspecified Shanghai woman believed to have some influence over Ciano.[102]

The fact that a 'peace conspiracy' was under way seems certain. Chen, who would eventually bolt the Guomindang to join Wang Jingwei's puppet government, was part of a group long opposed to Chiang Kai-shek. This was known by Ciano and he, Mussolini and Ribbentrop agreed to try to use him in whatever way possible. On 15 November and the very next day, Chen and Ciano discussed the gloomy battle reports and the fact that the only hope seemed to rest in Italian or German mediation.[103]

In rapid succession during the month of December, Rome instructed her military advisers to leave China, Nanjing recalled Liu Wendao and Ciano ordered the confiscation of the last shipload of arms destined for his former friends.[104] A new expanded trade agreement was signed with Japan in the first week of the new year and in March 1938 an Italian fascist goodwill mission, led by Marquis Paulucci de Calboli, arrived in Tokyo. There, he introduced the latest analogy: 'It is not without good reason that the Empire of the Rising Sun and the Imperial Italy of Mussolini find themselves so close at the present time'. 'The history of Rome', like that of the Japanese empire, 'was blessed by the favours of Heaven'. After visiting Japan, the delegation toured not only Manchuria but Japanese-occupied territory in China. The welcome flags in Harbin announced the newest relationship in Asia: 'Bienvenito alla missione fascista Italiana'.[105]

For their part, and responding to Chiang Kai-shek's overtures, the Germans tried to turn a tenuous position to advantage. Italy would have liked to have played a similar role. Thinking that they had an original idea, the British approached Ciano in mid-November 1937 to ask if he could use his contacts to ease the crisis.[106] Mussolini had, in fact, already told the German ambassador in Rome that the only hope for peace in the Far East was through the mediation of Germany and Italy. Ciano also confirmed that he was in touch with Tokyo.[107] Thus, to this extent, the visit of Jiang Baili had not been in vain. But Mussolini's rash statements and some foolish actions cost Rome her chance. On 15 September, over seven hundred Italian grenadiers landed in Shanghai, ostensibly to evacuate Italian subjects. Yet, when the cruiser *Mortecuccoli* tied up at a Japanese naval buoy and the troops were billeted in a Japanese primary school, an unfavourable Chinese reaction was assured. Rumours quickly circulated that the grenadiers gave bread to Japanese regulars then across Suzhou Creek.[108]

Although the Italian ambassador in Berlin insisted that his government be kept up to date on peace moves initiated by Germany, the German Foreign Ministry agreed with its diplomats in Asia that 'the participation of Italy cannot increase the present operation but may well jeopardise it'.[109] Ciano also recognised the sad truth: 'Hirota has entrusted the Germans with a message to Chiang Kai-shek containing terms of peace...the explanation given is that our bad relations with China make us unsuitable to act as peace makers'.[110] As it turned out, the Germans had better relations but no more success as mediators.[111]

Probably the most important meeting of the late 1930s, from a Chinese perspective, took place in Paris beginning on Christmas Day, 1937. There, together with Gu Weijun (Wellington Koo) and the Chinese ambassador to England, Guo Taiqi, General Jiang Baili, Cheng Tianfang, Chen Gongbo and five others gathered to discuss the turn of events. Chen chaired the conference—perhaps because he arrived with the latest information. The meeting is still clouded in mystery. Jiang Baili is known to have summarised Japanese strategic capability. Guo, fresh from a conference with Jiang Tingfu, now ambassador to the Soviet Union, brought the disappointing news that Moscow would not become entangled with Japan. He most likely pressed for closer ties to the Western democracies. We also know that Jiang presented details of his conversations with Ciano and Ribbentrop and, in his own subsequent report to Chiang Kai-shek, abandoned his personal ties to the fascist powers in order to recommend that China seek the assistance of Britain, France and the United States.[112]

No reader should be surprised to learn that all the symbolic language about common destinies was the first to be sacrificed on the alter of Chinese nationalism. Thus, relations with Italy serve to underscore some important features of Chinese foreign policy including the nation's on-going vulnerability to those sudden changes in the international weather entirely beyond her own control. In September 1937, at about the time Jiang Baili and de Stefani left China on the *Conte Rosse*, the *Conte Verde* was driven upon the rocks in Hong Kong by a typhoon.

While there are those who, for personal or factual reasons, steadfastly maintain that Nationalist China aspired to be a fascist state, events made it impossible to continue the Italian connection. After all, Chiang Kai-shek had already become a Methodist. But the Italian and Chinese ships of state did more than just pass in the night for the Eastern and Western courses reveal a good deal about the nature of China's response to the West. If in the 1930s fascism was a modernising force about to sweep the earth, there were Chinese who wished to identify with it. The fact that the Soviet Union once played the Italian role and that communism inevitably took on Chinese form moves us closer to our conclusion. The Middle Kingdom has been willing to emulate foreign models only as long as it has served practical purposes and supported a belief in the enduring glory of China.

NOTES

1. This account of Jiang's meeting with Mussolini is the one provided by his translator. See Xue Guangqian, 'Jiang Baili xiansheng de wannian' [The final years of Jiang Baili], Xue and Jiang Fuzong, comp., *Jiang Baili xiansheng quanji* [The complete works of Jiang Baili] (Taibei, 1970), VI, 104-108.

2. Lloyd E. Eastman, 'The Kuomintang in the 1930s' in Charlotte Furth, ed., *The Limits of Change: Essays on Conservative Alternatives in Republican China* (Cambridge, Mass., 1976), 191-210. See also his monograph, *The Abortive Revolution: China under Nationalist Rule, 1927-1937* (Cambridge, Mass., 1974). Mary Wright's arguments first appeared as 'From Revolution to Restoration: The Transformation of Kuomintang Ideology', *Far Eastern Quarterly*, XIV:4 (1955).

3. Jiang Baili, 'Xiandai wenhua zhi youlai yu xinren shengguan zhi chengli' [The origins of contemporary culture and the establishment of a new man] in Niu Sienchong, ed., *Jiang Baili xuanji* [Selected works of Jiang Baili] (Taibei, 1967), 29-34.

4. Xue and Jiang, comp., VI, 603.

5. For a short history of the Sino-Italian relationship, see Frank M. Tamagna, *Italy's Interests and Policies in the Far East* (New York, 1941).

6. See Earl Albert Selle, *Donald of China* (New York, 1948), p. 284.

7. Edda Mussolini Ciano, *My Truth as told to Albert Zarca* (New York, 1977), p. 101.

8. US Department of State, *Foreign Relations of the United States, 1932* (Washington, 1948), III, 210-211, 422, 686; Selle, pp. 274-275.

9. *North-China Herald*, 10 May 1932; Tamagna, p. 15.

10. Hui-lan Koo, *An Autobiography as told to Mary van Rensseleaer Thayer* (New York, 1943), p. 279.

11. Edda Ciano, pp. 105-106; *China Press* (Shanghai), for example, 3, 10, 11, 13 April 1933.

12. *China Press*, 28 July, 1, 4-7 August 1935; *North-China Herald*, 31 July and 7 August 1935. Arthur N. Young, *China's Nation-Building Effort* (Stanford, 1971), p. 354, claims that Chiang was afraid to fly in the plane preferring an American aircraft and pilot.

13. Yu Liang, *Kong Xiangxi* (Hong Kong, 1955), pp. 41-42.

14. *Ibid.* See also Young, pp. 353-354 and *China Press*, 11 April 1933.

15. Edda Ciano, pp. 104-105; For Jiang Baili's interest in Italian aviation, see Wang Ranzhi, *Jiang Baili Jiangjun yu qi junshi sixiang* [General Jiang Baili and his military thought] (1975), pp. 122-124.

16. *China Press*, 9 June 1933.

17. *Ibid.*, 9 January 1934.

18. *Ibid.*, 16 and 19 February 1934. See 18 October and 7 November 1933 for information on Boscarelli's arrival in China.

19. *Foreign Relations of the United States*, 1932, IV, 609, 612; Young, pp. 114-115, 379.

20. *China Press*, 29 September 1934.

21. *Ibid.*, 31 October 1934. Liu Wendao provides more details in 'ZhongYi guanxi de huiyi' [Memoir on Sino-Italian relations], *Zhuanji wenxue* [Biographical Studies], 11:4 (October 1967), 104.

22. For Liu's career see Howard L. Boorman, ed., *Biographical Dictionary of Republican China* (New York, 1968), II, 419-421. His life as a diplomat is sketched by Wu Xiangxiang, 'Shouren juYi dashi Liu Wendao' [Liu Wendao, first ambassador to Italy], *Zhuanji wenxue*, 11:2 (August 1967), 14-17. See also Liu Wendao, *ZhjongYi guanxi huiyi* [Recollections on Sino-Italian relations] (Taibei, 1956).

23. *Documents on German Foreign Policy, 1918-1945*, Series C (London, 1957), I, 643-644.

24. Wu Xiangxiang, p. 16; Xue and Jiang, VI, 48-49.

25. *Opera Omnia di Benito Mussolini* [The complete works of Benito Mussolini] (Florence, 1958), XXVI, 155.

26. *China Press*, 13 and 17 July 1933.

27. *Ibid.*, 24 November 1933.

28. *Ibid.*, 25 and 26 January 1935. See also Liu Wendao, 'ZhongYi guanxi de huiyi', p. 104.

29. Liu, *ibid.*

30. Cesare Galimberti, 'Sino-Italian Relations', *China Quarterly*, II (Summer 1937), 479-486.

31. See Liu Wendao, 'ZhongYi quanxi huiyi' and Liu Wendao, ed., *ZhongYi wenhua lunji* [Essays on Sino-Italian culture] (Taibei, 1956).

32. Sih Kwong-chin [Xue Guangqian], 'A Summary of Relations Between China and Italy', *China Quarterly*, II (Summer 1937), 488.

33. See Maria Hsia Chang, 'Fascism and Modern China', *China Quarterly*, no. 70 (September 1979), 553-67 and Lloyd E. Eastman, 'Fascism and Modern China: A Rejoinder', *China Quarterly*, 80 (December 1979), 838-842.

34. For example, Gilbert Allardyce, 'What Fascism is Not: Thoughts on the Deflation of a Concept', *American Historical Review*, 84:2 (April 1979), 367-398.

35. James S. Barnes, *The Universal Aspects of Fascism* (London, 1929), pp. xxviii and 240. The chapter 'Fascism and Democracy', for example, was translated as 'Faxisi zhuyi yi minzhu zhengzhi' and published by *Zhengzhi pinglun* [Political critic], 159 (20 June 1935), 155-162.

36. *North-China Herald*, 15 March 1933; For similar statements, see also 11 January and 5 July 1933.

37. *China Press*, 5-7 September 1934.

38. *Ibid.*, 14 January 1934.

39. See, for example: Hung-mao Tien, *Government and Politics in*

Kuomintang China 1927-1937 (Stanford, 1972), pp. 54-64; James C. Thomson, Jr., *While China Faced West: American Reformers in Nationalist China 1938-1937* (Cambridge, Mass., 1969), passim; Lloyd E. Eastman, 'Fascism in Kuomintang China: The Blue Shirts', *China Quarterly*, no. 49 (January-March 1972), 1-31; Harold R. Isaacs, 'Blue Shirts in China', *The Nation* (17 October 1934, 433-435; and the *New York Times*, 18 September 1932. There were also some worried dispatches from American and British diplomats in China.

40. Chiang Kai-shek, 'Xiandai junren xuzhi' [What the modern soldier should know] in *Jiang Zongtung ji* [Works of President Chiang] (Taibei, 1961), I, 648.

41. *China Press*, 2 March 1934. See also *North-China Herald*, 12 July 1933 and 17 October 1934.

42. *North-China Herald*, 5 April 1933. See also the strong 'anti-fascist' argument in the pro-Wang periodical, *The People's Tribune*, 16 March and 16 June 1933.

43. *The People's Tribune*, 25 July 1931.

44. *China Press*, 14 January 1934.

45. *The People's Tribune*, 16 March 1934.

46. Cheng Tianfang, *ShiDe huiyilu* [Reminiscences of the ambassador to Germany] (Taibei, 1967), 92.

47. 'Minzhu yu duzai' [Democracy and dictatorship], *Zhengzhi pinglun*, 140 (7 February 1935), 327-335.

48. See Eastman, *The Abortive Revolution*, pp. 140-180 and Jerome B. Grieder, *Hu Shih and the Chinese Renaissance* (Cambridge, Mass., 1970), chapter 8. The original arguments can be traced in the Chinese periodical press, especially, *Duli pinglun* [Independent critic], 80 (10 December 1933) through 133 (30 December 1934).

49. *China Press*, 14 January 1934.

50. Cited by Selle, p. 285.

51. This is the implication made by his confidant Donald, as reported in Selle, and confirmed when Zhang took on leadership of the 'anti-bandit' suppression campaign in the Northwest for Chiang Kai-shek.

52. Published originally in English by T.F. Tsiang [Jiang Tingfu]. 'The Present Situation in China: A Critical Analysis', *International Affairs*, XIV (July-August 1935), 505.

53. *Shehui xinwen* ['The Society Mercury'], 24 August 1933. Eastman suggests that this was a Blue Shirt publication, *Abortive Revolution*, pp. 325-326, no. 20.

54. Maria Hsia Chang, pp. 559-567.

55. Summarised in Wm. Theodore de Bary, ed., *Sources of Chinese Tradition* (New York, 1965), II, 121-124.

56. *China Press*, 14 January 1934.

57. 'The San Min Chu I in the light of Fascism', *The People's Tribune*, 1 July 1934.

58. *North-China Herald*, 11 January 1933.

59. Chu Chia-hua [Ju Jiahua], 'The New Life Movement', *The People's Tribune*, 1 June 1934.

60. Cited in Eastman, *Abortive Revolution*, p. 42.

61. *China Press*, 16 March 1934 and 19 June 1935.

62. See Donald G. Gillin, *Warlord: Yen Hsi-shan in Shansi Province 1911-1949* (Princeton, 1967), pp. 166-167.

63. See Wang Ranzhi, pp. 115-118.

64. See Chow Tse-tung, *The May Fourth Movement: Intellectual Revolution in Modern China* (Cambridge, Mass., 1960), pp. 217 and 341.

65. Immanuel C.Y. Hsü, trans., *Intellectual Trends of the Ch'ing Period*

(Cambridge, Mass., 1959), pp. 11-13.

66. Liang Qichao, *Yinping shi wenji* [Collected essays of the Ice-Drinker's Studio] (Shanghai, 1948), IV, 3-24.

67. *Gerarchia*, XVII:1 (January 1937), 38-39.

68. Liu Wendao, 'ZhongYi guanxi huiyi', p. 104.

69. Galimberti, p. 485.

70. Liang, *Yinping shi wenji*, III, 124-176.

71. *Shehui xinwen*, 15 May 1933. See also 18, 21, 30 May and 3, 12 June 1933 for similar comments.

72. Jiang Baili, 'Xiandai wenhua' in Niu, ed., p. 34.

73. Liang Qichao, 'Sanshi zishi' [Autobiography at the age of thirty]. The translation is from Joseph R. Levenson, *Liang Ch'i-ch'ao and the Mind of Modern China* (Berkeley, 1970), p. 15. Levenson notes that the date for Italy is wrong.

74. 'Xiandai wenhua' in Niu, ed., p. 50.

75. Xue and Jiang, comp., I, 395-402.

76. *Ibid.*, 423-434.

77. 'Xiandai wenhua' in Niu, ed., p. 40.

78. Zou Rong, *The Revolutionary Army*, John Lust, trans. (The Hague, 1968), p. 99.

79. *China Press*, 14 January 1934.

80. Eastman, 'Fascism in Kuomintang China', p. 20.

81. *Jiang Zongtong ji*, I, 733. *China Press*, 16 March 1934.

82. As reported in *The Missionary Review of the World* (July-August, 1937), p. 357.

83. *Ibid.*, pp. 357-358. See also 'Xinshenghuo yundong zhi yaoyi' [Essentials of the new life movement] in *Jiang Zongtong ji*, I, 733-734.

84. Liang Qichao, 'Yidali jianguo sanjie zhuan' in *Yinping shi wenji*, III, 132.

85. See 'Xiandai wenhua' in Niu, ed., p. 50.

86. See Chen Li-fu, *Philosophy of Life* (New York, 1948) and the general discussion of his brand of conservatism by Eastman in Furth, ed., *Limits of Change*.

87. Cited in Eastman, *The Abortive Revolution*, p. 68.

88. *Shehui xinwen*, 12 June 1933.

89. Contrast, for example, *Xin Zhonghua* [The new China], 23 December 1934, pp. 5-10 with its long essay on the 'New Roman Empire' with the later coverage of the invasion of Ethiopia in this and other magazines.

90. Liu Wendao, 'ZhongYi guanxi de huiyi', p.105. For general background see *China Press*, 27, 28, 30 November and 1, 6 December 1936.

91. *North-China Herald*, 26 April 1937.

92. *Ibid.*, 2 June 1937 and *China Press*, 30 May and 1 June 1937.

93. See Xue and Jiang, comp. VI, 78-100.

94. *1937-38, Diario* (Bologna, 1948), p. 5.

95. *Foreign Relations of the United States, 1937*, III, 447.

96. *Documents on German Foreign Policy, Series D*, I, 763-764.

97. Xue and Jiang, comp., VI, 104-107.

98. It is worth noting that Jiang Baili who had flown to Xi'an with his latest intelligence on events in Europe, also played a role in securing Chiang's release.

99. *North-China Herald*, 30 December 1936; *Foreign Relations of the United States, 1936* (Washington, 1954), IV, 432-433. Zhang Xueliang reportedly responded that an Italian-German-Japanese entente and the recognition of Manchukuo would bring about the end of fascism in China. See Nym Wales (Helen F. Snow), *Historical Notes on China, II: Notes on the Chinese Student Movement 1935-36* (1961), p. 2.

100. Malcolm Muggeridge, ed., *Ciano's Diplomatic Papers* (London, 1948), pp. 142-143.

101. *Documents on German Foreign Policy, Series D*, I, 735.

102. Related by Hollington Tong, *Dateline: China* (New York, 1950), p. 13. There is no evidence that Ms X made the trip.

103. See Gerald E. Bunker, *The Peace Conspiracy: Wang Ching-wei and the China War, 1937-1941* (Cambridge, Mass., 1972). *Ciano's Diplomatic Papers*, 143. *Diario*, p. 51.

104. *China Press*, 15 December 1937; *North-China Herald*, 22 December 1937; *Diario*, p. 76.

105. *North-China Herald*, 5 January, 23 March, 20 April, 11 and 18 May and 8 June 1938. Palucci de Calboli cited in Tamagna, pp. 32-33.

106. *Ciano's Diplomatic Papers*, p. 132.

107. *Documents on German Foreign Policy, Series D*, I, 782, 785-787.

108. *North-China Herald*, 3 November 1937 and China Press, 15 and 16 September 1937.

109. *Documents on German Foreign Policy, Series D*, I, 776, 800, 804-805, 809.

110. *Diario*, p. 75.

111. For the history of the German mediation effort, see James T.C. Liu, 'German Mediation in the Sino-Japanese War, 1937-48', *The Far Eastern Quarterly*, VIII:2 (February 1948), 151-171. The Chinese political situation is assessed in Bunker and Cheng Tianfang's role in Germany can be read in *ShiDe huiyi lu*, chapter 17.

112. See Cheng Tianfang, *ShiDe huiyi lu*, pp. 238-243 and William L. Tung, *V.K. Wellington Koo and China's Wartime Diplomacy* (New York, 1977), pp. 18-38.

PART 2

THE STATE AND POLICY IMPLEMENTATION

5

THE NATIONALIST STATE AND REGULATION OF CHINESE INDUSTRY DURING THE NANJING DECADE: COMPETITION AND CONTROL IN COAL MINING
Tim Wright

In their search for a rich and strong China, many Chinese in modern times have looked to the state to be the main agent of the transformation of society and the economy. The possibility of effecting such a transformation in this way drew into politics many who had earlier sought other roads to modernisation, for instance, in the case of Sun Yat-sen, through science and medicine. The coming to power of the Nationalists in 1928 raised new hopes that China now had a state strong enough to modernise the country. The fate of such hopes raises the question of how effective an actor the state really was in pre-communist China, and how far did it rather conform to the typology discussed by Myrdal in the case of South Asia, that of the 'soft state', in which 'policies decided on are often not enforced, if they are enacted at all, and in which the authorities, even when framing policies, are reluctant to place obligations on people'.[1]

Economic development was a key aspect of the search for wealth and power, and government sponsorship of economic change was by no means a new concept in China, as the first efforts at modernisation took place under the auspices of the Qing state in the late nineteenth century. The Beijing governments of the warlord period, however, were too weak to initiate even limited projects, and private enterprise came by 1927 to dominate most sectors of the economy.[2] But in 1928 the Nationalists came to power committed in theory to a programme of economic change, reconstruction and development as outlined by Sun Yat-sen in his 1918 lectures entitled 'Fundamentals of National Reconstruction'.[3] This paper examines one part of that ambitious programme, that part concerned with the control of private industry. It traces Nationalist thinking on this subject on the one hand to Sun's idea of the 'regulation of capital', a more general concept which he saw as one of the two basic means of attaining the Principle of People's Livelihood,[4] and on the other to the influence of European experiments in macro-economic management and counter-recessionary measures, as well as to more immediate political and personal considerations. Through an examination of the implementation of these policies in several industries and by means of a special case study of the abortive coal mining cartel of 1936, it brings into focus the relationship between government action and economic change in a country where two decades later a very powerful new regime was to initiate an almost unprecedented economic transformation.

'Economic Control' under the Nationalists

The Nationalist government adopted Sun's ideas for state-initiated and controlled industrialisation as the best way to achieve equitable growth and avoid the sort of class conflict that plagued Europe. In this scheme the state would establish a heavy industrial sector, and also give guidance and supervision to private enterprise in light industry.[5] Despite the ambitious plans put forward by Kong Xiangxi and Chen Gongbo during their tenures as Minister of Industry (1928-1931 and 1932-1935, respectively) the state was in reality in no better position to raise the huge sums needed for heavy industry than were private investors. Proposals for massive government investment to set up iron and steel plants and to electrify the whole country were totally unrealistic in view of the very limited resources available to the planners.[6] The only plant actually in operation in 1936 was an alcohol plant in Shanghai, though some progress had been made towards setting up machine shops.[7]

Regulating the operation of private enterprise within individual industries was more within the government's abilities, though even here serious problems were to be encountered. In addition to the Nationalists' long-term development strategy for China, two other currents of thought made a perhaps more immediate and direct contribution to the formation of policy on the issue. In the export industries the Chinese had long been concerned at their inability to control export prices even of commodities of which they were the major world supplier. Economic nationalism as well as self-interest therefore induced them to attempt to control trade in major export products as a way to raise prices and increase foreign currency earnings. Although this aim was seldom openly acknowledged, the policy led to frequent clashes with foreign commercial interests and diplomatic representatives.

Other countries' experience in the regulation of industry, first in wartime and then in response to the effects of the depression, also influenced Chinese thinking on this subject. Such concepts went under the name of 'economic control' in China in the 1930s,[8] a term which first became fashionable in the context of Roosevelt's New Deal.[9] It encompassed more than just the regulation of private industry, and indeed some interest was also shown in Soviet planning, though a number of authors differentiated the terms 'controlled economy' and 'planned economy'.[10] Closer to home, the success of the Japanese government in promoting industrialisation held, it seemed to many, lessons for China,[11] and industrialists were particularly impressed with the cartel arrangements worked out there in individual industries. By the mid-1930s the rapid development of Manchuria must also have heightened Chinese interest in the role of the state in the economy. Most influential of all, however, were the fascist policies of Italy and later of Germany; indeed the Americans feared the establishment in China of an Italian-style 'corporate state'.[12] Such thinking was used as a justification for the extension of short-term regulation well outside the sphere of export industries and especially to those industries supplying the domestic market which had been most severely affected by the depression. In such cases the government, aware of the positive role foreign capital could play in industrial development, attempted to integrate foreign firms in China into the scheme.

Probably nowhere is policy determined solely or even mainly on the basis of long-term theoretical considerations such as these, and Nationalist China was no exception. The struggle for political power by the government vis-à-vis other regional centres of power and other social groups outside Nanjing's control certainly informed much policy-making throughout the period.[13] More personal gains also played an important part, to the extent that some regard 'squeeze' as the primary motive for Nationalist economic policy. The illegal elements in such activity are of course difficult to document, but it is hardly likely to have been a coincidence that, for example, cigarette taxes were reduced so soon after Song Ziwen's acquisition of a large holding in the Nanyang Brothers Tobacco Company.[14] Nevertheless such direct considerations of personal gain were not always apparent, and many of the policies were aimed at least in part at attaining more general economic goals.[15]

The major institutions through which the Nationalists carried out their economic policy included both government ministries and special commissions established as co-ordinating bodies. After some changes in structure in the late 1920s and early 1930s the Ministries of the Interior, of Finance, of Industry, of the Railways and of Communication emerged as the ones with the most important economic functions. In addition the National Reconstruction Commission was established in 1928 with particular responsibility for electric utilities and for water conservancy. It later lost several of its responsibilities to other newer bodies, but continued to run its most important enterprises—the Nanjing power plant and the Huainan coal mine and railway—almost up to the war.[16] In 1931 the National Economic Council was established under Song Ziwen with the aim of co-ordinating planning. It made little progress in this, but the Cotton Industry Commission (Control Commission in Chinese), which it set up in 1933 amid assurances to the industry that it did not envisage nationalisation but merely planned to use political power to aid industry, did achieve positive, if limited, results.[17]

Provincial governments also initiated policies of 'economic control' within their own borders. Sometimes, these were unco-ordinated with or even in partial opposition to central government plans, as with Yan Xishan's programme for development in Shanxi.[18] Guangdong was another province outside the Nationalists' sphere of control, and its proposals for controlling cigarettes, sugar, cement and orange juice met with little support from Nanjing.[19] The lower Yangzi provinces, on the other hand, initiated schemes which were later taken over by the centre. A scheme for tea control in Jiangxi and Anhui was initiated in 1936 by the Anhui government, with the co-operation of Jiangxi and the National Economic Council. Opposition from foreign interests delayed its implementation, but the next year the National Tea Company of China was set up by the Ministry of Industry with private participation.[20]

In most cases the government joined with private interests to establish a company to control the distribution of the product, and sometimes to set quotas for production. The new company was sometimes nominally owned by private interests, while in other cases the government held a direct share: 50 per cent in the case of the National Tea Company.[21] In either case the government was to play a central role in policing the cartel, and thus would have a strong say in its direction. Moreover, as the United States minister in China remarked:

> Present conditions in China are not such as would stimulate the launching of projects that were not possessed of official connections to an extent guaranteeing their undisturbed functioning on a profitable basis.[22]

Many of these plans did, in fact, draw complaints from Chinese and foreign interests against the establishment of so-called government monopolies.

Complaints from foreigners over government monopolies were particularly vehement in the case of the export industries. American diplomats voiced opposition to the formation of ostensibly private companies to control the trade in tungsten and antimony, of both of which China was the world's largest producer. The initial moves to form the companies were made by the provincial governments of Jiangxi and Hunan, where the production of the two minerals was concentrated, but it was difficult for a provincially-run cartel to prevent the smuggling of the minerals across provincial borders, so in both cases the national government also became involved. Particularly with antimony the Chinese press saw the aim of the syndicate as to regain control of antimony prices, which had been at a low level since the end of the First World War. While in diplomatic communications the Chinese government denied direct involvement, other Chinese sources described the antimony syndicate as an organ of the provincial government, the National Economic Council and mining interests.[23]

Similarly when a China Vegetable Oil Corporation was established in 1936 ostensibly to prevent the industry from suffering a slump like that in the silk industry and to ensure exports which were dependable in both quality and quantity, both foreign and Chinese interests saw it rather as an attempt by government officials to seize control of the trade, partly in their own personal interests, partly in those of the government.[24]

Industries catering primarily to the domestic market in which attempts were made at regulation included tobacco and sugar. In 1936 the government was examining the possibility of promoting the Chinese tobacco industry by monopolising tobacco grown in China from American seed and by putting a protective tariff on imported tobacco.[25] Imports of sugar were also subjected to control, though critics pointed out the shortcomings of a scheme that did not cover domestic producers.[26]

More important was the match industry, where the initiative was taken by private interests. The history of this cartel shows many interesting parallels to what happened in coal mining.[27] China's 'match king', Liu Hongsheng (who was also an important figure in the coal trade), had proposed a cartel as early as 1933, with the aim mainly of protecting the market share of his Da Zhonghua Match Company. In the next year he won over match manufacturers in central China, but north Chinese factories and foreign interests remained aloof. Japanese companies in China were persuaded to join a national Match Sales Union in 1936, but their adherence had to be bought with exceptionally favourable terms, giving them a larger share of the market than they initially held. American match interests negotiated with the group throughout, reaching agreements with central Chinese producers in 1935 and (again on very favourable terms) with the national cartel in 1937; the American government, however, remained opposed to the idea and refused support to their businessmen.

Most of these industries either exported a large part of their output or relied substantially on imported materials. The government was, through its control over foreign trade licenses and procedures, more able to influence developments in them than in industries relying on domestic markets and materials. Insofar as there was a pattern to the government's efforts, therefore, it was a function less of the intrinsic importance or problems of a particular industry than of the opportunities it offered for the exercise of official power. How limited that power was can be seen in the case of the coal cartel.

The Coal Industry: Economic Organisation up to 1936

Coal mining was one of China's largest industries,[28] so the attempt in 1936 to regulate competition there represented the most ambitious plan to date. In 1933 only the cotton yarn and tobacco industries produced more in terms of net value added than did modern coal mining. Coal mines employed about 200,000 workers, as many as did the cotton mills, and far more than any other industry. Foreign interests also held a large stake in the industry: up to 1931 over 70 per cent of the coal produced by modern collieries came from ones wholly or partly owned by foreigners.[29] After the Japanese occupation of Manchuria in 1931, their mines there were excluded from the calculations of the Chinese government, so that in the 1930s just over 50 per cent of modern mine output in China came from foreign or Sino-foreign mines. The size and dispersion of the industry and the foreign interest in it all made coal mining a difficult industry for the Nationalist government to regulate.

The emergence of cartels in the coal industry in China can be traced back to the 1910s, when the KMA (Kailuan Mining Administration—an Anglo-Chinese company in Hebei and the largest producer of coal in China at the time) reached an agreement with the major suppliers of Japanese coal to regulate sales in the coastal market.[30] In 1918 the SMR (South Manchurian Railway Company, whose Fushun collieries overtook the KMA mines as the largest producers in China from 1922) adhered to the arrangements. Conferences between these parties were held annually up to 1931, though, as it was not in the interests of the participants to publicise their arrangements, little is known about them.[31]

Although we cannot judge the success of this cartel in terms of price control, its existence over a decade and a half suggests its continuing usefulness to the participants. The background to its presumed success was the extraordinarily high degree of concentration of both coal output and the coal market in China. While in most countries the coal industry is cited as almost the perfect example of atomistic competition,[32] in China the KMA and SMR mines accounted for 60 per cent of the output of modern mines between 1918 and 1931, and for 40 per cent of total output, including that from small unmechanised mines. Shanghai was by far the largest competitive market for coal in China, and cartel agreements were mostly aimed at that market;

statistics for coal imported by sea (by far the largest part of the total) show that Kailuan, Fushun and Japanese coal between them accounted for 95 per cent of the market in 1916 and for 86 per cent between 1924 and 1927.[33]

High coal prices caused by the boom during and after the First World War and, to a lesser extent, by the operation of the cartel did, as economic theory predicts, attract new investment into the industry, and many Chinese coal mines rapidly expanded their capacity in the early 1920s. Just as the resulting output was beginning to come on to the market, however, the civil wars which wracked north China in the mid and late 1920s brought a virtual halt to transport on the main north-south railway lines: freight traffic on the Beijing-Hankou line between 1926 and 1930 was on average less than one quarter of the 1923 level, and even in 1932-1933 traffic was running at under two-thirds of that level.[34] Similarly in 1927 coal production along that line fell to 24 per cent of output in 1923. Mining companies along this and other railways in China proper were forced to cut or even to close down their operations, and many were brought to bankruptcy, needing large bank loans to enable them to survive. On the other hand, the transport of coal from the KMA and Fushun, being under foreign protection, was much less seriously affected, so that coal from these two producers, and from Japan, was able to dominate the coastal market for seven or eight years longer than it might otherwise have been, so prolonging the effective life of the cartel. Other Chinese mines accounted at this time for only a small part of the market, and the phenomenon of a small competitive fringe is by no means uncommon in cases of oligopolistic collusion, and does not necessarily negate the advantage of collusion to the major participants.[35]

The expansion, with the gradual recovery of the railway network from the early 1930s, of that small competitive fringe into a major influence in the market was the basic factor behind both the collapse of the old cartel and the attempts to form a new one. But instabilities in China's foreign trade in coal and the effects of the world depression also greatly contributed to the industry's problems and formed the immediate background for both these events.

Japanese coal exports were badly hit by the steep rise in the value of the gold yen from 1929. Although exporters cut the yen prices of coal sold to China to below cost, prices in Shanghai still rose by as much as 40 per cent between 1929 and 1931.[36] Imports of Japanese coal into China fell, though the continuing physical constraints on the supply of Chinese coal meant that they fell less than might have been expected. In December 1931, however, the Japanese went off the gold standard and the yen started a precipitous fall against the silver yuan. So Japanese coal, which had in 1931 been barely competitive in Shanghai despite the fact that its price in terms of yen indicated that it was being dumped, now plummeted in price by as much as 50 per cent during 1932, and in the latter part of that year took a sharply increasing share of the market. This provoked a storm over Japanese dumping and, by threatening the KMA's profits and market share, led to their refusal to renew the Conference agreement, and to increased competition in the Chinese market.[37]

On 16 May 1933 China promulgated a new tariff schedule, which for the first time was avowedly protective. In this context the strong lobbying by the National Mining Association against Japanese dumping also achieved steep rises in tariffs on coal, which were increased from Y1.6 to Y3.5 per tonne.[38] This raised the price of Japanese coal in China by about 25 per cent, and clearly gave Chinese coal a decisive edge, as the share of imports in the market declined very sharply. Moreover, since Manchurian coal was, from September 1932, regarded as foreign coal, and so subject to the tariff, a gap was opened in the market for which different Chinese coals were able to compete. In this situation those interested in cartelisation inevitably turned their attention away from importers towards other mining companies in China.

While the effects of the transport crisis and the dumping controversy were still being felt in the mid 1930s, by 1934 the main concern was the fall in industrial demand caused first by the Japanese attack on Shanghai in January 1932, which closed down most industry there for three months. Two other factors soon also added to the troubles of Chinese industry and thence of its demand for coal. The loss of Manchuria cut off a major part of the market, particularly of many small-scale industries in north China.[39] Also the impact of the world depression began increasingly to be felt from 1932. First, rural areas went to recession as silver flowed into Shanghai and the terms of trade for farmers deterioriated sharply. From 1934 the further rise in world silver prices attracted silver out of China altogether, forced prices down in the cities as well, and initiated a full-scale industrial recession that lasted until mid 1936.

Table 1. The Effects of the Depression on Industrial Demand for Coal

Year	Index of output of consumer goods (1933 = 100)	Imports of coal by sea into Shanghai (1000 tons)	Consumption of coal in five major cities (1000 tons)	Price of Kaipang slack in Shanghai (¥/ton)
1930	85.3	3403	5700	10.3
1931	91.7	3617	5810	12.9
1932	93.7	2942	5260	11.3
1933	100	3323	5100	10.1
1934	98.1	3229	5130	8.8
1935	93.5	3303	5585	8.8
1936	99.5	3204	n.a.	10.6

Sources: John Key Chang, *Industrial Development in Pre-Communist China* (Chicago, 1969), p. 79; *Shina sekitan shijō ni taisuru kongo no hōsaku* [Plans in relation to the Chinese coal market], SMR, keizai chōsakai ed. (Xinjing, 1936), p. 18; *Shanghai jiefang qianhou wujia ziliao huibian* [Collected materials on prices in Shanghai before and after liberation], Zhongguo kexue yuan, Shanghai jingji yanjiu suo with Shanghai shehui kexue yuan, jingi yanjiu suo comp. (Shanghai, 1958), pp. 255-256; Tezuka Masao, *Jihen zen ni okeru Shina sekitan no seisan to ryūdō* [Pre-war coal production and marketing in China] (Tokyo, 1940), pp. 252-253.

Table 1 summarises the effects of these various influences on demand. Consumer goods output, a reasonable proxy for the level of activity in coal-using industries in the major cities, was falling between 1933 and 1935. As a consequence consumption for coal in Shanghai and the other major cities was at best stagnant throughout the 1930s, while low demand also forced down prices, which reached a nadir in 1934-1935.

By the mid 1930s, then, the situation in the coal industry was one where an increasing amount of Chinese coal was competing at low prices for a stagnant market. Though the decline of imports of Japanese and Manchurian coal eased the pressure a little, the return of the north China mines to the market undermined the KMA's quasi-monopoly position, which had earned them high profits throughout the 1920s, and initiated what the KMA's management foresaw as a prolonged period of oversupply in East Asia.[40] Moreover those north China mines, still in grievous financial difficulties resulting from the civil wars, were eager to sell coal at any price,[41] thus making it difficult for either the established firms or the new arrivals to make a profit. Table 2 shows the effects of these forces on the structure of the Shanghai market; the established mines such as the KMA and Zhongxing, in southern Shandong and the largest Chinese-owned mine in the country, were beginning to lose their share of the market, and the rapid rise in sales of coal from Anhui and central Shandong in particular to take over the place previously occupied by imports also held uncomfortable longer-term implications for the companies.

Table 2. Structure of the Shanghai Coal Market, 1933-1937

Year	Japan	Fushun	KMA	Zhongxing	central Shandong	Anhui
1933	15.7	13.0	33.5	9.5	9.7	2.5
1934	8.0	5.5	35.5	11.8	16.8	3.4
1935	4.5	2.3	36.5	12.5	19.1	5.5
1936	3.4	1.1	28.0	7.5	27.3	8.3
1937*	2.2	1.7	28.6	8.0	28.7	9.0

Percentage of coal sales accounted for by coal from

* January-May

Sources: KYZB, no 391 (21 July 1936), 102-104; Leonard G. Ting, 'The Coal Industry in China', *Nankai Social and Economic Quarterly*, X:2 (July 1937), 218; Kuboyama Yūzō, *Shina sekitan chōsa hōkokusho* [Report on Chinese coal] (Tokyo, 1940), p.102; *Tōyō keizai shimpō* [East Asian economic journal], 21 August 1937, pp. 678-679.

The Nanjing Government and the Abortive Coal Cartel of 1936

Nanjing's involvement with the industry reflected the changing nature of the problems and of perceptions of them. Up to 1932 the difficulties of the mines were clearly part of China's general problem of internal peace and stability, and any solution had to come in a wider context than that of the industry alone. With the restoration of a degree of order and stability in north China, however, problems more specific to the industry came to the fore, and mining interests began more seriously to approach the Nationalist government, which they hoped would be more favourable to their interests than had been previous administrations, for help in solving these problems, and to this end the Chinese Coal Relief Association was founded by the government and the coal trade in 1932. Successive Ministers of

Industry also came up with various plans to aid coal mining, and in 1933 conferences were held on improving the provision of railway transport and on the more general problems of the industry.[42]

The problems they aimed to tackle in the early years were mainly those of imports, of railway capacity and charges and of tax rates. Probably the greatest practical contribution made by the government to the industry's well-being was the tariff of 1933, which removed imports as a serious threat in the Chinese market, a fact not always clearly perceived, as for instance when the National Economic Council's 1934 proposals for increasing sales of Chinese coal centred on reducing imports. Complaints about excessive tax rates met with little response from a government whose income already fell short of expenditure, but the railways, though in as poor shape as the mines after the civil wars, did reduce charges through a series of discounts roughly to the level of the early 1920s.[43]

Mining companies were as worried about railway capacity as they were about freight rates. Although the railways began regular operations again around 1932, there was still a serious shortage of rolling stock because of the depredation of previous years. So several schemes were advanced for the government to raise or to guarantee loans to finance the industry in the purchase of more rail cars. While, however, shortage of transport capacity certainly limited the amount of coal particular mines could send to the market, it is less clear that by the mid 1930s it resulted in any serious shortage of coal in the main markets. In any case these schemes were rather unrealistic in the light of competing demands on the government's financial resources.[44] Moreover, in a foretaste of later difficulties, the Japanese minister objected to the raising of a loan on the grounds that it contravened the contract under which the Sino-Japanese Luda Company had been established in 1923; the objection seems to have been withdrawn when Chen Gongbo explained that the government's role was merely to guarantee the loan, which would be raised and repaid by the coal industry itself.[45]

So by 1934 attention was coming to be focussed on what was now the basic problem of the industry—over-production and the consequent low prices and profits. Several attempts were therefore made to regulate excessive competition in order to keep up prices. In 1933 and 1934 the Shandong provincial authorities encouraged the formation of a company to control sales of coal produced within the Shandong fields, but the various proposals put forward all foundered upon their inability to integrate the Sino-Japanese mines into the arrangements.[46] In Shanxi the price of Yangquan coal had fallen sharply in 1934-1935 and this had precipitated discussion of the formation of a joint sales company; such a company was established on 1 January 1936, and during that year did succeed in raising the prices of Shanxi coal both in Shijiazhuang and in Tianjin.[47] There were other arrangements made between individual mines. The KMA and Zhongxing reached an agreement in 1934 to regulate sales in the Yangzi valley, renewed it in 1935 and in 1936 extended it to cover also south China and Japan.[48] The KMA also reached a tentative agreement with the Sino-German Jingxing Mines in southern Hebei for regulation of the north China market, but the failure of Jingxing to reach a similar agreement with their neighbour, the Zhengfeng Company, reduced the scope of the agreement and made the KMA less eager to go ahead.[49]

Such schemes did, in 1935, excite discussion among members of the Coal Relief Association,[50] and Wu Dingchang, the Minister of Industry 1935-1937, initiated in 1936 an attempt to bring together these various projects to help the industry by the formation of a national cartel. Wu's interest in economic control went back at least to 1933 when he addressed the Institute of Banking on the subject. He had been a prominent north Chinese banker and had close ties with the so-called 'Zhejiang financial clique', a somewhat loose term encompassing at its widest most of those connected with China's banking system.[51] Members of this group held, through their banking jobs, strategic positions in the mining industry: most notably, the bankers Qian Yongming and Zhou Zuomin controlled the management of Zhongxing during the 1930s. Qian and Zhongxing's company secretary did indeed take away a very favourable view of the operation of the Japanese coal cartel from a trip to that country in 1935.[52] Politically, Wu, along with other bankers, gravitated towards the Political Study Clique, the group within the Guomindang (the Nationalist Party) which was the most urban and attractive to the bourgeoisie. Domination of financial and industrial activities in China's major cities was one of their chief goals.[53]

For the government as a whole the scheme, as well as being

a way of dealing with the problems of the industry, also offered an opportunity to extend its influence in north China, an area in which it was weak. In a similar way Song Ziwen's Huanan Rice Company, ostensibly aimed at improving the efficiency of rice production and marketing in south China, also enabled the government to strengthen its grip on the politically sensitive Guangdong-Guangxi region.[54] With several other organisations as well, political and economic aims overlapped, and it is not possible clearly to weigh the importance of each.

After having canvassed opinions from mining interests,[55] Wu convened a National Coal Conference in Nanjing, which was held between 1 and 3 June 1936.[56] In attendance were representatives of the twenty-eight major coal mining companies in China, as well as of four mining associations, the Ministries of Railways, Finance and Industry, and the Resources Commission. Sino-foreign mines in China, which earlier schemes had wished to exclude,[57] were explicitly included in the new proposals. In its preliminary statement, the ministry pointed out that the problem of imported coal had largely been removed since the raising of the tariff in 1933, and the minister's opening speech, while acknowledging the industry's concern with transport costs and taxes, said that excessive competition was the basic factor behind the stunted development of coal mines.

So the main task before the conference was the organisation of a scheme to regulate competition. After three days of discussion the delegates agreed in principle to the ministry's plan, and elected a committee to prepare a pilot project in Shanghai, the articles for which were to be drawn up within three months. In his closing speech Wu said that he hoped the industry would be able to regulate its own affairs and that the government would only play a guiding role.

The committee drew up draft regulations for the national sales control organisation and for the Shanghai office, which they planned to set up first. The regulations themselves were not specific as to the allocation of quotas, merely saying that quotas would be drawn up by a committee half-yearly. The earlier ministry proposals, however, made it clear that the existing shares of the market would be frozen, and only 5 percent of total sales would be allocated to small mines outside the scheme or for extra sales by the large mines in exceptional circumstances. Regulation was to be organised separately for bituminous and for anthracite coal. In total the scheme was very ambitious, dividing up the country into major market areas, each of which would be controlled by a branch office. The sanctions attached to the plan were that a 75 per cent majority of companies in any one area could ask the Ministry of Industry to take action against any one of their members in case of infringement. In a letter to Boshan coal guild the committee stressed the role of the government in the cartel, and the way these mines might expose themselves if they did not participate.[58]

Despite this, discussions following the conference showed that the mines in central Shandong and those in Anhui, while ostensibly approving the principle of regulation, were unwilling to participate in the scheme as proposed. The problems now encountered say much both about the economics of the coal industry and about the political history of state 'economic control' in the 1930s. Despite strong support for the idea, many economic factors were against the successful operation of a cartel. Collusive price agreements work better, other things being equal, in a concentrated industry where entry is difficult.[59] But the degree of concentration in the Chinese coal industry, although still high, was lower in the 1930s than it had been previously. Now that the Manchurian market was separated from China, the KMA, while still predominant, accounted for only about 30 per cent of output from modern mines. In Shanghai the two largest suppliers, now Kailuan and Zhongxing, supplied under 50 per cent of the market in 1934-1935 (see Table 2). No other single supplier accounted for as much as 10 per cent of the market . So the conditions for collusive arrangements among the market leaders were less favourable than they had been in the 1920s.

Entry into the industry was also relatively easy. There were many areas with coal reserves close enough to the surface to be accessible to medium-sized mines. There were therefore no very lumpy capital requirements. Economies of scale operated more in transport than in production, and given similar geological conditions small or medium-sized mines could operate as cheaply as large ones.[60] Entry might have been limited by the government, as a mining permit was required. But the weakness of central *fiat* in many mining areas made the use of such powers difficult. More importantly, the expansion of an existing small or medium-sized mine into one capable of competing in the national market (as, for instance, happened with the Yuesheng mine in central Shandong) had an effect similar to the entry of an entirely new operation, and this possibility made collusive arrangements between existing major mines inherently unstable.

A cartel might still have been viable had a strong government been willing to police it. The Nationalist government was indeed interested in encouraging a cartel, but lacked the strength to act as an effective policing agent. Internally the Guomindang was divided between the military/rural and urban/industrial groups.[61] Even the latter group was far from united in their plans for industry, and there was no co-ordinating body powerful enough to impose a common policy on the various disparate elements. Notwithstanding initial opinions that the Huainan mine in Anhui, which was run by the National Reconstruction Commission, would, as a government mine, have to join the scheme despite its expressed reservations,[62] this did not prove to be the case. The mine was rapidly expanding its share of the Yangzi market: sales of Anhui coal in Shanghai rose by five times between 1933 and 1937. This growth would be halted by an agreement to freeze market shares. Nevertheless, as the chief manager of the KMA pointed out, it was symptomatic that the Ministry of Industry did not even have the power to enforce its will on an enterprise run by another central government organ:

> Significantly it was a mine managed by the National Reconstruction Bureau in Nanking which refused to attend the Conference called by the Ministry of Industry, and together with the Japanese-controlled mines who did likewise, blocked the Government's efforts.[63]

Externally the government had to deal with the major foreign interests in coal mining. Of these, the British strongly favoured the cartel.[64] British economic influence in China had been reduced by the effects of the depression on the home economy. This led to a somewhat passive policy in China in the early 1930s, but by the middle of that decade the British were attempting to expand their influence: Major-general Hammond visited China to report on the condition of the railways, and suspicions of Britain were reflected by the belief, on the part of both the Americans and the Japanese, that the 1935 currency reform involved a Sino-British deal. In view of the increasing influence of the Japanese, however, British activities were mainly designed to prevent any further erosion of their position in China. Indeed British companies consciously tried to ally themselves with the Nanjing government through, for instance, participation in Song Ziwen's China Development Finance Corporation as a way of warding off Japanese pressure on their interests.[65] In this way they saw the cartel as a means of protecting the KMA, their largest direct investment in north China, and the KMA and the British were among the first to raise the question of the regulation of the coal industry with the Minister of Industry. Like Zhongxing's managers, Liu Hongsheng, the KMA's sales agent in Shanghai, had come back from a trip to Japan in 1935 very impressed with the cartel there and pledged himself to work for a similar arrangement in China, though the KMA's chief manager felt that the situation in China was much more 'undisciplined'.[66]

The Japanese took a different view. Concerned both in general and in coal mining with expanding their influence rather than with maintaining an existing situation, a cartel was much less suited to their aims. Since the separation of Manchuria from China, the main Japanese stake in Chinese coal had been in central Shandong: in Boshan, the Bodong Company, only one of the very many companies operating in the field; and in Zichuan the much larger Luda Company. The Japanese had seized the Zichuan mines from the Germans in 1914, run them for eight years, and handed them over in 1923 to Luda, a Sino-Japanese company formed specially to take over the mines; from 1923 their consuls had been active in protecting and furthering the interests of the company.[67]

Sales of coal from the central Shandong mines in general in the Shanghai market were expanding rapidly in the mid 1930s, being almost 50 per cent higher in 1936 than in 1935. This meant that they would be disadvantaged by an agreement to freeze the market. Nevertheless the proprietor of the largest Chinese-owned mine in Boshan was persuaded to co-operate, ostensibly for patriotic reasons. For the cartel to be successful, however, all the major mines in the area would have had to participate, and the failure to integrate the Sino-Japanese mines into the 1934 scheme for a provincial cartel boded ill for this. The Japanese remained opposed, both because the proposed project was inimical to the economic interests of Luda, and because it did not fit in with broader Japanese plans to extend their economic and political influence in China. The inability of the Chinese to apply sanctions to a partly Japanese-owned mine left Luda free to refuse, and thus to prevent any participation by central Shandong mines in the scheme.[68]

After the preparatory committee had agreed on the regulations, the second coal conference was held on 15 August 1936.[69] The Shandong mines and, at the last minute, Huainan refused to send delegates, though Huainan said that they would be willing to adhere to the scheme later if their sales in Shanghai in 1937 reached the target level of 400,000 tons. But the representatives now of nineteen mines and of the Ministry of Industry voted to set up offices first in Shanghai and then for the Beijing-Tianjin area, for Wuhan, for Shandong and for Guangdong. A month later the Shanghai office published its regulations, following the plans earlier outlined. The refusal of Huainan and the Shandong mines, which between them supplied over 30 per cent of the market, and whose share was expanding rapidly, to adhere to the scheme made the decision to proceed an empty one. Continued government attempts to persuade the Shandong mines to join were to no avail, and this industry wide organisation came in practice to nothing.

At the same time, the KMA, now convinced that the failure to win over Luda and Huainan had made national agreement impossible,[70] decided to go ahead on its own on the basis of private enterprise and without direct government involvement.[71] They planned, together with Zhongxing and the Chinese banks most closely involved with the industry, to form a syndicate, in which the KMA's say would be dominant, to buy up the coal of their main competitors and so to dominate the Shanghai market. On 4 November 1936 the KMA, Zhongxing and the Jincheng (Kincheng) Banking Corporation, which already traded in coal through a subsidiary, formed a holding company to become the chief shareholder of the Huazhong Coal Industry Company, in which the National Bank of Shanghai also had a holding. The KMA nominated two managing directors to the company, Zhongxing one. A further agreement with the Shanghai's leading coal trading concern whose owners, being men from Ningbo, could be expected to be close to the bankers of the Zhejiang financial clique,[72] gave the combine control of about 2.3 million tons out of the 3 million shipped annually by sea into Shanghai; of the rest all but 100,000 tons was supplied on contract.

In north China the KMA set up the Huabei Coal Company to fulfil a similar function, but here they were the only important participants, and the refusal of the Datong mines in north Shanxi, whose sales were the most rapidly increasing, to join created problems similar to those which had emerged in Shanghai. The earlier agreement with the Jingxing Mines continued, however, and Jingxing coal was also traded through the Huabei Company.

Later, in spring 1937, the KMA, Zhongxing and four major banks—the National Commercial, Zhongfu, Jincheng and the Salt Bank—formed the Zhonghua Industrial Company. This new holding company took the interests both of Huabei and of the holding company in central China, and was able to plan control of the market on a national basis.

The operations of these various organisations had some success, at least in Shanghai. The aim was to buy up as much as possible of the output of the Shandong and Huainan mines, and thus force through a rise in prices. In November 1936 E.J. Nathan, the KMA's chief manager, reported:

> We ought in a week or two from now be in a position to instruct our sales departments both here and in Shanghai and possibly also in Canton to raise prices by a considerable margin.[73]

And indeed December 1936 saw an almost 20 per cent rise in the price of Kaiping slack in Shanghai and in north China.[74] Although this rise was in part due to a general improvement in business conditions, the syndicate also contributed.[75] Its major coup was to undermine the credibility of Luda in the Shanghai market. Luda had won a large contract with the Shanghai Power Company, China's largest single coal consuming enterprise, and planned to supplement any shortfall in its own output with coal bought from other mines in Shandong. Since the syndicate had bought up all such spare coal, Luda was forced to default on its obligations. And as a result the KMA won their second largest share for thirteen years of the 1937 Shanghai Power Company contract.

These gains were, however, in their nature temporary—there

was no way the KMA and its associates could continue to buy increasing amounts of competitive coals in order to sustain prices. In the long term output restrictions would be necessary if the market did not expand rapidly enough. The KMA recognised this, fearing severe problems from the Sino-Japanese mines in 1939-1940, but seeing that the expansion of the market, particularly in Japan, might take some of the pressure off them. One plan considered by the KMA and Zhongxing was to buy up small mining concessions in Boshan in order to prevent the amalgamation of concessions necessary for the expansion of output. Rumours of their intentions, however, drove up the price of such concessions and no progress was made in this direction before the outbreak of war.[76]

Even should such a scheme have been carried through it would probably have had little more long-term effect than the regulation of sales, and for the same reason: it would only have stimulated the opening of new mines and coalfields to take advantage of the artificially sustained price of coal. It was this problem which in other countries had led to the close involvement of the government in schemes for coal control. It was only a strong government which could impose output quotas on the industry.

Conclusion

Nanjing pursued policies of control over industry which showed its ambition to be just such a strong government. It saw the export-oriented industries of antimony, tungsten and vegetable oil as suitable candidates for cartelisation in order to increase China's income from those exports, and also believed that those industries serving the domestic market which were hardest hit by the effects of the depression required government intervention in order to aid their recovery. The programme of intervention in the economy upon which the government embarked alarmed many vested interests. Even at the time it provoked the United States ambassador several times to use the term 'state capitalism' to describe the Chinese economic system.[77] Moreover with hindsight many Chinese scholars and politicians came to see the Nanjing decade as the prelude to the wartime and post-war domination of 'bureaucratic capital' over the economy.[78] Some Western scholars have put forward a similar view:

The trend toward bureaucratic capitalism, a historical model of government relationship to business with much precedent in China, flourished under the blessing of Sun Yat-sen's name and party resolutions. Its objective was control by the few rather than the expansion of output.[79]

Even Parks Coble, while providing a balanced and measured overall judgment, describes a high level of effective government intervention at least in the Shanghai economy in the mid-1930s.[80]

This view of the Nanjing government's role in the economy was belied, for most of Chinese industry, by a reality which prevented the implementation of most of even the less ambitious policies. Several major factors constrained the government's freedom of action in industry and limited its effectiveness as a promoter of economic change. Each also had a wider significance in reducing the power of the state to act in other areas.

The inability of the pre-1937 Chinese state to gain control over more than a very small part of national income denied it the financial means to undertake ambitious programmes in either the economic or other spheres. Great difficulties were experienced in funding many of the schemes for industrial control, as for example in the case of antimony, where the influence of the syndicate in the industry waned rapidly because of its financial difficulties and the failure of its negotiations with a foreign firm to establish a monopoly agreement for antimony exports. Similarly in Shandong one of the reasons for the failure to establish a provincial coal cartel was the difficulty encountered in raising funds for the proposed organisation.

Nor was Nanjing able to impose its will over the whole country; its sway was strongest in the lower Yangzi provinces and relatively weak in the areas of north China where coal mining was concentrated. The problems involved are well illustrated in the case of the match cartel, where the Ministry of Industry's order to all match companies to join the (privately organised) cartel carried insufficient weight to force the thirteen factories operating in Shandong into the arrangement. Indeed the economic programmes of the provinces were sometimes not only unco-ordinated with those of the centre, but, notably in the case of Shanxi, actually in tacit opposition. The Nanjing government and the Southwest Political Council in Guangzhou openly competed for control of the tungsten trade, each establishing its own monopoly and trying to enforce it against the interests of the other.[81]

An even more serious weakness of the government was in relation to foreign interests. Japanese opposition to the coal cartel was the single most important cause of its failure to get off the ground. Similarly in the match industry a very high price had to be paid to win the co-operation both of Japanese and of American interests. Foreign governments always expressed opposition to the proposed control organisation, citing the provisions against the establishment of monopolies written in the treaties with the United States of 1844 and with France of 1858. Indeed Japanese researchers believed that the greatest obstacle to 'economic control' was those clauses in the unequal treaties which allowed foreign governments to object to the establishment of monopolies in China.[82]

Weak, therefore, in its financial base, in its ability to impose its will on the whole of China, and in its dealings with the foreign powers, the Nationalist government was, for all its ambitions, in a poor position to promote economic change, or even to protect Chinese industry from the effects of the world depression. It is quite wrong to read back wartime and post-war levels of state power over the economy into the pre-1937 period, while the contrast with the state-initiated programme of industrialisation after 1949 is even more marked. The Nationalist state before 1937 was a rather ineffective agent of economic change, and the development that did take place during the period owed little to government action.

NOTES

The author would like to thank the members of the Department of Far Eastern History (Australian National University) seminar and of the 'China in Transformation' workshop for many helpful comments. He is also and particularly indebted to Shannon R. Brown and David Pong for their careful readings of earlier drafts and for their constructive criticism. Responsibility for overall interpretation and for any mistakes that remain is, of course, his own.

1. Gunnar Myrdal, *Asian Drama* (London, 1968), I, 66, 116 and II, 895-890.
2. Parks M. Coble, Jr, *The Shanghai Capitalists and the Nationalist Government, 1927-1937* (Cambridge, Mass., 1980), p. 20.
3. Sun Zhongshan (Sun Yat-sen), *Sun Zhongshan xuan ji* [Selected works of Sun Yat-sen] (Beijing, 1956), I, 104-419.
4. *Ibid.*, II, 788.

5. See the report of an interview with the Minister of Industry in US Department of State, *Foreign Relations of the United States, 1937* (Washington, 1954), IV, 584.

6. Gideon Chen, 'Chinese Government Economic Planning and Reconstruction', in *Problems of the Pacific, 1933*, Bruno Lasker and W.L. Holland eds. (London, 1934), pp. 352-354.

7. H.D. Fong, *Toward Economic Control in China* (Shanghai, 1936), p. 68; *Mantetsu chōsa geppō* [South Manchurian Railway Research Department monthly], XVII:7 (July 1937), 66.

8. Fong, *passim*; see also the papers of the National Conference of the Chinese Economic Society on economic control, in *Jingjixue jikan* ['Quarterly Journal of Economics of the Chinese Economic Society'], V:4 (March 1935), 61-176.

9. Chen Gongbo, *Sinian congzheng lu* [My four years with the government], (Shanghai, 1936), p. 42.

10. Chen Changheng, 'Minsheng zhuyi zhi jihua jingji ji tongzhi jingji' [Planned economy and controlled economy in the principle of people's livelihood], *Jingixue jikan*, V:4 (March 1935), 83. On the other hand Ma Yinchu regarded them as synonymous; see his *Zhongguo jingji gaizao* [Economic reform in China] (Shanghai, 1935) p. 191.

11. Zheng Dubu, 'Riben tongzhi jingji de jiantao' [A discussion of the controlled economy in Japan], *Dongfang zazhi* ['Eastern Miscellany'], XXX:23 (1 December 1933), 56.

12. US Department of State, *Foreign Relations of the United States, 1936* (Washington, 1954), IV, 607; Zhu Tongjiu, 'Tongzhi jingji sheng zhong zhi Deguo laodong tongzhi' [Labour control in Germany within the context of the discussion of the controlled economy], *Jingjixue jikan*, VII:4 (February 1937), 113-125.

13. Coble, pp. 208-209.

14. *Ibid.*, p. 232; Sherman Cochran, *Big Business in China: Sino-Foreign Rivalry in the Cigarette Industry, 1890-1930* (Cambridge, Mass., 1980), p. 197.

15. Coble, pp. 248, 257.

16. Chen, 'Chinese Government Economic Planning', pp. 360-361.

17. George E. Taylor, 'The Reconstruction Movement in China', in *Problems of the Pacific, 1936*, W.L. Holland and Kate L. Mitchell, eds. (London, 1937), pp. 381-382; *Yinhang zhoubao* [The banker's weekly], XVII:39 (10 October 1933): 'guonei yaowen', 4-6. The results included some progress towards improving seeds and cultivation methods, but very little towards regulating the operation of the cotton spinning industry, see Chen, *Sinian congzheng lu*, pp. 51-52.

18. Donald G. Gillin, *Warlord: Yen Hsi-shan in Shansi Province, 1911-1949* (Princeton, 1967), chs. 9-10; *Mantetsu chōsa geppō*, XIV:5 (May 1934), 215-221.

19. *Yinhang zhoubao*, XVIII:43 (6 November 1934), 'guonei yaowen', 1-2; *Gongshan banyuekan* [Semi-monthly economic journal], VI:12 (15 June 1934), 133-134; VI:23 (1 December 1934), 151; VI:24 (15 December 1934), 93.

20. *Yinhang zhoubao*, XX:21 (2 June 1936), 'guonei yaowen', 15-16; XXI:7 (23 February 1937), 'guonei yaowen', 1-3; *Geoji maoyi daobao* [The foreign trade journal], VIII:5 (15 May 1936), 103-108; IX:3 (15 March 1937), 248-250.

21. *Yinhang zhoubao*, XXI:7 (23 February 1937), 'guonei yaowen', 1-3.

22. US Department of State, *Foreign Relations of the United States, 1935* (Washington, 1953), III, 783.

23. *Ibid*, 778, 784-788. *Foreign Relations of the United States, 1936*, IV, 611; *Kuangye zhoubao* [Mining weekly] (hereafter KYZB), no. 132 (28 February 1931), 571; no. 151 (21 July 1931), 876-879; no. 249 (7 August 1933), 135; no. 285 (7 May 1934), 706. See also the report, 'The Hunan Antimony Syndicate',

enclosed in Despatch no. 3441 from Minister Johnson, US State Department file 893.6359 Antimony/18. The report is a translation from the 'Hunan Guomin Daily News', Changsha, 26, 27, 28 February 1935. For the earlier history of antimony in Hunan, see Angus W. McDonald Jr., *The Urban Origins of Rural Revolution* (Berkeley, 1978), pp. 67-79.

24. *Foreign Relations of the United States, 1936.* IV, 608-10; Howard L. Boorman, ed., *Biographical Dictionary of Republican China* (New York, 1967), III, 453; Coble, p. 244.

25. *Foreign Relations of the United States, 1936*, IV, 603-606, 615-623.

26. Zhu Boneng, 'Zhongguo zhi zhetangye ji qi tongzhi' [China's sugar industry and the control of it], *Dongfang zazhi*, XXXIII:3 (1 February 1936) 65; *Guoji maoyi daobao*, VIII:8 (15 August 1936), 246.

27. For the match industry see *Foreign Relations of the United States, 1936*, IV, 600-603; *Yinhang zhoubao*, XIX:33 (27 August 1935), 'guonei yaowen', 3-4; XX:33 (25 August 1936), 'guonei yaowen', 5-6; XXI:5 (9 February 1937), 'guonei yaowen', 10-12; Ma Bohuang, 'Lun jiu Zhongguo Liu Hongsheng qiye fazhan zhong de jige wenti' [Characteristics in the growth of the capitalist Liu Hongsheng's enterprises in China before liberation], *Lishi yanjiu* [Historical research], 1980:3 (May-June 1980), 50-60.

28. For the history and development of modern coal mining in China, see Shannon R. Brown and Tim Wright, 'Technology, Economics and Politics in the Modernization of China's Coal Mining Industry: The First Phase, 1850-1895', *Explorations in Economic History*, XVIII:1 (January 1981) and Tim Wright, 'Growth of the Modern Chinese Coal Industry: An Analysis of Supply and Demand, 1896-1936', *Modern China*, VII:3 (July 1981), 317-350.

29. Liu Ta-chung and Yeh Kung-chia, *The Economy of the Chinese Mainland: National Income and Economic Development, 1933-1959* (Princeton, 1965), pp. 426-428, 569, 575; Yan Zhongping, *Zhongguo jindai jingji shi tongji ziliao xuanji* [A collection of statistical materials on the modern economic history of China] (Beijing, 1955), p. 124.

30. The main Japanese suppliers were Mitsui, Furukawa and Mitsubishi, see Tōa dōbunkai, *Shina shōbetsu zenshi* [Complete gazetteer of China], XV, *Kōsō shō* [Jiangsu province], (Tokyo, 1919), 917.

31. For what is known see Nathan Papers (hereafter cited as NP), Bodleian Library, Oxford, especially Nathan to Young, 28 June 1925 and Shirosaki to Nathan, 15 August 1933.

32. Joe S. Bain, *Industrial Organization*, 2nd ed. (New York, 1968), pp. 27-28, 473-475.

33. Tōa dōbunkai, *Shina shōbetsu zenshi*, XV, *Kōsō shō*, 905; *Chiku-Hō sekitan kōgyō kumiai geppō* [Monthly journal of the Chiku-Ho Coal Mining Association], XXIV:288 (June 1928), 103.

34. *Ping-Han tielu nianjian* [Yearbook of the Beijing-Hankou railway, 1932], Ping-Han tielu guanli weiyuanhui, ed. (Hankou, 1932), p. 633; *Kita Shina keizai sōkan* [An economic overview of north China], SMR, sangyōbu, ed. (Tokyo, 1938), appendix, tables, pp. 66-72.

35. Bain, p. 123.

36. This is for Kishima lump, see the list of prices given in *Mei yu meiye* [Coal and the coal trade], Shanghai shangye chuxu yinhang, diaocha bu, ed. (Shanghai, 1935).

37. For the dumping controversy, see Wu Bannong, 'Rimei qingxiao zhong zhi guomei wenti' [The coal problem in China: Japanese dumping and the situation in foreign-owned and Chinese-owned collieries], *Shehui kexue zazhi* ['Quarterly Review of Social Sciences'], III:4 (December 1932), 479-532. For the end of the cartel, see NP, Nathan to Turner, 8 May, 26 September, 22 October 1932, and *Minami Manshū tetsudō kabushiki kaisha daisanji jūnenshi* [History of

the third ten years of the SMR], Minami Manshū tetsudō kabushiki kaisha, ed. (Dalian, 1938), p. 2014.

38. NP, Pryor to Turner, 22 June 1935; *Guoji maoyi daobao*, VI:4 (10 April 1934), 257; Coble, p. 125.

39. For cotton textiles, see Chao Kang, *The Development of Cotton Textile Production in China* (Cambridge, Mass., 1977), p. 200; for silk see Lillian M. Li, *China's Silk Trade: Traditional Industry in the Modern World, 1842-1937* (Cambridge, Mass., 1981) p. 123.

40. NP, Nathan to Turner, 26 September 1932; NP, 'Memorandum on the History and Prospects of the KMA' (1938).

41. NP, 'Memorandum on the History and Prospects of the KMA'.

42. *Shi nian lai zhi Zhongguo jingji jianshe* [Ten years of economic reconstruction in China], Guomindang zhongyang dangbu jingji jihua weiyuanhui, comp. (Nanjing, 1937), 'shiye', p. 64; *Chinese Economic Bulletin*, 3 June 1933, 347; KYZB, no. 367 (21 January 1936), 869.

43. KYZB, no. 287 (21 May 1934), 739; no. 367 (21 January 1936), 869; *Chinese Economic Bulletin*, 29 April 1933, 261; *Yinhang zhoubao*, XVIII:19 (22 May 1934), 'guonei yaowen', 1-2.

44. Chen, *Sinian congzheng lu*, pp. 55-56; KYZB, no. 349 (7 September 1935), 577, and other issues of the same magazine.

45. Chen, *Sinian congzheng lu*, p. 56; Chen was not more specific on the subject of the Japanese objections. For Luda, see Tim Wright, 'Sino-Japanese Business in China: The Luda Company, 1921-1937', *Journal of Asian Studies*, XXXIX:4 (August 1980), 711-727.

46. Wright, 'Sino-Japanese Business', 725-726.

47. KYZB, no. 351, (21 September 1935), 610-611; no. 364 (28 December 1935), 823; no. 378 (14 April 1936), 1150; no. 381 (7 May 1936), 1196.

48. NP, Nathan to Turner, 15 November 1933, 31 December 1935.

49. NP, Nathan to Turner, 1 November, 31 December 1935.

50. *Gongshang banyuekan*, VI:2 (15 January 1934), 116-117.

51. Boorman, ed. III, 452-53; Tien Hung-mao, *Government and Politics in Kuomintang China, 1927-1937* (Stanford, 1972), pp. 65-71; *Yinhang zhoubao*, XVII:37 (26 September 1933), 1-6.

52. *Shisen Hakusan Shōkyū, tanden chōsa shiryō*, Minami Manshū tetsudō kabushiki kaisha, Chōsabu, ed. (Dalian, 1937), p. 581.

53. Yamagami Kaneo, *Sekkō zaibatsu ron* [On the Zhejiang financial clique] (Tokyo, 1938), *passim*; Tim Wright, 'Entrepreneurs, Politicians and the Chinese Coal Industry, 1895-1937', *Modern Asian Studies*, XIV:4 (October 1980), p. 598.

54. Coble, pp. 229-230.

55. *Shi nian lai zhi Zhongguo jingji jianshe*, 'shiye', p. 64.

56. For the first coal conference, see KYZB, no. 385 (7 June 1936), 1-3; no. 386 (14 June 1936), 17-19; *Shisen Hakusan Shōkyū*, pp. 585-599.

57. *Yinhang zhoubao*, XVIII:19 (22 May 1934), 'guonei yaowen', 2.

58. *Shisen Hakusan Shōkyū*, pp. 603-609.

59. Collusion is very difficult in an atomised industry with easy entry, see Bain, pp. 27-28.

60. Similarly in England, see Patrick Fitzgerald, *Industrial Combination in England* (London, 1927), p. 35.

61. Taylor, pp. 385-386.

62. *Shisen Hakusan Shōkyū*, p. 610.

63. NP, 'Memorandum on the History and Prospects of the KMA' (1938).

64. *Shisen Hakusan Shōkyū*, pp. 576-579; Arthur N. Young, *China's Nation-building Effort, 1927-1937: The Financial and Economic Record* (Stanford, 1971), pp. 231, 246.

65. Coble, p. 221.

66. NP, Nathan to Turner, 28 November 1935.
67. Wright, 'Sino-Japanese Business', *passim*.
68. *Shisen Hakusan Shōkyū*, pp. 581, 613.
69. For the second coal conference and its aftermath, see *Shisen Hakusan Shōkyū*, pp. 614-622; KYZB, no. 395 (21 August 1936), 161-162; no. 399 (21 September 1936), 228-230.
70. 'Attempts at cooperation both privately and official through the Conference called by the Ministry of Industries have proved abortive.' NP, Nathan to Turner, 29 October 1936.
71. For the history of the companies set up by the KMA see NP, C. Ku, 'Memorandum of Arrangements Made for Dealing in Competitive Coals', 7 January 1937, enclosed in Nathan to Turner, 30 January 1937; 'Notes by C. Ku on Chung-Hua Industrial Co.', enclosed in Nathan to Turner, 10 March 1937; Nathan to Turner, 30 January, 10 March, 9 May, 27 May 1937.
72. Tōa dōbunkai, *Shina shōbetsu zenshi*, XV, *Kōsō shō*, 920.
73. NP, Nathan to Turner, 11 November 1936.
74. See *Shanghai jiefang qianhou wujia*, p. 257; and *1913-1952 nian Nankai zhishu ziliao huibian* [Nankai index numbers for 1913-1952], Nankai daxue jingji yanjiu suo, comp. (Beijing, 1958), pp. 128-129.
75. *North-China Herald*, 7 April 1937.
76. NP, Nathan to Turner, 9 July 1936; 'Note by C. Ku'.
77. Despatch no. 413, 6 April 1937, from Ambassador Johnson on 'Trend to State Capitalism in China' (State Department file 893.00/14100); *Foreign Relations of the United States, 1936*, IV, 614; *Foreign Relations of the United States, 1937*, IV, 573-574, 583-584.
78. Xu Dixin, *Guanliao ziben lun* [On bureaucratic capitalism] (Shanghai, 1949), pp. 29-48; He Ganzhi, *Zhonggyo xiandai geming shi, 1911-1956* (A history of the modern Chinese revolution, 1911-1956), 2nd ed. (Beijing, 1956), p. 182.
79. Douglas S. Paauw, 'The Kuomintang and Economic Stagnation, 1928-37', *Journal of Asian Studies*, XVI:2 (February 1957), 220.
80. Coble, chs. 7 and 8.
81. Confidential report of 24 August 1934 from Vice-Consul Mitchell at Hankou on 'Important Developments in Chinese Tungsten Trade' (State Department File 893.6359 Wolfram Ore/35).
82. *Foreign Relations of the United States, 1935*, III, 771-772; *Foreign Relations of the United States, 1936*, IV, 601-609; *Shisen Hakusan Shokyu*, p. 564, William F. Mayers, ed., *Treaties Between the Empire of China and Foreign Powers*, 5th ed. (Shanghai, 1906), pp. 63. 79.

6

EDUCATION IN THE GUOMINDANG PERIOD, 1928-1949
Colin Mackerras

This chapter seeks to anwser two sets of questions concerning Chinese education during the period of the National Government, 1928 to 1949. The first is in the realm of policy and practice. What were the specific aims which the Chinese government laid down for its education system and were these specified objectives met in practice? In other words, can Chinese education from 1928 to 1949 be considered a success in terms of the criteria it hoped to meet?

The answer to these questions will yield clues to solving the second, wider and consequently more complicated, set. Did the education system genuinely assist the processes of modernisation and social change? Was education a leading element in Chinese society and political culture at the time, or was it but another aspect to the catalogue of the National Government's failures?

The Aims and Content of Education

The National Government's was the third major attempt to institute a new educational system since the fall of the Qing dynasty, the earlier ones being in 1912 and 1922.

Among the first acts of the new Republican government's Ministry of Education was to hold a National Education Conference in July and August 1912. Shortly after, on 2 and 3 September, the Ministry issued orders regarding 'disciplinary regulations' and the 'school system'. First among the regulations was a statement of aims. It read as follows:

> The educational aim of the Republic of China is to pay

special attention to the development of morals, supplementing it with technical and military training, and completing it with a cultivation of the aesthetic powers.[1]

At about the same time the ministry issued a statement of its general policy in which it laid down 'the aim of general education' as 'to train students in such a manner as to fit them for present conditions, and render them good citizens of the Republic'.[2]

These aims are rather vague, but they do make clear overall thrusts which are both moral and functional. Education must make good citizens and is thus a socialisation process geared to the nation's needs. It also aims to give students skills which will strengthen China. The reference to technical and military training is important. In a statement on education in January 1915 President Yuan Shikai highlighted patriotism and respect for the military (*shangwu*). The criteria for a country's prosperity and strength, he said, were 'the progress or faltering of the people's virtue, the people's wisdom and the people's strength'. If these three qualities were to grow in China, 'then we must give them due weight in our national education'.[3]

Within a few years pressures began building up for changes in the aims of education. The May Fourth Movement and the simultaneous strong feelings against Japanese imperialism brought discredit on the Japanese tone of the 1912 educational system; while the visit of the famous American educationalist and philosopher, John Dewey (1859-1952), to China in mid-1919 was one factor in favour of an American model. Reflecting the impact of these pressures was the recommendation of the Fifth Congress of the National Federation of Educational Associations (*Quanguo jiaoyu hui lianhehui*) held in Taiyuan from 10 to 25 October 1919 calling for the abolition of the 1912 aims and transfer of the emphasis towards 'the cultivation of a healthy personality and the development of the spirit of democracy',[4] quite different from the moral and military bent of the earlier period. As a result of the changing climate a presidential mandate promulgated a new educational system early in November 1922. Among the seven aims the mandate laid down, the first were: '(1) To adapt itself to the needs of changes in society; (2) to promote the spirit of mass education; and (3) to develop individuality'.[5]

With the Northern Expedition and the establishment of Chiang Kai-shek's National Government in 1926-1928, new educational aims were formulated and adopted. On 25 March 1929, at the Third National Congress of the Guomindang (held on 15-28 March), the Party formally adopted a series of aims which were promulgated, unchanged, by the National Government one month later on 26 April. They read as follows:

> Education in the Republic of China, according to the Three Principles of the People, should take as its aims: to replenish and enrich the people's life; to foster social existence; to develop the livelihood of the citizens; and to continue the life of the nation. [We] aspire to national independence and the widespread realisation of the people's rights, and the development of the people's livelihood, in order to promote the Great Harmony on Earth (*datong*).[6]

Already at a government-sponsored National Education Conference held in May 1928, high-sounding aims such as these had been categorised into slightly more concrete compartments which included the promotion of nationalism, the maintenance of old cultural traditions, the raising of moral and physical standards, the attainment of democracy, and the realisation of social justice. The conference had specifically opposed any possible Marxist interpretation, which had been so recently significant during the period of the united front (1925-1927), when it declared one aim of education as 'to enlighten the people on the interdependence and harmony of economic interests of various classes'.[7] These were principles specific enough to allow their success or failure to be tested. Clearly they were interrelated with the vague ideas of the Guomindang as earlier enunciated.

In addition to aims, the National Government laid down some guiding principles. On 1 June 1931 it promulgated twelve educational points. The first is an inevitable restating of the validity of the Three Principles of the People. Some of the others antedated even this one as government policy. All appeared to demonstrate the Guomindang's determination to remould society in its own image. They included the following items:

> There must be equality of opportunity in education between

the two sexes. All educational organisations throughout the country, whether private or state, must accept state supervision... Children who have reached school age should all receive compulsory education... Those among the people who have not yet received compulsory education should be given supplementary classes by adults... The state should give encouragement and subsidies to those among the private schools which have made superior achievements... Schools throughout the country, whether state or private, should arrange for certain students to receive free tuition or scholarships... The state should protect and preserve those ancient remains and relics relevant to history, culture and art.[8]

The new government actually took some time to work out the guidelines and the specifics of their implementation. Provisional regulations had been issued in 1928 to cover primary and secondary education. However, it was not until 24 December 1932 that the National Government issued its Law on Primary Schools.[9] This declared, among other points, that they should 'be based on developing the bodies and minds of children and fostering national virtue', and set the period for lower primary at four years, upper at two. Primary schools should be organised at municipal, county or village level.

In March the following year the Ministry of Education issued its 'Primary School Regulations' in 14 chapters and 106 articles.[10] The fifth chapter set out the curriculum and the number of minutes to be spent on each subject per week in each of the six years. National language (*guoyu*) was to occupy by far the most time (390 minutes per week in each year), followed by physical education (150 from years one to four, increased to 180 in the last two years). Other subjects were citizenship, hygiene, society, nature, arithmetic, manual labour, fine arts and music. A certain amount of regional variation was allowed, but under Article 31 any textbook that was local needed to be checked and approved by the Ministry of Education.

Secondary education was slightly more complicated. For a start there were several different kinds recognised, including normal and vocational schools, and laws governing each were issued in 1932. Moreover, 'several kinds of normal school were permitted, to suit special local conditions in various parts of the country and to supply the need for teachers'.[11]

The Law on Secondary Schools was issued, with its primary counterpart, on 24 December 1932.[12] It laid down a period of three years for each of junior and senior secondary school, and directed that they be organised at provincial, municipal or county level. On 21 June 1935 the ministry promulgated its Revised Regulations on Secondary Education.[13] Curricula are there specified in great detail in the annexes, including the number of periods to be spent on each subject per week. Subjects added to the primary school list included, for junior secondary, 'scouts' (*tongzi jun*), English, a second foreign language, history, geography, mathematics in place of arithmetic, and, to replace 'nature', botany, zoology, chemistry and physics. In senior secondary military training, or for girls military first aid, was taught instead of 'scouts', and both history and geography were divided into Chinese for the first three semesters (the first one and a half years) and foreign for the fourth, fifth and sixth. In the final semester logic was added.

Among these subjects, 'scouts' deserves special mention as an arm of nationalism. It was in fact not too different from the military training which replaced it in higher grades. It could even be construed as militaristic. One scholar writes that 'the zeal of Boy Scouts in the urban middle [secondary] schools of the lower Yangtze proved that military regimentation had considerable appeal for Chinese adolescents'.[14] This suggests a degree of effectiveness for the subject in at least one part of China.

The ministry laid down not only which subjects should be taught but also standards. It attempted to make them consistent throughout the country, including in private secondary schools. As in the primary schools, all textbooks required Ministry of Education approval before use.

One American study, prefaced by its author in January 1932, saw this need of approval as connected with the broad aim of nationalism in Chinese education. Based on research in textbooks, including many from the early years of the National Government, he writes:

> In order to arouse this spirit of nationalism among the students the curricula and textbooks have been consciously controlled by the educators. Not only has a fair treatment of the world at large, its history and its contributions been

consciously eliminated in favor of the nationalistic emphasis, but also material designed to fit the student to his more vital life in the family and community has been reduced to a minimum, so that the conception of the nation as the supreme form of social grouping may be indoctrinated and all vital problems be seen as national ones which the state alone can solve through its political machinery.[15]

There are quite a few coloured words in this passage which suggest that the author does not like what he sees. However, the overall point that successive Chinese governments were specific and deliberate in their attempts to inspire nationalism through their handling of curricula and textbooks need not be challenged. The reference to the state and its political machinery suggests that nationalism meant loyalty both to the nation and the Party which ruled it.

Though the nationalist aim was constant, there were several major differences between the curricula of the new system and that of 1922. One was that all electives were abolished on the grounds that careful consideration of curricula by the ministry made choice unnecessary. Another was that English became compulsory for all six years of secondary school, whereas previously it had been only an elective.[16]

The last level of education to consider is tertiary. In 1929 the National Government specified two types: universities and technical schools. A university was defined as consisting of at least three colleges, including one of science, agriculture, technology or medical science. It must have permission to establish post-graduate research facilities. The government provided for four types of technical schools. The first included those of engineering and architecture, the second for agriculture, forestry, horticulture and fishery, the third for professional skills in the commercial world, and the fourth for the arts, music, painting and so on.

The Administration of Education

The mechanisms for implementing the policies and systems just described existed on three levels: central, provincial and local, that is county (*xian*). The first of these was dominated by the Ministry of Education (*Jiaoyu bu*), headed by the minister. It was first set up on 6 December 1905, just after the abolition of the traditional examination system signalled the Qing regime's intention to modernise the education system. With a brief interregnum from March 1926 to December 1928, the ministry lasted throughout the Republican period.

Under the ministry were several sections (*si*). These varied slightly from period to period; from 1928 they were the sections of general affairs, higher education, general education, social education and Mongolian and Tibetan education. The section of general education was in charge of primary education and kindergartens, the section of social education of adult and civic education.[17] The last of the sections was new to the Chiang Kai-shek government, symbolising an interest in bringing the minority nationalities under closer tutelage and control. New also was an office in charge of compiling and translating textbooks and works of reference, and standardising technical and scientific terms.[18]

Each province had its own department (*ting*) of education. The commissioners who ran them were members of the provincial government and enjoyed considerable autonomy and initiative even though they were appointed by the National Government and under the supervision of the Ministry of Education.

Lower down were bureaux (*ju*) of education in each county. Their directors were appointed by the department of education of the relevant province. Even lower were several districts within the county. According to one source,

> The school districts in China are usually not vested with sufficient power to cope with their local situations. They are loosely and inefficiently organised. Shansi [Shanxi] province has the best organisation of the local units. There every village in the county and every street in the city has responsible persons to look after educational matters, given adequate power to perform their proper function.[19]

One Chinese scholar writing near the height of Guomindang power (the author's preface is dated 5 March 1933) noted several major features of the progress of the administration of education in China since 1912 and of its situation under Chiang Kai-shek. His major point was that the system had become more centralised. In 1912 the Ministry of Education had been reformed 'but the provincial and local organizations were still in chaos'.[20] By the 1930s, however, a clear hierarchy of appointments had been established and reform extended to the local level. The pyramid followed a political model, and among the advantages was that the 'centralized feature is adaptable to the political situation in China'. This made for the removal of 'provincial and sectional feeling' and for 'more unity', so that 'the principle of unity in essentials and liberty in nonessentials is well observed'.[21]

On the other hand, from September to December 1931 a mission of educational experts appointed by the League of Nations' International Institute of Intellectual Co-operation visited China and derived a somewhat less sanguine impression than the one just cited. They appear to have believed that the system was *not centralised enough*, and their first proposal for reform was that 'the manner of appointment and dismissal of officials of the Education Administration ought to give greater influence than at present to the Ministry of Education'.[22] The mission criticised overstaffing at provincial and lower levels. In schools, for instance, there were far too many administrative servants—on average one for every two teachers and not quite ten students—who tended to clog, not facilitate, the processes of learning and teaching. They were badly equipped for their task, often ignorant and lacking in initiative.

The mission considered the whole system far *too* political in that 'the education official in the province or district is often completely at the mercy of different factors ... of a political nature'. Such people should, the mission argued, be given protection from 'the present arbitrary procedure of the higher officials towards them'.[23]

It is striking that two sources reach such different conclusions when the situation they are observing coincides in time so nearly. The reason is that the judgments are made against different backgrounds and criteria. The Chinese scholar takes 1912 as the standard and sees progress, the League of Nations mission assesses with a Chinese ideal and reality in certain advanced countries in mind. It is not the facts but the judgments that differ, and all that seems clear is that there was a sharp difference between reality and the wishes of government policy-makers.

It appears to follow from the Chinese account that there was a recognisable system of government primary and secondary education in Nationalist China, at least some of the major features of which could be identified. On the other hand, the League mission's suggests that there was far more local variation, backsliding and corruption than anyone could have desired.

One of the areas where the League mission criticised the lack of centralisation in educational administration was budgetting and finance. The mechanism was that funds for universities came from the central government, for secondary schools from the provincial, and for primary schools from the county authorities. The province did contribute a little towards primary education, but the central government nothing. The mission observed correctly that, according to the experience of all governments, 'where a department does not contribute in the matter of financial resources it can exert no influence',[24] so the National Government's input into primary education could hardly be great.

Another aspect of finance to come under the mission's scrutiny was that a totally disproportionate sum went to the universities, at the expense of the primary schools. The ratio of the amount spent on the average primary school pupil to that on a university student was 1:200, as opposed to 1:8 or 1:10 in European countries. 'This shows the extraordinary neglect of the primary school that is destined for the masses of the people',[25] bemoaned the mission.

A Chinese scholar of the time explained the 'signs of bankruptcy' which he saw 'everywhere, whether at national or local level', in terms of the recent history of China, that is, incessant aggression from abroad and civil war, natural disasters, social instability, and so forth. The general budget was in chaos and without good sources of revenue, so how could education be financed properly? The government itself was not consolidated and 'society has not yet been able to uphold education'.[26] The verdict is a good deal harsher even than the League of Nations mission's. It suggests that the problems went considerably deeper than the mission imagined.

The mission estimated expenditure on public education as about 9-10 per cent of budget expenses, lower 'than in most countries possessing well organised education systems' and 'too low'.[27] The fact is that the government could not afford more, and was not prepared to distribute expenditure more evenly among the various levels of education, because its class interests dictated otherwise.

Non-government Schools

One of the implications of the government's poverty was that the non-government schools continued to flourish. By way of examples, I propose to deal briefly with the traditional schools called *sishu* and the missionary schools.

The first of these two were relics of the past, surviving since well before the Western influence which affected Chinese education so deeply. Although the private system was tolerated as such, many edicts were issued by national and local governments against these schools. However, the *sishu* continued to play an important role in society, especially the rural areas, and government authorities frequently found it in their interests to use rather than suppress them. There is no reason to doubt the conclusion of T'ai-ch'u Liao, the only major writer on the *sishu*, that the movements by the authorities against them were motivated by fear that they could compete successfully with government schools.[28]

There were four main types of *sishu*. The first was those run by a single teacher who charged fees from the students, the second was mainly funded by local rich people, and tuition was free. The third and fourth types were family schools run either for the children of one specific clan or of relatives and close friends or for those with the same surname. Categorising them next by level, we find that there were the equivalent of primary, secondary, tertiary and normal schools among the *sishu*. This meant that the ages of the students ranged from as low as seven to as high as thirty.

Curricula varied vastly. Because they often existed despite the wishes of the government, the *sishu* did not necessarily follow official dictates or approvals in the courses they offered. Liao's studies of Wenshang county in Shandong, from which we can probably extrapolate a similar situation in at least some other areas, show that teachers could tailor the courses to suit the needs of individual students' parents. But in any case the content of curricula was likely to be far more old-fashioned than in a government school. For instance, classical Chinese was the language used, even the old eight-legged essays of imperial times were still taught in some *sishu*.

It is perhaps not surprising that the teachers were in general considerably older than in the government schools. In Liao's sample Shandong county, Wenshang, 26 per cent of the *sishu* teachers were over sixty, 48 per cent between forty and sixty, and only 26 per cent below forty, while in government schools some 70 per cent were below thirty, and less than 10 per cent above forty.[29]

Their greater age gave them far weightier authority in a still traditional society which they were explicitly trying to preserve. They were, indeed, not merely teachers but general social advisers and confidants, and one of their jobs was to negotiate against government officials who might try to interfere in any way. T'ai-ch'u Liao notes the various ways in which government officials in Wenshang were seen by the people as trying to exploit them. He goes on:

> In dealing with all these cases, the teacher in the szu shu [*sishu*] was definitely 'the choice made by God'. He was the one and the only one who had the qualifications, who could read, talk, write, lie and even bribe. Little by little an ambitious teacher would have brought all administrative details of the village to his desk in the szu shu pending his opinion and wisdom.[30]

In fact there was good reason why the government distrusted the *sishu*.

The quotation's reference to villages shows that the *sishu* were mainly rural. But this does not mean they were open equally to rich and poor peasants and landlords alike. The fact that some were family schools and that in others fees were charged already shows bias in favour of the rich. Yet there were poor peasants who could go, if they were lucky enough to find a school subsidised by a rich neighbour. Nobody cared if the demands of the poor peasant's life made absences by the children inevitable, because there was no formal progression from one grade to another, or graduation.

Since these schools were so informal it is impossible to find out exactly how many there were. The proportion of government education to *sishu* varies wildly from place to place. Liao states that in Wenshang there were about three times as many students in the *sishu* as in the government schools[31] whereas in a district he studied in Chengdu there were about equal numbers of students in the new primary schools and the *sishu*.[32] Statistics for Yunnan province show a few counties where figures are available for both *sishu* and lower primary schools. According to these there were, in the mid-1930s, 79 of the former and 1171 of the latter.[33] Possibly the government source has found only a few *sishu* because most preferred not to reveal themselves. Whatever the reason, the discrepancy is very large indeed, not only between the two types of schools but with Liao's findings.

Statistics are much more readily available for the other type of non-government school, that run by missionaries. In 1933 there were 102 Catholic colleges and universities, 362 higher primary schools and 3,135 primary schools, instructing respectively 14,739, 18,769 and 115,793 students. The total number of primary students was 1.7 per cent of the total number in all China.[34] In 1936 there were 2,795 Protestant primary schools, reporting 173,228 pupils, or about 2.5 per cent of the national total.[35]

Missionary educational institutions developed a generally good academic reputation, and some of the Christian-run universities and colleges were famous not only in the West but in China itself. However, they did labour under the stigma of being foreign and thus possible arms of cultural imperialism.[36] Chiang Kai-shek was himself a Christian, but it was still essential for a government which espoused nationalism to oppose ideologies which could be seen as supporting more the interests of the imperialist powers than those of China.

The National Government laid down strict rules on requirements for the registration of private educational institutions. Those applied to foreign schools were particularly stringent. Thus foreigners were not permitted to establish primary schools which educated Chinese children. In those secondary schools or above set up by foreigners, a Chinese must be appointed principal or director. For missionaries the most difficult rule was the following:

> Private schools may not make religious subjects compulsory, nor undertake religious propaganda in class. If there are religious services in schools established by religious bodies, it is forbidden to compel or induce

students to attend. It is not permitted to hold religious services in primary schools or schools of the same level.[37]

These rules and the need for registration were regarded by Christian missionaries as infringements on religious freedom. Certainly the regulations were designed to ensure the promotion of nationalism, and were in conformity with the general requirement for government approval for curricula which extended to missionary as to government schools.

Many missionary schools resisted the regulations. Many closed down, but many others became self-supporting or were taken over by local Chinese Christian churches. The number of Chinese principals grew, and also the proportion of Chinese to foreign academic staff rose in the missionary universities. In the fourteen Protestant Christian colleges there was an approximate ratio of one Chinese to one foreign teacher in 1923-1924, which changed to two to one by 1932 and four to one by 1936.[38]

Apart from their image of being foreign and so anti-nationalist, the main problem with the missionary schools, especially those of the Protestants, was their elitism. The class breakdown of the parents of the Protestant primary schools students was: merchants 41-50 per cent, officials 1-10 per cent, scholars and professionals 1-10 per cent, labourers 1-10 per cent, and farmers 1-10 per cent.[39] The League of Nations mission was undoubtedly right in its observation that 'it was children belonging to the higher and middle classes' who attended the mission schools. 'The effect', it concluded, 'was rather to create a social élite, a governing intelligentsia class'.[40]

Both the *sishu* and the Christian schools thus tended to accentuate the uneven class spread of education. Both types were also influential. Yet the direction of their influence was diametrically opposed in that the former strove to preserve traditional Chinese values, the latter to spread Western notions. Generally speaking the *sishu* were rural, the Christian schools far more, though by no means exclusively, urban. Partly for this reason the former could escape the eye of the government and its rules more readily than the latter. But actually neither can be regarded as an example of the success of Guomindang aims in education. The *sishu* did breed love of China, certainly, but more the culturalism of former times than the nationalism of the Guomindang. They do not appear to have paid positive dividends in terms of loyalty to the Party. As for the mission schools, they conformed more closely to the class interests of the Guomindang in 1949 than they had done in 1927, but they were never really transmitters of nationalism; they fostered loyalty neither to the Chinese nation nor to the Party which ruled it.

Compulsory Education

The private schools were important complements of the state system. They did contribute to some extent towards what we have already seen as a prime aim of Guomindang education, that it should be compulsory, even if they did not make this objective anything like a reality.

Already in 1902 the Imperial Regulations on Primary Schools had included, in their sixth article, the stipulation that 'all children from the age of six *sui* on..., no matter of what kind, must receive these seven years of [primary] education'.[41] The ideal was repeated numerous times after that, in the different laws, although the length of time varied from a minimum of one year to a maximum of six.[42]

Law is one thing, implementation another. The first detailed plan to make compulsory education a nationwide reality was put forward by Minister of Education Tang Hualong in June 1915. It advocated compulsory education for four years with a province-by-province approach, accumulating into a nationwide compulsory education movement.[43] Another, introduced by the ministry on 2 April 1920, envisaged nationwide compulsory education for four years to be implemented in stages over an eight-year period. The principle was that the main cities go first, the countryside follows.[44]

The plan was more or less totally ignored. As far as cities were concerned, only in Guangzhou did primary schools become 'comparatively widespread', while among provinces only Shanxi 'actively implemented' the plan.[45] Actually Shanxi had developed its own stage-by-stage plan for compulsory education in 1918. Even by 1922-1923, there were already 780,962 children in junior primary, that being some 70 per cent of those in the relevant age group. But one scholar writing in 1926 bemoaned, justifiably, that 'unfortunately, in the last few years, partly because of the influence of war, and partly because implementation in the small villages has not been easy, progress has been extremely slow'.[46]

According to official statistics there were, in 1929-1930, 799,977 children in junior primary schools in Shanxi. The province's population in 1932, again according to official statistics, was 11,092,553.[47] So the proportion of the population in junior primary schools was approximately 7 per cent, by far the highest of any of China's provinces, but showing very little change since 1922-1923.

In view of the failure of the first plans the National Government made a further attempt to realise compulsory education. From 15 to 25 April 1930 the Ministry of Education held its Second National Education Conference in Nanjing under the chairmanship of the Minister of Education, Jiang Menglin. It retained the notion of four years' compulsory education but aimed for its realisation not in eight years, which was clearly unrealistic, but in twenty. The plan was to devote the first five years mainly to establishing normal schools and training teachers and only then, in the last fifteen years, to proceed towards universal education.[48]

In 1932 the ministry issued two more orders which in effect allowed each province to make arrangements suiting its own conditions. It became possible to insist on only one year's education. In subsequent years yet further regulations appeared as appropriate to an ever changing situation and very uneven adherence to earlier government commands.[49] It is notable that in fact the ministry had relatively little influence over what happened to make education compulsory. Primary school finance was arranged locally, not centrally. The ministry could receive reports of provincial or local intentions, but not much more.

It may be useful to examine two provinces in slightly more detail as case studies, Jiangsu and Yunnan.

Jiangsu was among the richest of China's provinces. The national capital was situated there and it was possibly the most firmly under Guomindang control of any area in the country.

On 12 August 1935, the head of the Jiangsu Department of Education made a report on compulsory education in the province. This man happened to be Zhou Fohai, one of the founding members of the Chinese Communist Party,[50] who went over to the Guomindang and had occupied his position in the Jiangsu Department since 26 December 1931.[51]

Zhou was anything but bright in the picture he painted of

the extent of education in Jiangsu. Only 12.6 per cent of children in the relevant age group were in primary schools in 1930, but the figure had not gone up much because natural disasters and other economic adversities had prevented the provincial government's allocating much more money to education. This would not change, so measures to expand education without increasing expense had to be found. Those he himself suggested included the following three. Firstly, class sizes must be raised. In some places classes were as small as eighteen or nineteen, but thirty should be a minimum and forty an ideal. Secondly, steps should be taken to improve the *sishu* as well as the quality of teaching in them. Thirdly, private individuals should be encouraged through rewards to set up their own primary schools, whereas at present 'there is a weakness in Jiangsu's education, which is that private people who run schools all like to go for secondary schools and do not want to run primary schools'.[52]

Yunnan was by comparison to Jiangsu a backward province where National Government control was weak. Yet in 1933 the proportion of children of relevant age in school was 27.73 per cent, much higher than in Jiangsu. A plan for compulsory education had been put forward by the provincial Department of Education in 1930 and another one followed in 1935. As in Jiangsu several specific measures were proposed to improve the situation. One was to run 'a system of short-term one-year schools', where children could gain at least one year's education. Another was to improve the *sishu* schools; and 'the comparatively superior ones must be changed into short-term or ordinary primary schools'. Thirdly, mobile schools and teachers must be instituted, especially for poor or remote villages where 'communications are inconvenient'.[53]

There is a striking similarity in the appeal of both provincial authorities to the traditional *sishu* schools to solve their problems. The slighting reference to 'improving' them reflected government attitude, but the important point is the recognition that use could and should be made of them for a specific purpose. Government authorities were clearly acknowledging the inadequacies of their own system.

Another parallel is that between the privately run school, proposed in Jiangsu, and the circulating school of Yunnan. Both depended on willing and competent individuals. The reference to remote villages in the case of Yunnan is a clear suggestion that those who did receive education were far more thickly concentrated in the cities than the countryside, but at least the authorities were aware of the problem. Both provinces were not surprisingly anxious to effect universal education as cheaply as possible.

The fact that backward and remote Yunnan was apparently further ahead, at least quantitatively, than advanced and central Jiangsu shows that there was no definite correlation between Guomindang control and success in implementing universal education. It may, indeed, be yet another pointer to the failure of the National Government's efforts.

Did all the regulations and measures produce any effect? Reliable statistics, free from political bias, are unavailable. The Guomindang claimed that at the end of the war, 1945, 61.76 per cent of children of the relevant age were in junior primary schools and that 37.25 per cent of illiterate adults were receiving some education.[54] The illiteracy rate, both children and adults, is claimed by a Guomindang source to have been about 34 per cent of China's population in 1944,[55] and continued to fall after that despite the war. On the other hand, one author writing on the People's Republic quotes Chinese Communist Party sources as giving figures of 85 to 90 per cent illiteracy at the time of liberation.[56] It is perhaps possible that many of those included as 'literate' by the Guomindang were actually only marginally so, and lost their skills or were counted as illiterate by the Chinese Communist Party. On the other hand, the gigantic discrepancies suggest that none of the figures can be given much credence. The social conditions were inappropriate for statistics collection, even apart from the political biases. What is clear is that none of the governments of Republican China ever achieved anything approaching compulsory or universal education. Only the extent of the failure is in dispute.

One feature of the educational system on which there is no doubt is that it favoured the rich and left the poor till last. This point was made strongly about private schools, but applied also to the government system. In theory state primary schools were free. But the League of Nations mission claimed that admission procedures of children into primary schools were such that 'when the number of applicants exceeds the number of places a selection is made whereby preference is given to children of parents who are more wealthy and influential'.[57] It pointed out also that the children of the poor were more likely to be set to work than those of the rich.

Even in successful Shanxi in the 1920s the smaller villages had been left out, and the same point emerged for Yunnan in the 1930s. In fact, the poor peasantry had virtually no chance to gain education. The emphasis on class harmony which the National Education Conference of May 1928 had formulated was a doctrine which helped only the rich against the poor.

In the discussion of illiteracy rates mention was made of adults as well as children. As a coda to this section it will be useful to note that the National Government placed some weight on what it termed social education (*shehui jiaoyu*).[58] One of the several aims was adult schools, which aimed to teach people from sixteen to fifty elementary knowledge, reading, writing and citizenship. They differed from province to province and could be private or state run. Textbooks needed the approval of the Ministry of Education. The League of Nations mission was impressed with China's social education describing it as 'one of the most satisfactory features of education in China'.[59]

Possibly the best known instance of social education was the pioneering mass education movement in Dingxian, Hebei province, in which the leading light was James Y.C. Yen.[60] It was much better financed than other similar ventures, having obtained money not only from the government but also from the China Foundation for Education and Culture, that is the remitted American Boxer Indemnity Fund, and the Rockefeller Foundation. It organised a broadly successful campaign against illiteracy, and there were also branches dealing with agriculture, citizenship, hygiene and art education.

The Education of Females

One of the features not only of the mass education campaign in Dingxian but of social education in general was that it was in theory open equally to men and women. We now come to another theme which looms large in the literature on education in Republican China, namely the attempt to overcome centuries of tradition and educate the female half of the population.

The first entirely Chinese run or financed school for girls began classes in Shanghai on 1 June 1897 with an enrolment of sixteen. It was a private school.[61] On 4 August 1906 the Ministry of Education laid down rules for female education,[62] thus formally encouraging it at government level. On 24 January the next year the ministry set down regulations for the running not only of primary schools for girls, but also of normal schools.[63] This marked the beginning of secondary education for girls and enabled their training as teachers.

In January 1924 the First National Congress of the Guomindang held in Guangzhou stated that it 'certifies the principles of equality between the two sexes in law, economy, education and society and promotes the development of women's rights'.[64] A Chinese scholar commented on the Congress that 'equality of education and vocational opportunity for both sexes are the most important remedies in the present [1933] situation'.[65] And it is true that equality of opportunity between the sexes remained the ideal and government policy through the Guomindang period. In the field of education it was earlier noted as among the major guiding principles promulgated in June 1931.

Did it become a reality? The answer will depend upon what 'equality' means. It is certain, however, that education remained much less difficult of access to boys than to girls right down to the time of liberation.

In primary schools, the national average of girls in the early 1920s was over 6 per cent.[66] According to government sources, the total number of pupils in and below primary schools in 1932 was 12,223,066 of whom 1,846,083 were girls, that is 15.1 per cent. And in 1945 the comparable figures had risen to 21,831,898, including 5,583,342 girls, or 25.57 per cent.[67] In fairness to the Christian schools one should point out they were far ahead of the state system in this respect. In 1933 girls were 35.32 per cent of all students in Catholic primary schools and, at about the same time, 39.2 per cent in Protestant.[68]

Looking next at college and university level we find a shift in proportions similar to that in state primary schools. In 1923 there were a total 34,880 students, of whom 887, or 2.5 per cent, were female.[69] In 1934, the proportion of girls was 15.02 per cent, and in 1947 17.8 per cent.[70] Again the mission institutions led the way, girls constituting 35.14 per cent of students in Catholic colleges, normal schools or universities in 1933 and 22 per cent in Protestant at about the same time.[71]

At both levels there was a sharp increase in the proportion of girls in state educational institutions comparing an early year of the Republican period with one in the early or mid 1930s. At the primary level there is another big rise for a late Guomindang year. It appears, however, that the early and middle 1930s, perhaps the years when the Guomindang was at or nearing its height, were not those of most spectacular improvement. Indeed, a Chinese study of female education in China from 1930 to 1933 concludes that 'there was no notable progress' in those years, no matter whether one looks at primary, secondary or tertiary level, at absolute figures or proportions with males.[72]

More detailed and revealing statistics are available for the 'numbers of students in vocational schools and above throughout the whole country'. Below is shown a sample of years and technical specialities.[73]

Table 1.

Year	Law	% female	Education	% female	Medicine	% female	Total	% female
1934	11,029	7.75	4,059	32.05	2,633	17.89	41,768	15.02
1936	8,253	8.88	3,292	34.17	3,395	20.32	41,922	15.21
1938	7,024	13.44	2,031	40.67	3,623	30.03	36,180	18.37
1940	11,172	14.45	2,606	44.78	4,271	28.40	52,376	19.47
1942	12,598	13.48	2,257	38.72	5,108	32.20	64,097	19.15
1944	15,990	12.44	2,608	42.18	6,343	32.11	78,909	18.81
1947	37,780	11.50	5,548	43.98	11,855	28.13	155,036	17.80

Although the point was earlier made of a substantial rise in the total population of female students at the tertiary level between 1923 and 1947, there is no dramatic change if the base year selected is 1934. In fact the proportion even peaked and began to decline. Of course in absolute terms the number of girls rose greatly, because the overall total did so.

What is just as interesting is the relative concentration of girls in particular areas. Thus the percentage of girls in law was very low in 1934 and remained so in 1947, despite a small rise. Medicine shows a somewhat higher proportion of girls, rising more substantially by 1947 than in law. In neither area is the latest proportion the highest. That is to say there is no consistent trend in favour of girls. The area where girls are best represented is education. The proportion of girls rises here least inconsistently. It is the only area to show even one year with an actual majority of girls: 50.5 per cent in 1946.

Since the overall percentage of girls in the total rose so little between 1934 and 1947 it is no surprise that there were areas where the proportion actually fell, or where a quite dramatic increase yielded very little in absolute terms for girls. An example of the latter is engineering: in 1934 a total of 5,910 including 99 girls, in 1947 a rise to 27,579, but only 692 girls.

All this suggests that there were indeed changes in the extent of education for girls and women during the Guomindang period. But in general they failed to catch up with expansion in opportunities for boys and men. Social biasses against female education in specific areas remained heavy. Only in a few isolated parts of the system was advance substantial.

Differences remained in the curricula not only in practice in vocational schools, colleges and universities but everywhere. The National Government was quite explicit that education for girls should not be the same as for boys. Article 6 of the 'educational aims of the ROC [Republic of China] and guidelines for their implementation', promulgated by the National Government on 26 April 1929 reads:

> Opportunities in education for males and females are equal. Education for girls must pay great attention to moulding a sound and healthy morality in them, to preserving the special qualities of motherhood, and also to building up good family life and social life.[74]

In other words equality for women, including in education, rested on the assumption that sex roles in society would and should remain. At no level did education seek to effect radical changes in women's or general societal attitudes. Given such conservative aims even success would hardly count as a major achievement of the Guomindang.

The Impact of the War on Education

The War of Resistance against Japan had the overall effect of rendering the Guomindang more demoralised, more debilitated than ever. It simply reinforced and intensified the conservatism to which reference has just been made. Yet ironically enough, if there was one sphere of life in which the war did force the National Government of Chiang Kai-shek to undertake some useful and efficient measures, it was education.

The most important point is that the education system did not collapse under the impact of Japanese occupation. On the contrary, resistance spurred the Chinese to unprecedented efforts and forced them to bring paper ideals closer to reality then ever before. Even before the war actually broke out, the Chinese had begun planning how they would use the education system against the Japanese. One important periodical devoted a whole issue to the topic. The lead article urged the people to intensify vital features of the normal peace-time system, such as 'developing a spirit of patriotism', 'the forging of a healthy physique', and so on.[75] So when war did in fact break out, it was immediately obvious that education was to be a tool for the defeat of the enemy.[76] One typical writer stated, at the beginning of the war, that because education was part of the general aim of the national liberation movement, its first major principle was that it 'must fit in with the whole national wartime organisational system'; and this meant teaching military affairs, anti-aircraft knowledge and production skills.[77]

When the Extraordinary Guomindang National Congress adopted its Programme of Armed Resistance and National Reconstruction on 1 April 1938 it devoted four articles to education. These declared that the educational system and teaching material should be revised to lay 'emphasis on the cultivation of the people's morals, and the enhancement of scientific research, and the expansion of necessary facilities'. In other words, resistance needed two prongs, one was the moral will, the other the practical techniques. Perhaps more interesting were the last two articles:

> 31. Youths shall be given training to enable them to work in the war areas or rural districts.
>
> 32. Women shall be given training so that they may be of service to social enterprises and thereby of help to the nation's war strength.[78]

It is likely that the improvement in the extent of education for women to which reference was made in the previous section was due, at least in part, to the exigencies of war. T'ai-ch'u Liao claims that in the *sishu* too it was as a result of the war that pressure on women and girls 'only to listen and to give assistance to their husbands' was gradually given up, and that the number of female students increased.[79]

The mention in the programme of the rural districts is

extremely important. It was the war which forced the Chinese to bring education to the remote villages of the interior, not only in government policy but to a large extent in reality.

In March 1940 a government-sponsored conference devised a plan to establish schools everywhere so that by August 1944 there would be a people's school in every *bao*, that is subdivision of a village. At the same time the mass education movement gathered momentum. The result was that basic literacy expanded more quickly and rose to peaks never known before the war.[80]

The other side of the coin was that urban students went to the rural areas in far greater numbers than ever before. 'Groups of twenty or more college or middle school boys and girls, sometimes accompanied by professors and instructors', were prepared to face the rigours of the countryside through the desire to resist Japan. There they undertook propaganda among the villages, and also learned something of conditions there.[81]

One of the reasons why middle school students could go thus to the countryside was that the number of institutions at secondary level not only grew greatly as a result of the war, but also schools became much more evenly distributed by region. Whereas earlier these had tended to be concentrated in the coastal provinces, the Japanese occupation forced development in the interior provinces.

The Guomindang used the opportunity to step up propaganda not only against the Japanese but in favour of its own by now utterly conservative value system. Secondary-level curricula were changed, and textbooks in courses such as citizenship and Chinese history 'were considerably modified to fit actual conditions, and instructive passages were selected from the teachings of Dr. Sun Yat-sen and other great leaders'.[82] In 1938 a tutorial system was introduced into all secondary schools to promote character cultivation, which meant indoctrination in the four major virtues of the New Life Movement: propriety, righteousness, integrity and self-respect. What mattered to the Chinese was resistance to Japan. The irrelevance of an attempted revival of the New Life Movement is obvious from the post-war disintegration of the Guomindang.

Turning finally to the tertiary sector, we find the same movement to the interior under very difficult conditions and a redoubled effort to make the most of scarce resources in the name of resistance to Japan. One example will illustrate the point. When Beijing and Tianjin were occupied in 1937, Qinghua and National Peking Universities in the former city and Nankai in the latter moved to Changsha, where they amalgamated into a single university. Early in 1938 they made another move, this time to Kunming. According to one source, the women students and weak men went by rail to Guangzhou, then through Hongkong and Vietnam to Guangxi, but over two hundred male students organised travel groups and walked to Kunming, led by the famous literary figure Wen Yiduo and others. This took them more than two months, but 'on the way the teachers and students came into contact with the people of the southwest under Guomindang rule and their cruel life, and received education in real life'.[83] Again the function of the war in bringing urban intellectuals and peasants and others together in a common cause becomes evident. The combined university in Kunming was known as the National South-west Associated University.

While it is true that amalgamations such as this and other causes reduced the number of institutions of higher learning from 108 before the war in 1937 to 91 later in the year, the number had risen to 143 by the middle of 1944.[84] Additions and other changes were made to curricula to fit war and reconstruction needs, and research geared to similar ends was both strongly encouraged and undertaken.

Conclusion

Actually, in recapitulating the aims of education as outlined in the first section, we find that meeting contemporary national needs runs through them as a strong thread at all times, not only during the war. The 1912 version may have emphasised respect for the military, that of 1922 more the spirit of individuality, but each claimed to perceive its own ideal as leading to China's greater benefit. The twin goals of nationalism and the growth of national strength are inherent in virtually all statements made on education not only in these years but also under the Guomindang.

There appear to be five headings under which the broad aims of education can be placed. The first is moral: the desire to train citizens of the future whose characters will fit them to serve the country well. The second aim, related to the first, is to use education as a major means of persuading the people to harmonise the economic interests of the various classes, a vehicle of class conciliation. The third is technical. The people need not only good characters but intellectual skills. They need knowledge of a practical kind which will help China modernise, as well as that which contributes to the retention of China's culture. Fourth is the physical level. Education should make the Chinese fitter, healthier and stronger in the interests of national development and prestige. Finally the aim of education appears to me to be frankly political. The constant harping on the Three Principles of the People under Chiang Kai-shek was more a mechanism for legitimating his own rule than a maintenance of respect for 'the national father' Sun Yat-sen. This is shown most clearly through the rather futile attempt to use the education system to keep the principles of the New Life Movement alive during the war against Japan.

Related to these five categories of aims, in a sense prerequisites to them, were the more concrete aims of compulsory or universal education, the wiping out of illiteracy, and equality of educational opportunity for women. We have seen that none of these was achieved, but nevertheless the extent of failure differed from place to place, time to time, and some of the attempts were genuine. In 1930 the National Government announced its intention to realise compulsory education within twenty years. The government itself did not last so long, but China was a good deal closer to that ideal in 1950 than in 1930. The efforts forced on the Chinese by the war were a major factor contributing to what success there was. The same comments apply to the limited and partial, but nonetheless real, success of the attempts to educate women. It needs to be said again that the idea of equal opportunity for women in no way envisaged or aimed at the elimination of social sex roles, but on the contrary sought to strengthen them.

So the questions can be framed thus: did the education system make the Chinese more moral, more skilled at their jobs, more developed, stronger physically or more supportive of their government? Did it contribute to class conciliation? Most of these questions are too big to be answered properly. There was economic progress in some of the years under discussion, but it was political and military factors which principally dictated how much, or indeed if any. The Japanese invasion impeded economic progress but it also showed that the Chinese had the moral will to resist. What is most questionable is whether the education system of the 1930s was itself a prime force in the creation of this moral will. The answer is surely that it may have been one factor, but not a major one. It was politics, the struggle with the Communist Party, the international balance of power, the Xi'an incident, but not education, which forced resistance to the Japanese. Possibly education had made the Chinese readier, fitter to fight. This is suggested by its reaction to the war, which was to expand against the challenge, and not to collapse, but no higher position than that can be accorded the education system in the priority of the causes of resistance to the Japanese.

Two points are crystal clear. One is that the period of the National Government is characterised not by class conciliation, but by its opposite, class struggle. The result was the success of one of the largest class revolutions of the twentieth century. The second point is that none of the numerous governments of the Republican period, and in particular that of Chiang Kai-shek, was successful in using the education system to indoctrinate the people in its own political ideology. All tried, all ultimately failed. A political regime requires popular support, which education can provide. But no amount of schooling can save a faltering or crumbling government, and the vast educational bureaucracy of the Guomindang did not save Chiang Kai-shek. Such support for him as survived in China after 1949 was due to the class interests of various groupings, not to education. According to T'ai-ch'u Liao, the success of the private *sishu* lay precisely in their freedom from interference by the government.[85] Nothing could exemplify better the failure of the government education system to instil feelings of solid and lasting support into the people.

One reason why the students had no real confidence in the government was that they knew they themselves were distrusted by the authorities. The Fourth Plenum of the Guomindang's Second Central Executive Committee, held in February 1928, forbade primary and secondary school students to take part in politics and attempted to strip student unions of all non-educational functions.[86] The Guomindang tried to thwart student radicalism and use the young intellectuals for its own purposes. One scholar aptly sums up its failure thus:

> The New Life Movement and other Kuomintang

[Guomindang] programs were most successful among middle-school students of the lower Yangtze Valley. Little impact was made upon sophisticated college students or in those areas of the country where Nanking's influence was weak. The party still suffered from internal contradictions: organizational efforts of political activists thwarted pedagogical aims of liberal educators ... The White Terror, immediately successful at ridding campuses of many insurrectionists and at frightening others into silence, was suicidal in the long run ... An aura of fear clouded government-student relations.[87]

The broadest aim of education was to stimulate nationalism, and this included loyalty both to the nation and the party, the Guomindang. Nobody would dispute that nationalism was a factor of critical importance in the China of Chiang Kai-shek. Moreover, it most certainly existed within the educational system. The various student movements of the period, such as the December Ninth of 1935 and after, were inspired by nationalism. But again one would need to ask whether it was the educational system itself which sparked off or fanned this nationalism, or was it merely the repository, the body where the nationalism grew. Once again the credit must go much more to the political situation than to education. It was hatred of Japanese encroachments and imperialism which sparked off the movement.

If the intellectual climate in 1935 favoured nationalism it was hardly the system that was responsible. There were of course progressive teachers and professors, and some of them are justly famous for their support of the student movement and its nationalism. But, by and large, governments and the Party or other authorities in the system whom they appointed favoured a nationalism quite different from that which actually took root among the students. Put in its bluntest terms, student nationalism tended to see the various governments and the Guomindang itself as targets rather than friends, as appeasers of Japanese or other imperialists not as genuine allies against them. This being the case, the educational system cannot possibly be considered as primary in the nurturing of nationalism. Once again that honour must go to politics.

All this leads to the conclusion that Chinese education from

1928 to 1949 cannot be considered a success in terms of the criteria it hoped to meet. It also suggests strongly that education was only a secondary factor in assisting the processes of modernisation and social change. Individuals within universities can certainly claim a leading role in the intellectual climate, but not education or the educational system as a whole. Progress in various areas of education was made in the 1930s, but it was the war against Japan that forced acceleration and important changes in the system. The impact of the war on education is much more real, more important and more visible, than *vice versa*. It was politics which was primary, not education.

The reasons for the essential failure of the educational system to achieve its aims or to take a primary role in the most vital social processes of the time lie partly in its administration. It was not that a bureaucracy was lacking. As shown earlier there was a complex administrative machinery. But it was too large, too inefficient, too corrupt, not well enough motivated. The administration included a mechanism for distributing that vital ingredient: finance. But it was too little, too badly and unevenly distributed. Like so much else in China under Chiang Kai-shek the real purpose of the educational bureaucracy and its budgeting was to serve the interests of the leading and ruling classes and sectors of society.

It would not be fair to put all the blame on the administration of education. The fact is that the failure of education in the Guomindang period was by no means total. Insofar as the experience did not succeed, the reason lay essentially in the political failure of the Guomindang and the disintegration of society as a whole. As a matter of fact, the education system is probably among the better achievements in the Guomindang's rather bleak record, among the lighter spots in a not very bright period of China's history.

NOTES

1. See the Chinese text in Ding Zhipin, *Zhongguo jin qishi nian lai jiaoyu jishi* [Chronology of education in China over the last seventy years] (Nanjing, 1933), p. 40 or Shu Xincheng, comp., *Zhongguo jindai jiaoyu shi ziliao* [Materials on the recent history of Chinese education] (Beijing, 1961), I, 226. Shu's compilation was first published in Shanghai in 1928. I have followed the translation given in H.T. Montague Bell and H.G.W. Woodhead, *The China Year Book 1913*, Kraus reprint (Nendeln, 1974), p. 387.

2. *The China Year Book 1913*, p. 390.
3. Shu Xincheng, I, 248.
4. Lu-dzai Djung, *A History of Democratic Education in Modern China* (Shanghai, 1934), p. 53.
5. See the Chinese text, among other places, in Fang Yuyan, *Xin jiaoyu shi* [A new history of education] (Shanghai, 1934), p. 389 and Ding Zhipin, p. 100.
6. See the Chinese text, among other places, in Fang Yuyan, p. 394. A translation into English, somewhat different from the above, is given by Theodore H.E. Chen, in 'Education in China, 1927-1937', in Paul K.T. Sih, ed., *The Strenuous Decade: China's Nation-Building Efforts, 1927-1937* (Jamaica, N.Y., 1970), p. 294.
7. See H.G.W. Woodhead, ed., *The China Year Book 1931*, Kraus reprint (Nendeln, 1969), p. 447.
8. *Jiaoyu faling* [Educational statutes] (Nanjing, 1946), p. 33.
9. See the text in *Jiaoyu faling huibian* [Collection of educational statutes] (Changsha, 1936), I, 267-268.
10. *Ibid.*, pp. 268-276.
11. Wang Shih-chieh, 'Education', in Kwei Chungshu, ed., *The Chinese Year Book 1935-36 Premier Issue*, Kraus reprint (Nendeln, 1968), p. 473.
12. The law is contained in *Jiaoyu faling*, p. 371 and *Jiaoyu faling huibian*, I, 154-155.
13. See the text in *ibid.*, pp. 156-171.
14. John Israel, *Student Nationalism in China, 1927-1937* (Stanford, 1966), p. 191.
15. Cyrus H. Peake, *Nationalism and Education in Modern China* (New York, 1932), p. 155.
16. See detailed comment and description on secondary curricula in Guomindang China also in *Dier ci Zhongguo jiaoyu nianjian* [Second educational yearbook] (Shanghai, 1948), II, 350-355.
17. See the Organic Law of the Ministry of Education in *Jiaoyu faling*, pp. 1-3 and H.G.W. Woodhead, ed., *The China Year Book 1934*, Kraus reprint (Nendeln, 1969), p. 313.
18. See Lu-dzai Djung, p. 25.
19. *The China Year Book 1934*, p. 313.
20. Lu-dzai Djung, p. 43.
21. *Ibid.*, p. 44.
22. C.H. Becker, M. Falski, P. Langevin, and R.H. Tawney, *The Reorganisation of Education in China* (Paris, 1932), p. 48.
23. *Ibid.*, p. 47.
24. *Ibid.*, p. 44.
25. *Ibid.*, p. 51.
26. Cheng Xiangfan, *Zhongguo jiaoyu xingzheng* [Administration of Chinese education] (Shanghai, 1930), pp. 304-305.
27. Becker *et al.*, p. 50.
28. T'ai-ch'u Liao, 'Rural Education in Transition, A Study of the Old-fashioned Chinese Schools (Szu Shu) in Shantung and Szechuan', *Yenching Journal of Social Studies*, IV (February 1949), 27.
29. *Ibid.*, p. 36.
30. *Ibid.*, p. 49.
31. *Ibid.*, p. 48.
32. *Ibid.*, p. 52.
33. See the figures in Yunnan Jiaoyu ting dier ke, 'Yunnan sheng shishi yiwu jiaoyu xianzhuang', [Present state of affairs in the implementation of compulsory education in Yunnan province] *Yunnan jiaoyu gongbao* [Yunnan education bulletin] IV:2 (16 October 1935), between 31 and 32.

34. The figures for the Catholic schools come from *The China Year Book 1934*, pp. 334-35. According to *ibid.*, p. 315 the total number of primary school students in China was 774,082 in higher and 7,118,581 in lower, or 7,892,663 altogether.

35. H.G.W. Woodhead, ed., *The China Year Book 1939*, Kraus reprint (Nendeln, 1969), p. 302.

36. See one treatment of this topic in William Purviance Fenn, *Christian Higher Education in Changing China 1880-1950* (Grand Rapids, 1976), pp. 111-120.

37. Article 8 of the 'Revised Regulations on Private Schools' of 19 October 1933. See *Jiaoyu faling huibian*, I, 343. Earlier regulations of the same import were issued in 1925 and 1927.

38. Fenn, pp. 112-113.

39. *The China Year Book 1939*, p. 302.

40. Becker *et al.*, p. 20.

41. The law is given in Shu Xincheng, II, 404-16, Article 6 p. 404.

42. See Wang Fengjie and Li Zhengfu, 'Woguo shishi yiwu jiaoyu zhi yange jiqi jinzhan', [Reform and progress in the implementation of compulsory education in our country] in Zhongguo jiaoyu xuehui, ed., *Yiwu jiaoyu yanjiu* [Research on compulsory education] (Taibei, 1961), pp. 44-45.

43. See Chen Jingpan, *Zhongguo jindai jiaoyu shi* [History of modern Chinese education] (Beijing, 1979), p. 294.

44. Ding Zhipin, p. 86.

45. Fang Yuyan, p. 419.

46. Zhuang Zexuan, *Jiaoyu gailun* [Outline of education] (Shanghai, 1928), p. 184. The introduction is dated October 1926 by the author.

47. *The Chinese Year Book 1935-36*, pp. 523, 123.

48. Ding Zhipin, pp. 215-16; Wang Shih-chieh, 'Education', in *The Chinese Year Book 1935-36*, p. 485.

49. See Wang Fengjie and Li Zhengfu, pp. 35ff.

50. See Shao Weizheng, 'The First National Congress of the Communist Party of China: A Verification of the Date of Convocation and the Number of Participants', *Social Sciences in China, A Quarterly Journal in English* I: 1 (March 1980), 121-123.

51. Ding Zhipin, p. 257.

52. Zhou Fohai, 'Zenyang tuijin Susheng yiwu jiaoyu', [How to promote compulsory education in Jiangsu province] *Jiangsu jiaoyu* [Jiangsu education] IV: 9 (15 September 1935), 1-2.

53. 'Yunnan sheng shishi yiwu jiaoyu xiankuang', pp. 24-25.

54. See *Dier ci nianjian*, I, 241.

55. *China Handbook 1937-1944, A Comprehensive Survey of Major Developments in China in Seven Years of War* (Chungking, 1944), p. 244.

56. R.F. Price, *Education in Modern China*, revised edition (London, 1979), p. 202.

57. Becker *et al*, p. 93.

58. See the enormously detailed treatment in *Dier ci nianjian*, III, 1085-1207.

59. Becker *et al.*, p. 188.

60. There is a substantial literature on James Yen's mass education campaign in Dingxian. See, for example, Pearl S. Buck, *Tell the People: Talks with James Yen about the Mass Education Movement* (New York, 1945).

61. Ida Belle Lewis, *The Education of Girls in China* (New York, 1919), p. 25.

62. See Guo Tingyi, *Jindai Zhongguo shishi rizhi* [Chronology of modern Chinese history] Taibei, 1963), II, 1256.

63. Ding Zhipin, p. 21.
64. Article 10, quoted in *ibid.*, pp. 109-110.
65. Lu-dzai Djung, p. 157.
66. *Ibid.*, p. 159.
67. *Dier ci nianjian*, IV, 1457.
68. See *The China Year Book 1934*, pp. 334-335, for the Catholic schools, and p. 340 for the Protestant.
69. Lu-dzai Djung, p. 154.
70. *Dier ci nianjian*, IV, 1403.
71. *The China Year Book 1934*, between pp. 334 and 335, 339.
72. See Yu Qingtang, 'Sannian lai zhi Zhongguo nüzi jiaoyu',. [The education of girls in China over the last three years] *Jiangsu jiaoyu* IV: 1-2 (February 1935), 126.
73. The figures come from *Dier ci nianjian*, IV, 1413, 1403. The proportions shown are my own calculations based on the figures shown there.
74. *Jiaoyu faling*, p. 34.
75. See Wang Maozu, 'Guonan yu jiaoyu', [The national trouble and education] *Jiangsu jiaoyu* V: 1-2 (15 February 1936), 3-4.
76. Yuan Zhe, *Kangzhan yu jiaoyu* [The war of resistance and education] (Changsha, 1937), pp. 7-9.
77. *Ibid.*, p. 17.
78. *China Handbook 1937-1944*, p. 47.
79. 'Rural Education in Transition', p. 62.
80. See some figures in *China Handbook 1937-1944*, pp. 243-244 and Hubert Freyn, *Chinese Education in the War* (Shanghai, 1940), pp. 117-118. The above statement allows for these figures to be inflated, such as Freyn's claim of Guangxi (p. 117) that 'by the end of 1938, the province's 3,369,999 illiterates were reduced to 1,863,995, who are expected to be all educated within another year'.
81. *Ibid.*, p. 120.
82. *China Handbook 1937-1944*, p. 242.
83. *Qinghua daxue xiaoshi gao* [Draft history of Qinghua University] (Beijing, 1981), pp. 291-292.
84. *China Handbook 1937-1944*, p. 231.
85. 'Rural Education in Transition', p. 64.
86. John Israel, 'Kuomintang Policy and Student Politics', in Albert Feuerwerker, Rhoads Murphy, and Mary C. Wright, eds., *Approaches to Modern Chinese History* (Berkeley, 1967), p. 295.
87. *Ibid.*, p. 300.

7

NATIONALIST FOREIGN POLICY, 1928-1937
Edmund S.K. Fung

Despite some notable achievements in treaty revision, the performance of the National Government in the sphere of foreign relations was a failure on the whole. Owing to a combination of factors, Nanjing's was the diplomacy of weakness. Internally, China faced the problems of political disunity, incessant civil strife, financial stringency and military inferiority. Within the Guomindang and the government it controlled, there were policy differences and factional struggle between the left and the right as well as personal antagonisms between individuals vying for power. Externally, although the Western powers were prepared to be conciliatory and friendly towards Nanjing, all of them soon found themselves in a worldwide economic depression while the crises in the Far East and Europe were coming to a head, which impeded their efforts to help resolve China's diplomatic difficulties presented by an aggressive Japan after 1931. As a consequence of China's weaknesses, the National Government throughout the Nanjing period was unable to formulate a concrete and well thought out policy and was obliged to approach foreign affairs in a piecemeal manner.

In line with the purge of the Communists in 1927, and with the rise to power of the right wing and the military faction, the Guomindang abandoned mass movement as a means of achieving foreign policy goals. Indeed, as it reviewed its position on anti-imperialism which had been an essential element in the revolutionary movement during the period of the united front, it eschewed the use of mob violence as far as possible and sought a peaceful solution to the decades-old question of treaty revision.

This called for a *rapprochement* with the West, particularly with Great Britain, which had for some years been singled out as the arch-imperialist in China. The breaking off of relations with Soviet Russia in December 1927 after the abortive communist-led Guangzhou uprising of that month further contributed to the reorientation of Nationalist foreign policy. Despite its determination to 'hem in, undermine, or otherwise restrict foreign rights and interests in China', as Edmund Clubb puts it, the Nanjing government was not as virulently anti-imperialist as he suggests.[1] In fact, the Guomindang's anti-imperialism subsided after 1927, even though it did not disappear. The party was prepared to compromise with imperialism and to revert to the earlier pre-1924 policy of international co-operation as an essential part of self-strengthening and national reconstruction. Once it was in power, the Guomindang was forced to recognise the reality of the military superiority of the powers and to deal with them through negotiations as far as possible, except in the case of the Soviet Union where the Chinese made very poor judgments diplomatically and militarily.

The foreign relations of the National Government can be conveniently divided into two major phases with the Japanese invasion of Manchuria in September 1931 as the dividing line. In the first phase Chinese diplomacy was principally concerned with treaty revision, focusing on the Western powers. Generally speaking, these powers, for a variety of reasons and also motivated by self-interests, desired to come to terms with China's new nationalism and were prepared to meet at least some of her grievances by negotiation. Britain and the United States were particularly inclined to pursue what they regarded as a 'liberal and conciliatory policy' towards China. Both the Soviet Union and Japan were, however, in different categories. Because of Nanjing's perception of the Soviet involvement in the activities of the Chinese Communist Party, Nationalist relations with Moscow deteriorated to the point of an armed conflict in 1929. Meanwhile, negotiations with Tokyo for treaty revision were impossible unless on Japanese terms. Indeed the Japanese invasion of Manchuria highlighted China's weakness and rendered impossible any Chinese attempts at effective diplomacy.

Foreign Policy Objectives

At the Fourth Plenum of the Second Central Executive

Committee held early in February 1928 the objectives of Nationalist foreign policy were broadly defined in terms of racial and national equality (*minzhu zhi pingdeng*) and national independence (*guojia zhi duli*), both of which were to be attained through the abolition of the unequal treaties. This was not a new definition, as it accorded with the wishes of Sun Yat-sen. Subsumed in it were considerations of national security and territorial integrity—the integral parts of the traditional concept of national interest—although it was not at all clear how these were to be maintained. The party emphasised China's inability to meet the foreign powers with force and that her only hope lay in national reconstruction. It further stressed that imperialism should be opposed with 'realistic reconstruction', not with communist means of violence, and that national independence and international equality were not something that could be gained without labour, hardship and perseverance.[2]

These objectives may be seen as a continuation of those which had been conceived by patriotic Chinese since the self-strengthening movement of the late Qing period—equal treaties and the recovery of sovereign rights, the war cries of China's new nationalism. The question of anti-imperialism, however, remained ambiguous in 1928 because of differences of opinion within the party, particularly in terms of policy implementation. This caused a lively debate at the Fifth Plenum of the Second Central Executive Committee held in August of the same year. A number of interrelated questions were raised; some of them were unreal, others were not really practicable. For example, the question was raised whether anti-imperialist slogans should be abandoned in view of China's inability to fight imperialism by force. Would the imperialists cease being an obstacle to the Nationalist revolution just because such slogans were dropped? Considering the 'contradictions' between imperialism and communism, should a united front with the imperialists be formed in order to oppose international communism? As it was the ultimate goal of the party to realise Sun Yat-sen's dream of the Great Harmony on Earth (*shijie datong*), should the Guomindang seek unity with all the weaker nations and oppressed peoples in the world in a common struggle against imperialism and the Comintern?[3]

No clear-cut answers were given by those who raised these questions. However, it was obvious that some party members were seriously concerned about the leadership's weakening stance on imperialism. This led Tan Yankai, a member of the Central Executive Committee, and Cai Yuanpei, the well-known educationist who served on the Central Supervisory Committee, to submit to the plenum a lengthy memorandum on foreign policy. The thrust of the memorandum was a strong recommendation for total and unconditional abrogation of all the unequal treaties in order to carry out the principles of the Nationalist revolution and to free China from the shackles of imperialism. Tariff autonomy and extraterritoriality were the two issues deserving immediate attention. Negotiations for the conclusion of new treaties to replace the old should be successfully completed within six months, otherwise, the memorandum urged, the government should declare the powers concerned as non-treaty countries and treat them accordingly.[4]

Other proposals were put forward to the plenum by a number of party branches and local committees in Nanjing, Ji'nan, Hangzhou and elsewhere, all calling for a vigorous, 'revolutionary' foreign policy. All these reflected not only the lack of a consensus on the means of carrying out the general policy defined earlier by the party leadership but also the growing disaffection of some significant sections of the party on foreign policy issues. Their differences were also indicative of the party leadership's reluctance, for a variety of reasons, to make use of such 'grass-roots' support as represented by these more 'radical' branches and local committees. The foreign policy debate was inconclusive, as were discussions of a number of domestic issues. The plenum, endeavouring to prevent matters from reaching an open deadlock, wound itself up with many resolutions on important issues passed after perfunctory deliberation or submitted to the Central Political Council for evaluation, while deferring others for future discussion.[5]

Despite the lack of a consensus, it was reasonable in view of the leadership's perception of China's weakness that the party should concentrate its efforts on the short-to-medium-term objectives of treaty revision. The Nanjing government claimed to be the legitimate heir to the Nationalist movement in which treaty abrogation had been the quintessential catchphrase of the 1924-1927 revolution. Chinese 'public opinion', too, desired a speedy end to the old treaty regime as Sun Yat-sen had wished.

On what may be regarded as long-term

objectives—ideological commitments, China's role in Asia or in the world, for example—the Guomindang was not in a position to say much. Sun Yat-sen's Three Principles of the People served as an ideological basis for Chinese foreign policy, but these principles, unless redefined in terms of reality and concrete solutions, were unsophisticated, imprecise and not particularly inspiring to the policy makers. Nevertheless, in their official pronouncements, the Nationalists paid due respect to Sun's lifelong desire for world peace based on a public spirit transcending national and racial boundaries (*tianxia weigong*), as well as on the equality of all nations and peoples. It was assumed that China would become wealthy and strong and attain the status of a world power after the unequal treaties had been completely abolished. When that time arrived, China would continue to oppose imperialism and, more significantly, revive the ancient tradition of 'helping the weak and raising the fallen' (*jiro fuqing*).

Sun had written, with some distortion of the facts, that imperial China, even in the heyday of her power, had never impaired the independence of Korea, Burma, Annam and Siam, all of which had been part of the extensive Chinese cultural empire. The Chinese empire, said Sun with a degree of Chinese chauvinism, had been achieved through the 'kingly way' (*wangdao*); by contrast the imperialism of modern times was based on 'military conquest and hegemonism' (*badao*) which resulted in colonialism. A strong and wealthy China would have a responsibility to the world in supporting the weak and small nations against the oppression and aggression of the mighty and the strong. And then, with morality and peace as the ideological foundations of her foreign policy, China would be well placed to help realise the Great Harmony on Earth.[6]

The Nationalist leaders might still regard China as a 'sub-colony' in the Sunist vein, but they appeared to realise the futility of talking about China's playing an active role in the national liberation movements overseas or in world affairs for many years to come. The grand unity with the oppressed peoples of the world called for by the Second National Party Congress in January 1926 was now regarded as impracticable and a thing only for the distant future. The concept of the Great Harmony on Earth was almost meaningless to the party leaders or to anyone else. Nobody really believed it to be more than a rhetoric or an abstract slogan, nor, indeed, was it relevant to China's immediate problems.

Revision of the Unequal Treaties

The Guomindang was divided on ways of repudiating the unequal treaties. The left wing adhered to the theory that imperialism was the cause of China's ills and the chief obstacle to the Nationalist revolution. With a view to a total abolition of foreign rights and privileges, the leftists advocated 'revolutionary diplomacy' based on mass support. Though not opposed to negotiations, they were prepared, as a last resort, to apply economic pressures, strikes, boycotts and mass agitation of various kinds.[7] Most of them, however, considered abrupt treaty abrogation involving armed conflict to be out of the question; only a small minority demanded total and immediate repudiation even at the risk of war.[8]

On the other hand, the right wing of the party and the military faction of Chiang Kai-shek which gained the upper hand insisted on what appeared to be a moderate approach. On 21 February 1928 Huang Fu, the newly-appointed Foreign Minister, declared that the Nationalist government would make all necessary preparations for the early opening of negotiations with the powers for the conclusion of new treaties. Expressing the government's desire to maintain and develop friendly relations with the powers, Huang pledged to protect foreign life and property and to recognise all treaties and agreements that might be concluded thereafter by regional authorities with foreign governments provided these had Nanking's prior approval.[9] From a Western point of view, the reasonable and compromising tone of Huang's statement contrasted markedly with the Guomindang's anti-imperialist polemics of earlier years.[10]

On 15 June, following the victory of the Northern Expedition, Nanjing declared that the time had arrived for new treaties to be negotiated on a basis of full equality and mutual respect for each other's sovereignty. On 7 July Wang Zhengting, who had succeeded Huang Fu as Foreign Minister the month before, declared that those treaties which had expired should be *ipso facto* abrogated. As for those which had not yet expired, the National Government would take immediate steps to terminate them. Pending the conclusion of new treaties, a set of interim regulations would apply.[11] These regulations were promulgated six days later.

The immediate steps Wang threatened to take to terminate those treaties which had not yet expired were described by the Chinese government as 'in accordance with proper procedure'. Certainly, the powers would not regard them as 'proper'. Nevertheless, seen in the context of domestic politics, Wang's declaration represented an uneasy compromise between the hardliners and the moderates within the party, a compromise which combined abrogation (*feiyue*) and revision (*xiuyue*) as a strategy. If the powers refused to revise the treaties on Chinese terms, Nanjing might invoke the principle of *rebus sic stantibus*[12] and denounce them unilaterally on the grounds that the circumstances in which these treaties were concluded had since changed significantly. This principle had been employed by some European nations before, although the powers never recognised its application as a normal diplomatic practice.

Owing to persistent demands by the general public, as well as by the left wing for a vigorous 'revolutionary' foreign policy, the Guomindang adhered to a policy of treaty abrogation but insisted at the same time that China must put her own house in order first through a long process of self-strengthening and reconstruction. Certainly, negotiations for treaty revision should proceed without delay, but the successful completion of these negotiations and the full attainment of treaty abolition would have to await what Chiang Kai-shek described as 'a preparatory period' of at least three years and possibly five or ten.[13] In other words, the rights recovery movement was to proceed in stages over a period of time. The powers favoured this approach. With the notable exception of Japan, they were prepared to come to terms with Chinese nationalism, but few saw the hope of China herself achieving peace and order within a reasonable period of time. And that explains why they chose to deal with China's treaty question item by item, each on its own merits.

Wang Zhengting, who belonged neither to the left nor to the right in Guomindang politics, was obliged to take this approach when he determined the priorities in the treaty revision programme. Foreign rights and privileges were divided into five groups, to be abolished in the following order: tariff control; extraterritoriality; presence of foreign troops on Chinese soil; navigation in the interior and coastal waters; and leased territories, concessions and settlements.[14] Later in 1928 Wang lowered the presence of foreign troops to last priority because of continuing civil strife in the country.[15] He also sought to negotiate simultaneously the rendition of foreign concessions and leased territories. In any case, he began with the tariff question which had been dealt with by the powers at the Beijing Tariff Conference (October 1926 to April 1927).[16] He met with a favourable response from the United States, which, acting independently of the other powers, signed a treaty with Nanjing on 25 July 1928 granting China tariff autonomy subject to the most-favoured-nation clause. Although the treaty gave nothing new to the Chinese, as they had already been accorded tariff autonomy in principle at the Beijing Tariff Conference, it helped to expedite Sino-British negotiations. On 20 December, an Anglo-Chinese treaty was signed, providing for the enforcement of a Chinese national tariff schedule as of 1 February 1929.[17] Similar treaties were signed in 1928 with Germany, Norway, Belgium, Italy, Denmark, the Netherlands, Portugal, Sweden, France and Spain. Negotiations with Japan proved more difficult because of the question of *lijin* (transit taxes levied by the local government) and China's unsecured debts which concerned Japan more than any other power. Japan did not agree to tariff autonomy until May 1930, after the debt question had been resolved.[18]

Before the end of 1928 Nanjing had also signed treaties of amity and commerce with Belgium, Denmark, Italy, Portugal and Spain, all of which agreed to renounce extraterritoriality if others would do so. Meanwhile, the National Government was recognised by many foreign countries, including the United States and Britain. Japanese recognition was extended in June 1929.

In all these negotiations the National Government sought to break the powers' tendency to act in concert. Unity of action was a traditional policy of foreign diplomacy in China. The Chinese had learned from past experience that they had no bargaining power when dealing with the powers as a bloc and at international conferences. Conversely, separate, bilateral negotiations would be more efficient and profitable and would, at times, enable them to play one power off against another. It should be pointed out, however, that the Chinese were able to do so only as a result of the growing divergence of interest between Japan and the Western powers in this period. The Chinese were quick to exploit their rivalries, but the powers would still act as a bloc when their collective interests were at stake or when the endangering of one power's interests had implications for those of the others.

As the prospects of treaty revision depended on international goodwill as well as on the progress of domestic reconstruction, Nanjing felt an urgent need to woo the West following its break with the Comintern and the Soviet Union. Wang Zhengting, a Yale-educated career diplomat,[19] was well disposed towards the West and was particularly interested in cultivating the friendship of Britain, which, in December 1926, had announced a new, conciliatory China policy. Anxious to get on with the task of treaty revision and cognizant of Britain's influence in the Far East, Wang considered British friendship and co-operation the best substitute for the now broken Russian connection.

The United States was also to be wooed. Wang believed that since American interests in China were mainly commercial, missionary and philanthropic, the United States would be among the first to agree to treaty revision. Germany had been forced to surrender her treaty status after the First World War, and Soviet Russia also treated China as an equal, at least in theory. China's difficulty lay with Japan. In view of Japan's ambitions on the Asian mainland, Wang wanted to avoid antagonising the Japanese as far as possible, for they could block any Chinese move towards treaty revision. His strategy was to negotiate with Britain, the United States and France first while keeping Japan in a friendly mood without arousing her suspicions. He therefore devoted a great deal of attention to improving relations with Britain in the hope that once British consent to treaty revision was secured, the Japanese could be persuaded to go along.[20]

The period 1929-1931 saw a remarkable improvement in Sino-British relations.[21] The Chinese recovered the British concessions in Hankou, Jiujiang, Zhenjiang and Xiamen and the leased territory of Weihaiwei. Changes to the municipal administration of the British concession in Tianjin were effected while Chinese representation on the municipal council of the Shanghai International Settlement was increased. An agreement concerning Chinese use of the Boxer Indemnity funds was also reached.

Negotiations on extraterritoriality, on the other hand, were lengthy and complicated, as the powers were not prepared to relinquish their rights without adequate safeguards. Nanjing, however, was anxious to present to the Chinese public and its political opponents a 'strong' stand. So, on 28 December 1929 a mandate was issued declaring that as from 1 January 1930 all foreign nationals in China were to abide by Chinese laws and regulations.[22] The mandate, coming immediately after an unsuccessful military revolt against the government, was clearly intended for domestic consumption, for two days later Wang Zhengting issued a separate statement to the effect that his government was prepared to consider and discuss within a reasonable time any representations from the powers in regard to the mandate.[23] Subsequent negotiations failed to yield satisfactory results, and this compelled Wang to announce on 10 April 1931 that there was still outstanding disagreement between China and the powers over a number of vital points, but he warned that unless the solution desired by China was completely in sight, he would be constrained to 'declare the present negotiations with the Powers concerned as dead-locked'.[24] This was a veiled threat to take unilateral action if necessary. As it turned out, on 4 May, the day before the People's Convention opened, the National Government took the much-heralded action by promulgating a set of regulations governing the exercise of jurisdiction over foreign nationals in China with effect from 1 January 1932.[25] Again, this was motivated by the need for some diplomatic success in the face of yet another internal challenge, the separatist Cantonese movement.[26] Negotiations with Britain and the United States were wound up because of the renewal of civil strife, and before long the Manchurian crisis forced the Chinese to announce, on 29 December, that the enforcement of the regulations of 4 May would be postponed.[27] Thus, once again, internal disunity, coupled with external threat, impeded the pursuit of a strong foreign policy.

War with the Soviet Union and Difficulties with Japan

While Nanjing enjoyed good relations with Britain and the United States, its relations with the Soviet Union and Japan were unsatisfactory. Guomindang leftists had been arguing for some time that, in spite of Soviet support of the Chinese Communists, the Soviet Union was the only power which had treated China as an equal and that although another alliance with Moscow was out of the question, there were merits, such as broadening

China's international contacts, in restoring relations with it on Chinese terms—non-interference in China's domestic affairs—at an appropriate time.[28] The party leadership, however, was too obsessed with the eradication of communism at home to appreciate the value of a *rapprochement* with the Russians and, instead, took an aggressive attitude towards the Soviet position in Manchuria. On 27 May 1929 Nationalist troops raided the Soviet consulate in Harbin and seized certain secret documents purporting to show Russian involvement in Chinese communist activities. On 10 July they suddenly took over the Chinese Eastern Railway, dismissed all the Soviet heads of departments and divisions and expelled other Soviet railway staff and citizens. Even now, the Chinese motives remain unclear, though ostensibly they resented Russian control of the Chinese Eastern Railway, which, under the terms of the Sino-Soviet Agreement of 1924, should have been jointly managed on an equal basis.

In statements made on 22 July and 20 August, Wang Zhengting attributed China's actions in Harbin to alleged Russian subversion, presumably in connection with the Chinese Communists, using the Soviet consulate as a centre. The Chinese objective was, then, to expel the Russian agents involved in subversive activities rather than seize control of the Chinese Eastern Railway. Backing up Wang's position, the Guomindang published a compendium of articles through its propaganda department, emphasising the political significance of the Sino-Soviet dispute and playing down the importance of the legal aspects of the 1924 Agreement.[29] Hu Hanmin, then chairman of the Legislative Yuan, also accused the Russians of having used the railway zone as 'headquarters' to further 'red imperialist interests'. If the issue had been over railway rights only, Hu asserted, his government would have resolved it by moderate means. Similarly, Chiang Kai-shek perceived 'red imperialism' as more 'treacherous' and 'rapacious' than 'white imperialism', but he attached more importance to the treaty question than did Wang and Hu, apparently in order to enlist popular support for the government in case of war with the Russians.[30]

In attacking the Soviet position in Harbin, the Chinese seem to have been encouraged by past performance. In April 1927 Zhang Zuolin, then in control of the Beijing government, had raided the Soviet embassy, and the Nationalists had also closed the Soviet consular and commercial establishments in areas under their control in December of the same year. On all occasions the Chinese had escaped retaliation, which might have led them to think that they could get away with it again. Moreover, Chiang Kai-shek is said to have been plotting against the Russians for some time with Zhang Xueliang, the 'Young Marshall', who had brought Manchuria into the Nationalist fold in December 1928. Feng Yuxiang, then Chiang's rival, had just defected from Nanjing and was thought to be moving into the Russian and communist orbits; so Chiang may have wished to shortcut the Russians to prevent such an alliance.[31]

Whatever Nanjing's motives, it made a blunder by attacking the Soviet position, thus violating the Sino-Soviet Agreement of 1924; the dispute then became a test case from the powers' point of view, that is, whether China was prepared to honour her contractual obligations.

So, contrary to Nanjing's expectations, none of the powers supported its actions. They were unimpressed by China's attempts to alter arbitrarily a situation governed by international treaties, even though the country affected this time was communist. The American Secretary of State, Henry Stimson, welcomed the strong Russian stand and warned China that by violating treaties, she was alienating her friends.[32] The British Foreign Office shared the American sentiment, believing that the unyielding Soviet stand would teach the Chinese a lesson and have a restraining effect on Nanjing's drive towards an early settlement of the question of extraterritoriality.[33] Likewise, Tokyo reacted to the Nationalist move with great disquiet because of its implications for the Japanese-controlled South Manchurian Railway.[34]

War broke out in the autumn. Chinese troops were no match for the Russians. On 22 December the Nationalists were compelled to sign the Khabarovsk Protocol, which restored the *status quo ante*. This was a sobering experience for them: the powers, communist or not, could not be provoked with impunity. From a diplomatic point of view, the Manchurian adventure was also a complete failure. No international sympathy was received. Moscow severed what remained of its diplomatic ties with Nanjing. Significantly, the imbroglio was closely watched by Japan, who could hardly fail to be impressed by the effectiveness of the Soviet military response to Chinese assaults on treaty rights.

As regards Sino-Japanese relations there was a basic conflict between Chinese nationalism and Japan's special interests in Manchuria and east Inner Mongolia which were threatened by the Nationalist drive to unify the whole of China. The Japanese intervention in Shandong in April 1928, ostensibly to protect Japanese life and property against possible attacks by undisciplined Chinese soldiers, boded ill for relations between the two countries. Following the Ji'nan incident of 3 May, in which clashes between Japanese and Nationalist troops resulted in the former's seizure of the city and the death of many Chinese, anti-Japanese feeling ran high throughout the year, with boycotts, strikes and demonstrations in various parts of the country. The incident provided ammunition for the leftists and government critics to attack not only Japanese imperialism but also Nanjing's 'weak-kneed' diplomacy.[35] Negotiations for the withdrawal of Japanese troops from Shandong yielded no results until 28 March 1929 when a settlement was reached.

The situation was complicated by Wang Zhengting's declaration of 7 July that all treaties which had expired were to be terminated, since this would subject the foreigners concerned, including the Japanese, to Chinese jurisdiction and taxation on a provisional basis until new treaties were concluded. It was thought by some observers at the time that Wang's 'revolutionary diplomacy' was intended mainly for domestic consumption and that the National Government had no desire to provoke the Japanese.[36] On 19 July, however, Wang boldly denounced the Sino-Japanese Commercial Treaty of 1896, which had been renewed by the former Beijing government for successive short terms since its expiry in 1926. The Tanaka government reacted strongly by describing the Chinese move as an 'outrageous' act which might lead to an abrogation of the more important treaties concerning Japan's Manchurian interests.[37] In response, Nanjing reinstated its treaty policy but felt compelled to give no effect to the interim regulations. Contrary to his intentions, Wang could not keep Japan in a friendly mood and instead succeeded in arousing Japanese apprehensions about the Nationalist threat to their special position in Manchuria. In fairness to Wang and the Guomindang, however, that was not really a failure on their part as it was hardly possible to keep Japan in a friendly mood without compromising China's national interests. The assassination of Zhang Zuolin on a train bound for Shenyang (Mukden) on 4 June 1928, carried out by junior officers of the Japanese Guandong Army albeit without the prior approval or even knowledge of Premier Tanaka, was a stern warning to the Chinese that Japan was determined to maintain her position in Manchuria by force, if necessary.[38]

As if to make the situation worse, the Chinese were at the same time pursuing a policy of economic competition through railway construction in Manchuria begun some years before, often in violation of the Treaty of 1905 whereby the Chinese government undertook to construct no lines parallel to the South Manchurian Railway. Little by little, the Chinese succeeded in forming a system linked to the port of Yingkou. As a former Nationalist minister of railways put it: 'These railways not only facilitated the free movement of Chinese troops in all parts of Manchuria but diverted a large share of traffic from the Japanese to the Chinese lines'.[39] By the end of 1930 another port, Huludao, immediately south of Jinzhou on the Beiping-Shenyang Railway, had begun construction to compete with the Japanese-controlled Dalian.

Tokyo was alarmed, as was the local press which was very sensitive to the question of Japanese rights and interests in Manchuria. In December 1930 there were rumours of an impending Sino-Japanese conflict, following persistent reports from China that Nanjing was negotiating with foreign capitalists for funds to construct additional railways to the detriment of the South Manchurian Railway.[40] The situation was complicated by the fact that the Chinese People's Convention meeting in May 1931 issued a declaration stating that the Chinese people should recognise none of the 'unequal' treaties and achieve China's complete independence and equality in the shortest possible time.[41] The Chinese pronouncement need not be taken at face value, but the Japanese could not help feeling alarmed, and the Guandong Army in particular was becoming restless and quickly exploited it. This, combined with other factors, led to a series of disputes in Manchuria, culminating in the incident of 18 September 1931 when the Guandong Army took matters into its own hands and occupied Shenyang.

Nanjing's Diplomacy since the Shenyang Incident

The Shenyang incident marked the beginning of a new phase in

Chinese foreign relations. Until then Nanjing's objectives had related principally to the rights recovery movement. Despite the fact that extraterritoriality and other special rights and privileges remained, Nanjing had succeeded in recovering tariff autonomy and a number of foreign concessions in the treaty ports, thus undermining the old treaty system. After the Shenyang incident, however, the Chinese realised that it was impossible to press on with treaty revision as they had to concentrate on the Manchurian and north China problem.

Nanjing did not want an armed conflict with Japan, as it lacked the military strength to fight the Japanese. Chinese critics deplored the fact that insufficient attention had been paid to the Manchurian question because of the government's preoccupation with tariff matters and extraterritoriality.[42] However, given Japan's special interests in the region, one wonders what the Nationalists could have done to check Japanese expansion unless they were prepared to risk war. Indeed, Chiang Kai-shek was not firmly anti-Japanese and had been at pains to avoid provoking the Guandong Army before the Shenyang incident.[43]

At the outbreak of the incident, Chiang was in Jiangxi preparing for the third anti-communist campaign. He rushed back to Nanjing on 21 September and immediately ordered the formation of a Special Foreign Affairs Committee under the chairmanship of Dai Jitao to deal with the crisis. He also halted the anti-communist push, sent a delegation to the south to reconcile with the separatist Guangzhou regime, and issued a national proclamation calling for calm, patience and unity. On the following day he addressed the party headquarters, asking the nation 'to grin and bear the adversity' while awaiting the decision of the League of Nations, to which the crisis had been referred.[44] Subsequently, on various occasions between October and November, Chiang time and again stressed his government's recourse to international peace treaties and collective security systems as a means of resisting the Japanese and that the solution to the crisis, whether through war or negotiation, lay first in China's internal unity.[45]

Nanjing's policy then was to offer no armed resistance and to hold no negotiations with the Japanese but to seek foreign support. Song Ziwen, the influential Finance Minister and deputy head of the Special Foreign Affairs Committee, who initially favoured negotiations with Japan, is said to have been misled by Dr Ludwig Rajchman, director of the health section of the League of Nations who happened to be in China at the time, into believing that the League would be eminently suitable to deal with the crisis and check Japanese aggression.[46] It is not clear how true this claim is, nor can one be sure that Song was so innocent. The important question is: Up to what point would Nanjing persist in this three-pronged policy? Let us see what the Special Foreign Affairs Committee thought.

Some time in November the committee submitted to the Central Political Council a secret report containing the following points: Tokyo's objective was to occupy Manchuria; the Japanese military, after refusing to evacuate the region, had come to dominate Tokyo's China policy; the Japanese army would attack Jinzhou and afterwards make a southern thrust into Tianjin, Beiping, Qingdao, Ji'nan, Shanghai, Ningbo and Wuhan, thereby threatening Nanjing. The League of Nations would try its best to frustrate the Japanese plans but its member nations, for a variety of reasons, were unlikely to go to war with Japan, and this would preclude any effective League measures against Japan. The United States, though not a member of the League, supported it and might invoke the Nine-Power Treaty and intervene. China would eventually win 'international victory' (sympathy?) and should under no circumstances declare war on Japan first but maintain good relations with the other powers and consider the reality of the situation. Military sacrifice, however, should be made when the intolerable stage was reached; if the Japanese went on to attack Jinzhou, China would have to resist to the best of her ability in order to win popular confidence in the government, as well as for national salvation. For the present, the government should nevertheless demonstrate publicly its trust in the League of Nations so that the Chinese people would not accuse the government of doing nothing. Meanwhile, good relations with the other powers should be maintained, and China could expect American support by invoking the Nine-Power Treaty. Finally, the report concluded, anti-military forces would one day re-emerge in Japan when Sino-Japanese relations would be normalised, but until then China should prepare herself for self-defence based on popular support.[47]

It can be seen with the benefit of hindsight that the report showed an error of judgment in regard to the likelihood of

American intervention. The committee did not explain why it was so confident about getting armed support from the United States. We can only suggest that it was probably because of the committee's perception of Washington's rivalry with and mistrust of Tokyo. It is interesting to note, on the other hand, that no undue confidence was placed on the efficacy of the League of Nations and that a limit to Chinese non-resistance was set beyond which China must fight back. And the limit was Japan's attack on Jinzhou. Was the limit to be strictly adhered to? How important was it? The report did not say clearly. What it did urge was that military preparations, albeit not immediate resistance, should be made. There was no mention of negotiations.

The report seems to have been adopted as a government policy at a time when Chiang Kai-shek was being forced to relinquish his office as chairman of the National Government in an effort to settle Nanjing's differences with the south. But the suggestion that China should prepare herself for self-defence based on popular support was not taken seriously and the limit to non-resistance was not adhered to. When Jinzhou was attacked and finally occupied by the Japanese army on 3 January 1932, no armed resistance was offered, nor were negotiations held.

The government's policy was criticised in various quarters. Patriotic students, the Communists, and even some sections of the Nationalist troops, notably the Twenty-ninth Army commanded by Song Zheyuan in north China, urged resistance from the very beginning.[48] Others, such as Hu Hanmin and the Chinese minister in Tokyo, Jiang Zuobin, favoured negotiations with Japan.[49] Indeed, some historians have criticised Nanjing's refusal to negotiate immediately following the Shenyang incident when the civilian leadership in Tokyo favoured direct negotiations. This, the the argument goes, gave the Guandong Army time to consolidate its gains in Manchuria and to present to the civil authorities in Tokyo a *fait accompli* which the latter had to defend.[50] However, while it is true that the Watatsuki cabinet desired to control or restrain the Japanese army, they differed more over means than over ends as far as their objectives in Manchuria were concerned.[51] Even if Nanjing had entered into negotiations with Tokyo, the Japanese terms would have been too harsh to be acceptable to any Chinese regime that called itself nationalist.

On 28 January 1932 the Japanese navy intervened in Shanghai partly in an attempt to deal with the anti-Japanese boycott organised by the local Chinese Chamber of Commerce with the backing of the National Government.[52] Two days later the government was transferred to Luoyang temporarily, while the intervention was stiffly resisted for thirty-three days by the *regional* Nineteenth Route Army led by Cai Tingkai and Jiang Guangnai, who withdrew only after the arrival of massive Japanese reinforcements. The extent to which the Fifth Army of the central government was involved in the fighting remains a controversy.[53] But it appeared that Nanjing was more interested in using economic weapons than in armed resistance.

Yet the Shanghai resistance clearly demonstrated the usefulness of taking a strong stand against the Japanese. For one thing it met with the approval of the Chinese people who hailed the commanders of the resistance force as national heroes. Despite their defeat, the Chinese now found themselves in a better diplomatic position than several months before and were able to negotiate a local settlement through the good offices of the British minister, Sir Miles Lampson.[54] The settlement was reached on 5 May, by which time the Nationalists had formed a new administration with Wang Jingwei as head of the Executive Yuan, Chiang Kai-shek as chairman of the Military Affairs Commission and Luo Wen'gan as Foreign Minister. Their new Japan policy, articulated by Wang Jingwei, was 'resistance on the one hand and negotiation on the other'.[55] They refused to recognise the puppet state of Manchukuo (Manzhouguo in Chinese, Manshū koku in Japanese), which Japan had created earlier in March.

In October the Lytton Commission set up by the League of Nations to enquire into the Manchurian affair published its findings, but the matter was not formally debated in the League Council until in early 1933. Japan rejected the Lytton Report, which essentially proposed a compromise solution, and withdrew from the League on 27 March. The Western powers, preoccupied with European affairs and their own domestic problems arising from the world depression, were not inclined to take any measures against Japan other than moral sanctions.[56] Even without these preoccupations, it was doubtful whether any of them would have wanted to go to war with Japan. Their vital interests in China were not seriously or directly jeopardised at this time; moreover, Nanjing had no intention of doing the fighting itself.

Nor did China succeed in obtaining help from the Soviet Union, with which diplomatic relations had been resumed in December 1932. The restoration of relations had been favoured by those, including Song Ziwen and Chiang Kai-shek, who hoped to manoeuvre Moscow into fighting China's war on the grounds that Japan's actions in Manchuria threatened Russian interests there.[57] Furthermore, resumption of relations would be useful as a good-neighbour policy, as an appeasement of the leftists within the Guomindang, as a demonstration of Nanjing's diplomatic success, as a political victory over Japan, and as something to play on Western fears of communism in the Far East.[58] From the very beginning, however, the Russians had no wish to be used as a Chinese cat's paw in the Sino-Japanese conflict. Nanjing's recourse to them only reflected its helplessness.

In January 1933 the battle of Shanhaiguan brought another victory to the Japanese army which swiftly moved into Rehe province. In the following months the Japanese moved south and, after crushing the stiff resistance of the Twenty-ninth Army led by Song Zheyuan, forced Nanjing to negotiate a cease-fire.[59] Huang Fu, a former foreign minister now charged with the peace talks, signed the humiliating Tanggu Truce on 31 May, whereby an area of some 5,000 square miles separating Beiping and Manchuria was declared a demilitarised zone to be patrolled by a police force friendly to the Japanese. Luo Wen'gan resigned as Foreign Minister; his portfolio was assumed *ad interim* by Premier Wang Jingwei concurrently.

The defeat of Song Zheyuan's troops, 300,000-strong against Japan's 50,000 men, exposed China's military weakness. Earlier on 8 May Chiang Kai-shek had made an important speech stressing that internal pacification of the Communists (*annei*) must be accomplished before resistance to Japan (*yangwai*) could be undertaken, for he believed that the Communists had contributed to the Japanese invasion by undermining China's defence capabilities. *Annei* and *yangwai* were not two independent things, and Chiang argued that internal disunity led to weakness and therefore had to be dealt with first.[60]

On 28 July Wang Jingwei joined Chiang in issuing a

statement to the effect that the government would continue to strive for China's stability and international peace and would not sign any treaty ceding or recognising 'the fruits of military aggression'. The Tanggu Truce, they believed, was a temporary measure which did not mean that the government had abandoned Chinese territory.[61] As officiating Foreign Minister, Wang described Chinese foreign policy thus:

> The Government is ready to admit that it is weak and powerless. To rectify this failing, there is only one thing to be done—to develop the strength of the people and consolidate the national vitality, which cannot, however, be achieved except by productive reconstruction. On this depends our ability to resist foreign aggression... Settlement and improvement of the domestic political situation must be the watchword of China's foreign policy.[62]

The truce, defended by an independent scholar, Hu Shi, as a necessary evil—the only pragmatic means of safeguarding the rest of north China, particularly the Beiping-Tianjin area, thus reducing China's losses[63] —was denounced by Chiang's political opponents and patriotic students. Feng Yuxiang emerged from retirement to organise a People's Federated Anti-Japanese Army for the dual purpose of resisting Japanese aggression and overthrowing the Chiang regime. After some initial success, however, Feng was forced, in August, to return to retirement after other national leaders had failed to respond to his call to arms.[64] In November Chen Mingshu, Cai Tingkai and Li Jishen launched a new rebellion and established a people's government in Fujian. As well as calling for the overthrow of Chiang Kai-shek, the insurgents proposed a united front against the Japanese. The rebellion soon collapsed, however, through lack of support from the other southern leaders who sniffed social radicalism in it.[65]

By mid-1933 Nanjing's policy towards Japan had changed from 'resistance on the one hand and negotiation on the other' to 'appeasement', a policy which raised two important questions. Should China abandon all hopes on the League of Nations and 'co-operate' with Japan by way of concessions as far as possible? Or should China continue to rely on the League for technical and financial assistance while at the same time seeking Japan's understanding? Some favoured the latter strategy;[66] others, while accepting the wisdom of continuously seeking the League's assistance, were not confident that Japanese understanding was forthcoming. Hu Shi, for one, criticised that Chinese diplomacy since September 1931 had neglected the cultivation of the Soviet Union, Europe and the United States, and urged the government to make as many friends as possible by expanding its diplomatic activities.[67] Hu was naive, however, in thinking that the United States, having recently improved relations with Moscow, might still be persuaded to fight China's war jointly with the Russians. China could not expect others to fight her battles while she herself made a minimum contribution. When the United States did eventually fight Japan in the Pacific War (and Japan's actions in China were a major cause of the increasing friction up to 1941), the Chinese had already done their own fighting for over three years.

Nanjing was interested not so much in taking new diplomatic initiatives as in seeking foreign aid for purposes of 'national reconstruction'. The Lytton Report had emphasised that a strong China was essential for the maintenance of peace in the Far East and that the best means of strengthening China in the sphere of economic development was through international co-operation. Thus in 1933 when Song Ziwen was in Europe for the World Economic Conference, he appealed to the League for further financial aid and technical assistance and proposed the creation of a special consultative committee that would obtain further credits for China and, in the long run, provide sufficient funds to undertake large industrial and railway projects and to settle China's outstanding foreign obligations. While *en route* to London, he made arrangements with the Reconstruction Finance Corporation in Washington for a US$50 million credit. When he arrived in the United States in early August, his primary aim was to raise money for the proposed consultative committee.[68]

Nanjing, moreover, was determined to build up a professional, modern army, but for the purpose of fighting the Communists, not the Japanese. With that in mind, Chiang Kai-shek turned to Germany and invited General von Seeckt, the former commander-in-chief of the Reichswehr, to spend three months in China in 1933, during which time a blueprint for the reorganisation of the Chinese army was prepared. In the following year von Seeckt returned to China as head of a

German military mission to assist the Chinese.[69] Meanwhile, arrangements had been made with Colonel John Hamilton Jouett and some thirteen other American aviators, all of the United States Reserve Corps, to come to China to assist in the founding and direction of a military aviation school in Hangzhou.[70] The Italian government, on the personal urging of Mussolini, had also decided to enter the field of military aviation in China. In October 1933 an Italian air mission supported by funds from the Italian Boxer Indemnity arrived in Nanjing, and its commander, General Lordi, was appointed chief aviation adviser to the National Government six months later.[71]

Whatever Nanjing's success or failure in obtaining foreign aid, Japan was alarmed and opposed any scheme from which she was excluded. As far as Japan was concerned, any foreign effort to strengthen China would only encourage the Chinese to persist in a hostile attitude. So, on 17 April 1934, Amau Eiji, a spokesman for the Japanese Foreign Ministry, issued a declaration proclaiming that Japan was responsible for maintaining peace in Asia and that she opposed any operations undertaken by the foreign powers in the name of technical and financial assistance to China and any projects such as detailing military instructors or advisers to China or supplying the Chinese with war planes.[72] The declaration was a warning to the powers, as well as to China, who was accused of attempting to play one country off against another.

Wang Jingwei refuted the Japanese accusation, pointing out that China, brow-beaten by Japan, was only crying for help.[73] The official Chinese statement also said that no country had the right to claim the exclusive responsibility for maintaining international peace in any designated part of the world and that China's collaboration with the other nations, whether in the form of loans or technical assistance, had been strictly limited to matters of a non-political nature. The purchase of military equipment and the employment of military instructors, the statement went on, had been for no other purposes than national self-defence and therefore should cause no concern to countries that harboured no ulterior motives in China.[74]

Without foreign intervention, and faced with a host of domestic problems, Nanjing had only two options: either appease Japan with further concessions or resist her by mobilising mass support and bringing all political parties into a united front. The latter option would mean co-operating with all anti-Japanese elements, including the Communists whose legal existence would have to be recognised. That would mean also stopping the anti-communist campaigns. Since the Nationalist leadership was not prepared to do so, it was left with the other option which necessitated a *modus vivendi* with Japan in the name of 'co-operation'. While adhering to non-recognition of Manchukuo, the Nationalists, in June and July 1934, reached a local agreement with the Japanese Guandong Army authorities to resume postal and train services in Manchuria.[75] Some months later, Chiang Kai-shek wrote an article entitled 'Enemy or Friend?', published under someone else's name in Nanjing early in 1935. In this article Chiang called on both countries to strive for a *rapprochement*, particularly urging Japan to take the initiative in breaking the present political stalemate by relinquishing the use of force and attempts at political control of China. He expressed a strong desire to co-operate with Japan in the cultural and economic spheres, his only condition being the return to China of the north-east provinces then under Japanese occupation.[76]

'Enemy or Friend?' was published at a time when there was much talk of a new Sino-Japanese *rapprochement* in both countries. The Japanese Foreign Minister, Hirota Kōki, had expressed the hope that China 'will re-establish stability within the country and, waking up to the actual situation of the Far East, will act in such a way as to meet our expectations. Japan, as a friendly neighbour, will render her the necessary assistance'.[77] Nanjing welcomed the opportunity to improve relations with Tokyo, and asked Wang Chonghui, formerly chairman of the Judicial Yuan, to visit Japan while *en route* to The Hague to resume his duties as a judge of justice of the International Court. At the end of a fortnight's exchange of views with Japanese leaders from various circles, he declared on 4 March: 'I leave the hospitable shores of Japan for The Hague happy in the belief that something has been accomplished to end the unfortunate estrangement which has prevailed between the two countries of the East'.[78]

While the politicians were searching for a *rapprochement*, fighting threatened to renew in eastern Chahar and Hebei. The local disputes were settled by the He-Umezu and the Qin-Doihara Agreements of 10 and 23 June 1935, respectively, which brought another political defeat to the Guomindang. Under the terms of the agreements, the Nationalists were excluded from these two provinces.

In the autumn of 1935 the National Government proposed to Japan through Ambassador Jiang Zuobin certain fundamental measures for the improvement of Sino-Japanese relations. In reply Hirota put forward three conditions:

    1. China must abandon the policy of playing one foreign country off against another;
    2. China must respect the fact of the existence of Manchukuo; and
    3. China and Japan must jointly devise effective measures for preventing the spread of communism in regions in the northern part of China.[79]

Nanjing considered these points too vague to serve as a useful basis for discussion and requested Japan to state the actual terms. No immediate response was received, but the Chinese were given to understand that Hirota's three principles were to be upheld.

It was futile to talk about *rapprochement* unless on Japanese terms quite unacceptable to the Chinese. Tokyo had no wish to change its policy towards Manchuria, while Nanjing, though anxious for peace, could not legalise the loss of the north-east provinces by recognising the state of Manchukuo, whose existence was a constant reminder of Japanese imperialism. 'Economic co-operation' and 'co-prosperity' were euphemisms for Japanese exploitation of the China market and cheap Chinese labour. What *rapprochement* meant for Japan was that China should, as Hirota neatly put it, 'act in such a way as to meet our expectations'. The Japanese army, in the meantime, was interested in seeking control of north China through a policy of establishing 'autonomous regions' which Nanjing resisted politically as hard as it could.[80]

Nanjing's policy of appeasement failed to contain the Japanese in north China or to provide itself a breathing space in which to undertake the task of 'unification through reconstruction'.[81] It is possible for the strong to appease the weak as the former can decide how far it wishes to go, but not *vice versa*. As one contemporary Chinese writer aptly commented, the appeasement of such a powerful and aggressive neighbour as Japan was tantamount to a flat submission to Japanese rule.[82]

Not surprisingly, Nanjing's policy was more and more violently opposed by anti-Japanese elements. On 1 November 1935 an assassination attempt was made on the life of Wang Jingwei, which forced him to resign all official posts in the following month to seek medical treatment overseas.[83] Zhang Qun from Chiang Kai-shek's inner circle was appointed Foreign Minister, but no policy change followed. On 19 November Chiang told the Fifth National Congress of the Guomindang: 'We shall not forsake peace until there is absolutely no hope for peace. We shall not talk lightly of sacrifice until we are driven to the last extremity which makes sacrifice inevitable'.[84] He added, however, that there were limits to China's patience and tolerance.

But what constituted 'the last extremity' and 'the lowest limit' of Chinese patience? Chiang did not elucidate on this until eight months later when, on 13 July 1936, he said at the Second Plenum of the Fifth Central Executive Committee that the lowest limit of Chinese diplomacy was the maintenance of territorial integrity. He declared that his government could not tolerate any further infringement upon China's territorial integrity or sign any agreement to that effect. He said specifically that the 'intolerable moment' would have arrived if China was forced to recognise Manchukuo, and he drew a line which went back to November 1935, the time of the last National Party Congress. Should Chinese territorial integrity again be encroached upon after that date, and should such encroachment fail to be stopped by political and diplomatic means, thus threatening China's very existence, then it would be time to make the 'ultimate sacrifice' of going to war with Japan.[85]

Chiang's statement raised more questions. Was the maintenance of territorial integrity not always a principal object of Nationalist foreign policy? Limits to China's patience and tolerance had been set before, but they were never adhered to. Why should, this time, the line be drawn in November 1935? Chiang did not explain.

Chiang's proclamation of 13 July was nevertheless significant in that it marked a shift in his attitude from the previous November. This shift was politically motivated and must be seen in the context of the revolt of the south-west provinces of Guangdong and Guangxi, which began the month before. Not only was the revolt anti-Chiang, but it had also proclaimed a determination to fight Japan.[86] As the revolt progressed, Chiang found it politically necessary to adopt a firm, if not exactly bellicose, stance towards the Japanese. Consequently, the suppression of the revolt, accomplished for the most part peacefully, caused a change in the national mood and contributed to Chiang's new image as a national leader. In November and December 1936 Chiang responded militarily to the Japanese attempts to establish an 'independent' state in Suiyuan under the Mongolian Prince De. Nationalist forces commanded by Fu Zuoyi routed the troops of Mongolians and Manchurians who were armed and supported by the Japanese Guandong Army, and restored Suiyuan to Chinese control. In the meantime, Nanjing rejected Japan's demands, including recognition of the autonomy of an area consisting of the five provinces of Hebei, Shanxi, Shandong, Chahar and Suiyuan, appointment by China of Japanese advisers, and sharp reduction of tariffs on Japanese imports. The government insisted that Chinese sovereignty should be fully respected and 'economic co-operation' be conducted on the principle of mutual benefit.[87]

Yet, while there was growing support for Chiang as a national leader in spite of the failings of the Guomindang and governmental maladministration, there remained an ambiguity in his attitude towards Japan. He was still convinced that internal pacification of the Communists should be completed before resisting foreign aggression and was indeed preparing for a sixth, and he hoped final, campaign against the Communists who had survived the Long March. This ignored the nationalistic mood of the Chinese people whose support Chiang could have used to unite the country and all the diverse political groups and parties behind his leadership for the cause of national defence. On 9 December patriotic students demonstrated in the streets of Beiping, clamouring for action against Japan; their demands were supported by the Chinese Communist Party, which was broadening its own appeal for an anti-Japanese united front.[88] Chiang responded by suppressing the student movement. It was not until he was kidnapped in Xi'an on 12 December by Zhang Xueliang, who was then in command of the North-west Bandit-Suppression Forces stationed in Shaanxi and Gansu, that Chiang felt compelled to enter into another alliance with the Communists to fight the foreign enemy.[89] The War of Resistance followed the Marco Polo Bridge (Lukouqiao) incident of 7 July 1937.

Conclusion

From the beginning of its rule in Nanjing, the Guomindang, in line with changes in its domestic policy, reappraised its stance on imperialism and took a moderate approach towards the treaty powers. In emphasising national reconstruction, domestic progress and international co-operation, the leadership recognised the need to put China's own house in order and to place her relationships with the foreign powers on good terms. The Guomindang failed not because of its desire to reconstruct China and to cultivate friendly ties with the imperialists but because of its inability to carry out what it pledged to do. Internally, many of the necessary reforms were either not fully implemented or never considered or simply remained on paper. Externally, the basic objects of national freedom, equality and independence were not achieved, in spite of some diplomatic successes in treaty revision. Recognising the realities of China's domestic problems and the military superiority of the powers, the National Government concentrated on the short- and medium-term goals of its foreign policy. Unfortunately, its efforts were marred by certain contradictions. For example, after proclaiming moderation towards treaty revision, Nanjing undermined its own position and alienated foreign sympathy by embarking on the anti-Soviet Manchurian adventure. In the case of extraterritoriality negotiations, it allowed domestic difficulties to encourage a stronger stand than it was able to see through. While wishing to avoid antagonising Japan, it boldly and unilaterally denounced the Sino-Japanese Commercial Treaty of 1896 and threatened repudiation of other treaty rights in many party statements without taking heed of Japanese sensitivities.

Incessant civil war, political instability and intra-party strife added to Nanjing's diplomatic difficulties. Unable to present a united front to the powers, the National Government was forced to conduct its foreign policy from a position of weakness, its success being dependent on the individual attitudes and goodwill of the powers with which it dealt. Where negotiations on the basis of reciprocity and mutual respect for sovereignty were possible as, for example, with Britain and the United States (whatever the real British and American motivations), the Chinese had some diplomatic successes. But where force was used, as in the case of the Soviet Union, China was simply asking for trouble. And in the case of Japan, which was determined to maintain its special Manchurian interests, negotiations were impossible unless on Tokyo's terms. Indeed, the Sino-Japanese conflict over Manchuria was basically a conflict between nationalism and imperialism.

Chinese policy towards Japan following the Manchurian crisis underwent several changes, from 'non-resistance and non-negotiation' to 'negotiations on the one hand and resistance on the other', and then from 'appeasement' and 'co-operation' to 'not forsaking peace until there is absolutely no hope for peace and not talking lightly of sacrifice until we are driven to the last extremity'. At all times the party leadership used slogans such as 'unity through reconstruction', 'obey the party', 'internal pacification before resistance' and so on. All these slogans and policy changes were open to criticism either for their contradictions or for their hollowness and irrelevance. None was convincing to the Chinese public as a practical foreign policy; all failed to produce their desired effect of gaining popular support. By failing remarkably to champion the cause of national defence and to mobilise mass support for it as the Chinese Communist Party did, Nanjing's foreign policy aggravated the division of the country instead of fostering national unity. By failing to come to grips with Japanese imperialism, the leadership of Chiang Kai-shek gave legitimate cause for doubting its seriousness about the maintenance of China's territorial integrity.

In the final analysis, the Nanjing decade was far from the 'golden decade' that some writers have depicted. Just as changes in the economic and educational spheres fell far short of set goals as the previous two chapters have shown, so did efforts to promote China's national interests in the area of foreign relations.

NOTES

The author wishes to thank Professor Wang Gungwu, David Pong and Tim Wright for their many helpful comments on an earlier draft of this chapter. The errors and shortcomings that remain are, of course, his sole responsibility.

1. O. Edmund Clubb, *Twentieth Century China* (New York, 1964), p. 158.
2. See the manifesto of the plenum in *Geming wenxian* [Revolutionary documents], Vol. 69, ed. Xiao Jizhong (Taibei, 1976), pp. 189-190.
3. Zhongyang mishuchu, ed., *Zhongguo Guomindang dierjie zhongyang zhixing weiyuan diwuci quanti huiyi jilu* [Proceedings of the Fifth Plenum of the Second Central Executive Committee of the Guomindang] (Nanjing, 1928), pp. 34, 83-85.
4. *Ibid.*, pp. 221-223.
5. Great Britain, Foreign Office Archives (hereafter cited as F.O.) 371/13173 F5824/7/10 Lampson to Lord Cushendun, 10 September 1928.
6. See, for example, the manifesto of the Fourth Plenum of the Second Central Executive Committee of February 1928, in *Geming wenxian*, LXIX, 189-190; the foreign affairs report adopted by the Third National Party Congress of March 1929, in Zhongguo Guomindang zhongyang zhixing weiyuanhui xuanquan weiyuanhui, ed., *Zhongguo Guomindang di yiersansi ci quanguo daibiao dahui huikan* [A collection of records of the first, second, third and fourth national party congresses of the Guomindang] (Nanjing, 1934), pp. 146-148. For Sun's views of *wangdao* and *badao* and of China's future role in world, see his first and sixth lectures on nationalism delivered on 27 January and March 1924, in Zhongguo Guomindang zhongyang weiyuanhui dangshi weiyuanhui, ed., *Guofu quanji* [The complete works of the national father] (Taibei, 1973), I, 2-4, 71-72.
7. Zhou Gengsheng, *Geming di waijiao* [Revolutionary diplomacy] (Shanghai, 1929). See also some of the articles in *Geming pinglun* [The revolutionary critic], a short-lived weekly journal edited by Chen Gongbo, a leftist, in 1928.
8. T'ang Leang-li, *The Inner History of the Chinese Revolution* (London, 1930), p. 332.
9. Shen Yunlong, comp., *Huang Yingbai xiansheng nianpu changbian* [A chronology of the life of Huang Yingbai] (Taibei, 1976), I, 322-323.
10. A member of the Far Eastern Department in the British Foreign Office remarked: 'So far as tones and professions go, Huang Fu's declaration of policy is a hopeful development. In itself perhaps it means little; compared with the diatribes, to which we were accustomed a year ago, from Ch'en Yu-jen [Eugene Chen, Chen Youren], it is an indication of the *great change* that has taken place in the *KMT* [Guomindang]'. (original italics) F.O. 371/13165 F929/7/10 minute by Toller.
11. Waijiaobu, *Guomin zhengfu jinsannianlai waijiao jingguo jiyao* [A brief account of the diplomacy of the National Government during the last three years] (Nanjing, 1929), pp. 37-39.
12. Under this doctrine, treaties are made with implied conditions that when the circumstances in which they were made have so radically altered that they become incompatible with the independence, welfare and development of a contracting party state, that party state may request the other contracting state or states for revision or termination; and if the request is denied, the former may declare the treaty null and void. For contemporary Chinese writings on this, see R.T. Huang 'Termination and Revision of China's Unequal Treaties', *China Weekly Review*, 10 October 1928, pp. 22-24; Wang Chonghui, 'The National Government from a Legal, Diplomatic and Reconstruction Standpoint', *China Weekly Review*, 9 February 1929, pp. 462-463; Zhu Shiquan, 'Duiyu guomin zhengfu chenglihou waijiaoshang jingguo zhi ganxiang ji weilai zhi xiwang', [Reflections on the diplomacy of the National Government since its founding and hopes for the future], *Zhongwei pinglun* [The international critic], 25 (10 August 1929) 15-20.
13. Jiang Zhongtong yanlun huibian weiyuanhui, ed., *Jiang Zhongtong yanlun huiban* [The collected speeches and writings of President Chiang Kai-shek]

(Taibei, 1956), IX, 109-110. Hereafter cited as Chiang Kai-shek.
14. F.O. 371/13173 F5911/7/10 Lampson's telegram to Foreign Office, 30 October 1928.
15. *The Times* (London), 12 January 1929.
16. For the Special Beijing Tariff Conference, see Stanley F. Wright, *China's Struggle for Tariff Autonomy, 1843-1938* (Shanghai, 1938), ch. 6.
17. For Sino-American tariff negotiations, see Dorothy Borg, *American Policy and the Chinese Revolution*, second revised edition (Stanford, 1961), pp. 401-404. For a summary of Sino-British negotiations, see F.O. 371/13893 F1056/11/10 Lampson to Chamberlain, 4 January 1929.
18. For Sino-Japanese negotiations, see Akira Iriye, *After Imperialism: The Search for a New Order in the Far East 1921-1931* (Cambridge, Mass., 1965), pp. 241-242, 246-248, 262-263, 271-272.
19. For a brief biographical account of Wang, see Howard L. Boorman, ed., *Biographical Dictionary of Republican China* (New York, 1970), III, 362-364. See also Wang's unpublished memoirs, 'Looking Back and Looking Forward', in the custody of Columbia University as part of the oral Chinese history project.
20. Wang Zhengting, 'Looking Back and Looking Forward', ch. 14, pp. 5-6.
21. See Edmund S.K. Fung, 'The Sino-British Rapprochement, 1927-1931', *Modern Asian Studies*, XVII:1 (February 1983), 79-105.
22. *Documents on British Foreign Policy, 1919-1939 Second Series*, Vol. VIII, ed. Rohan Butler (London, 1960), pp. 252-53, Docs. 182-183.
23. *Ibid.*, p. 257, Doc. 188.
24. *Ibid.*, pp. 570-571, Doc. 460.
25. *Ibid.*, p. 514, Doc. 417.
26. The house detention of Hu Hanmin, a prominent right-wing opponent of Chiang Kai-shek's, on 28 February 1931 precipitated a rebellion of the Cantonese who subsequently set up an opposition government in Guangzhou. The separatist movement represented a conglomeration of elements from the left, the right and the southern militarists. In early autumn it took a more aggressive turn, preparing for a military expedition against Nanjing.
27. F.O. 371/16234 F4981/4981/10 Annual report on China for 1931, pp. 24-26.
28. See, for example, Chen Gongbo, 'Zailun disandang', [On the third party again] *Geming pinglun*, 8 (1928), 1-2.
29. See Zhongyang xuanquanbu, comp., *Zhongdonglu wenti zhongyao lunwen huikan*, [A compendium of important articles on the Chinese Eastern Railway question] (Nanjing, 1930). Wang's statements are on pp. 26-27, 66-68.
30. For Hu's articles on the dispute, see *ibid.*, pp. 6-16, 40-50; for Chiang's, see *ibid.*, pp. 1-3, 51-58.
31. Clubb, *Twentieth Century China*, p. 161; also O. Edmund Clubb, *China and Russia: The Great Game* (New York, 1971), pp. 254-265; Iriye, p. 264.
32. US Department of State, *Foreign Relations of the United States*, 1929 (Washington, 1943), II, 222-223.
33. *Documents on British Foreign Policy, 1919-1939 Second Series*, Vol. VIII, p. 180, Doc. 110.
34. Iriye, pp. 267-268.
35. These criticisms led to Foreign Minister Huang Fu's resignation in May. Earlier he had been criticised for being too 'weak' towards the Americans in settling the Nanjing incident of 24 March 1927.
36 Wang Yunsheng, 'Zhongguo Guomindang waijiao zhi huigu', [A review of the Guomindang's foreign policy] *Guowen zhoubao* [National news weekly], IX:1 (1 January 1932), 6-7; Shigemitsu Mamoru, *Japan and Her Destiny* (New

York, 1958), pp. 58-59.

37. William F. Morton, *Tanaka Giichi and Japan's China Policy* (New York, 1980), p. 141.

38. On Zhang Zuolin and the Japanese connection, see Gavan McCormack, *Chang Tso-lin in Northeast China, 1911-1928: China, Japan and the Manchurian Idea* (Stanford, 1977), pp. 222-249.

39. Chang Kia-Ngau, *China's Struggle for Railway Development* (New York, 1943), p. 84.

40. *Foreign Relations of the United States*, 1929, II, 303-308; Morton, p. 165.

41. *Geming wenxian*, LXIX, 227-230.

42. See, for example, Jiang Tingfu, 'Jiuyiba di zeren wenti', [The question of responsibility for the 18 September incident] *Duli pinglun* [The independent critic], 18 (18 September 1932), 13-17; by the same author, 'Jiuyiba—liangnian yihou', [18 September—two years later] *Duli pinglun*, 68 (17 September 1933), 2-5; Hu Shi, 'Quanguo zhenjing yihou', [After the national shock] *Duli pinglun*, 41 (12 March 1933), 2-8.

43. Liang Jingchun, *Jiuyiba shibian shishu* [A historical account of the 18 September incident] revised edition (Taibei, 1968), p. 107.

44. Correspondent, 'Liaoji beizhan jishi', [A factual account of the occupation of Liaoning and Jilin] *Guowen zhoubao*, IIX:38 (28 September 1931), 11-13; *Geming wenxian*, LXIX, 248-250.

45. Chiang Kai-shek, X, 32-36, 37-45, 46-47.

46. Yan Huiqing, *Yan Huiqing zizhuan* [The autobiography of Yan Huiqing] (Taibei, 1973), pp. 164-65; Jiang Zuobin, *Jiang Zuobin huiyi lu* [The memoirs of Jiang Zuobin] (Taibei, 1967), pp. 17-19.

47. Chen Tianxi, ed., *Dai Jitao xiansheng wencun* [The collected works of Dai Jitao] (Taibei, 1959), I, 373-375.

48. Li Yunhan, *Song Zheyuan yu qiqi kangzhan* [Song Zheyuan and the war of resistance] (Taibei, 1973), p. 22.

49. Liang Jingchun, pp. 112-113; Jiang Zuobin, pp. 53-54; Jiang Yongjing, *Minguo Hu Zhantang xiansheng Hanmin nianpu* [A chronology of life of Hu Hanmin during the republican period] (Taibei, 1981), 511.

50. See, for example, Fu Qixue, *Zhongguo waijiao shi* [A history of Chinese foreign policy] (Taibei, 1972), II, 477. Lin Han-sheng, 'A New Look at Chinese Nationalist Appeasers', in Alvin D. Coox and Hilary Conroy, eds., *China and Japan: Search for Balance Since World War I* (Santa Barbara, 1977), p. 225.

51. Gavan McCormack, 'The Crisis of Japan's Liberal Imperialism: China Policy in the 1920's', unpublished paper delivered to the workshop on 'China in Transformation' held at the Australian National University on 24-25 October 1981.

52. Donald A. Jordan, 'China's Vulnerability to Japanese Imperialism: The Anti-Japanese Boycott of 1931-1932', in F. Gilbert Chan, ed., *China at the Crossroads: Nationalists and Communists, 1927-1949* (Boulder, 1980), pp. 91-123.

53. Qiu Guozhen, *Shijiu lujun xingwang shi* [The rise and fall of the Nineteenth Route Army] (Hong Kong, 1969), pp. 78-90. According to some accounts, it was not the Nineteenth Route Army but the National Government's Fifth Army that bore the brunt of the fighting. Chiang Kai-shek is said to have actually supported resistance to the Japanese, but he posed as an advocate of appeasement in order to avert a full-scale war with Japan. See Lloyd E. Eastman, *The Abortive Revolution: China Under Nationalist Rule, 1927-1937* (Cambridge, Mass., 1974) p. 91.

54. David Steeds, 'The British Approach to China Period, 1926-1933, with Special Reference to the Shanghai Incident of 1932', in Ian Nish, ed., *Some*

Foreign Attitudes to Republican China (London, 1980), pp. 26-51.

55. Jingchi, 'Zhengfu qianluo shiyu baoRi juedou', [The removal of the government to Luoyang determined to fight an oppressive Japan] *Guowen zhoubao*, IX:7 (22 February 1932), 11; Shen Yunlong, comp., II, 480.

56. For foreign diplomacy towards China and the Far Eastern crisis, see Dorothy Borg, *The United States and the Far Eastern Crisis of 1933-1938* (Cambridge, Mass., 1964); Henry L. Stimson, *The Far Eastern Crisis* (London, 1936); C. Thorne, *The Limits of Foreign Policy: The West, the League and the Far Eastern Crisis of 1931-33* (London, 1972); S.L. Endicott, *Diplomacy and Enterprise: British China Policy 1933-1937* (Manchester, 1975); and Ann Trotter, *Britain and East Asia 1933-1937* (Cambridge, 1975).

57. Clubb, *China and Russia*, p. 271.

58. Werner Levi, *Modern China's Foreign Policy* (Minneapolis, 1953), p. 200.

59. For Song's resistance, see Li Yunhan, pp. 27-30.

60. Chiang Kai-shek, X, 172-185.

61. Wang Ching-wei [Wang Jingwei], *China's Problems and Their Solution*, ed., T'ang Leang-li (Shanghai, 1934), pp. 120-121; Shen Yunlong, comp., II, 599.

62. Wang Ching-wei, p. 104.

63. Hu Shi, 'Baoquan huabei di zhongyao', [The importance of safeguarding north China] *Duli pinglun*, 52-53 (4 June 1933), 2-6.

64. James E. Sheridan, *Chinese Warlord: The Career of Feng Yu-hsiang* (Stanford, 1966), pp. 270-273; Li Yunhan, pp. 31-42.

65. For details of the Fujian Rebellion, see Eastman, ch. 3.

66. See, for example, Junheng, 'Zhongyang waijiao fangzhen ruhe zhuanbian?' [How should the central government change the direction of its diplomacy?] *Duli pinglun*, 66 (3 September 1933), 2-4.

67. Hu Shi, 'Shiji xinxing shili di Zhongguo waijiao fangzhen', [Chinese foreign policy direction in the new world situation] *Duli pinglun*, 78 (26 November 1933), 2-5.

68. Borg, *The United States*, pp. 60-65, 69.

69. F.F. Liu, *A Military History of Modern China, 1924-1949* (Princeton, 1956), ch. 10; US Department of State, *Foreign Relations of the United States, 1934* (Washington, 1950), III, 288.

70. US Department of State, *Foreign Relations of the United States, 1933* (Washington, 1949), III, 455; *Foreign Relations of the United States, 1934*, III, 288.

71. *Foreign Relations of the United States, 1933*, III, 285, 300; *Foreign Relations of the United States, 1934*, III, 315; Claire Lee Chennault, *Way of a Fighter* (New York, 1949), p. 36.

72. H.G.W. Woodhead, ed., *The China Year Book, 1934*, Kraus reprint (Nendeln, 1969), pp. 725-726.

73. Wang Ching-wei, pp. 120-121.

74. *The China Year Book*, 1934, p. 726.

75. H.G.W. Woodhead, ed., *The China Year Book, 1935*, Kraus reprint (Nendeln, 1969), p. 129-131.

76. For the full text of the article, see Chiang Kai-shek, IV, 146-178.

77. Hirota's speech in the Japanese Diet on 23 January 1935. See *The China Year Book, 1935*, p. 135.

78. *Ibid.*, pp. 135-136.

79. H.G.W. Woodhead, ed., *The China Year Book, 1936*, Kraus reprint (Nendeln, 1969), p. 176.

80. For the Japanese efforts, see Winston Kahn, 'Doihara Kenji and the North China Autonomy Movement', in Coox and Conroy, eds., pp. 177-207. For

Chinese resistance to the movement, see Li Yunhan, pp. 92-116.

81. I take an oppostie view to Lin Han-sheng's in Coox and Conroy, eds., p. 236.

82. Zhang Xiruo, 'Tanggu xieding yilai di waijiao', [Chinese diplomacy since the Tanggu truce] *Duli pinglun*, 144 (31 March 1935), 5.

83. Howard L. Boorman, 'Wang Ching-wei: A Political Profile', in Chun-tu Hsueh, ed., *Revolutionary Leaders of Modern China* (New York, 1971), p. 308.

84. Chiang Kai-shek, XII, 275.

85. *Ibid.*, p. 378.

86. For the south-west revolt which lasted from June to mid-September, see Eastman, pp. 251-262.

87. *Ibid.*, pp. 262-265.

88. For the student demonstrations, see John Israel and Donald W. Klein, *Rebels and Bureaucrats: China's December 9ers* (Berkeley, 1976).

89. For the Xi'an incident, see Tien-wei Wu, *The Sian Incident: A Pivotal Point in Modern History* (Ann Arbor, 1976).

PART 3

SOCIO-POLITICAL GROUPS AND COMPETITION FOR POWER

8

THE DIPLOMACY OF CHINESE NATIONALISM, 1900-1911
Louis T. Sigel

A major transformation occurred in the nature of Chinese foreign policy after 1900; from the turn of the century, Chinese diplomats assumed an openly nationalistic stance and demonstrated a new determination to strengthen China and safeguard its sovereign rights. Altered diplomatic objectives and modes of dealing with Chinese external relations comprised this momentous shift. This change, however, came as a result of the heightened urgency of foreign affairs for the central government. The critical state of Chinese security forced the imperial authorities to rely on the diplomatic skills that personnel recruited from the modern, treaty port commercial community could provide; for the first time, Chinese from this community attained positions of authority in significant numbers and gained extensive responsibility over diplomatic negotiations. Nevertheless, like the more passive 'mainstream approach' of the nineteenth-century reformers that it replaced, this actively nationalistic and anti-imperialistic approach, which became the dominant feature of Chinese foreign policy after 1900, was also a reflection of the fundamental changes in international politics and rivalry of this era.

The 'Mainstream Approach', 1860s-1890s

The main characteristic of foreign affairs management from 1860 until the late 1890s was the reliance on the treaty system as a bulwark of Chinese territorial integrity and administrative autonomy. This basically flexible and pragmatic strategy pursued by the high imperial functionaries charged with the conduct of

China's international relations, the modernising regional self-strengtheners and the reformist metropolitan statesmen, was moderately successful in defending China's interests up to 1895. This approach was embodied in the views advanced by Li Hongzhang, Zeng Guofan, Prince Gong and the majority of the Zongli Yamen, China's proto-foreign office; they advocated rigid compliance with treaty stipulations. Their aim was to avoid incidents, which the foreign powers might use as a pretext for demanding further concessions, and to control the foreigners by peaceful manipulation and limit their activities to only those stipulated in the treaties. By adopting this strategy, the reformers hoped they could gain a breathing space for China to build up her defences. But by acquiescing in and supporting the treaties to deprive the foreigh powers of valid grounds for greater encroachments, the advocates of the 'mainstream approach' had in effect conceded a role to the foreigners in China's administrative and legal affairs as embodied in the unequal treaties.

Despite a certain amount of openness towards the West in line with their generally instrumental and pragmatic mode of thought, this outlook did not involve any significant reorientation as far as central values and central world view were concerned. So, although this period witnessed an increasing interest and support for Western knowledge, in the eyes of the reformers, foreigners remained barbarians that had to be kept under Chinese control. And despite the recognition that Western military and scientific technology were superior, and therefore desirable, the foreigner did not represent any threat to their basic sense of Chinese cultural superiority. This Sinocentric aspect of their thinking was later a significant transformative element in the development of gentry and secret society nationalism.

The scope of self-strengthening expanded during the 1870s and 1880s with the launching of government and of government-sponsored *(guandu shangban)*, literally, official supervision and merchant management) projects in steamships, mining, telegraphs, cotton textile production and railways, but the basic rationale remained the military-orientated struggle for dominance over the intruders. As Li Hongzhang wrote in 1872 in defending steamship development to the Throne:

> The method of self-strengthening lies in learning what they

can do, and in taking over what they rely upon ... If we can really and thoroughly understand their methods—and the more we learn, the more improve—and promote them further and further, can we not expect that after a century or so we can reject the barbarians and stand on our own feet?[1]

In his effort at 'enriching the nation and strengthening the army' (*fuguo qiangbing*), Li reasoned that commerce and industry could provide the tax base for funding the means of China's self-protection. By the development of coal and iron mines, for example:

> A source of profit will naturally be opened. Taking the surplus funds from the new source we can even use it to maintain our ships and train our soldiers.[2]

In his mind, spending on all other activities of the state could be economised but China should never try to save funds on defence measures. Basically, without military preparation, 'the nation will never have anything to stand upon, and we shall never be strong'.[3]

The Approach of the Treaty Port Commercial Community Before 1900

The relative success of the 'mainstream approach' up to 1895 was dependent in part on Britain's international economic supremacy. As the mightiest industrial and mercantile power in the world, Britain utilised its diplomatic and military prowess to establish a world economy providing for maximum liberty for trade and investment. The forced opening of China and imposition of the unequal treaties upon it between 1842 and 1860 were one aspect of Britain's 'imperialism of free trade'. Although this treaty system was imposed upon China through military force and was maintained by the use of gunboat diplomacy, the foreign powers, with the significant exception of Czarist Russia, made negligible territorial acquisitions. There was only limited intervention in China until very late in the nineteenth century because the aim of the dominant British interests was to trade with and not to govern China; the goal of military and diplomatic policy in China was the removal of impediments to expanded trade by establishing treaty ports, gaining extraterritoriality, maintaining 'most-favoured-nation' status, and keeping tariffs and duties at minimal and insignificant levels.

In response to this international environment, and in contradistinction to the kind of defensive, tradition-orientated and inward-looking world view which prevailed among the higher officialdom, the merchants and intellectuals in China's treaty ports began to develop a profoundly altered outlook and attitude towards the West. This modern commercial community which emerged in these foreign enclaves along the coast and on the Yangzi was composed primarily of businessmen involved in foreign trade. As compradors, translators, agents and private merchants, their ability in gaining expertise in Western techniques and foreign languages determined their mercantile fortunes. Tang Tingshu, Xu Run and Zheng Guanying were the most prominent of the entrepreneurs, advisers and intellectuals with prior comprador experience which enabled them to be among the first to formulate a different sort of perception regarding the character of the threat posed by the foreign powers.

Another source of the modern commercial community was the treaty-port Christian community and those who came into more direct contact with Western thought and institutions through the agencies of the missionary movement. The outstanding nationalistic individuals from this group include Ma Jianzhong and his elder brother, Ma Liang, as well as figures like Wang Tao and He Qi. The Ma family was an old scholarly family of Jiangsu which had converted to Catholicism in the late Ming period through the efforts of the Jesuit pioneer Matteo Ricci. Both of the Ma brothers studied in Jesuit schools in Shanghai and served as foreign affairs experts in the late Qing. Wang Tao and He Qi, on the other hand, came to Christianity and Western learning through involvement with the London Missionary Society in the mid-nineteenth century and were primarily active as advocates of Chinese reform and writers of reform essays, propagating their programmes in the earliest Chinese-language newspapers which they played a major role in launching.[4]

Gradually during the later nineteenth century as the foreign trade based in the treaty ports flourished and as Western studies became more respectable and accepted, the modern commercial community was enhanced by the acculturation of the leading gentry families in the areas closely linked economically and socially with the treaty ports. The Xue family of the Jiangsu silk filature centre of Wuxi near Shanghai is the most outstanding example of this latter group. Xue Fucheng, one of the leading reform writers of the self-strengthening movement, served in the administrative network of Zeng Guofan and Li Hongzhang and was one of the earliest Chinese diplomats to Europe. His son, Xue Nanming, was active as a founder of the modern silk-raising and weaving industry in Wuxi and was one of the leaders of the Wuxi business faction in Shanghai. The grandson, Xue Shouxuan, studied in America and was the major silk producer in Wuxi in the early twentieth century.[5]

Similar in social background to this latter group and with personal ties with the modern commercial community as a whole were the bureaucratic industrialists and offical capitalist administrators. This group, however, was separate and distinct from the modern commercial community in its perception and understanding of the West and in its goals for China. In ability, performance and outlook, these mandarin promoters were closer to the self-strengtheners under whose authority they operated.The dominating and most infamous figure from this group in the late Qing period was Sheng Xuanhuai, who exerted influential control over steamships, telegraphs, mining, banking and railway affairs. The proposals and activities of these official managers differed in many respects from those of individuals from the modern commercial community who identified the bureaucratism of these men as one of the evils inhibiting China's economic competition with the West.

The self-strengthening statesmen and their agents heading official enterprises could agree with men from the modern commercial community on the goal of creating 'a rich country and a strong military', but the two differed considerably on the priorities of the reform programme to achieve this objective. In particular, they held diametrically opposing views regarding the role of commerce and industry in the overall development of China. To the reformist bureaucrats, economic activities were the expedient for generating income which the state could tax to finance military modernisation. In the writings of Ding Richang, one of the most enlightened of the nineteenth-century reformist officials, the emphasis is on 'providing for new sources of wealth and limiting expenditures' (*kaiyuan jieliu*). It is in this context that he advocated economic development. He supported the establishment of spinning and weaving mills, for example, with the argument that the value added would remain within China and accrue to the Chinese rather than being lost to foreigners if China could export silk cloth rather than floss silk. The government could then claim part of the increased profits as tax revenue. Similarly, he sought a government policy of building railways and developing mines, further warning that otherwise the ownership and profits would fall into the hands of foreigners, depriving China of needed sources of wealth. In Ding's programme, moreover, as in Li Hongzhang's and those of other prominent self-strengtheners, industrial enterprises were to be operated by the government itself or under the *guandu shangban* system, an updated version of a traditional Chinese mechanism and consistent with earlier state monopoly practice. This active and dominant role for the state is evident in his plans for the development of Taiwan and the founding of banks.[6]

In contrast, the modern commercial community stressed the dynamic economic function of commerce and industry and the important part played by the merchant and entrepreneur. Although almost all of the leaders of the modern commercial community were associated with the undertakings of Qing self-strengthening, they advocated release from the dependent status this type of economic administration imposed upon them and sought an end to the stultifying influence that the bureaucratic supervision exerted. They saw that commercial and industrial activities were the source of wealth in Western countries, and this made them strong. Attaining wealth for the nation through economic development was seen as an end in itself, not a means. Competing with the foreign powers for markets and profit or waging 'commercial warfare' (*shangzhan*) was given a higher priority than learning military warfare.

Unique to the modern commercial community in China before the 1890s were intellectual currents which challenged the Confucian ideological basis of the imperial social and political order and their willingness to adopt certain aspects of Western civilisation as valid critiques of China and to advocate fundamental changes in the sphere of traditional values while not consciously rejecting Confucianism. Writing in 1879, Xue

Fucheng commented favourably on British practice as an example for China to follow, explaining:

> Formerly when the Lord Shang discussed wealth and power, he regarded ploughing and warfare as fundamental. However, when Westerners plan for wealth and power, they regard industry and commerce as primary with ploughing and warfare being established upon this foundation... the fundamental principle of the Westerners' technique for gaining wealth is that industry be sufficient for opening up trade; moreover, industry is considered the base and commerce the application. Recently in managing their international affairs, the British have fully, wholeheartedly and with all their energies exhaustively planned for industry and commerce. There is a growing improvement in their wealth and power, and they are first among the nations of the world.[7]

China, likewise, must 'definitely struggle in competition with the Westerners' and fulfil the principle of 'promoting that which is profitable for the people' (*weimin xingli*). Only with these kinds of policies adopted could one have hope for China's future: 'If China is prosperous, then all later problems can be successively handled'.[8]

The leaders of the modern commercial community who were politically active in the nineteenth century lacked official rank gained through the civil service examination but had titles by purchase to operate within the traditional society which placed merchants at the bottom of the orthodox social hierarchy. They felt merchants should be given proper recognition for the vital role they played in strengthening and safeguarding the nation. They should be accorded elite status like gentry with access to political authority and protection in pursuit of profit. The developing of wealth by private entrepreneurs should be encouraged, assisted and protected; merchants should not be subjected to the Confucian axioms impugning profit-making nor forced to suffer extortionate demands from officials.

Prior to the 1890s, the reformist thought of the treaty port society with its impetus coming from ideas of progress rather than tradition was relatively isolated from the thinking of the reformist essayists influential in the elite circles in the provinces or in Beijing. Even within the port centres of the coastal provinces there was only a limited flow of ideas; a great cultural gulf existed between reformers from commercial and bureaucratic backgrounds. Wang Tao offered his opinions for political and economic change to Ding Richang, Zeng Guofan and Li Hongzhang in direct and indirect correspondence, and Rong Hong, Tang Tingshu and Zheng Guanying had access to these reformist officials; but this communication from treaty-port intellectuals was private and specific. Tang Tingshu, Xu Run and Zheng Guanying were all men upon whom Li Hongzhang relied in proposing, establishing and running his self-strengthening enterprises; with their purchased degrees, they did not hold posts which entailed formal bureaucratic responsibility. They operated largely as consultants within Li's *mufu* (privately hired specialists) and their effect on policy was limited to the pressure they could exert on him through personal and informal persuasion. The relationship of the treaty port Chinese to the self-strengtheners was described by Tang Tingshu in a comment on his influence on Li Hongzhang as: 'The viceroy leads, but I am the man who pushes'.[9]

By way of contrast, in 1887, Liang Qichao entered the Xuehaitang, the largest academy in Guangzhou, where he spent three years as a faithful and brilliant scholar. Persevering in this bastion of Han learning, Liang had no contact at all with Western learning, which he encountered for the first time in the spring of 1890 during a visit to Shanghai. Similarly, Zhang Zhidong, as provincial commissioner of education in Sichuan, compiled a selected bibliography of basic Chinese works as a guide for learning in 1875; this work, *Shumu dawen*, considered the most important and most widely used bibliography of the late nineteenth century, contains nothing on Western learning.[10]

Only with the considerable intellectual ferment of the decade of the 1890s was there a wider circulation of the thought of the modern commercial community to the more classically orientated reformist gentry. The writings of both Wang Tao and Zheng Guanying were included in the new compilations of statecraft essays; the informed knowledge of the West that they possessed became recognised as legitimate and essential. Treaty-port figures played a prominent role in the development of elite journalism which brought attention to Western learning on a nation-wide scale for the first time, and they contributed to the new gentry institutions generated by the scholarly agitation of the time—schools, academies and study societies.

The Intellectual and Social Links between the Treaty-Port Community and the Post-1900 Leadership

After 1900, the active drive to protect and regain Chinese authority over China displaced the earlier, defensive 'mainstream approach' of merely utilising Western international law to curtail further foreign encroachments beyond the limits of the unequal treaties. The problem of heightened foreign incursions after the Treaty of Shimoneseki of 1895 served to accelerate the rise of a new generation to positions of social, intellectual and political leadership, and this new Chinese elite felt that the very survival of China was threatened by Western and Japanese imperialist aggression. This sense of trial and urgency led to the rejection of the makeshift concepts and the *ad hoc* peripheral institutions grafted onto the Qing imperial state by the conservative reformers earlier. Instead, the new leadership carried out a more thorough-going renovation of the bureaucratic machinery, particularly where the formulation and implementation of Chinese foreign policy were concerned.

Chinese diplomacy after 1900 was in many ways the fulfilment of the earlier desires and efforts of the modern commercial community and was brought into realisation by the second generation of this community specially trained for this purpose. Individuals from the comprador-merchant sector had been working to safeguard and recapture China's national rights since the middle of the nineteenth century. Members of the Sino-Western hybrid society developing in the treaty port commercial centres had the most direct and most extensive contact with the foreign threat to China and were the earliest to understand the nature of the Western impact and to formulate constructive programmes to deal with it. They called for the adoption of Western institutions as a means of achieving national strength and prosperity as well as of asserting their own interests in this new order. This modern Chinese sector sought active government support to overcome the trade advantages enjoyed by their foreign competitors and advocated the elimination of the restrictions of the traditional economy. They realised the potentials of modern industry in a nation's growth and sought government encouragement for their enterprises.

It was the Chinese treaty-port society that first generated a call for far-reaching reforms to regain China's legitimate prerogatives in asserting its national rights politically and economically. They called for the abolition of extraterritoriality and for the return of economic sovereignty through Chinese tariff autonomy and the exclusion of foreign vessels from intranational shipping. Their proposals stressed industrial development, urging government protection for private initiative in railway, mining, banking and textile undertakings. In addition, they protested against the injustices and humiliations suffered by the Chinese at the hands of the foreigners and called for a government strong enough to prevent the Westerners from committing offences forbidden by Western law. The commercial experience of the comprador-merchants led them to appreciate the important economic roles of the state and the significance of a strong government willing and able to support but not dominate or monopolise mercantile activities. The nature of the nationalism adopted by these men was conditioned by their awareness of the dynamic role of trade and industry in Western societies as well as by an appreciation of the higher political and social status enjoyed by merchants, particularly in Great Britain and the United States.[11]

The programme of reforms drawn up by Rong Hong in 1870 at the urging of Ding Richang was one of the early articulations of the views of mercantile nationalism held by the treaty port community. Ding had hoped that the crisis in foreign relations generated by the Tianjin Massacre, in which violent rioting broke out over alleged abuses by Catholic missions, leaving twenty-one Westerners dead, including the French consul, might make his colleagues more receptive to change. These suggestions included the proposal for a Chinese-owned and Chinese-managed steamship company to compete with foreign shipping lines and to dominate Chinese coastal waters. This company would be organised on a joint stock basis and would be supported by government through a franchise to carry tribute rice. Rong Hong also sought to induce the government to utilise the mineral wealth of the country in the hope that this would indirectly pave the way for the introduction of railways for transporting the ore from the interior to the coastal ports. Rong Hong further emphasised the need to restrict missionaries encroaching upon the sovereignty of China and wanted to prohibit them from exercising any jurisdiction over their converts. Most essential to him was the plan to send Chinese youths abroad to be educated for the public service. In the realisation of the various reforms advocated by Rong, the comprador-merchants played a decisive role.[12]

Tang Tingshu, one of the most prominent of the comprador-merchants in the nineteenth century, and his colleagues demonstrated their determination to strengthen China and safeguard China's sovereign rights although this did not emerge as the dominant theme of Chinese foreign policy until after 1900. The early projects for industrial development to which these pioneer comprador-entrepreneurs devoted their wealth were in and of themselves seen as challenges to the threat of foreign domination in shipping, mining, insurance, railways and other enterprises. As Zheng Guanying recounted to Tang Shaoyi: 'I heard that your uncle [Tang Tingshu] said that China was daily losing her economic rights and must necessarily promote industry'.[13] The comprador-industrialists emphasised the need for China to preserve her economic sovereignty and felt that control over China's wealth was of vital concern, particularly in the development of railways and mining. With the founding of the Kaiping Mines and the Tangshan railways, Tang Tingshu set the example by his scrupulous effort to deny any degree of foreign ownership and to minimise foreign participation in management.

The comprador-merchants in the nineteenth century took the initial steps for the recovery of China's national sovereignty in other fields as well and laid important precedents to be followed by their successors. One obvious target of their anti-imperialist attitude was the right of the foreign traders to import opium into China which was guaranteed by the early unequal treaties. Tang Tingshu and other members of the modern Chinese sector participated in the Anglo-Oriental Society for the Suppression of the Opium Trade founded in 1875, and they circulated copies of its publication, *Friend of China*, among their colleagues in the treaty port community. When Tang Tingshu visited England in 1883, he addressed the society and affirmed the importance of its work and the activity it was generating among his fellow Chinese. The treaty-port community showed an interest in rolling back the tide of imperialism on China's frontiers as well. One of the foci of Chinese relations with the foreign powers in the late nineteenth century was the encroachment on Chinese security through political and economic penetration in the traditional Qing frontier buffer states. In the 1880s, pressure on these tributaries within the strategic sphere of the Qing imperial order came from France in Vietnam and from Japan in Korea. Prominent treaty-port personalities participated in both crises and urged the Chinese government to adopt the policies and techniques of the Western nation-states to achieve and institutionalise Chinese colonial control and assert Chinese authority in this modern way in these previously autonomous kingdoms. Tang Tingshu went to Korea in December of 1882, for example, and carried out a mining survey of the interior. He submitted a report advising mining and railway development of Korea but in a way which would amount to Chinese economic domination. In his capacity as managing-director of the China Merchants' Steam Navigation Company, he sought to demand control over the use of the loans the company would extend to Korea for these industrial enterprises, and he would give the money only on the guarantee of the Chinese government.[14]

The increase in strength and influence of the treaty port Chinese was related to the acquisition of foreign learning. The projects to send students abroad to train officials with new Western-orientated skills were part of the self-strengtheners' response to the lack of foreign expertise. The hope was that young Chinese would become fluent in foreign languages and skilled in the conduct of foreign affairs and would solve the manpower problem. Most Chinese, however, did not appreciate the importance of foreign studies, but the comprador-merchants were one of the few groups who saw the value of a Western education in the 1870s and 1880s. They actively supported the various projects for providing Chinese with foreign training, and it was largely the younger generation of this community which received the benefits of these programmes. The movement for the recovery of Chinese sovereignty after 1900 was born out of the power in the hands of this foreign-educated younger generation which emerged as the officials responsible for managing China's diplomatic relations. In the case of the Chinese Educational Mission to the United States in the 1870s, Rong Hong was appointed to administer the scheme after his proposal was accepted while Tang Tingshu and Xu Run had the responsibility for selecting the hundred and twenty students sent and for logistical support. Friends and relatives of Tang and Xu also provided all of the youths who left to study in America under the programme. The alumni of the Chinese Educational Mission who returned to China on its cancellation in the 1880s were among the most prominent of the nationalistic diplomats after 1900.[15]

The New Imperialism

During the late nineteenth century, many of the premises upon which the existing international system was based were seriously eroded. The rapid growth in world trade and remarkable progress towards freer trade under British economic hegemony in the period up to 1880 continuously expanded the size of the world market, but Britain's dominant position was increasingly challenged as European and American manufactured goods displaced British products in the markets of the developed economies. The relatively free flow of goods declined in the face of tariff barriers and other discriminatory measures erected with ever greater frequency and height after 1880. Country after country protected their domestic markets to shield their emerging industries from competition, and the continental European powers rushed to divide up Africa as well as parts of Asia and the Pacific into their formal colonies and 'spheres of influence'. The world economy was gradually splitting into exclusive and competing imperialistic economic systems; with the waning of Britain's 'imperialism of free trade', the threats to Chinese security, in particular, grew dramatically.

The major shift in Chinese foreign policy after 1900 was partly a reflection of the significant decline in the British position in Chinese foreign trade. While remaining one of China's most important trading partners, the British share of both the import and export trade dropped steadily. By the late nineteenth century Britain was no longer predominant in the China market. In terms of direct trade, Great Britain was the destination of more than half of Chinese exports in 1870 (52.5 per cent), but of only about 15 per cent of Chinese exports in 1890 and only about 6 per cent in 1900. As a source of imports into China, the British similarly declined in importance from providing a bit less than half (45.8 per cent) in 1870 to barely more than one-fifth (20.5 per cent) in 1900. Correspondingly, substantial increases in their shares of Chinese foreign trade were registered by the aggressive imperialist powers of Japan, Russia, France and Germany.[16]

Another significant factor contributing to the striking alteration in China's approach to diplomacy which distinguishes the post-1900 era was the radical transformation in China's international economic relations in the late nineteenth century. During the nineteenth century, as China's foreign trade was gradually expanding, the balance of trade was generally in China's favour. This aspect of Chinese external economic intercourse is often overlooked because of the focus on the growth of the illicit opium trade and the outflow of silver from the mid-1820s as China's balance of trade became negative; the severe social and economic repercussions of the resulting monetary deflation as background to the Opium War of 1839-1842 are well known. The attention paid to the trade deficit of the second quarter of the last century, however, has tended to obscure the fact that with the opening of the treaty ports the balance of trade returned to China's favour in the late 1840s. The treaties imposed upon China had the ironic effect of eliminating the trade imbalance as the export of tea and silk expanded rapidly. Silver again began to flow into China from the middle of the nineteenth century despite the growth in opium importation.[17]

From the viewpoint of international payments, China continued to record favourable trade balances with consistency until the late 1880s. Subsequently, from 1888 until the end of the nineteenth century, Chinese foreign trade expanded rapidly with total trade approximately doubling in the last decade of the century. During these years, however, the trade balance fluctuated erratically from year to year but, as a whole, a sizable net trade deficit was registered. The unfavourable trade balance was not excessive, and the value of exports tended to move fairly closely with the value of imports, with both generally on the increase. Up to the turn of the century, then, foreign trade in China continued to be largely characterised by commodity exchange.[18]

From the beginning of the twentieth century, the Qing economy experienced a steady widening of the gap between imports and exports; the total net trade deficit of this last decade of imperial rule amounted to several times that of the earlier years. This huge trade imbalance, moreover, was a reflection of the shift in the nature of China's economic interaction with the rest of the world. No longer were China's links mainly of a commercial or financial character; increasingly these ties took on a political colouration. The massive shortfall between exports and imports in the early twentieth century was financed by the heavy influx of foreign capital as the imperialist powers increasingly attempted to entrench themselves in exclusive spheres of influence within China.

Between 1901 and 1911, China experienced an acceleration and intensification of imperialist pressure in all spheres. Economically, culturally and politically, the foreign powers were posing an ever more concrete and serious threat to Chinese territorial integrity and administrative independence. In terms of treaty ports, for example, twenty-one ports were opened to foreign trade and residence by treaty between 1842 and 1895 compared with twenty-eight between 1896 and 1911. Of these later-opened ports, seven were opened by treaty in 1896 and 1897 while the remaining ones were all opened between 1902 and 1907.[19] Likewise, foreign shippers increased their already dominant share of steamship tonnage in Chinese waters, and foreign investors came to own or control almost all of China's railways.

The rapid growth in Christian mission efforts is also indicative of the much greater encroachment on China in the decade prior to the fall of the Qing monarchy. The Roman Catholic church in China nearly doubled in size from 720,540 baptised Catholics in 1901 to 1,421,258 in 1912; this increase compares with that of only around 40 per cent between 1890 and 1901. The much smaller Protestant churches in China grew even more rapidly, more than doubling their size in the six years between 1900, when there were 85,000 Chinese converts, and 1906, when there were 178,251. The number of Protestant missionaries rose substantially from 1,296 in 1889 to 3,445 in 1905 and to 5,144 in 1910. The network of Protestant missions, too, expanded considerably in this period. More mission stations (274) opened in the period 1901-1910 than had opened in the eighty-three years before 1891 (270), rivalling the number that had opened in the 1891-1900 decade (225). In 1902, Kaifeng in Henan became the last provincial capital to admit Protestant missionaries, and by 1903, with one exception, every prefectural city in China was either 'occupied' or about to be 'occupied' by missionaries.[20]

The New Generation of Foreign Affairs Officials and the Diplomacy of Nationalism

It was under circumstances such as these that a far more effective protection of Chinese sovereignty than was possible under the 'mainstream approach' became necessary. This post-Boxer situation provided for the rise of Yuan Shikai to preeminent status as key adviser to the central government in foreign affairs, military development and institutional innovation. Backed by the power and prestige of the Beiyang establishment and enjoying the factional support of Prince Qing as well as the trust of Empress Dowager Cixi, Yuan was able to assume and maintain his leading position in domestic reform. But his political success was also based upon his effectiveness in dealing with the problems that arose and his ability to handle the responsibilities assigned to him. Yuan and other leading officials of this period were sensitive to the inroads of the foreign advances and the dangers to China posed by the rising onslaught of imperialism. The administrative success of government reformers like Yuan Shikai was significantly dependent upon their ability to recruit into their bureaucratic networks men who possessed the technical expertise in diplomacy and modern industry which an effective anti-imperialistic policy demanded. Besides, Yuan needed these Chinese experts to insulate his domestic political concerns from the impact of foreign intervention. This meant that, to a large extent, Yuan had to look to the modern commercial community where this talent was concentrated.

The growing pressure of foreign imperialism at the turn of the century required a more vigorous response from the Chinese government which in turn led to a greater reliance on men capable of coping with foreigners. The new generation assuming leadership after 1900 had a number of men with more formal and extensive Western education, many of whom, including those who had studied abroad, had come from families with a treaty port background. They were able to gain admittance into political life in substantive bureaucratic posts rather than the peripheral, advisory roles to which their predecessors had been relegated. Rising to meet the challenge of imperialist encroachment, they defended the increasingly imperiled frontiers and developed a Chinese resistance to the mounting foreign demands for concessions in mining, railways, loans and telegraphs. This critical international situation had brought the modern commercial community to political prominence and enabled individuals from this group, now vested with decision-making authority, to implement policies the community had long been advocating. In no small degree, they contributed to the new nationalistic approach to international affairs.

It calls for little surprise, then, that their rise to positions of influence was warmly greeted by the earlier generation of treaty-port based reformers. As Zheng Guanying congratulated Tang Shaoyi—the Chinese Education Mission-educateed younger clansman of Tang Tingshu—who had just been appointed a provincial governor in the North-east:

> The Court knows the value of men and thus it appoints a 100 per cent supporter of the 'wealth and power' group to carry out reforms. In the past, they avoided formulating policies that smacked of opening the sources of wealth and nourishing and feeding the people; but now they regard the development of fallow land, mining production and pastoralism as most urgent and foremost. Now in building 'wealth and power', it is necessary to care for the people first. The people are the basis of the state, but wealth and the national life are what support them. My book *Shengshi weiyan* had already discussed this in detail.[21]

These men, characterised by the foreign press as Young China, were from a social stratum that had largely detached itself from its native roots. In spite of this, they were able to acquire a significant place in government and play a crucial role in the post-1900 reforms because they were both prepared and equipped to adopt Western diplomatic practices and deal with foreign powers on those grounds. They sought for China the same rights, privileges and prerogatives that were accorded to sovereign states by Western theories of international law. It was in large part their efforts that made the late Qing monarchy a viable mechanism for checking the foreign threat and preventing the feared 'carving up of the Chinese melon'. Diplomatically and politically they fought to protect China's borderlands and actively forced a weakening in the foreign hold over China's development.

Among the major problems faced by the nationalistic Chinese diplomats of the early twentieth century were the privileges China was forced to yield to the foreign powers in the 'scramble for concessions' of the late 1890s. After 1900, Chinese negotiators and administrators attempted to obstruct and offset the foreigners' effort at consolidating control over their spheres of influence. In re-examining the noteworthy Chinese success in containing German imperialism in Shandong, for example, one should bear in mind that the provincial governors whose names were attached to the memorials containing the proposals for handling the Germans were usually not the authors of these policies; Yuan Shikai, Zhou Fu and Yang Shixiang were dependent upon officials with foreign skills to formulate concrete plans for defending Chinese sovereignty in such matters as railway and mining development, international trade and missionary activities. As Yuan emphasised in his initial memorial concerning Shandong, it was important to select officials who 'fully understand the terms of the treaties and are knowledgeable about current affairs.[22] In addition to personnel, new provincial institutions were introduced to check the Germans and to encourage Chinese competition with the foreigners. The administrative bodies responsible for implementing the policy of blocking German aggression and for handling the negotiations that succeeded in limiting the German advance were the Negotiation Bureau (1900), the General Bureau of Foreign Affairs (1901), the Bureau of Commerce (1901), the Bureau of Railways and Mines (1902), and the Bureau of Mine Supervision (1906).[23]

The officials who staffed these agencies were by and large men with a personal knowledge of the West and frequently from the treaty-port society. It was largely to the efforts of these individuals that the success in Shandong was due. For example, when Yuan Shikai arrived in Ji'nan as the province's governor, he found the diplomatic matters of the province so unwieldy that he had to memorialise for the transfer of Tang Shaoyi, the foremost Young China official, to assist him. Yuan appointed Tang director of the foreign affairs bureau and later reported to the throne:

> He is very knowledgeable about foreign affairs. After he came to Shandong, he was assigned to handle a variety of

foreign and commercial matters. In all these situations he was extremely competent.[24]

In late 1901 when Yuan Shikai was promoted to Governor-general of Zhili and Tang Shaoyi joined his staff as Tianjin Customs Daotai, Tang's cousin, Tang Ronghao, succeeded to the Shandong post.[25]

By the beginning of 1898, two years before Yuan became governor, the Germans had already acquired their desired colony at Jiaozhou with the great port of Qingdao and had also extracted important economic and political advantages for expanding from their base to dominate all Shandong. But thanks to the skills and services of the Western-trained officials, Yuan and his successors were able to assert China's interests and nullify most German advantages.

The Chinese aggressive counter measures in Shandong forced the German government to reassess its goals, inducing it to curtail expansion in the interest of its broader concerns in China and elsewhere. The concerted Chinese campaign forced the Germans to renounce military interference in the interior, curtailed their railway construction, abolished the thirty-*li* zone for mining along the railroad routes, eliminated their rights of priority in the province, and destroyed the tariff autonomy of the German leasehold. Although the Chinese drive failed to attain all of its goal of effacing German power in Shandong, it did succeed in cancelling German political influence on the province and in seriously infringing upon the independence of the German concession itself.[26]

In the final decade of Qing rule, Chinese officials from the modern commercial community with expertise in foreign techniques were active within the metropolitan and provincial governments pressing for Chinese control over foreign activities in China. Tang Shaoyi and his fellow returned-students were the most outstanding of what foreign observers called the 'sovereign rights' party, and *The Times* correspondent, George Morrison, noted that this Young China group was directing its abilities towards the advancement of 'China for the Chinese'. It was Tang, however, 'who perhaps more than any other stands for Chinese reform'. As Morrison further noted, Tang was particularly dogmatic in his assumption of China's sovereign rights and of its complete ability to control its own destinies.

Characteristic of this attitude, according to Morrison, was Tang's retort to the Russian minister to China, Pokotilov, during the early stages of negotiations in 1906 concerning Russian rights in the North-east after the Russo-Japanese War:

> No government that calls itself a government can submit to dictation in such matters [as the right of bondholders to control foreign concessions]. We do not repudiate, we acknowledge the agreements but will carry them out in our own way.[27]

Tang Shaoyi's efforts to contain the imperialist threat covered a broad spectrum of issues. He was largely responsible for the negotiations in most points of contention which arose between China and the foreign powers during the last decade of Qing rule. He firmly and consistently opposed the extension of foreign influence and succeeded in eliminating the worst aspects of foreign domination in many areas. Regarding the control of railway and mining development, for example, he could exploit the public agitation and provincial gentry protests, using them as a leverage in bargaining with the representatives of the foreign concession holders. In countering such other significant aspects of intrusion as control over the customs service and the foreign right to import opium into China, the initiative was taken by the foreign-trained Young China diplomats with public support generally emanating from the modern treaty-port communities.

One of the early successes of the nationalistic foreign policy of the late Qing was in regaining diplomatic recognition of Chinese suzerainty over Tibet. When the British military invasion of Tibet from India, the Younghusband Expedition of 1904, resulted in the Lhasa Convention between Tibet and British India on terms which amounted to a British protectorate over Tibet, the Young China nationalists pressed for action to protect the endangered frontiers of the Qing Empire. It was largely due to the energetic pressure of the junior Vice-president of the Waiwubu, Wu Tingfang, a member of the modern commercial community with Overseas Chinese background and British legal credentials, that China mounted a forceful diplomatic offensive against the British. Wu was also instrumental in having Tang Shaoyi selected as envoy to Calcutta to negotiate a settlement. Tang's strong opposition to the forward policy of Lord Curzon, the Viceroy of India, helped to create the opportunity for the assertion of Chinese influence in Tibet as embodied in the Beijing Adhesion Convention of 1906. Tang then assigned his subordinate, Zhang Yintang, to investigate and reform the situation in Tibet with an eye to increasing Chinese authority.[28]

Tang Shaoyi also took an active part in the effort to end the foreign right to import opium, which was one of the most glaring examples of the loss of Chinese jurisdiction within China. He realised that the question required careful and deliberate moves by Chinese foreign affairs specialists. While in India for the discussions over Tibet, Tang made systematic inquiries to determine the nature of opium production, the importance of opium revenues to the Indian economy, and the attitudes of the British administrators towards abolition. In this, he worked with Sir Edward Baker, the Indian Finance Secretary, who was also interested in ending opium cultivation in India. Tang later pressed for the elimination of India's opium trade during his negotiations in Beijing to settle the Tibetan controversy and established ties with foreign anti-opium societies to encourage them in their struggle to end the opium trade. Under mounting pressure, the British were forced to announce their willingness to co-ordinate their policies with any Chinese initiatives in restricting cultivation, importation and consumption of opium. Tang Shaoyi was the leading official responsible for persuading the Empress Dowager to issue an edict on 30 September, 1906, calling for the ban on opium within ten years. He was also the one who drafted the set of eleven regulations issued by the Grand Council in November of that year for enforcing the decree. He remained active in the following years maintaining pressure both on provincial governors and on the British to ensure that opium would be eradicated.[29]

The Young China group resented the authority over China's foreign trade the powers had gained through the unequal treaties and found the fact that customs collection was placed in the hands of foreigners particularly galling. As part of their programme to regain economic control, they hoped to end the independence of the Imperial Maritime Customs Service. Tang Shaoyi frequently displayed his bitterness over the lack of Chinese employed on the indoor staff of the Imperial Maritime Customs and upheld the opening of the customs service to Chinese as one of his reform goals. In 1906 Lancelot Carnegie,

Secretary of the British Legation in Beijing, informed Sir Edward Grey, the British Foreign Secretary, of Tang's attitude:

> Why, he wanted to know, should any Portuguese, Spaniard or Japanese be admitted while equally well or possibly better qualified Chinese were excluded. At first these were wanting, and China had to rely on foreigners, but now there were 4,000 Chinese students abroad, many of them having University degrees; why should they not be given a chance if they could pass the necessary examination... Chinese candidates would have to be permitted to take their chances with those of other nationalities... Mr Tang's arguments... seemed reasonable, but... I preferred not to enter into a discussion on the subject, which is evidently a grievance of long standing, as he continued to enlarge upon it at great length until it was time for me to end the visit.[30]

When Sir Robert Bredon, the acting head of the customs service, informed Tang that some of the foreign powers were claiming a representation in the higher ranks of the Imperial Maritime Customs proportionate to the amount of their trade, Tang angrily retorted, 'Tell them that China has herself a fair share of the trade and no representative'.[31]

Tang Shaoyi was instrumental in the issuance of the imperial decree of 9 May 1905, which established the Shuiwuchu (Board of Customs Control) as an agency to oversee the activities of the customs service and to bring it under the authority of the Chinese government. Subsequent to this governmental order, Tang served as co-administrator of this board under the titular direction of Tieliang as administrator-general. Tang dealt diplomatically with the protests raised by the British, asserting that China was a sovereign and independent power and could not allow interference with her rights in exercising authority. Through the Board of Customs Control, Tang introduced changes which undermined the independence of the customs administration and which limited the access of the foreign consuls to the trade statistics from the various treaty ports. Tang further made it clear that he intended to restore full administrative authority over the Imperial Maritime Customs to Chinese officials on the expiration of the loan agreements for which customs revenue were pledged, and that the question of a successor to Sir Robert Hart as inspector-general would be decided by the Chinese on the basis of enhancing Chinese influence.[32] When Tang was appointed Premier of the Republic of China in 1912, Sir John Jordan, the British minister in Beijing, reported:

> I fully anticipate that his next move will be an attack upon the Customs Service, for which he has no love and anything of that kind must be met firmly if we are to avoid a repetition of the 1906 experience when he succeeded in establishing the so-called Revenue Council. He has been intriguing in Shanghai with King and Taylor, two British Commissioners, who would be only too willing to become his tools in giving the Service the Chinese complexion Tang desires.[33]

As railway and mining development became a main focus of domestic nationalism, Tang took an active part in building a new professional and nationalistic bureaucracy recruited from the Young China group and served as chief negotiator for most railway and mining affairs between 1905 and 1907. In these various diplomatic discussions, Tang played one power off against another and one foreign firm off against another. As well, he took advantage of specific contract terms and of particular crises experienced in the development of certain railway lines in order to improve the terms on which funds were borrowed and especially to enhance Chinese control over the operation of the railways. In his capacity as Director-general of Railways, Tang introduced foreign-trained Chinese into the management of the important railway enterprises which resulted in greater Chinese authority over personnel recruitment, purchasing policy, financial matters and the setting of freight rates. Tang and his colleagues were thus able to stymie the efforts of the foreign concessionaires from consolidating their economic advantages in China, reversing many of the outrageous terms negotiated in the pre-Boxer period and containing the imperialist threats to Chinese integrity.

The concerted anti-imperialist drive of the Young China diplomats was most successful in blocking the encroachments of those countries motivated by a desire to promote themselves as maritime and commercial powers. Britain and Germany, for example, were primarily concerned with their opportunities to trade and invest in China and demonstrated a marked reluctance to risk a major and costly military confrontation as long as their economic interests were not significantly endangered. They were more amenable to accommodating the growing assertion of Chinese nationalism. In contrast, the Young China officials found Japan and Russia far less conciliatory. The more aggressive imperialism of these two powers was prompted by territorial and continental concerns. Particularly in the Northeast, the Russians and Japanese evinced a willingness to resort to the use of force in safeguarding their interests because they considered these interests to be strategic priorities. Unlike the other powers enjoying special economic privileges in other parts of China, Japan and Russia regarded hegemony over the Northeast as vital to the security of their respective empires and emphasised the exercise of effective political authority rather than the enjoyment of economic advantage. Even in the Northeast, however, members of the Young China group were able to implement a forceful policy in defence of Chinese sovereignty and to prevent Japan and Russia from consolidating their spheres of influence.

The Fall

The diplomatic successes of Young China in preserving China's territorial integrity and in resisting imperialistic inroads into its internal administrative affairs were an essential aspect of dynastic survival in the political environment of the post-Boxer era. For while the achievements of the Young China group continued, the provincial elites continued to recognise some obligations of loyalty to the dynasty. Progressive reformers dominated the provincial assemblies and the railway and mining companies working to check foreign encroachments, and they favoured a constitutional monarchy. Their commitment to the monarchy ceased to be an integral part of their commitment to the Confucian cosmological myth. Rather, it was a commitment conditioned on the success of the Qing house in proving that it was still the most useful vehicle for securing and safeguarding Chinese sovereignty.

In the wake of the death of Empress Dowager Cixi in 1908, many of the prominent Young China diplomats and negotiators from the modern commercial community lost their positions as part of the purge of the Yuan Shikai faction within the bureaucracy. The removal of these capable and effective officials commited to Chinese sovereignty left the Qing bureaucracy tangibly less able to counter foreign pressures, and the anti-imperialist effort lost ground in many areas. As George Morrison commented in early 1911, 'Never has the Wai-wu-pu [Waiwubu] been more badly represented than now'. After noting that Prince Qing, the head of the Waiwubu, had apparently only been there once in the last six years, he elaborated:

> Na Tung, the Senior Assistant President, had a stroke of paralysis some three years ago which has slightly affected his speech, and he also is doing his best to shun the Foreign Office. He only comes to the Wai-wu-pu when a Minister writes specially asking that he shall be there. Next to him comes Tsou Chia-lai, a cock-eyed incompetent, whom I would not engage as head boy, whose claim to the post is that he has from time to time discovered in the Archives documents which have passed out of sight for years. A more hopelessly incompetent imbecile it would be difficult to imagine in any position of responsibility, even in Persia in its worst days.
> Next to him comes Hu Wei-te, an amiable little man... But he lacks ability, authority and personality, nor has he any quality whatever, so far as I can discover, which would entitle him to confidence in the negotiation of a serious interational question.[34]

The loss of effectiveness and commitment to pursue a nationalistic foreign policy became widely evident in the closing years of the dynasty. The movement to recover China's lost mining rights which was actively supported by the provincial elites and which had succeeded in redeeming a number of major mining concessions up to this period could no longer look to Young China diplomats in Beijing for co-operation and encouragement. The failure to regain control over the Kaiping mines in Zhili is a case in point. When Tang Shaoyi was forced to leave government, he was replaced by the notorious industrialist, Sheng Xuanhuai, as Minister for Posts and Communications, with responsibility over mining. Sheng was unwilling to provide the necessary financial guarantees for the

Lanzhou mine in its competition with Kaiping. Under these circumstances, the shareholders of Lanzhou decided upon a merger with Kaiping, and the Kailan Mining Administration was formed with distinctly greater British control and advantages in the new Sino-foreign enterprise. Sheng can rightly be blamed for what was referred to as the 'loss of Lanzhou'.[35]

A reversal in the fortunes of China's anti-imperialist struggle of the late Qing was similarly experienced in the North-east where Chinese security was most gravely threatened by Japanese expansionism. The active stance assumed by Tang Shaoyi and his Young China foreign affairs specialists in 1907 and 1908 in resisting Japanese claims altered under their successors in the last years of the dynasty. In the case of the Yanji border dispute, Tang, as Governor of Fengtian and with diplomatic responsibility for the entire North-east, aggressively opposed Japanese encroachment from their protectorate in Korea both through negotiations and military confrontation. In the face of overwhelming documentary evidence to support the Chinese claims regarding the Sino-Korean frontier, the Japanese shifted their position. Arguing that it was their obligation to protect Korean settlers in the Yanji region, they sought Chinese recognition of Japanese rights over the Koreans similar to those they exercised over Koreans resident in the treaty ports.

Tang Shaoyi vigorously denied the Japanese demands made by Komura Jutaro, the Minister of Foreign Affairs, in their negotiations in Tokyo in the fall of 1908. According to Tang, the main desire of Japan was to station Japanese officials in Yanji. He, therefore, strongly urged the Waiwubu to resist Japanese pressures. As he stated, resident Japanese officials exercising consular rights over Koreans in that region would pose a major obstacle to Chinese authority since there were twice as many Koreans there as Chinese. To assert Chinese control, he advocated that steps be taken to open one or two trade marts in Yanji as self-opened ports and to provide for public works, police, and hygiene solely under Chinese regulation. Limitations on the migration of Koreans across the border should also be enforced.[36]

Despite the earlier firm opposition to Japanese demands, the privilege of exercising consular protection over the Yanji Koreans was conceded to Japan in an agreement that settled the dispute in September 1909, after Tang's departure from the scene. Japan recognised the disputed region as Chinese territory but was allowed to establish consulates and branch consular offices of the consulates in four designated places. Japanese consular officers were permitted to intervene in civil and criminal cases involving Koreans, and Japan secured Chinese acquiescence in the construction of a railway connecting the Jilin-Changchun Railway with the Korean line via Yanji.[37]

Finally, in the field of railway construction, the final years of the monarchy were marked by a complete reversal of the rights recovery movement. With Sheng Xuanhuai as its architect, the Court sought to enforce a policy of railway nationalisation. This scheme, which entailed mortgaging China's railway development to foreign bondholders, could but be seen by the provincial elites as an imperial sell-out to foreign interests. It forcefully demonstrated that the Manchu rulers, without the help and the prodding of the Young China group, were ineffectual in safeguarding Chinese sovereignty.

During the last three years of Manchu rule, the dynastic clan appeared determined to assert its own narrow self-interests regardless of the national consequences. The provincial gentry leadership rapidly lost their confidence in the Throne; Qing management of the country's affairs increasingly seemed to be detrimental to China's survival. The removal of the Young China diplomats and the related shift away from the foreign policy consistently advocated by the modern commercial community therefore proved to be a decisive factor in the ultimate rejection of the ruling house and with it the monarchy itself in 1911.

NOTES

1. Ssu-yu Teng and John K. Fairbank, *China's Response to the West* (Cambidge, Mass., 1961), p. 109.
2. *Ibid.*, p. 110.
3. *Ibid.*, p. 109.
4. Paul A. Cohen, 'Littoral and Hinterland in Nineteenth Century China: The 'Christian' Reformers' in John K. Fairbank, ed., *The Missionary Enterprise in China and America* (Cambridge, Mass., 1974), pp. 201-205.
5. Wang Jingyu, *Zhongguo jindai gongye shiziliao dierqi 1895-1914* [Historical materials on modern Chinese industry, second collection, 1895-1914] (Beijing, 1957), pp. 944-945.
6. Lu Shiqiang, *Ding Richang yu ziqiang yundong* [Ding Richang and the self-strengthening movement] (Taibei, 1972), pp. 235-238. Similarly, Feng Guifen, one of the outstanding reform essayists of the mid-nineteenth century statecraft

thinkers ridiculed the ideas of Wei Yuan on political strategy for dealing with the barbarians saying: 'Only one sentence of Wei Yuan is correct: 'Learn the strong techniques of the barbarians in order to control them''. But in urging the establishment of shipyards and arsenals for the manufacture of foreign implements, Feng's emphasis was on military weapons. Even when he advised the adoption of farm tools, weaving equipment and steamships, the focus was on strengthening the state's revenue base and the transport taxes in kind. Teng and Fairbank, pp. 102 and 53; Feng Guifen *Jiaobinlu kangyi* [Straight-forward words from the lodge of early Zhou studies] (1897), pp. 68b-69a, 73b-74b.

7. Xue Fucheng, *Yongan quanji* [Complete collection of writings of Xue Fucheng] (1884-1898), II, 10b-11b.

8. *Ibid.*

9. W.A.P. Martin, *A Cycle of Cathay* (New York, 1900), p. 351.

10. Hao Chang, *Liang Ch'i-ch'ao and the Intellectual Transition in China (1890-1907)* (Cambridge, Mass., 1971), pp. 58-59; Hao Chang, 'The Intellectual Context of Reform', in Paul A. Cohen and John E. Schrecker, eds., *Reform in Nineteenth-Century China* (Cambridge, Mass., 1976), pp. 148-149.

11. Hao Yen-p'ing, *The Comprador in Nineteenth Century China* (Cambridge, Mass., 1970), pp. 201-206.

12. Yung Wing, *My Life in China and America* (New York, 1909), pp. 170-181.

13. Zheng Guanying, *Shengshi weiyan houbian* [Revised edition of words of warning in a seemingly prosperous age] (1969 Taibei reprint of 1911 edition), II, 1087.

14. *The Friend of China*, VI (1883), 209-210, 218-228; Louis T. Sigel, 'Ch'ing Foreign Policy and the Modern Commercial Community: T'ang Shao-yi in Korea', *Papers on Far Eastern History*, 13 (March 1976), 80-81.

15. Xu Run, *Xu Yuzhai zishu nianpu* [An autobiographical chronology of Xu Run] (Xiangshan, 1927), pp. 15-22.

16. Based upon figures in Hsiao Liang-lin, *China's Trade Statistics, 1864-1949* (Cambridge, Mass., 1974), pp. 22-23, 141-163.

17. Wang Yeh-chien, 'The Secular Trend of Prices during the Ch'ing Period', *Xianggang Zhongwen daxue Zhongguo wenhua yanjiusuo xuebao* [Journal of the Research Institute of Chinese Culture of the Chinese University of Hong Kong], IV:2 (December 1972), 347-368. Similarly, the Jardine, Matheson and Company archives reveal that silver bullion exports to England ceased by 1849. Small shipments of silver began to be imported from England in 1850, and the flow of silver back to China grew larger and more regular in 1852 and in 1853. Edward Le Fevour, *Western Enterprise in Late Ch'ing China* (Cambridge, Mass., 1970), p. 10.

18. Hsiao Liang-lin, pp. 268-269; Cheng Yu-kwei, *Foreign Trade and Industrial Development of China* (Washington, 1956), pp. 13-14.

19. Stanley F. Wright, *Hart and the Chinese Customs* (Belfast, 1950), App. 3, p. 894.

20. Kenneth S. Latourette, *A History of Christian Missions in China* (New York, 1967), pp. 537-605.

21. Zheng Guanying, II, 728.

22. John E. Schrecker, *Imperialism and Chinese Nationalism: Germany in Shantung* (Cambridge, Mass., 1971), p. 113.

23. *Ibid.*, p. 154.

24. Shen Zuxian, *Yangshouyuan zouyi zheyao* [Major memorials of Yuan Shikai] (Taibei, 1966), pp. 306-307.

25. Yung Shang Him, 'The Chinese Educational Mission and its Influence', *Tien Hsia Monthly*, IX:3 (October 1939), 225-256.

26. Schrecker, pp. 158-209.

27. *The Times* (London), 18 January 1907, p. 5.

28. Louis T. Sigel, 'Ch'ing Tibetan Policy (1906-1910)' *Papers on China*, 20 (1966), 177-201.

29. *The Times*, 13 February 1909, p. 8; *North-China Herald* (Shanghai), 19 October 1906, pp. 147-148, 23 November 1906, p. 458.

30. Great Britain, Foreign Office, FO 405, Confidential Prints on China and Korea; No. 167, Carnegie to Grey, 19 May 1906.

31. FO 405, No. 190, Jordan to Grey, 21 January 1909.

32. FO 405, No. 183, Jordan to Grey, 24 September 1908.

33. Sir Francis B. Alston Papers, No. 246, Jordan to Langley, 16 April, 1912.

34. Lo Hui-min, ed., *The Correspondence of G.E. Morrison, I, 1895-1912* (Cambridge, 1976), pp. 587-588.

35. Ellsworth, C. Carlson, *The Kaiping Mines, 1877-1912*, Revised ed., (Cambridge, Mass., 1971), pp. 127-137.

36. *Qingji waijiao shiliao* [Historical materials on foreign relations in the Qing period] comp. by Wang Yanwei and Wang Liang (Beijing, 1932-1935), 217: 19-20.

37. John V.A. MacMurray, ed., *Treaties and Agreements with and Concerning China 1894-1919* (New York, 1921), I, 796-797.

9

SOME REFLECTIONS ON POLITICAL CHANGE 1895-1916
K.S. Liew

Beijing gossip regarding the founding of the Republic of China in 1912 runs thus: some workmen were ordered to remove from one of the gates into Beijing a tablet, the 'Great Qing Gate', and replace it with a new one, the 'China Gate'. On completing their task they asked their foreman what they should do with the old one. Mindful of the uncertainty of the new regime and the responsibility that would be his if the Qing dynasty were restored, he instructed his men to leave the tablet in the loft above the gate. Much to their surprise, there was already one there covered in thick dust. It turned out to be the 'Great Ming Gate' which had been taken off the same entrance nearly three hundred years before when the Qing dynasty replaced the Ming dynasty.[1]

This story, told by C.P. FitzGerald, is repeated here to emphasize the sameness in the ordinary man's response to change despite the distance of time that separated the fall of the last two dynasties. It tells much about the limits of the influence of nationalism or anti-Manchuism on ordinary folks. If city dwellers, particularly residents in the national capital, had so little understanding of the forces of change, how much less their impact was on the population at large.

The foreman's precaution was understandable and excusable even with hindsight. Were there not two attempts to restore the monarchy within the first decade of the Republic? The ghost of the Qing dynasty lingered on in the Republic for a further decade to materialise in the form of Manzhouguo [Manch Kingdom] in the 1930s. Although it was set up, not by the

Chinese themselves, but by the Japanese, could it not be argued that even the Japanese were unconvinced of the depth of Chinese nationalism or anti-Manchuism, still less that of Chinese republicanism?

Moreover, seventy years after the founding of the Republic, historians are still debating in earnest on the nature of that change. Indeed as one American scholar observes:

> The dialectic of writing on 1911 has made it first the revolution, then 'no revolution', then 'something of a revolution', and now back to 'not much of a revolution' and 'paltry achievements'. I think it is time to negate yet another negation: 1911 was not so trifling a revolution.[2]

Some historians of modern China attempt to steer a middle course in the debate. Thus another scholar writes: 'The great revolutions of the Western world—the American and the Russian—have all taken aim at the monarchical form of government. China too had a revolution which transformed a monarchy into a republic. The Revolution of 1911 has since been eclipsed by the far more significant Chinese Communist revolution. But the Revolution of 1911 was only less significant. It was not insignificant'.[3] The same author further adds: 'As we turn from causes to the significance of the revolution it will become clear that in some respects 1911 was a most unrevolutionary revolution.'[4]

These are some indications of the extent of historians' disagreement on the nature of the 1911 Revolution. Some see substantial departures from tradition. Others doubt the significance of the changes marked by this event. This chapter focuses on the development of the period 1895-1916. It aims to elucidate some of its historical features, partly by narrating and analysing the forces at work, and partly by reviewing the influential opinions and theories advanced by some historians.

The choice of dates delimiting the period for this discussion is necessarily arbitrary but not without some justification. The year 1916 signals the commencement of the collapse of central authority for a decade and beyond, while 1895 marks the end of an era during which the traditional Confucian elite, the scholar-bureaucrats, were still exercising firm leadership in state affairs and confident in their own ability as well as in the general strength of tradition, both cultural and political, to cope with China's internal and external problems. But in 1895 this traditional leadership was discredited and their confidence shattered as Japan resoundingly defeated China's most modern forces, including the famous Beiyang Navy, the fruit of three decades of self-strengthening. Consequently, Li Hongzhang, who had led the movement in search of wealth and power since the 1860s, was forced to admit failure and beg the throne to look for alternatives.

Political Change before the Boxer Uprising

The year 1895 saw the appearance of movements in different quarters and the introduction of measures which were to affect and change China's political scene for the next twenty years and more. Significantly, from the non-official gentry came the reform movement led by Kang Youwei, Liang Qichao and other newly qualified members of the gentry. Perhaps even more significantly, from among the overseas Chinese arose the first Chinese revolutionary organisation initiated by Sun Yat-sen, a Western-educated man outside the pale of Chinese tradition. Both the reformers and the revolutionaries represented the emergence of two new types of men who were to become or to seek to be China's new elite. One was nurtured in China's traditional Confucian environment but modified by Western influences while the other grew up in Western-dominated centres where traditional Chinese influences were weakest. Their different origins had a profound influence on their political behaviour.

The reformers, being disgruntled members of the non-official gentry and having already one foot on the bottom rung of power and influence in China's political and social structure, preferred to challenge the leadership of their superiors from within. They wanted to liberalise the governmental structure, get rid of the dead wood and make room for men like themselves who had managed to break through the web of tradition. Thus Kang Youwei wrote in one of his petitions to the throne in 1895:

> In order to rally the support of the nation the Throne's first act should be to issue a decree confessing its own inadequacy. The next step is to reward those who merit reward and to punish those who have erred so that people's

grievances may be aired. Then he should attend to the neglected and humbly and widely search for advice. Expand the advisory institutions to gather as many men of talents as possible to serve the government, and establish deliberative organs to facilitate the exchange of opinions, particularly those from below.[5]

The reformers wanted to retain the traditional monarchy and, through peaceful reform directed from Beijing, to bring about constitutional government with expanded opportunities for political participation by men from the ranks of the non-official gentry.

In contrast, the revolutionaries, with little or no stakes in the traditional political structure and no prospect of gaining access to the seats of power in the traditional regime, wanted to overthrow the monarchical system of government and replace it with a democratic republic. It is true that even a man like Sun Yat-sen had traversed the path of reform before choosing the course of revolution. He had suggested to Li Hongzhang a programme of reform and offered himself in his sesrvice. Without a doubt Sun had hoped through persuasion to gain entry into the political world of the gentry. But once rebuffed, he gave up this path believing that there was no room in the traditional order for a man like him.[6] He never looked back to that day when a slight recognition from Li Hongzhang might have averted him from a revolutionary career.

Neither the reformers nor the revolutionaries achieved much before 1900. The latter attempted their one and only revolt in Guangzhou (Canton) in 1896 but failed. The former managed to gain the ear of the Emperor in 1898 and exercised nominal power for a hundred days. Then their effort also aborted in the face of conservative reaction which forced them to flee for their lives.

Besides reform and revolution, which were the results of voluntaristic actions of groups of individuals aspiring to be the serious leaders of modern China, there were two other developments which were not immediately significant but had unforeseen consequences for China in the twentieth century. Both were the results of deliberate governmental actions.

In the wake of defeat by Japan and with the continuing aim of strengthening China's defensive capability, the central government's first action, with the apparently unanimous support of the entire bureaucracy and the gentry, was to train a new national army to replace the decimated Beiyang forces as well as the older imperial armies. It included the establishment of modern military academies to train officers and also the sending of military students abroad to acquire the latest developments in military affairs.[7] The man entrusted with the task of training the central government's metropolitan units was Yuan Shikai, an unorthodox man in Confucian eyes. He did not enter officialdom through the normal regular channel, the imperial examination system, but through military service and with a purchased degree.[8] This unorthodox beginning of Yuan's official life had more than personal significance. Military service formerly held in contempt by Confucians was becoming a respectable alternative path to the seat of power and influence.[9] Yuan made his first impression on China's governing circles and foreign diplomats with his deft handling of the Korean crises in the early 1880s when he, as a junior official in the Chinese army stationed in Korea, skilfully and decisively smothered a pro-Japanese plot to seize power.[10] This display of boldness and decisiveness in face of a delicate foreign crisis stood him in good stead in the tottering Qing officialdom. His ability won the praise and confidence of the gentry despite the fact that some of them despised his non-literate background or found a certain trait in his character repugnant.[11] With the army he trained in the 1880s and after, and with the support of new provincial army units which were to come into existence in the 1890s and the early years of the twentieth century, he was to play a central role in deciding not only the fate of the Qing dynasty but also that of the infant Republic after 1911.[12]

The other important development under the aegis of officialdom was in the realm of education. It was partly initiated by some reform-minded provincial officials such as Zhang Zhidong and Huang Zunxian, who introduced a new type of school or training programme with an emphasis on practical knowledge rather than on pure moral content.[13] It was also partly encouraged by the reformers who hoped, through newspapers, study societies, schools and translation bureaux, to politicise and enlighten their fellow-countrymen, particularly members of the literate class, so as to create a wider basis for their reform movement and to realise their goals by an alternative road, namely reform firmly supported by the lower official or unoffical gentry class. For a time the reformers' activities attracted wide attention and it looked as if the bureaucratic and the non-official gentry were united for a firm programme of action.[14] Leading bureaucrats such as Sun Jia'nai, Weng Tonghe, Li Hongzhang, Zhang Zhidong, Yuan Shikai, and prominent gentry leaders like Zhang Jian and Chen Sanli, all expressed their enthusiasm by giving financial and other forms of support.[15] The Governor of Hunan, Chen Baozhen, also put his authority behind the reformers for a time in the hope of making Hunan a model province for the rest of China.[16]

But the political climate of the 1890s was not yet ripe for these reformist efforts to succeed. The first manifestation of opposition from the bureaucratic gentry to the reformers' activities occurred in 1896 when the latter's barely three month old Society for Strengthening Learning (Qiangxuehui) in Beijing and Shanghai was ordered to close on the charge of breaching the law prohibiting private societies.[17] This was however only a small chill in comparison with the sudden frost of conservative reaction in 1898 in which six reformers lost their lives. Kang Youwei and Liang Qichao managed to escape unharmed only with foreigners' help.[18]

Conservative opposition in the Manchu court was instrumental to the collapse of the 1898 reform, which was unfortunately caught up in the power struggle between Emperor Guangxu and the Empress-Dowager Cixi.[19] But the ultimate cause of its failure was not the conservative Manchu court but the lack of support from the rank and file of China's ruling elite which had a strong vested interest in maintaining the old order. Generally the bureaucrats disliked the presumptuous young upstarts and the challenge to their leadership, while the local gentry, as pointed out by Ichiko, were appalled by the reformers' threat to their power and the local autonomy on which much of their authority depended. For example, the abolition of sinecures would deprive many of their livelihood and social status, while education reforms would ruin the future of numerous aspirants to office.[20] After the collapse of the 1898 reform, Liang Qichao, in despair, almost opted for the path of revolution while Tang Caichang, another reformer, plotted an uprising in central China.[21]

Fortunately for the cause of reform, a kind of spring soon

followed the blizzard of 1900: the Boxer Rebellion and the invasion of China by the joint forces of eight foreign powers catalysed the force of change in the provinces and forced the Manchu court to adopt fundamental reforms. Of course, Marxist historians in China argue that the Boxer Uprising was a landmark in a long, consistent and continuing peasant movement and mass struggle against feudal and imperialistic aggression and that it failed because of the lack of proletarian leadership. Some also view it as the beginning of modern Chinese nationalism. But they also admit that it was not until the rise of the Chinese Communist Party that the peasantry was welded into an invincible force for revolution. Therefore, as far as the development of the 1900s was concerned, peasant power remained a dormant force.[22] Nevertheless, the Boxer outbreak did serve China's political development in some unexpected ways.

Confronted with the powerful foreign forces and having to cope with an irresolute central government, Li Hongzhang, Viceroy of Guangdong, Zhang Zhidong, Viceroy of Hunan and Hubei, Yuan Shikai, Governor of Shandong, and Liu Kunyi, Viceroy of Liangjiang, decided to flout the order of the court to wage war on the powers. Instead, they took the unprecedented step of declaring neutrality for central and south China. Arguing that Beijing's declaration of war was an illegitimate order—it being the result of a subversion of the court by a small band of evil men—these provincial leaders openly concluded a pact among themselves for the mutual preservation of the provinces in their control and entered into an agreement with the powers as if they were an independent, sovereign state.[23]

In contrast with the behaviour of the provincial authorities in the 1911 Revolution, the action of these provincial heads in 1900 was but a very subdued demonstration of independence, and probably should not be taken as evidence of provincialism and regionalism, at least not in the sense of a deep estrangement between central and regional authorities. Although this challenge to central authority represents a stage in China's centrifugal process since the provincial authorities gained military and fiscal power for suppressing the mid-century rebellions, the seriousness of this growth of regional power is still a subject of debate.[24] It may be argued that the action of these provincial officials were taken with national as much as regional interests at heart. As a

Marxist historian puts it:

> Under the strong pressures of the Boxers there seems to be a split between the Beijing government and the powerful faction of southeast China, but in practice they were acting in complete unison. The Empress-Dowager temporarily adopted the deceptive stand of supporting the Boxers in order to deflect the attack of the masses [on her regime], while [her officials in south China] were bent on appeasing the imperialists, by opposing the Boxers from beginning to end and by maintaining good relations with the powers.[25]

Whatever the court's view was of this provincial challenge to its authority, the incident could not but fill Beijing's ruling clique with apprehension.[26]

Reform and Revolutionary Movements After 1900

The forces of change that had emerged in the 1890s thus received from the traumatic experience of 1900 not a kiss of death but a new lease of life with even greater vitality.[27] Their opponents were now checked. For their unwitting part in the Boxer Uprising, the conservative forces in the Manchu court were disarrayed and weakened. Some die-hards were executed, and the rest, still shocked and confounded, dared not oppose further the demands for reform.[28] Thus the Manchu court headed by the now seemingly repentant Empress-Dowager Cixi swung to the support of reforms she had opposed so vehemently in 1898, though still refusing to pardon their principal architects, Kang Youwei and Liang Qichao.[29] Of the measures taken, the most important and far reaching were undoubtedly educational changes and the decision to adopt constitutional government. The abolition of the traditional examination system was no less an act of revolution. It struck at the bastion of Chinese conservatism, removing in one stroke a vital stabilising element that had sustained the Confucian state and ensured the political and social dominance of the scholar-gentry for the past millenium.

The abolition of the imperial examination system also gave Western learning a new impetus. The modernised school curricula now included not only subjects of obvious practical, technical content but also those with a political and social emphasis. This new learning, whether obtained in China or abroad, offered the Chinese intelligentsia a new road to power and social prestige. Further it swelled the rank of radicals committed to rapid change since the new learning diluted the students' traditional loyalties and aroused their hostility towards an apparently incompetent alien ruling house. Even the Emperor Protection Society of Kang Youwei and Liang Qichao should not be interpreted as a firm commitment by the reformers to the preservation of the Manchu dynasty.[30] The Hundred Days' Reform, as Jerome Ch'en puts it,

> proposed to expand the basis of government to include the participation of the unofficial gentry in political deliberations. They wanted to change the Qing dynasty based on the Mandate of Heaven to a nation state governed by the will of the people. They wished to change the examination system in order to select talented officials of a new kind. These were the reform proposals branded by the conservative political clique as 'revolt' because what they aimed to preserve was China, and not necessarily the 'great Ch'ing [Qing] dynasty'. The focus of their attention was the complete sovereignty of the Chinese nation and not necessarily the maintenance of the Chinese culture in its entirety.[31]

As far back as December 1897 Liang Qichao had already 'toyed with the idea that the failure of the dynasty to prevent aggression had already vitiated its right to rule'.[32] Kang and Liang wanted to protect the reformist Emperor Guangxu, who was willing to co-operate with them in political reform and in transferring the power of government to an elected parliament, but their programme did not necessarily also mean the retention of the Manchu ruling house.

Revolutionary radicals of course were not so ambivalent. They vowed to get rid of not only the alien Manchu ruling house but also the long enduring monarchical system of government.

Gentry, Bureaucrats and Bourgeoisie

While circumstances favoured change, reformers and revolutionaries alike remained minorities among the civil elites in the decade leading to the Revolution of 1911. The chief reason was that the deeply-rooted Confucian leadership had not yet disintegrated sufficiently for reformers to take their place, still less for republicanism to take hold.

Some studies express the opinion that the majority of the Chinese elites were conservative but were compelled to swim with the tide in an effort to preserve their status and privileges. Thus they supported 'new schools to train their progeny, local police to protect their lives and property and local self-government institutions to exercise greater formal control over local government than everbefore possible'.[33] Deprived of their major path to political power and influence via the traditional examinations, the gentry looked elsewhere for alternatives. They found them in the proposed constitutional institutions. As Chuzo Ichiko points out, they realised that through participation in local self-governing institutions as well as provincial and national assemblies, they could exercise greater power and influence than that which their traditional qualifications entitled them.[34]

Social homogeneity is no guarantee for unity even in the best of times. Perhaps it is not surprising to find that in times of change, even China's traditionally closely connected gentry elites should have parted ways in their efforts to adjust themselves to the new situations confronting them. A recent study draws our attention to a bifurcation of the non-official gentry, the division between the reformist elite who operated in the treaty ports and provincial capitals, and the 'local gentry' of the self-government associations who operated mostly at prefectural and lower regional levels. The distinction between them was not that between higher and lower degree holders but that the latter 'never came to possess the progressivism and enthusiasm for Western style constitutionalism or developmental concern for economic rights recovery that urban reformist elite displayed'.[35] In other words, the former had wider objectives with the main or at least some national interests at heart, while the latter had their interests more narrowly and locally focused.

This hard-core conservative gentry, most noticeable among members of the bureaucratic gentry and the court in Beijing before 1900, now came to the fore among the local gentry. Confronted with the impending loss of the prospect of advancement on the imperial ladder and the imminent threat to their interests, and deserted by many of their own ranks who had turned to reformism, the conservative local elites were forced to fall back on their own resources. In addition to participation in local self-governing institutions to preserve their influence, they also utilised their traditional prestige to influence or encourage the discontented masses to disrupt social order or to attack specific targets.[36] A well-known case was the Changsha Rice Riot in which rioters, led or directed by the gentry, attacked selected foreign properties and government schools. If the court's support for the Boxer Uprising in 1900 was the desperate act of the bureaucratic gentry and the Manchu aristocrats against imperialism, the mob violence of the Changsha kind represented the conservative local gentry's last-ditch battle to save their own hides, and the results were almost as disastrous to themselves. In the case of the Changsha gentry, its leading members were demoted and disgraced for their part in the riot, never recovering their former prestige to challenge the reformist gentry.[37]

But even the reformist gentry were divided: there was a modern national elite and a modern provincial elite. The latter group, as Daniel Bays points out, lacked 'the interprovincial connections of the national elite [of the older gentry] and found it natural to operate entirely within the province.'[38] At least in attitude on China's internal affairs, this group was provincial—rather than national-oriented, and constituted an important centrifugal force in twentieth-century China's political life.

It remains to draw attention to the most untraditional force for change, namely the bourgeoisie comprising compradores, merchants, bankers, industrialists and overseas Chinese. Whether these social groups constituted a bourgeois class or not is open to debate. There is little argument, however, whether from the Marxist or from the non-Marxist standpoint, that these new groups were a weak nationalistic force. Coming into being either in China's own semi-colonial environment or in colonial situations overseas, the Chinese bourgeoisie were economically dependent on the capitalist-imperialist powers. This economic dependence is held to account for both their nationalistic sentiments and their inability to embark on a thorough-going revolution. They resented obstacles to their fuller development but were powerless to remove them on their own. They threw their support behind whatever leadership, gentry, reformist or revolutionary, to achieve their aspirations for independence and freedom, but they had not enough resources to see them through.[39]

Of the political forces outlined above, the revolutionaries and the reformists were highly politicised and firmly committed to political change, though by different means. In contrast the bureaucrats, particularly those of the 1860s generation, were not so well disposed towards political change. As Andrew Nathan suggests, some of these men had acquired professional administrative or technical qualifications because of their exposures to new influences from the West. But they were also steep in Confucian education, and, in addition, 'had passed too long a time in the service of the Ch'ing [Qing] to be anything but ambivalent republicans' or constitutionalists.[40]

The bourgeoisie were interested in either reform or revolution but an inner weakness condemned them to be half-hearted supporters. With the exception of those infiltrated by revolutionaries, the armed forces, especially the new armies brought into existence after 1895 and 1903 by the central and provincial governments, were generally apolitical in the sense that they were not deeply committed to a particular faction or cause although they were supposed to be the defenders of the state's interests. They were open to subversion of various kinds and from various sources.[41] For this reason they easily became private armies with the inclination to fight, not for political principles, but for personal loyalty to their officers, or at best for provincial or regional interests. The Manchu court professed to support constitutionalism but aimed for a greater centralisation of government, thereby enhancing its own power. The local gentry opposed radical changes, but were prepared to discard the dynasty if it failed to support its conservatism.

Of these socio-political groups, only the new armies were better able to realise their goal provided they had one or were given one; none of the rest was capable of fulfilling its aspirations on its own. Thus, repeated attempts of the revolutionaries at uprisings before the 1911 Revolution failed dismally.[42] The constitutionalists' unsuccessful demand for parliamentary government only added to their own frustration. Even the local gentry who were supposed to have real local power suffered reverses in their confrontation with bureaucrats as shown in the Changsha Riot, while neither the Manchu court nor the bureaucracy could hope to go their own ways with success.[43]

China had been a restive society since the beginning of the

nineteenth century. Population increase, official corruption, economic and technological stagnation, unfavourable external trade and foreign incursions had already set in motion massive social discontents. The White Lotus Rebellion of 1793-1802 and the Taiping Revolution of 1851-1864 were major manifestations of many of these discontents. The dynasty, with the aid of the gentry elite, was able to suppress these rebellions. By early twentieth century, however, the gentry itself was no longer a cohesive force. The three-tier power structure of traditional China, the central, the provincial and the formal and informal sub-provincial apparatus of government, had already begun to fall apart. The split between the formal and informal strata of government has been noted by some historians as particularly serious. It has prompted an historian to write:

> The real political watershed which is relevant for our understanding of the late nineteenth and early twentieth centuries is that between the entire formal apparatus of government and the informal system of local administration below the level of the district magistrate. This informal system depended upon the quasi-governmental functions of the gentry class in local society. A degree-holding individual, when appointed to office, was part of the central apparatus; when not in office, and living at his provincial home, he was a key part of the local system of government, complementary to the central one. The balance between these two separate but vitally linked polities began to change in the late nineteenth century, and by 1911 it had shifted so drastically that the dynasty itself could be sloughed off. The reason for this was the mobilization of the gentry class, in particular at the provincial level, and its willingness to act as an interest group outside the old formal structures linking it to central dynastic authority.[44]

In general terms, most historians appear to agree with this interpretation of twentieth-century China's political trend. It is indisputable that the ruling elite was becoming fractious. There are, however, doubts as to the depth of this split within this elite before 1911, or even before 1916 which marks the beginning of the warlord period. There is the counter-opinion that after 1900 the trend was toward consolidation of central power which did not fall apart until 1916.[45]

On the surface these seem to be diametrically opposed opinions with each following or emphasising a particular line of enquiry or reasoning. An effort has been made to resolve these contradictory findings by recognising that there was in this period a 'triple-levelled expansion of power', or 'three simultaneously expanding and overlapping nodes of power', namely central, provincial and local segments at the expense of the peasantry but not necessarily at the expense of one another.[46] It is certainly an ingenious approach but whether the history of this period can be explained in terms of such a neat model is questionable. The tentative picture sketched in the preceding pages is not contradictory to or incompatible with the findings of most historians. It portrays a scene of fragmented and delicately-balanced forces competing for power and leadership in their attempts to save China from foreign encroachments, or simply to protect their own respective regional or group interests. As pointed out previously, although these competing groups were germinating, growing and expanding their influences before 1911, none had any success in their bid for power. A combination of these diverse groups was required for success. Revolutionary leaders such as Sun Yat-sen obviously understood this even if their rivals such as Kang Youwei, whose support Sun tried to obtain, did not.[47] Sun established relations with secret societies, overseas Chinese, young student groups, and also attempted to subvert Manchu troops.[48] But all these proved to be insufficient to topple the dynasty. It was not until the more powerful splinter groups of the gentry elite, the constitutionalists in the provinces threw in their lot with the revolutionaries that the scale was tipped in favour of the anti-dynastic and anti-monarchical cause.

This was precisely the phenomenon of the 1911 Revolution. The Manchu efforts to centralise the reins of government into their own hands and the railway nationalisation issue finally antagonised the provincial and local elites, conservative and reformist alike, and convinced the constitutionalists that hopes for attaining participatory government peacefully had faded. They seized the opportunity of the Wuchang Uprising in 1911 to join up with the revolutionaries in open revolt. The impact of this alliance was astonishing. In less than two months, fifteen provinces became independent. In another two months it was all over. Deserted by its own bureaucrats and the new armies, and deprived of support from any foreign powers, the Qing dynasty came to an abrupt end.

The Significance of Yuan Shikai's Rise and Fall

In this alliance and its swift victory, however, also lay the dilemma of the 1911 Revolution. The alliance was a marriage of convenience. Even before the fall of the Manchu dynasty, the anti-dynastic camp, beset by financial difficulties and divided by regional and personal allegiances was already drifting apart with the constitutionalists and the bourgeoisie gravitating towards an obviously strong, if not stronger, combination of Yuan Shikai's Beiyang army and the bureaucrats in Beijing.[49] The immediate result was the so-called north-south compromise which brought about the cessation of hostility between the anti-dynastic provinces in south China and the residual forces of the outgoing dynasty led by Yuan Shikai, and handed over the infant Republic to the care of this ex-Manchu bureaucrat.

Once the revolutionaries had decided to hand over the presidency to Yuan Shikai, political events occurred in rapid succession, mostly to the detriment of the republican cause. The Manchu emperor abdicated on 12 February 1912; Sun Yat-sen, the provisional president of the republic at Nanjing, stepped aside in favour of Yuan on the following day. On 15 February Yuan was unanimously elected to take Sun's place by delegates representing seventeen provinces. On 2 April, the provisional parliament was moved from Nanjing under the control of the revolutionaries to Beijing, the hub of Yuan's power. The first cabinet under Yuan's presidency, consisting of important revolutionaries such as Song Jiaoren, collapsed in less than three months. In March 1913 Song, as the actual leader of the reorganised revolutionary party, now renamed the Nationalist Party which had just won the first national election to become the dominant political party in the first formal parliament of the Republic, was assassinated. Before the year was over, Yuan had consolidated his position by provoking and smashing the revolutionary republican forces in the so-called 'second revolution', and by expelling Nationalist members from the national parliament, which was in effect dissolved because it did not have sufficient members to form a quorum. From then on,

Asia's first democratic republic inspired by Western examples was systematically dismantled and turned into a personal dictatorship. By 1914, preparation for a return to a monarchical form of government was under way.[50]

The attempt to restore monarchy did not succeed, however. Yuan's reign lasted merely eighty-one days from 1 January to 23 March 1916, and he was forced to step down. It was surely one of the rare examples of history which repeated itself within such a short time. Yuan went almost the same way the last Manchu emperor did. Reformers, revolutionaries, constitutionalists and military leaders, including Yuan's own, all rose to oppose the monarchy, and province after province declared their independence. It was Yuan's turn to taste the bitter fruit of desertion by his former collaborators, followers, and supporters, both Chinese and foreign, and the drama with Yuan as its central figure ended only with his death on 6 June 1916. His immediate legacy to China was, through his destruction of the Republic of China, the beginning of a long period of warlordism.[51]

Different Views on the 1911 Revolution

How much of a revolution was the Revolution of 1911? As pointed out at the opening of this chapter, historians are divided on this question. In China both orthodox and neo-orthodox Nationalist and Communist writers are unwavering in their belief that it was a great national democratic revolution which aimed to modernise China's political system along Western liberal lines in order to regenerate China.[52] Admittedly it was not a great success, but it did rid China of a two-thousand-year-old monarchical system which was never to return despite efforts to revive it.[53] Nationalist and communist views differ, however, in three major respects, namely the nature of the revolution, the causes of its failure, and the legitimacy of its successors. The Communists believe that it was a bourgeois-capitalist revolution led by a small elite with aspirations to build a republic based on the French-American model and on the ideals of individual freedom, equality and fraternity. But the Chinese bourgeoisie, developing in a semi-feudal and semi-colonial environment, was weak. It was narrowly based and so closely tied to the foreign capitalists that it had not the strength to assert its own will. Their revolution, therefore, ultimately failed, and it was not until the rise of the proletarian class that the Chinese revolution was brought to a successful conclusion.[54] Thus Sun Yat-sen widened the structure of the Nationalist Party in 1924 to take in the Communists in order to tap the support of the workers and the peasants as well as to obtain Russian aids. But the high tide of the Chinese revolution had to wait until the rise of the proletariat and the peasantry.[55]

Nationalist historians deny the class character of the 1911 Revolution, insisting that it was a revolution brought about by a broad cross-section of the Chinese people, including modern intellectuals, students, secret society members, traders and artisans, overseas Chinese, the new armies, and on the eve of the revolution, supported by constitutionalists at all levels and even bureaucrats of the Qing dynasty. It was neither a proletarian nor a bourgeois revolution but a national revolution on behalf of the interests of the whole people.[56] It did not achieve all its goals because of the collapse of this broad alliance due to inter and intra-party rivalries, foreign or fear of foreign threats, and above all Yuan's treachery.[57] Not only did Nationalists claim that they were the lawful custodians of the Republic, but they also maintain that the Tongmenghui was their own party's direct predecessor, both ideologically, organisationally, and even in terms of personnel.[58]

Outside China few other countries could compare with Japan in the study of Chinese history and culture, and to Japanese scholarship on the 1911 Revolution we shall next turn. Japanese debates on the revolution centre on its internal and external causes.[59] One school argues that the impetus for the revolution came from imperialist pressures on China. As China lacked the democratic elements of a modern industrial society, namely a mature bourgeois-capitalist class, the revolution could not have been a democratic bourgeois-capitalist one. Another school emphasises the development of capitalism and a bourgeois-capitalist class as the main driving force even though this class failed to achieve its objectives. A third school feels that the other two overemphasise the bourgeois-capitalist revolution of the West as a model of modernisation. In equating modernisation with Westernisation, they fail to take into account the unique aspects of the historical environments of the East. It argues that the main force for modernisation in China came from the masses and an advanced revolutionary element of the bourgeois class, with anti-imperialism and anti-feudalism as its content. The process of modernisation in China therefore differs from the Western pattern. The 1911 Revolution was merely an important stage in this process. It prepared the way for the later New Democratic revolution of the proletariat.

A fourth Japanese view represents a compromise of the preceding three, but with a particular slant of its own. It agrees with the first school that the event of 1911 was not a revolution, with the second that there was in Chinese society a democratic bourgeois-capitalist class, and with the third that the main impetus for modernisation in China came from the masses, and that it was both anti-imperialist and anti-feudal. But it rejects the idea that 1911 should be labeled a bourgeois-capitalist revolution. It argues instead that 1911 saw a kind of change similar to the Meiji Restoration of modern Japan and the rise of new absolutism in seventeenth-and eighteenth-century Europe. Some horse-trading was done but the riders remained.

Yokoyama Suguru, a principal proponent of this view, asserts that real political power after 1900 had passed from the Manchu court into the hands of the 'New Westernisers' (*Xinyangwupai*) represented by men such as Yuan Shikai, Zhang Zhidong and Liu Kunyi. Hence they, rather than the Manchu court should have been the target of the Revolution. Since it was not the case, and Yuan Shikai was chosen to head the Republic, the event of 1911 could not be accepted as a revolution.[60] While recognising that there were multiple forces at work in late Qing society, he argues that there were only three major ones: the revolutionary party (Tongmenghui) representing the interests of petty bourgeoisie; the constitutionalists representing a faction of big landlords and big bourgeois-capitalists, and the new Westernisers behind whom were the other factions of the big landlords and big bourgeois class. Their relationship to one another was neither one of total friendship nor one of outright enmity, for whereas they had much in common in their aspirations, they were also rivals in the race for political power. The revolutionaries appealed to latent anti-Manchu sentiments and hoped to gain leadership by overthrowing the dynasty and establishing a republic. The constitutionalists sought to share political power with the Manchu court through constitutional reform, while the new Westernisers were already exercising power on behalf of the Manchu court by instituting new reform measures, particularly the establishment of new armies. Contrary to Chinese orthodox views, Yokoyama emphasises the constitutionalists rather than the revolutionaries as the major force in the 1911 Revolution. He argues that the new Westernisers were generally cautious and marking time, waiting for an opportunity to seize power. The revolutionaries were active in instigating uprisings and in agitation but with only limited influence and result. Only the constitutionalists in whose ranks were landlords, regional bureaucrats and bourgeoisie, with deep social roots in Chinese society and wielding considerable influence through such modern political machines as the provincial and national assemblies, local self-governments and such pressure groups as the chambers of commerce and the press, could have exercised effective influence on China's internal political development.[71]

Western opinions on the 1911 Revolution are no less varied if not more diverse. The tones and directions of research, especially in America, were set by the controversies of the 1960s arising from debates on the revolutionary leadership, less about its nature as about its composition and personalities, and from discussions at the 1965 Portsmouth conference on the 1911 Revolution.[62] Some examine or re-examine the roles of individual revolutionaries, reformers, constitutionalists, bureaucrats, and some focus on more impersonal forces in terms of group interests, class divisions, regionalism, provincialism, militarism, nationalism and intellectual change. So far no last word can yet be said on any aspect as scholars continue to differ. The best effort at synthesizing these conflicting opinions on the nature of the history of this period was by Mary Wright, who suggested that it be treated as the 'first phase' of China's twentieth-century revolution, a much bigger phenomenon the tail end of which has only just begun to appear scores of years later.[63] Tying the 1911 Revolution to this much larger political phenomenon, however, seems to be just another way of saying that it was an 'unsuccessful revolution' which the Chinese have been saying all along and had formally recognised it in Sun Yat-sen's will in 1925. It does not suffice to satisfy historians and still less the dissenting ones, especially the followers of Ichiko's 'no revolution' school.[64]

Since the thoughtful survey of studies on early twentieth-century revolutionary movements in China by Stuart R. Schram in 1972,[65] and the provocative review of works on the subject by Joseph Esherick in 1976,[66] nearly another dozen of monographs on this period have appeared. Four of them are in some way concerned with the political and social developments of China's gentry elite and masses in the central provinces of Hunan and Hubei; two examine the basis and implications of Yuan Shikai's role and power; two discuss respectively the roles of the overseas Chinese and the military; and lastly a latest arrival on the scene which emphasises the strong roots of liberalism in twentieth-century China.[67] The immediate impression these works and others before them give us is a confused historiographical landscape of contradictions with a dialectic of its own. The roles of individual personalities of the period have been debated without conclusion; the earlier emphasis on regional separatism as the source of China's disintegration is now disputed by evidence showing a trend towards centralisation and the revival of central power in the late Qing period. Former focus on the revolutionary forces as the main driving force for change is now strongly challenged or even replaced by studies on conservatism or conservative reformism as the main spring of political life in early twentieth-century China. It often seems to historians that the historical threshold of great discovery and understanding was only a short tantalising distance away, and yet when approached, it turns out to be a mere mirage disappearing before their very eyes.

Interpretation Reconsidered

In conclusion, some views may be scrutinised further to clarify some major aspects of this period.

Among the historians who hold different views on the importance of regional separatism, centralising trend, and class disintegration or conflict, there is considerable common ground. The most important is the common notion that the 1911 Revolution was an elitist affair with little involvement of the masses. But historians disagree on the extent or even the existence of disunity among this elite. Even among those who emphasise the fragmentation within this elite, there is no agreement as to where the main front line of conflict lies. Some argue that it was between the central and the provincial authorities.[68] Others assert that the crevasse was between the formal and the informal apparatus of traditional government, with the latter, being much larger numerically and having gained much greater power and influence from constitutional reforms and local self-government, exerting a decisive influence on the developments of 1911. Once it had decided to operate independently, the old imperial structure had to go.[69] This interpretation was taken even further by another historian who, taking a longer view of history, argues that the influence of this sector was decisive enough in overthrowing the dynasty but, itself estranged from the masses, was unable to sustain a unified national structure in the face of foreign pressures and demands from below; hence the Republic collapsed in 1916.[70] This view is not, however, widely shared. To some, it seems to have put too much emphasis on the division between the formal and the informal arms of late Qing polity. An alternative view is that Yuan Shikai's rise to power in 1911-1912 was due to his ability to draw support from all centres of power, support which was solid enough until he attempted to increase the power of the central government at the expense of the provincial and local centres.[71]

The differences between these views, based on still rather partial evidence, at best, have made it hard for a more consistent interpretation of the period to emerge. But it may be pointed out that these views, with emphasis on the continuation of the traditional gentry's political and social leadership, are basically in agreement with the 'no revolution' school. The biggest concession this school would make to its opponents is to admit that ties between them were loosening, though not sufficiently so for a real revolution to take place in 1911.[72]

The parallels and contrasts between the revisionist view on Yuan Shikai and Yokoyama's analysis of the leadership of the 1911 Revolution are particularly striking. Both agree that it was not a revolution and that Yuan's rise to power had the consent and tacit support of the elites of all shades. They also substantially agree on the basis of this general consensus even if the reasons given are couched in different phraseologies. The political cells of power, whether seen as horizontally diffused organisations such as Yuan's bureaucratic group, the revolutionary faction and the reformist constitutionalists, or as vertically stratified associations of national, provincial and sub-provincial local elites, are held to have shared the same nationalistic aspirations and concerns: the defence of Chinese sovereignty and economic interests and the development of national wealth. Behind these broadly shared national concerns was an understanding, or perhaps a misunderstanding, that the maintenance of the *status quo* was the main basis of collaboration between the 'groups' or the 'nodes' of power, each hoping as Stephen MacKinnon puts it, to be 'simultaneously expanding' though perhaps not necessarily at each other's expense.[73] It is hardly conceivable that this could actually have been the case. The power relationship between the central and regional authorities had always been a problem for Chinese rulers. It seems simply beyond common sense to suggest that each could have expanded its power at no one's expense except that of the peasantry. The latter had never possessed any real political power except perhaps in times of rebellions. In what sense then does one talk about the expansion of 'power' at the peasant's expense, except in terms of increasing the latter's suffering and economic hardship?

Historians' perceptions of the strength of liberalism and democracy in this period also differ greatly. The influence of liberal ideals was evident enough in the constitutionalist movement, in the appearance of provincial and national assemblies, and in republicanism. But with a very few exceptions most historians doubt its importance in 1911. Yokoyama has clearly rejected it as an important element in his emphasis on the continuing dominance of the military faction in this period. Ernest Young sees liberal influence in provincialism and in republicanism, but diagnoses its slender root and its imcompatibility with centralism: it was eclipsed by or discarded in the interest of nationalism in the early republic.[74] Joseph Esherick, on the other hand, echoes the Chinese Marxist view that elitist liberalism was doomed to failure because of the size of China's problem, including strong foreign pressures and sharp internal divisions, which could be overcome only with the support of China's broad masses.[75] This view is, however, questioned by others such as Edward Rhoads, who did not regard China's domestic reform 'as destined for failure even if in the end it did fail'. He contends:

> The alienation of the gentry elite from the masses did not become wide enough to engender a social revolution for another decade or two. Furthermore, while it is true that

the political reforms of the late Qing and early Republic were narrowly based, it must be remembered that they were only a beginning. The nationalist movement, in particular, politicized more than simply the elite. As the process of politicization expanded, so did the concept of 'people' (min). What in 1898 had meant only members of the elite developed by 1913 to include a much broader segment of the population. For example, the franchise for the provincial election of 1912, though still restricted, was significantly more liberal than that for the election of 1909.[76]

Rhoads blames Yuan Shikai and his imperialist supporters for the failure of China's constitutional movement which might otherwise 'have continued to expand, as happened in Japan'. To Rhoads, 'the era from 1900 to 1913 was, with the possible exception of the mid-1920s, the most hopeful time for China in the hundred years from the Opium War to the Communist revolution'.[77] But this is a rather negative defence of the liberal cause of this period. With the publication of John Fincher's new book on Chinese democracy, liberalism during this period seems to have been a much stronger political force than perceived at first by other historians. He writes:

> Elected assemblies appeared in China at the local level by 1907, at the provincial level in 1909, and at the national level in 1910. Most historians have either forgotten or, like me, had never known the impact of elections for these assemblies on Chinese politics during 'the period off the 1911 Revolution'...the elections of 1909 mobilised a non-official elite of nearly two million capable of seizing the initiative from the bureaucracy and the Court when it came time in late 1911 to ponder the future of monarchy in China. The elections of 1912 and 1913 were based on those of 1909 as much as they were influenced by the 10 October 1911 Wuchang uprising and the abdication of the last Chinese emperor on 12 February 1912. They enlisted in politics some tens of millions of Chinese, who may not have been 'the masses' but whose numbers will not let us dismiss China's 'old' liberal democratic republics as merely 'elitist'.[78]

He further concludes: 'Close study of the self-government movement from 1905 to 1911 shows that liberal democracy was not so short-lived as the Liberal Republic of 1911-13'.[79]

Fincher's arguments strengthen considerably the position of some historians such as Mary Wright's perception of the 'new forces' at work in this period, Edward Rhoads' 'most hopeful time' interpretation, and my own that it was a genuine democratic revolution even if we disagree on the extent of its success as well as on its historical significance. I look upon the 1911 Revolution as the first and last chance of Western liberalism in China whereas Fincher sees the continuation of liberalism as an important force in Chinese political life long after 1913.[80] Despite the impressive scholarship John Fincher has brought to bear on this subject, there can be no conclusive answer until Chinese history unfolds itself further. In the meantime, students of history, particularly those of the 'no revolution' school, should certainly take seriously his contention that 'it is a mistake to argue that they [the liberal republics of China] were never there or could never be there'.[81]

As noted previouosly the 'no revolution school' emphasises either the continuous dominant political role of the traditional conservative gentry or the futility of liberal reform without the support of the masses. Fincher's contention may not demolish this argument completely but it is enough to throw it into grave doubt. The strength of the 'no revolution' school rests mainly on the traditional character and the role of the local gentry at sub-provincial levels. But it is very doubtful that leaders operating at the provincial and national levels can be described as traditional gentry. Chang Peng-yuan's analysis of the first Republican parliament of 1913-1914 clearly shows how untraditional the parliamentary elites of early Republican China were. In terms of age the combined average of both houses was a mere 36.45 years (*sui*) old. Only six per cent of the members were fifty years (*sui*) or over and less than one per cent of the total older than sixty. The youthfulness of this parliament reflected not only 'the origins of the political elite in revolution—a young man's enterprise', as Chang puts it, but also the very untraditionalness of this elite, especially when it is taken together with their educational background. Available data on 499 members of parliament show that 48.5 per cent were entirely new-style educated and lacked traditional degrees, and 51.5 per cent had traditional degrees. Of the latter category, most had also received new-style education whether in China or overseas, and only 18.84 per cent were exclusively traditional degree-holders.[82] If there is still any doubt about either the significance or the influence of these elites because of the apparent ease with which this parliament was dissolved in 1913, one should bear in mind that these elites represented, as pointed out by Fincher, over forty million voters based on property and educational qualifications.[83] The cause of the apparent political impotence of these elites obviously lay somewhere else: the interplay of internal forces and foreign pressures, and above all, the disunity among the forces which these parliamentary elites represented.[84]

Another argument which negates the significance of the 1911 Revolution is, as mentioned before, Yokoyama's view that the revolution did not represent any kind of political change because real political power had already shifted from the Manchu court into the hands of a military clique headed by Yuan Shikai long before 1911, and that 1911 was no more than a formal recognition of this fact.[85] Jerome Ch'en, when explaining the change in China's political power structure from the gentry-dominated gentry-military-coalition since mid-nineteenth century to the military-led military-gentry collaboration of the early twentieth century, was at first also inclined to agree with Yokoyama but has since changed his mind. In view of new evidence showing that the Manchu regime had never really lost political control over the military, he now traces this change to 1912, not 1895.[86] Regional armies led by civilian leaders such as Zeng Guofan, Zuo Zongtang, Li Hongzhang were allowed to exist only because they served the interests of the central government. Once they had outlived their usefulness, some were disbanded without difficulty while others were sent to fight the Japanese in 1894-1895 and were, as a result, decimated. In early twentieth century, the ease with which the Manchu court was able to relieve Yuan Shikai of his viceroyalty of Zhili in 1907 and to force him into retirement in 1908 shows that the Manchu court was still firmly in control of political developments until 1911.[87] Even in the 1911 Revolution military leaders in the provinces had yet to assert clearly their power over civilian authorities, though at a national level the Beiyang army had begun to make its influence felt by first petitioning the throne for constitutional monarchy and later by demanding the abdication of the Manchu emperor.[88]

Edmund Fung's study on the role of the military in the 1911 Revolution, the fullest on this subject to date, also observes that 'once the Republicans had resolved to accept Yuan as the president, most military leaders throughout the country pledged their support for him'.[89] Why, despite the fact that fifteen of the twenty-two provincial governors were military men and only seven were gentry leaders, was the military so submissive to the political decisions of the civilian leaderships in Beijing and Nanjing. Undoubtedly a variety of factors came into play. For example, nationalism, fears of foreign intervention, a desire to restore order and stability as soon as possible, concerns for financial difficulties and the devastations and dangers of a prolonged civil war were shared by all Chinese, including the military. But perhaps equally important was the role played by the gentry in 1911. Both the works of Ichiko, already referred to, and myself, here and elsewhere, have shown how this civilian elite played a crucial and even decisive role in toppling the Manchu dynasty.[90]

If primary importance is given to the gentry, did the other forces including the military play only secondary roles? Though any attempt at answering this question must be highly qualified at this stage of our scholarship, in Fung's opinion, the new armies in Wuchang played a crucial role in the initial phase of the 1911 Revolution because they held off the attack of the imperial forces long enough to give other provincial forces time to make up their mind and declare their stand.[91] Similarly, perhaps it could be said that the gentry played crucial roles in the revolution by switching firstly to the anti-Manchu camp to enable the Nanjing Provisional Government to be formed, and then to the Beiyang faction to enable Yuan Shikai to snatch the presidency of the Republic of China.[92] The first move was aimed to grab provincial leadership, the second was to hand over national political leadership to the Beiyang group at the expense of the revolutionary faction. At least in the second part of the gentry's dealing, the military played hardly any part. The armies of both camps stood still awaiting the decision of their political leaders. As is well known, Yuan Shikai did not win the presidency on the battle-field but through negotiations in Xiyintang [Time-caring Hall] in Shanghai, the house of Zhao Fengchang, a gentry member and a cashiered bureaucrat from the provincial government of Hubei years earlier, when Zhang Zhidong was the viceroy of Hunan and Hubei.[93]

Even in the early Republican period Yuan's power was not based on naked force alone. He exacted obedience from all quarters including the military because he was the President of China rather than just the commander of the Beiyang army. The despatch in 1914 of a few thousand of his men under Chen Yi and Tang Xiangming to Sichuan and Hunan respectively could hardly suffice to control provinces as large as France, if traditional respect for central political authority were not there.[94] To a high degree it was Yuan's own frequent use or misuse of the military for political and personal ends and to undermine national civil authority that brought about his own downfall and ushered in the period of warlordism.[95] Herein lay Yuan's personal responsibility for the ascendancy of the military during and after his presidency, and the source of harsh historical judgment on his person, his moral character as well as his statesmanship.[96]

Recent trends of scholarship on the 1911 Revolution tend to emphasise impersonal objective forces at work. In this regard Edmund Fung's conclusion on his study of the military dimension of the Chinese Revolution is worth quoting at length as an example:

> The Chinese had always preferred civilian rule by moral sanctions based on the Confucian system... The Revolution of 1911 almost irrevocably altered the traditional relationship between the army and the state bureaucracy, the result of which was the ascendancy of the military as illustrated in the period of 'warlordism'...The ascendancy of the military has been attributed to the existence of an ideological vacuum after the abolition of the imperial system and the concept of the Son of Heaven. The new Republic lacked the traditional sanctions for the exercise of supreme power. Neither the President nor the provincial authorities could rely on Western-style democratic institutions which were yet to be established; they invariably relied increasingly on the support, or at least goodwill, of the army commanders. The revolution had destroyed the traditional patterns of government and disrupted Chinese society to the extent that the Chinese

people had lost their political and psychological orientations. During the period of political instability in the early Republic, the military was naturally inclined and better equipped than the civil organisations to compete for political power. Certainly, in the absence of a new satisfying ideology, any successors to the Son of Heaven were bound to have serious problems in government. Yuan Shikai was no exception, nor were the rulers of Peking after 1916.[97]

Fung has clearly demolished the view that the ascendancy of the military or warlordism antedated the 1911 Revolution, and he is unequivocal on the irrevocability of the change brought about by the 1911 Revolution, albeit not the result desired by the republicans or the constitutionalists. In his explanation of the rise of the military, he shows his share of a fatalistic view of history current among some Western liberal historians including a leading American scholar, John King Fairbank.[98]

Yet, for the reasons outlined in the preceding pages, I remain sceptical of the opinion that democracy or for that matter reformism was bound to fail before the Second Revolution in 1913. Is it purely an historian's fantasy in speculating that had Yuan Shikai been a personal equal to Bismarck in his understanding of his political and social environments, and possessing the vision, ability and diplomatic skill to deal with them, and had he had the idealism, integrity and steadfastness of Washington, would the result of the 1911 Revolution have been different and more positive? The majority of historians seem to think it otherwise or outright impossible, and history cannot be recalled to prove the point. Yet it is still an important and reasonable question one should ask, and Fincher's new look at this issue has certainly reopened the question. Thematic and regional studies are in vogue at present but more researches on the historical personalities also ought to be done. Historians should not, like the social scientists, focus only on the so-called impersonal or objective forces larger than life, whether in the form of groups and regions, or in terms of economic, social or ideological pressures. It is only when the words and actions of key historical figures such as Yuan Shikai, Song Jiaoren, Sun Yat-sen, Huang Xing, Zhang Jian and others are also properly and thoroughly examined and appraised that a more balanced interpration of the events could result and the significance of the period clarified.

NOTES

I would like to thank all the participants in the October 1981 workshop hosted by the Department of Far Eastern History, Australian National University, for their constructive criticisms and encouragement. I wish also to thank my colleague, Asim Roy of the History Department, University of Tasmania, for the many hours he has spent in discussing with me some of the issues raised in this paper. I remain, however, responsible for the view and errors contained in this chapter.

1. C.P. Fitzgerald, *Revolution in China* (London, 1972), pp. 1-2.
2. See Michael Gasster's comment in 'Comment from Authors Reviewed', *Modern China*, II:2 (April 1976), 205.
3. Joseph W. Esherick, *Reform and Revolution in China: The 1911 Revolution in Hunan and Hubei* (Berkeley, 1976), p. 1.
4. *Ibid.*, p. 8.
5. Zhou Hongran, *Zhongguo minzhu sixiang yundongshi* [A history on the development of democratic thought in China] (Taibei, 1964), p. 254.
6. Shao Zhuanlie, *Sun Zhongshan* [Sun Yat-sen] (Shanghai, 1980), pp. 22-25; Harold Z. Schiffrin, *Sun Yat-sen: Reluctant Revolutionary* (Boston, 1980), p. 36.
7. Marianne Bastid-Bruguiere, 'Currents of Social Change', in *Cambridge History of China*, XI: Late Ch'ing 1800-1911, Part 2, John K. Fairbank and Kwang-ching Liu, eds., (Cambridge, 1980), p. 542; Edmund S.K. Fung, *The Military Dimension of the Chinese revolution: The New Army and its Role in the Revolution of 1911* (Vancouver, 1980), 12ff.
8. Liu Housheng, *Zhang Jian zhuanji* [Biography of Zhang Jian], (Reprint, Hong Kong, 1965), pp. 6-9; 14-19.
9. Ernest P. Young, *The Presidency of Yuan Shih-K'ai: Liberalism and Dictatorship in Early Republican China* (Ann Arbor, 1977), p. 53, points out that contribution to military organization and training figured largely in his rise to high posts, but adds that his claim to prominenece did not rest on his expertise in military administration alone. Cf. Andrew J. Nathan, *Peking Politics 1918-1923: Factionalism and the Failure of Constitutionalism* (Berkely, 1976), p. 9.
10. Jerome Ch'en *Yuan Shih-k'ai* 2nd ed. (Stanford, 1972), pp. 3-17.
11. For example, Zhiang Jian. See Liu Housheng, pp. 20-25; Song Xishang, *Zhang Jian di shengping* [The life of Zhang Jian] (Taibei, 1963), pp. 38-46.
12. Some recent monographs tend to minimise the importance of the military in Yuan Shikai's rise to power in the 1911 Revolution and emphasise the support of the gentry. See Young in n.9 and Stephen R. MacKinnon's *Power and Politics in Late Imperial China: Yuan Shi-kai in Beijing and Tianjin, 1901-1908* (Berkeley, 1980), pp. 5-6.
13. William Ayers, *Chang Chih-tung and Educational Reform in China* (Cambridge, Mass., 1971) pp. 167-79; Chang Hao, 'Intellectual Change and the Reform Movement', *Cambridge History of China*, XI; Late Ch'ing 1800-1911, Part 2, pp. 303-304.
14. Zhou Hongran, pp. 254-260; Chang Hao, pp. 292-293.
15. On these men, See Arthur W. Hummel, ed. *Eminent Chinese of the Ch'ing Period* (Washington D.C. 1943) and Howard L. Boorman, *Biographical Dictionary of Republican China* (New York, 1967).

16. Chang Hao, pp. 300-301.
17. *Ibid.*, p. 294; Zhou, p. 255.
18. Chang Hao, p. 328.
19. *Ibid.*, p. 325. Zuo Shunsheng, *Zhongguo jindaishi sijiang* [Four lectures on modern Chinese history] (Hong Kong, 1962), pp. 154-156. According to Sue Fawn Chung,, the tarnished image of Cixi was the result of a very successful propaganda campaign against her by the reformist group led by Kang Youwei and Liang Qichao. Chung, 'The much Maligned Empress Dowager: A Revisionist Study of the Empress Dowager Tz'u-hsi (1835-1908)', *Modern Asian Studies*, XIII:2 (May 1979), 177-196.
20. Chuzo Ichiko, 'The Role of the Gentry: An Hypothesis', in Mary C. Wright, ed. *China in Revolution: The First Phase, 1900-1913* (New Haven, 1971), p. 299; Daniel H. Bays, *China Enters the Twentieth Century: Chang Chih-tung and the Issues of a New Age, 1895-1909* (Ann Arbor, 1978), pp. 5-6.
21. Edmund S.K. Fung, 'The T'ang Ts'ai-ch'ang Revolt' *Papers on Far Eastern History*, I (March 1970) 70-114; Earnest P. Young, 'The Reformer as a Conspirator: Liang Ch'i-ch'ao and the 1911 Revolution', in Albert Feuerwerker, Rhoads Murphey and Mary C. Wright, eds. *Approaches to Chinese History* (Berkeley, 1967), pp. 239-267, especially p. 241.
22. Few historians, Marxist or liberal, would challenge this view. This is, however, not to say that peasant unrest did not contribute to political change. It certainly did, as ably argued by Marianne Bastid-Bruguiere. See above n.7. See also J. Lust, 'Secret societies, popular movements and the 1911 Revolutions', in J. Chesneaux, ed., *Popular Movement and Secret Societies in China, 1940-1950* (Stanford, 1972). According to Edward Friedman, *Backward Toward Revolution: The Chinese Revolutionary Party* (Berkeley, 1974), p. 4, 'a radical union between rural insurgents and radical urban intellectuals had to be rethought [after the 1911 Revolution] before the former could serve as the basis for revolution'.
23. The idea of insulating south and central China from the turmoil of the north apparently came from Zhao Fengchang, an ex-official and protege of Zhang Zhidong, and a resident of Shanghai. His idea quickly gained the support of gentry leaders such as Zhang Jian, Tang Shouqian, Chen Sanli, as well as that of provincial heads of the region and Chinese envoys to Britain, Japan, Germany and the United States. See Zuo Shunsheng, pp. 212-215. For a Marxist account and interpretation, see *The Yi Ho Tuan Movement of 1900* comp. by the Compilation Group for the 'History of Modern China' series, (Peking, 1976), pp. 62-70. On the Boxer Rebellion, see Victor Purcell, *The Boxer Uprising: A Background Study* (London, 1963).
24. On this subject see Kwang-ching Liu, 'The Limits of Regional Power in the Late Ch-ing Period: A Reappraisal', *Tsing Hua Journal of Chinese Studies*, New Series, X:2 (July, 1974). See also Mackinnon, pp. 6-8.
25. Liu Danian, 'Yihetuan yundong shuomingle shimo' [What was explained by the Boxer movement?], in Zhongguo Kexueyuan Shangdong fenyuan lishi yanjiusuo comp., *Yihetuan yundong liushi zhounian jinian lunwenji* [Commemorative essays on the sixtieth anniversary of the Boxer movement] (Beijing, 1961), pp. 15-16.
26. Chen Zhirang, *Junshen zhengquan: Jindai Zhongguo di junfa shiqi* [The military-gentry coalition: modern China's warlord period] (Hong Kong, 1979), p. 10 states: 'During the Boxer war, a new development which perturbed the government of the conservative faction most was the 'Mutual Preservation Pact of the Southeast''.
27. For discussions on this subject, see Wright, ed., *China in Revolution*, pp. 11-19, 30-44.
28. For the post-Boxer retributions, see Tan, pp. 137-156.
29. Zhou Hongran, pp. 275-277.

30. John Fincher, 'Political Provincialism and the National Revolution', in Wright, ed., *China in Revolution*, p. 168.

31. Chen Zhirang, pp. 10-11.

32. Angus W. McDonald, Jr., *The Urban Origins of Rural Revolution: Elites and the Masses in Hunan Province, China, 1911-1927* (Berkeley, 1978), p. 14.

33. Esherick, p. 112.

34. Ichiko, p. 300.

35. Esherick, p. 112. For definitions of higher and lower gentry according to degrees obtained in traditional examination, see Chung-li Chang, *The Chinese Gentry*, second printing (Seattle, 1970), pp. 6-32.

36. Ichiko, p. 302; Esherick, p. 133. Yixian [Sun Zhongshan], 'Zhina baoquan fenge helun' [A discourse on the preservation or cutting up of China] *Jiangsu*, VI (November, 1903), 13-21; Schiffren, p. 357.

37. Esherick, pp. 133-135, 140.

38. Bays, p. 178.

39. Marie-Claire Bergere, 'The Role of the Bourgeoisie' in Wright ed., *China in Revolution*, pp. 231, 237, 287-288.

40. Nathan, pp. 8-10.

41. On the subject of military subversion, see Fung, *The Military Dimension*, pp. 5-10.

42. Stuart R. Schram, 'Some Recent Studies of Revolutionary Movements in China in the Early Twentieth Century, *Bulletin of the School of Oriental and African Studies*, XXXV (October, 1972), p. 602. For more detailed studies on the role of the military, see Yoshihiro Hatano, 'The New Armies', in Wright, ed., *China in Revolution*, pp. 365-382, but especially Fung, *The Military Dimension*. See also Fincher, pp. 253-260 for a different view of the military.

43. For example the attempt of Zhang Zhidong, Viceroy of Hunan and Hubei, to raise a foreign loan in 1905 was frustrated by a public outcry from the provincial gentry and students. See Bays, pp. 178-181.

44. *Ibid*.

45. The same conclusion is arrived at by MacKinnon, pp. 223-224. McDonald, Jr., pp. 58, places the beginning of warlordism in 1913.

46. McDonald, Jr., pp. 7-11.

47. For relations between the revolutionaries and reformers in this period, see Schiffrin, pp. 148-167; Chang P'eng-yuan, 'A Typological Hypothesis on the Elites of the 1911 Revolution in China', *Journal of the Oriental Society of Australia*, IX:1-2 (1972-1973), 32-38.

48. On the role of the secret societies in the 1911 Revolution, see Jean Chesneaux, *Secret Societies in China* (Ann Arbor, 1971), pp. 135-159; on overseas Chinese, see Yen Ching Hwang, *The Overseas Chinese and the 1911 Revolution with Special Reference to Singapore and Malaya* (London, 1976); on students and intellectuals,' the following works may be added to those already cited: Chun-tu Hsueh, *Huang Hsing and the Chinese Revolution* (Stanford, 1961); Michael Gasster, *Chinese Intellectuals and the Revolution of 1911* (Cambridge, Mass., 1969); K.S. Liew, *Struggle for Democracy: Sung Chiao-jen and the 1911 Chinese Revolution* (Berkeley, 1971; Mary Backus Rankin, *Early Chinese Revolutionaries Radical Intellectuals in Shanghai and Chekiang, 1902-1911* (Cambridge, Mass., 1971).

49. Bergere, pp. 286-295; Mark Elvin, 'The Revolution of 1911 in Shanghai', a paper read at the Fourth Biennial Conference of the Asian Studies Association of Australia, 10-14 May, 1982 at Monash University, Melbourne; Shen Weibin, Yang Liqiang, 'Shanghai Shangtuan Yu Xinhai Geming' [Shanghai Volunteer Corps and the 1911 Revolution], *Lishi Yanjiu* (Historical research), 3 (May-June 1980), 67-88.

50. See Li Chien-nung, pp. 266-345.

51. Jerome Ch'en, pp. 214-15.

52. Winston Hsieh, *Chinese Historiography on the Revolution of 1911: A critical Survey and a Selected Bibliography* (Stanford, 1975), pp. 25-63.

53. For the latest emphases on this aspect of the 1911 Revolution, see Hu Yuebang, 'Zai Beijing gejie jinian xinhai geming qishi zhounian dahuishang di jianghua' [Speech to the gatherings of various peoples in Beijing for commemorating the seventieth anniversary of the 1911 Revolutional], *Beijing Review*, (9 October 1981), pp. 3-4.

54. For a Chinese Marxist definition of the bourgeoisie, see Edmund S.K. Fung, 'Post-1949 Chinese Historiography of the 1911 Revolution', *Modern China*. IV:2 (April 1978), 185, 211. See also Lin Zengping, *et al.*, *Xinhai gemingshi* [History of the 1911 Revolution] (Beijing, 1980), I, 44-73, cited in Wu Anjia, 'Zhonggong weishimo yao "jinian" xinhai geming' [Why do the Chinese Communists need to commemorate the 1911 Revolution?] *Zhongguo dalu* [Mainland China], 70 (October 1981), 6.

55. Li Shu, *Xinhai geming qianhou di zhongguo zhengzhi* [Chinese politics before and after the 1911 Revolution] (Hong Kong, 1978), pp. 148-152. See also Zhang Kaiyuan, 'A General Review of the Study of the Revolution of 1911 in the People's Republic of China', *Journal of Asian Studies*, XXXIX:3 (May 1980), 525-529.

56. Ye Botang, 'Lun xinhai geming di xingzhi: Zhongshan xiansheng lingdao di geming shi quanmin geming' [A discourse on the nature of the 1911 Revolution: The Revolution led by Sun Yat-sen was a revolution of the whole people] *Zhongguo dalu*, 171 (November, 1981), 17-18.

57. Hsieh, 'Introduction' especially pp. 6-13, and conclusion, particularly p. 86. See also Li Chien-nung, pp. 290-303. For a recent example of historical writings on the 1911 Revolution, particularly the causes of its failure, see Zhang Pengyuan, *Lixianpai yu xinhai geming* [The constitutionalists and the 1911 Revolution] (Taibei 1969), pp. 240-246; Zhang Yufa, *Zhongguo xiandai shilue* [An outline history of contemporary China] (Taibei, 1978), pp. 2-3; Shen Yunlong, *Xiandai zhengzhi renwu shuping* [A critical narrative of contemporary political personalities] (Taibei, 1960), p. 76. Cf. Li Dingyi, pp. 232-243.

58. Hsieh, pp. 5-8. See also Zou Lu, *Zhongguo guomindang shilue* [A brief history of the Chinese Nationalist Party] (Taibei, 1951), p. 242.

59. This analysis of Japanese historiography is based on Satoi Hikoshichiro, 'Chukoku kintaikatei ni kansuru mittsu no toraekata ni tsuite' [On the three ways of grasping the processes of modernisation in China], *Rekishigaku kenkyu* [Historical studies] 312 (May 1966), cited in Lin Qiyan's translation of the concluding chapter 'Iwayuru shingai kakumei' [The so-called 1911 Revolution] of Yokoyama Suguru's *Shinhai kakumei kenkyu oboegaki* [A note on study of the 1911 Revolution] (Hiroshima, 1976). See *Dousou* [Shake up] 31 (June, 1979) 17.

60. Yokoyama Suguru in *Dousou*, 31:17. New Westernisers seem to differ from the Westernisers of the Tongzhi and early Guangxu periods, both in the direction of reform and in the greater degree of influence they had on the court as extremely conservative opposition had greatly weakened after 1895, especially after 1900.

61. *Ibid*, p. 22. Cf. Zhang Pengyuan, *Lixianpai*, pp. 218-225 and Ichiko, pp. 311-312.

62. On the Portsmouth conference see Wright's Preface in Wright, ed. *China in Revolution*, pp. vi-vii. On debates on leadership in the early 1960's, see *Journal of Asian Studies*, XXII:3 (May 1963), 373-375 and XXI:3 (May 1962), 374-376; *Modern China*, II:2 (April 1976), 221-225.

63. Wright, ed., *China in Revolution*, pp. 62-63. For continuity in a special sense by joining the beginning of liberalism in the 1911 period to its

manifestation in contemporary China, see John Fincher, *Chinese Democracy: The Self-Government Movement in Local, Provincial and National Politics, 1905-1914*, (London, 1981).

64. For Ichiko's view, see Wright, ed., *China in Revolution*, pp. 312-313.

65. Schram, pp. 588-605.

66. Joseph W. Esherick, '1911: A Review', *Modern China*, II:2 (April 1976), 141-183.

67. The books referred to are Charlton M. Lewis, *Prologue to the Chinese Revolution: The Transformation of Ideas and Institutions in Hunan Province, 1891-1907* (Cambridge, Mass., 1976); McDonald, Bays, Esherick, Young, Mackinnon, Yen, Fung and Fincher already cited.

68. Robert A. Kapp, *Szechuan and the Chinese Republic: Provincial Militarism and Central Power, 1911-1938* (New Haven, 1973), pp. 2-3, 11; Young, p. 24; see also Ernest P. Young, 'A Summing Up: Leadership and Constituencies in the 1911 Revolution', *Modern China*, II:2 (April 1976), 223-225; Fincher, 'Provincialism and National Revolution' in Wright, ed., *China in Revolution*, p. 219.

69. Bays, pp. 5, 178.

70. Esherick, *Reform and Revolution in China*, p. 258.

71. MacKinnon, p. 224.

72. Young, *The Presidency*, p. 25; Ichiko, pp. 312-313. It should be pointed out that their views are not identical. Young emphasises the odds against revolution in 1911 including not only internal but also external forces, while Ichiko emphasises the interests of the provincial and sub-provincial gentry in maintaining status quo.

73. MacKinnon, pp. 9-10. Fincher, *Chinese Democracy*, p. 12, holds the view: 'In a polity as large as China's...some separatism would be expected and some provinces showed it. But nationalism limited its results,...In China the self-government movement advanced...through a three-level hierarchy of local provincial and national politics... It seems clear that loyalty to groupings at one level was compatible with loyalty to groupings of another level'. What Fincher tells us is that 'nationalism can have a more complex social basis than its historians have usually allowed'.

74. Young, *The Presidency*, pp. 243-244.

75. Esherick, *Reform and Revolution*, p. 243.

76. Edward Rhoads, 'Two Cheers for 1911', *Modern China*, V:1 (January 1979), 135.

77. *Ibid.*

78. Fincher, *Chinese Democracy*, p. 16.

79. *Ibid.*, p. 251.

80. *Ibid.*, pp. 252-273 and Preface. For other opinions referred to in this connection, see Wright, 'Introduction', in Wright, ed. *China in Revolution*, pp. 30-44. Wright does not emphasise liberalism as an important force but the very mention of the various groups at work suggests elements of a liberal society in the making. Rhoads in his review essay, 'Two Cheers for 1911', obviously indicates his appreciation of liberalism as a moving force behind the event of 1911. My own belief in the liberal phenomena of 1911 is expressed in Liew, particularly ch. 12.

81. Fincher, *Chinese Democracy*, p. 273.

82. Chang P'eng-yuan, 'Political Participation and Political Elites in Early Republican China: The Parliament of 1913-1914', translated by Andrew J. Nathan, *Journal of Asian Studies*, XXXVII:2 (February 1978), 293-313.

83. Fincher, *Chinese Democracy*, p. 252.

84. Chen, Zhirang, pp. 18-21.

85. Yokoyama, p. 18.

86. Chen Zhirang, pp. 3-4, 20. For his earlier review, see Jerome Ch'en, *The Military-Gentry Coalition: China Under the Warlords* (Toronto, 1979), and Ronald Suleski's review of it in *Journal of Asian Studies*, XL:1 (November 1980), 98-101.

87. Ch'i Hsi-sheng, *Warlord Politics in China, 1916-1928* (Stanford, 1976), p. 15 states that Yuan had already established a considerable military following by the time of his dismissal in 1908. He points out that of 'some sixteen divisions and sixteen mixed brigades were considered to be loyal to Yuan personally'. Accordingly he describes Yuan's dismissal as 'semi-retirement'. My argument is that he certainly had potential influence within those units of the new army but without the events of 1911, the extent of his influence would have remained unknown as he would not have had an opportunity to exercise or exploit that influence.

88. Chen Zhirang, pp. 18-19.

89. Fung, *The Military Dimension*, p. 227.

90. Ichiko, p. 312. Liew, pp. 197-199.

91. Fung, *The Military Dimension*, pp. 256-257.

92. Liu Housheng, pp. 194-195 cited in Liew, p. 197. Before the start of the north-south peace negotiation in 1911, Tang Shaoyi representing north China, went to see Zhang Jian first as instructed by Yuan Shikai. Zhang Jian was alleged to have said to Tang, 'The so-called north-south peace negotiation is really a negotiation between Xiangcheng [Yuan] and the Tongmenghui. It has little to do with Jiangsu and Zhejiang. The independence of these two provinces is a passive rather than an active act with the aim of avoiding the ravages of war, especially in Jiangsu in which there are eight persons assuming the title of military governors with their troops all over the province. If we do not support Cheng Dequan, we would not have known how to put the place together. For this reason, we have no demands at all on Xiangcheng. I could only offer some opinions on behalf of the people of Jiangsu and Zhejiang, but cannot guarantee that the Tongmenghui would listen. This matter would depend entirely on your skill and ability'. See Liu, p. 194. This account suggests the gentry's fear of the military as a threat to their leadership, but should not be interpreted as evidence of the loss of general civilian authority. See also pp. 180-184 for the existence of a previous understanding between Zhang Jian and Yuan Shikai before the revolution. Cf. Zhang Pengyuan, pp. 244-245.

93. Liu Houseng, pp. 194-195 cited in Liew, p. 197. See also Xu Zhucheng, *Jiuwen zayi* [Miscellaneous recollections of old times] (Hong Kong, 1980), pp. 202-204.

94. See Kapp, pp. 14-15; McDonald, Jr., pp. 24-27. On Chen Yi's position in Sichuan, see Liu Yusheng, *Shizaitang zayi* [Miscellaneous recollection of the Age-laden Hall], (Shanghai, n.d., Preface by Doug Biwu, dated 1959), pp. 198-199.

95. Hsi-sheng Ch'i, p. 15; see also Chen, Junshen Zhengquan, p. 19; Fincher, *Chinese Democracy* p. 254, sees Yuan and the anti-Yuan revolutionaries as competitors in the subversion of troops for their own political purposes. It is intriguing to derive from it the possible conclusion that each thereby had its own shares in contributing to the rise of the military and the militarists' contempt for civilian authority. Yet, is there no distinction between the revolutionaries' instigation of troops against Yuan for the cause of the republic and Yuan's deployment of his own soldiers against parliamentary democracy?

96. See Jerome Ch'en, *Yuan Shi-Kai*, pp. 206-215. See also Herbert Huey's review of Ernest P. Young's book on Yuan Shikai, *Journal of Oriental Studies*, XVII: 1-2 (1979), 61-62. Cf. Lyon Sharman, *Sun Yat-sen: His Life and Its Meaning* (Stanford, 1968), p. 169, and Xue Jundu [Hsueh Chun-tu] 'Xinhai geming xinlun' [New discourse on the 1911 Revolution], in *Dousou*, 47

(November 1981), 1-12, especially p. 3.
97. Fung, *The Military Dimension*, p. 258.
98. John King Fairbank, *The United States and China*, 3rd edition (Cambridge Mass., 1973), pp. 195-96. I was myself inclined towards this view at one time in a slightly different way. See Liew, ch. 13, especially pp. 197-201. Despite profuse qualifications in his argument, Barrington Moore, Jr's Basic historical approach in explaining the development of modern China is also a fatalistic or even a deterministic one. See his *Social Origins of Dictatorship and Democracy* (Harmondworth, 1977), ch. 4.

10

THE HAKKA CHINESE OF LINGNAN: ETHNICITY AND SOCIAL CHANGE IN MODERN TIMES
S.T. Leong

The progressive breakdown of China's imperial order and the remaking of a socio-political system from the mid-nineteenth century onwards opened up a competition for power by various groups in varying contexts. Formerly disadvantaged groups thrust themselves forward to seize opportunities for socio-economic advancement. The Hakkas were one such group who in this period played obtrusive roles at various times, only a few of which can be discussed in this chapter. The reader should be alerted from the outset that the available data permits no more than a sketch of Hakka ethnic history in modern times and the conclusions drawn are more suggestive than definitive.

Generally it is possible to examine Hakka activities in two broad phases, one in the nineteenth century when they sought to minimise the risks to their survival as a group by means of ethnic mobilisation, and the other in the twentieth when they responded to the opportunities presented by a new political environment. Common to both phases were a readiness on their part to accept new ideas with a revolutionary potential, and an emphasis on ethnic assertiveness—two of their strategies for surviving or enhancing their socio-economic status. Thus, the Taiping Rebellion with its Hakka leadership core reflected both strategies: a ready acceptance of a foreign religion, Christianity, and mobilisation by means of the God Worshippers' Society in the upper West River basin (Guangxi), where Hakkas were in strife with neighbouring groups.[1] In the same period, the Hakkas at the Lingnan core were similarly mobilising during the Hakka-Punti War (1854-1867).[2] Receptiveness to new ideas as a means of social advancement predisposed many Hakkas to join Sun Yat-sen's revolutionary movement.[3]

In the early twentieth century, ethnic self-awareness and a predisposition to social change attuned the Hakkas mentally to the opportunities presented by the military profession, the introduction of modern education and associated new professions, the rise of new political structures which opened up careers for talent, and opportunities of acquiring commercial wealth which were closed to them in Lingnan but open in Southeast Asia and elsewhere. In these early decades, the Hakkas succeeded in achieving a degree of political and military influence out of all proportion to their numbers. In the Fujian-Jiangxi and Hunan-Jiangxi border regions, where the Hakkas were predominant, the location of the communist rural soviets in the 1930s offered them new political opportunities there. Both the Guomindang and the Chinese Communist Party military-political establishments were to end up with substantial Hakka representation.

This paper will focus primarily on the Hakkas in the Lingnan Region where numbers of this group achieved a strong regional presence, and even a measure of national prominence before the Sino-Japanese War. The subject is treated in five sections: first, a conceptualisation of the Hakkas and competing groups; second, the Hakka position in Lingnan in the nineteenth century; third, the articulation of a Hakka ethos by the Hakka elite; fourth, the Hakkas as nationalists, and finally the new Hakka position in Lingnan in the 1930s before the outbreak of the Sino-Japanese War.

Cultural/Ethnic Groups in Lingnan

Scholars and laymen observers have long been aware that the 'Cantonese', 'Hoklos', and 'Hakkas', along with sprinklings of diverse non-Han aborigines populate Guangdong province. Conceptualising these groups has remained a problem. The basis and significance of these categories are elusive, while the labels themselves, both as to their origins and symbolic loads, remain imprecise, not to mention the confusion over whether they are self-ascriptions or ascriptions by others. A few preliminary remarks are necessary to clear up some of the confusion.

To begin with, each of these groups entered Guangdong at different times and occupied a separate ecological niche. The earliest of the Cantonese ancestors arrived before Han times, although in significant numbers only from Tang onwards. Intermixing with the numerous pre-existing aboriginal tribes, collectively known as the Baiyue, and linguistically influenced by them, they occupied the Guangzhou (Canton) delta lowlands before fanning out.[4] The Hoklos of eastern Guangdong immigrated mainly from southern Fujian, beginning probably around the ninth century, and they maintain to this day a strong linguistic affinity with that area; they occupied the only other lowland, the fertile lower basin of the Han River.[5]

The ancestors of the Hakkas are said to have migrated in waves from the north, starting in the fourth century, settling first in the Gan River highlands (southern Jiangxi), overflowing then to the Ting River basin (western Fujian); migrants of both areas then settled in the North River highlands and the Mei River basin in north and north-eastern Guangdong from the time of the Song-Yuan transition.[6] This theory of course ignores the considerable intermixing with pre-existing non-Han aborigines. In any case, by the end of the fifteenth century, it may be assumed that the Hakkas of all contiguous areas had developed a common culture and tradition, including a distinctive speech.[7]

The Hakkas' initial disadvantage therefore stemmed from the limited resources of their ecological niche in the hills and mountains of the Guangdong-Fujian-Jiangxi borderland. Their society and culture, while having much in common with Chinese society and culture in general, showed distinctive features that were the result of ecological adaptations—the Hakka dialect, non-binding of women's feet to maximise the labour value of women, distinctive gender roles compared to what prevailed among their neighbours, occupational non-discrimination, tradition of sojourning, and so on.

Migrating out in search of opportunities, they generally settled as agriculturalists, cash-croppers, or miners in the hillier and less productive lands than those of their neighbours. Thus, in the sixteenth century, some of them migrated and settled close to the South-east Coast lowlands, in response to economic opportunities near Chaozhou, Fuzhou, and Wenzhou; others moved further inland to the highlands separating the Gan and the Xiang drainage basins (Hunan-Jiangxi border area); and still others settled on the uplands of the West River (Guangxi). Their advance down the East River towards the Lingnan core began late in the sixteenth century, but in significant numbers only in the late seventeenth and eighteenth centuries, when many also headed for Sichuan, Taiwan, and South-east Asia. A final wave took place in the second half of the nineteenth century following the Hakka-Punti War, when displaced Hakkas were relocated by the authorities in the poorer parts of the Leizhou peninsula and on Hainan island.[8]

Two millenia of Han Chinese colonisation and assimilation of the older natives had produced a complex cultural landscape in Lingnan. Contributing significantly to this complexity were the adoption of Han names by the non-Han, and intermarriage between Han and non-Han. None of the Han Chinese groups can claim the possession of a purely Han ancestry no matter what their ethnic rhetoric. But nothing had shaped inter-ethnic relations so much as the forced migration of lesser groups. The Cantonese had, for example, disinherited the Zhuang people of the lowlands and the Yao of the higher ground; in the northeast, the Hakkas, and to some extent the Hoklos, had all but displaced the She aborigines. This environment engendered a sense of racial defensiveness, stronger in some ethnic groups than in others, to be sure, but all the Han Chinese in the area at times felt the need to assert their racial purity with categorical certainty. One and all they were 'Tangren' (people of Tang culture), descendants of migrants from the 'Central Plain' (*zhongyuan*), that is, the cradle of ancient Chinese civilisation in the North, and their ancestors were upper-class gentry families (*yiguan zhi zu*). Both the Cantonese and Hakkas had an implausible lore about how their ancestors entered Guangdong.[9] The history of settlement of the area makes intelligible the singular preoccupation of these groups with racial and cultural purity, which then accentuated the racial aspect of nationalism when it did emerge at the turn of the twentieth century.

The above historical survey enables us now to discuss the meaning, or lack of it, in the classification of the groups. The label 'Cantonese' derives from the now-forgotten old Western name for Guangdong province. In the literature, it serves two functions: it refers broadly to the preponderant group, but at the same time narrowly to the speech of the Guangzhou metropolis, which happens to be only one of several dialects, some varying to the point of mutual non-intelligibility. A Cantonese, however, would identify himself to others of the province as 'Punti', meaning 'native', or as 'Guangfuren' (a person of Guangzhou prefecture), and to outsiders as 'Guangdongren' (a person of Guangdong province).

'Hoklo', a term of confused origin and uncertain rendering in Chinese, and capable of connoting respect or contempt, depending on the context, is others' designation of the natives of Chaozhou (excluding of course the Hakkas) in eastern Guangdong, but the label often includes the inhabitants of southern Fujian. The Hoklos of Chaozhou refer to themselves as 'Tiechiu', the local pronunciation of the prefecture.

Finally, 'Hakka', commonly mistaken as a label given by others, is a term of self-designation. The Cantonese in fact referred to them in the past by the derogatory name 'Aizi', relenting only in recent times in order to preserve communal harmony. How the term 'Hakka' originated and why members of the group continue to refer to themselves by a label that implies 'sojourning', despite centuries of residence, remain inexplicable even to the Hakkas themselves.

Next to the problem of unravelling the meaning of these labels is the more important question of the nature of these entities in sociological terms. They are variously called 'ethnolinguistic',[10] 'subcultural',[11] or more commonly in anthropological literature 'ethnic' or 'sub-ethnic' groups.[12] Caution is undoubtedly called for, but one should have no difficulty labelling them 'ethnic' provided the meaning behind this shorthand ascription is borne in mind. A distinction must first be drawn, as Orlando Patterson has argued, between a 'cultural' and an 'ethnic' group. A group that shares, consciously or unconsciously, a common culture and tradition is but a cultural group. It only becomes ethnic when members of the group identify themselves consciously as belonging to the group, and seek to promote group identity and solidarity for the purpose of enhancing the group's socio-economic status or minimising the threats to its survival.[13] Ethnicity is thus 'essentially a form of interaction between cultural groups operating within common social contexts'.[14] The 'choice of ethnic allegiance', as Patterson puts it, is contextual;[15] ethnic salience varies with time and place depending on the needs of the groups concerned. In short, the Cantonese, Hoklos, and Hakkas, while being cultural groups, may only be ethnic groups some of the time. Moreover, 'the fact that a segment of a cultural group becomes an ethnic group', says Patterson, 'does not mean that all members of the cultural group thereby become an ethnic group'. Nor is the group ethnic, even if perceived by others as one, unless members of the group choose to interact with others in ethnic terms.[16]

The Hakka Position in Lingnan

With these preliminary remarks we may now examine briefly the position of the Hakkas in Lingnan early in the nineteenth century. I have shown elsewhere that the situation of the Hakkas and their ethnic expressions can best be illuminated by using William Skinner's regional systems framework.[17] Instead of viewing them within the administrative, provincial boundary of Guangdong, we look at them within the physiographic, economic macro-region of Lingnan, a region that comprised the drainage basins of the West River (including most of Guangxi), the North River, and the East River. The basin of the Han River, including the Mei and Ting tributaries, fell physiographically within the South-east Coast and is therefore excluded (see Map 1).

An essential feature of the regional systems framework is the structuring of time and space to better understand various social phenomena. Thus, as of the early part of the nineteenth century, China divided physiographically into nine relatively unintegrated macro-regions, each internally differentiated into a core and a periphery. Compared to the periphery, the core was characterised by a greater population and population density, higher concentration of resources (i.e. arable land), transport network, and investment, and a great degree of commercialisation. Each region also had its distinct developmental cycle. An important aspect of systemic interactions, from our point of view, was the demographic movement (a) from the periphery towards the core by highlanders seeking to exploit new opportunities associated with an economic upturn, and (b) away from it during an economic downturn. An economic downturn would be accompanied by what Skinner calls 'community closure', and at such a time ethnic mobilisation and inter-ethnic conflict became salient.[18]

In Lingnan economic contraction did set in early in the nineteenth century, following an expansionary phase from the late seventeenth through the eighteenth centuries. It was caused, among other things, by a silver shortage, opium consumption,

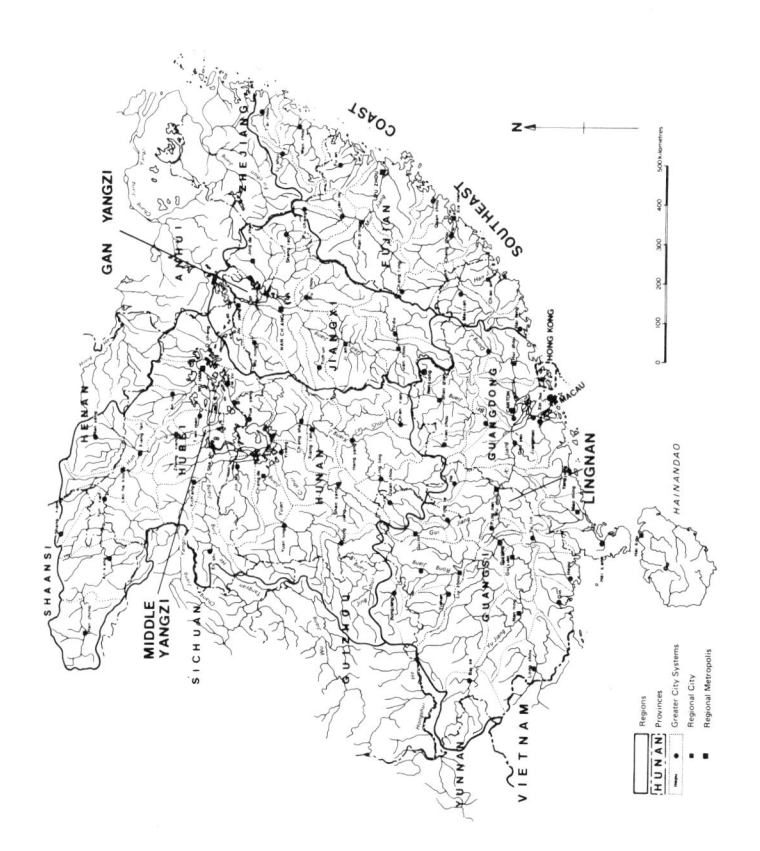

Map 1. The Lingnan, Southeast Coast, Gan and Middle Yangzi Macroregions, ca. 1893, showing the approximate extent of greater-city trading systems

piracy, and the loss of Guangzhou's pre-eminence in foreign trade to Shanghai. Economic insecurity gave rise to massive emigration overseas, widespread local dissidence, inter-lineage and inter-ethnic feuding. The Hakkas at the Lingnan core and up and down the West River basin interacted with their neighbours in ethnic terms. The usefulness of the regional systems framework is underlined by the fact that at no time did all the Hakkas unite in ethnic solidarity, partly because the Hakkas straddled three different macro-regions, each with a different developmental cycle. Hakkas and Hoklos, for instance, interacted without a single incident along the isogloss all through the second half of the nineteenth century.[19] One reason among several was that the South-east Coast regional cycle, unlike that of Lingnan, began an upturn following the Opium War, with the creation of treaty ports along the coast.

To press the point further, there is much ambiguity in the use of the name Hakka in the existing literature. By not drawing the cultural/ethnic distinction, or mistaking ethnic rhetoric for reality, the literature describes Hakka distribution as spread across the adjoining borderlands of Jiangxi, Fujian, and Guangdong, and yet when discussing other matters, attention is focused entirely on what pertains to Guangdong. This confusion is cleared up once the spatio-temporal dimension of each constituent of the cultural group is recognised. As I have argued elsewhere, 'Hakka' originated as an ethnic label peculiar to the immigrants from these borderlands to the Lingnan core and the lowland of the Han River. This symbol of ethnic identity, which had emerged in a situation of contact and conflict with lowlanders, was subsequently transmitted to the homeland, primarily the basin of the Mei, a tributary of the Han, and secondarily the basin of the Ting, the other main tributary. The 'Hakkas' of the upper Gan basin never identified themselves as such; instead, they called themselves 'bendi' ('natives') in relation to immigrants, a large proportion of whom had in fact come from the Mei and Ting basins. The label was carried by these immigrants to various parts of the Gan basin, but was subsequently eclipsed by the label 'keji'. Even more significantly, the 'Hakkas' in the North River uplands, though within the Lingnan macro-region and Guangdong province, dissociated themselves from the label when Hakka ethnic self-awareness reached one of its peaks. This may be explained by the fact that the North River 'Hakkas' had migrated to the Lingnan core in far fewer numbers, owing to the relatively advantageous economic position of the Shaozhou sub-region on the north-south artery of trade. In sum, Hakka ethnic assertiveness in Lingnan in the nineteenth and early twentieth centuries should not be construed as an all-Hakka phenomenon. The 'Hakkas' were segmented by regional context of time and place, and some had more reasons than others to behave in ethnic terms.[20]

To continue with a characterisation of the Hakka position in Lingnan, one feature to be underlined is that Hakka disabilities were primarily economic. This was true of Hakkas everywhere: the home base was invariably described by the stock phrase *shanduo tianshao*, that is, more mountains than arable land, and close to the Lingnan core the Hakkas were typically tenants of Punti landlords, a dependency-relationship that lay at the root of Hakka-Punti conflict. The Hakkas everywhere were not specially disadvantaged by any deliberate government policy. Indeed, the institutional arrangements and imperial policies maintained fairly open and equal opportunity structures and were sensitive to inter-ethnic rivalry. Hakkas in the home base were of course able to acquire gentry status by means of the prefectural examinations, and in such predominantly Hakka prefectures as Jiaying, Huizhou, Nanxiong, and Shaozhou in Guangdong, Tingzhou in Fujian, and Ganzhou and Nan'an in Jiangxi, they competed among themselves. In mixed prefectures where Hakkas formed a substantial minority, special quotas were set aside for them, usually following inter-ethnic altercations, in order to defuse tensions. This procedure was first adopted for the 'Hakkas' in Yuanzhoufu (Jiangxi) in 1730.[21] Later the precedent was extended to the Guangzhou and Zhaoqing prefectures in Guangdong. Thus, civil and military examination quotas were set aside for Hakkas of the counties Xinning (1788),[22] Dongguan (1801),[23] Xin'an (1802),[24] Kaiping (1807),[25] and Gaoming (year unknown).[26]

The Hakkas of Lingnan were differentiated by spatial and temporal variations in migration and settlement (see Maps 2 and 3). The isogloss of Hakka and Cantonese can be fairly accurately delineated immediately beyond the all-Hakka areas, that is, along the line of the Guangzhou regional core, cutting through the East and North River basins. (The exception was that the western basin of the North River above Yingde had a large Yao

Map 2. The Lingnan, Southeast Coast, Lower, Gan, and Middle Yangzi Macroregions, showing the approximate county boundaries, ca. 1893

THE HAKKA CHINESE

Distribution of the Hakkas

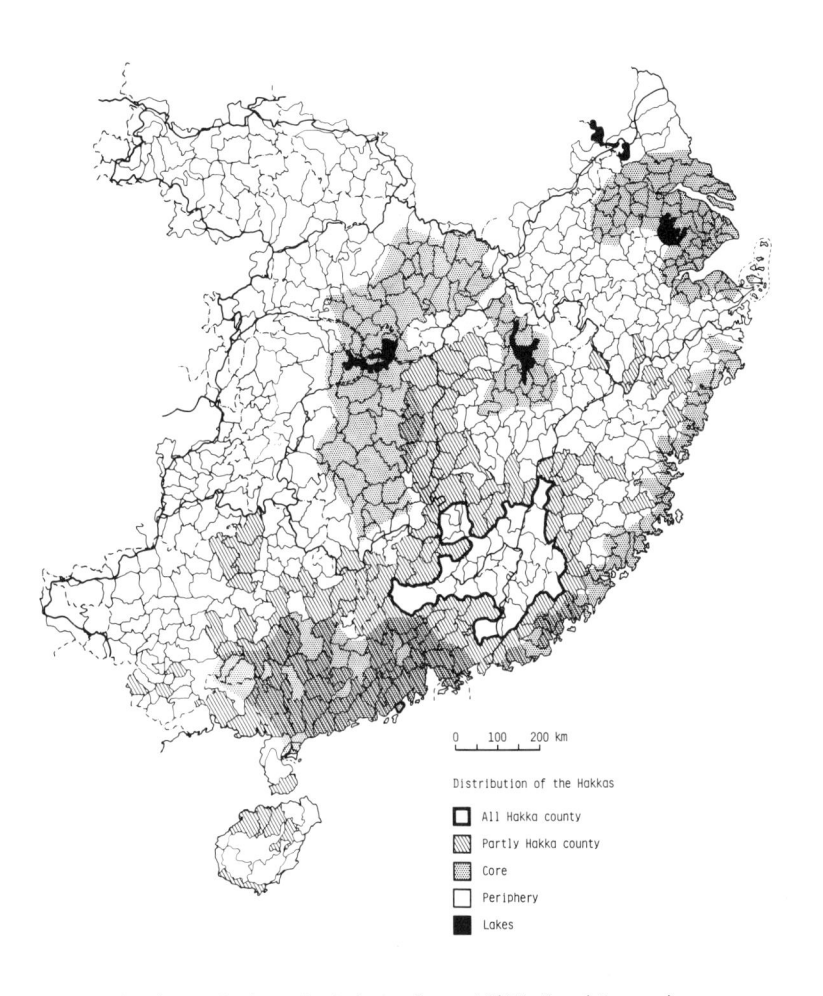

- All Hakka county
- Partly Hakka county
- Core
- Periphery
- Lakes

Map 3. The Lingnan, Southeast Coast, Lower, Gan, and Middle Yangzi Macroregions, showing regional cores and the distribution of the Hakkas, 16th to 19th centuries

population.) Moving inward from the first line of inter-group contact, there are significant variations in the comparative numerical strength of Hakkas vis-à-vis the Cantonese. Reliable demographic data are of course unavailable; the impression given by the sources is that by the mid-nineteenth century, Boluo county was the only one with a Hakka majority and, according to one source, they were paying ground rent to Punti owners residing in the towns. Nearly equal numerical balance appears to be the case in Zengcheng, Conghua, and Hua xian; slightly fewer in Dongguan and Xin'an, and as much as a third in Xinning, Kaiping, and other surrounding counties.[27]

The relative size of the Hakka community was obviously of critical importance in its effect on the resources available, the scope and duration of ethnic mobilisation, and in deciding the choice between confrontation or accommodation. Hakka settlement patterns, too, enhanced the potential for inter-ethnic conflict, as Myron Cohen has elucidated.[28] As migrants of a culturally different population, Hakka settlements initially tended to be small and widely interspersed among the Cantonese who were already organised in localised agnatic groupings. This did not mean, however, that Hakkas and Cantonese generally lived in the same villages. On the contrary, Hakka settlements tended to be segregated from Cantonese villages. Indeed, in some counties for which gazetteer information is available, the layout of the Hakka community may be seen to occupy an entire section of the county, generally cleaving to the hillier and poorer lands.[29] What this pattern of settlement suggests is that the pure Hakka villages facilitated the endurance of distinctive cultural traits, forming the basis for ethnic identification and mobilisation.

This settlement pattern stemmed from the fact that the land available to the Hakka immigrants was generally limited to the marginal type, not yet in use but already claimed by the Cantonese. Initially, the relationship was symbiotic: Hakkas worked the land in permanent tenure and the Cantonese collected ground rent. A great many of the settlers had arrived under government sponsorship in the eighteenth century; these were given the right of landownership upon the land being brought under cultivation and the taxes paid. But, as so often happened, no sooner was the 'waste' land made productive than prior unknown claimants asserted their claims, the reason cited by one local official in the eighteenth century why settlers hesitated in responding to the official call for settlers.[30]

These initially small and dispersed Hakka communities would subsequently grow, drawing a constant stream of immigrants who congregated, in the stock imagery used by Cantonese, 'like ants and bees'. The pressure on the part of the Hakkas to develop village settlements of size and to increase their landholdings became increasingly difficult to resist, while the rapacity of Cantonese landlords grew with economic contraction. As E.J. Eitel of the London Missionary Society wrote in 1867:

> The Hakkas are everywhere to be found, either dispersed in small villages between the hills and paying ground-rent to the Puntis, or congregated in large villages, and then continually fighting with the Puntis for the ownership of the hills and fields occupied by them.[31]

One government official endeavouring to reason with the Puntis and mediate in the Hakka-Punti War remarked:

> Concerning these feuds, are the Hakkas entirely to blame? For decades, the natives (*te*) have been treating the Hakkas like slaves. Native humiliation and oppression of the Hakkas are no different from the present Hakka treatment of the natives.[32]

One other factor which facilitated extra-local organisation for inter-ethnic conflict was the institution of *xiangyue*, a form of social control promoted by the government in the countryside.[33] Residents of different villages came together periodically for moral lectures by elders. These inter-village 'compacts' had the capacity to federate, to use Philip Kuhn's term, into 'multiplex' organisations,[34] providing a ready forum for ethnic issues and the emergence of ethnic leadership.

The scene was now set for widespread and uncontrolled conflict that lasted from 1854 to 1867, and engulfed, like 'a prairie fire', as many as eight countries, Xinning, Gaoming, Heshan, Yangcun, Yangjiang, Enping, Kaiping, and Xinxing.[35] The ethnic consciousness of the Hakkas more than made up for their inferior numbers. At the height of the conflict, speaking to an official sent to mediate, a Cantonese leader observed:

> Peace is possible where the two groups are equally strong or equally weak, or where one is stronger than the other. Where the natives are stronger than the Hakkas, the former offer to discuss peace if the latter so wish. But here the natives are weaker and the Hakkas reject peace proposals from the natives.[36]

These may have been self-serving remarks made by a member of the group bent on extirpating the enemy, but Hakka strength could scarcely be exaggerated.

Ethnic antagonism between the two groups was absolute. As observed by Eitel, Punti animosity was as extreme as their well-known xenophobia towards Westerners:

> If you were to ask a thorough-bred Punti about the character of the Hakkas, he would certainly, in the case of his condescending to acknowledge that he ever heard of such people, turn up his nose and tell you that the Hakkas are quite beneath your notice, that they are a kind of semi-barbarians, living in poverty and filth.[37]

The Hakkas, on their part, reciprocated with an image of the Puntis as 'a clever but malicious and sneaking set of people', calling them 'those snakes'.[38] As the Puntis 'refused to be sheltered by the same heaven with them',[39] the solution had to match the depth of ethnic division. After 200,000 dead on each side, a new independent department was carved out of a section of Xinning county at the edge of the sea, called Chiqi ting.[40] Hakkas were urged to exchange acre for acre and move to Chiqi. Others were resettled in the Leizhou peninsula and on Hainan island. Many no doubt remained behind in fortified villages but at a safe distance from the Cantonese for, as W.F. Mayer subsequently noted, 'wherever their clans have been intermingled with a Punti population, they have been ousted and overwhelmed'.[41]

Articulation of the Hakka Ethos

The most disastrous aspect of the conflict in the western districts of the Lingnan core was that the gentry on both sides engaged directly in mutual belligerence. This signified extreme community closure of the 'coercive' kind, culminating in the militarisation and fortification of one group against another.[42] In times of community openness the gentry might be expected to use their extra-local contacts to perform the expected role of mediation. Now, as heads of warring groups along a cultural divide, and imperial authority at the local level being at its most impotent, they provided the leadership and resources for large-scale, organised, and uncontrolled warfare. Hereafter, the most visible area of Hakka ethnicity lay in the Hakka elite articulating a particularistic ethos that would bolster Hakka pride and cohesiveness. Successive generations of Hakka elites would seek to foster a uniformity of self-perception for Hakkas everywhere. In discussing Hakka 'cultural orientation' as perceived by Hakka ethnic writers, it is well to bear in mind Patterson's distinction between an ethnic and a cultural group. The culture of an ethnic group tends to be of a myth-making nature, while the traits of a cultural group are objectively verifiable.

Associated with the symbolic articulation of Hakka identity was the rise of the county Jiaying (also the name for the prefecture) as the spiritual centre of the Hakkas. The emergence of what Frederik Barth calls 'ethnic boundary' occurs in a situation of interaction between cultural groups.[43] One would therefore expect ethnicity to arise, in the first instance, not at the heart of Hakka homeland but in the zone of contact. Thus, 'Hakka' as an ethnic label was first recorded in Yong'an (Zijin) in the late sixteenth century: when the county was formed (1567) after the area had been cleared of the She aborigines, its initial migrant settlers came from the two Hakka cultural areas of Jiangxi and Fujian, the former designating themselves 'Shuiyuan' ('source of the river'), the latter 'Kejia'.[44] It next appeared in Dongguan where Hakka immigrants first arrived in 1680s; the natives there referred to them as 'Ailao'.[45]

Ethnic sentiments, however, do get transmitted to the home community; the humiliation of members of a group at the hands of another reflect upon the group as a whole. Thus, by the mid-nineteenth century, according to Eitel, 'Hakka' as an ethnic label was prevalent 'even in the Department of Kiaying-chow'.[46] Jiaying's prestige among the Lingnan Hakkas was based, in part, on its academic success, and in part on the multitude of emigrants from the Mei Basin. According to one computation, over a two-hundred-year period from the Shunzhi to the Daoguang reigns, this economically deprived county outperformed Panyu and, to some extent, Nanhai, two of the metropolitan counties, as the table below shows.[47]

Late in the eighteenth century, in a series of examinations for the *juren* degree in Guangzhou, four Hakka candidates from Jiaying and one from Dapu contiguous to it performed the consciousness-raising feat of carrying off first prize in succession, to the discomfort of their Cantonese rivals.[48] The beleaguered Hakkas at the Lingnan core and elsewhere would increasingly look to Jiaying, in American Baptist missionary George Campbell's words, 'for vindication from calumny'.[49]

county	juren graduates	jieyuan (first place in juren exams.)	jinshi graduates
Jiaying	302	9	49
Panyu	300	1	37
Nanhai	402	9	47

The first spokesman for the Hakka ethnic group was not in fact a native of Jiaying. Although Hakkas had been roused before, the first ethnic statement did not appear until the early nineteenth century, following inter-ethnic feuds in Boluo and Dongguan in 1808. The spokesman was Xu Xuzeng, a native of Heping in the East River upland and *jinshi* of 1799. As director of the Fenghu Academy in Huizhou, he considered in a lecture the question of why, despite centuries of settlement, the Hakkas were still known by a name that denoted 'sojourning'. In his lecture, which is preserved together with his genealogy,[50] Xu introduced all the themes that would be repeated tirelessly in Hakka ethnocentric writings. Like all such statements, it is neither all myth nor all truth. It is a statement of all the essential elements of Hakka self-identification, of the claim to Chineseness that was equal, if not superior, to that of other Chinese.

Xu began with origin, a search for greatness. First, the Hakkas were descendants of northerners, bearers of the ancient civilisation of the Central Plain. Their migration to the south was motivated by the spirit of patriotic loyalism. Some of the Hakka ancestors in the south were Song loyalists, old upper class families who had accompanied the Northern Song Court in the move to Hangzhou in the early part of the twelfth century, in the wake of barbarian invasion, but mostly they had migrated during the Song-Yuan transition to avoid Mongol rule. To continue in Xu's own words:

> Then the Mongol armies came further south, the Song Court moved hither and thither, finally to the Southern mountain ranges. The old upper class families along with commoners uprooted themselves and followed...battling the Mongol armies with their bare hands on the way... Accompanying the emperor to the south, only one in ten thousand survived, scattering everywhere. Though bereft of family and country, they did not emulate the five hundred on Tianheng Island, who committed suicide, but instead determined to live on and nurse their vengeance. [Avoiding the unhealthy climate of the lowlands and unwilling to live among people of different customs and speech] they selected an area [in the highlands of the Guangdong-Fujian-Jiangxi border] to be in close proximity to provinces of the interior. Moreover, as survivors of the same cause, they felt they should reside together, preserve their customs and speech...so that their patriotic spirit would not diminish.

The Hakka brand of loyalism was in fact patriotic anti-foreignism. It was not one that was unique to them by any means, for their Punti neighbours also exhibited it in their 'origin myth'. Unlike the Hakkas, however, the Puntis never felt the need to assert repeatedly this aspect of their origin, or indeed any other, displaying the serenity and self-assurance of a dominant group.

The existence of anti-foreign patriotic sentiments among the Hakkas may be historically significant, although the extent to which the Taiping leaders acted out of this tradition is unclear. What is certain is that the patriotic anti-foreignism of the Hakkas predated the rise of anti-Manchu nationalism. Moreover, this view of the past has been carried forward to a historical view of the Taipings and of Sun Yat-sen and his Hakka followers that fits in with that tradition.

As to the timing of the departure from the centre of Chinese civilisation, most Hakka writers would agree that the majority of the Hakkas were descendants from the migrants of the Song-Yuan transition. The claim was already made in Xu's time, however, that some Hakkas were descended from earlier immigrants. Xu stated that his Hakka contemporaries, the renowned poet-scholars, Song Xiang of Jiaying and Zhou Shenxuan of Qujiang, were of the belief that some of the 'keren' of Jiaying, Tingzhou, and Shaozhou prefectures traced their origin to the fall of the Western Jin Dynasty early in the fourth century A.D., a significant indication that Xu was not alone in being concerned with the question of the group's origin.[51] The circumstances in the fourth century, when the earlier immigrants arrived, resembled those of the later migration in essential detail. Then, as in the twelfth century, the reigning Chinese dynasty had been forced out of the Yellow River valley by barbarian invasions, one to be restored in the present-day Nanjing, the other in present-day Hangzhou. In each instance, the expelled court was accompanied by loyal officials and their families, to whom the Hakkas traced their ancestry.

The assertion of an origin in the north by all Han sub-ethnic groups in the south was in part a function of their forced co-existence with non-Han aborigines. The claim was made by Hakkas, Cantonese, and Hoklos alike. Moreover, the story of their entry into Guangdong province was simplicity itself. Major Hoklo lineages would trace their descent from the state-sponsored colonists of the late Tang, who emigrated from Henan to the Zhangzhou-Quanzhou and Chaozhou areas in the southeast.[52] Similarly leading Cantonese lineages propagated the lore of descent from the ninety-seven families, made up of thirty-three surnames, who foregathered, after the long trek from the north following the Mongol invasion, at an obscure place on the Guangdong border, Zuzixiang (Pearl Ward) in Nanxiong, before arriving in the Lingnan lowlands.[53] The Hakkas, on their part, propagated the lore of Shibicun (Stone-wall Village) in Ninghua county, Fujian, where their ancestors had found shelter from the Huangchao Rebellion in the late ninth century. Subsequently, at the time of the Mongol invasion, they crossed the provincial border to the counties of Jiaying and beyond.[54] The claims of all these groups were carefully recorded in the genealogies of their families and lineages.

To return to Xu's elaboration on Hakka origin, isolated physically in the peculiar highland ecology of their new homeland, Hakka society evolved distinctive values and customs. No Hakka ever served the Mongol regime: Hakka refusal to do so was celebrated as a mark of patriotic loyalism. No matter how destitute, Hakkas combined the high culture of scholarship with farming and martial arts. Hakka women, rich or poor, did not practise foot-binding, which Xu implied was in response to early Qing decrees.[55] Consequently, Hakka women unlike others excelled in fieldwork, in addition to household management, handicrafts, and child-rearing. Frugal by habit they had never had to resort to prostitution. Finally, in the language of the Hakkas was preserved the speech of the ancient north. 'In essence', exulted Xu, 'the Hakkas are diligent by habit, thrifty and unostentatious in customs, courteous, modest, elegant and polished by disposition'—all the prized virtues believed to inhere in the uncorrupted people of the Golden Age of great antiquity.[56]

This elaborate articulation of an ethos for the Hakka group by a *jinshi* of the realm marked a new level of ethnic consciousness that was to fragment the Lingnan elite along ethnic lines. The feuds in Boluo and Dongguan, which had prompted Xu Xuzeng's ethnic statement, had been quickly brought under control, thanks to the presence of the imperial military units stationed close at hand, but also to the mediation by the elite on both sides.[57] Those that erupted in the western districts in mid-century, however, were to prove unmanageable. The imperial forces were then preoccupied with the Taiping rebels. Other local dissidents could only be put down by *ad hoc* recruitment of local mercenaries. Incredible as it may seem, Hakka and Punti braves were among the recruits used to suppress the Red Turban (*Hungtou*) rebels, who were ethnically Punti.[58] It was in the nature of the Chinese local elite that, in times of extreme local instability, loyalty to lineage and community tended to overshadow that towards the regime, impelling some to cultivate the dissidents in the interest of self-preservation. In these circumstances Hakka braves could not suppress the rebels without at the same time attacking their Punti elite supporters. In a situation of simmering inter-ethnic tensions this spelt disaster. The Puntis, alarmed by the 'excessive zeal' of the Hakka mercenaries in going after the rebels and their supporters, real or imaginary, responded by declaring war on all Hakkas. The battle line was drawn on the sound of one's speech alone. This thirteen-year long war was to leave a legacy of mutual hatred that imbued high and low on both sides beyond the immediate battle zone.

In the mid-1860s, when a less beleaguered government was able finally to intervene to bring about a settlement, two Hakka officials who were not native to the region of warfare spoke up to ensure a fair deal for the Hakka group. Ding Richang, a native of Fengshun and Governor of Jiangsu province, wrote to his opposite number in Guangdong, cautioning an even-handed approach and enlightening him on Hakka origins and culture so that there would be no danger that the Hakka would be treated disadvantageously as if they were non-Han aborigines.[59] Lin Daquan, a native of Dapu and *juren*[59] of 1861, who was in Ding's employ, circulated a treatise on the Hakkas and expressed strong criticism of the official handling of the feuds. He attacked the local authorities in particular for referring to the Hakkas involved in the feuds as 'Hakka bandits' (*fei*), and for aiding the Puntis in driving them out. Like Xu's lecture, Lin's treatise was a spirited glorification of the Hakkas: true sons of the Golden Age, descendants of the upper class of the Central Plain, and a speech that showed a clear affinity with the ancient speech of the north.[60]

The Punti gentry on their part were decided in their characterisation of the Hakkas as bandits, thiefs, and beyond the Chinese racial and cultural pale. This stereotype was fostered in the county gazetteers, which served as an important repository of local particularism. Thus, in the section recording the feuds, Hakkas were labelled as *fei* in the gazetteers of Gaoyao (1863), Xinhui (1871), Xinning (1893), and Gaoming (1894).[61] Subsequently the Gaoyao gentry, in the Xuantong edition, improved on that of 1863 by describing the Hakkas as Yao aborigines.[62] The Yangjiang gazetteer of as late as 1925 still referred to the Hakkas as bandits (*kefei*).[63] But the Enping gazetteer of 1934 topped them all: the name 'Hakka' was written as Chilao, a sub-branch of the Lao aborigines; a dozen verses by one Punti talent at the time of the feuds, which cursed the Hakkas for causing the calamity, were included in the section containing the literary works of the country.[64]

The publication of the gazetteer of Jiayingzhou in 1898, by then the undisputed spiritual centre of the Lingnan Hakkas, was something of a milestone in the articulation of the Hakka ethos. Its chief compiler Wen Zhonghe was a Hanlin academician. The gazetteer included an extensive treatise on Hakka customs and manners and a detailed exposition of all the main rituals, to dispel any doubt of Hakka Chineseness. The Hakka language had received its first scholarly treatment by the Hakka poet-classicist, Huang Zhao, in his Zhenping (Ziaoling) county gazetteer of 1862.[65] Wen's chapter on the Hakka dialect carried it a step further. The tonal affinities of Hakka with Sui-Tang speech were set out to show unmistakably northern origin of the dialect. Finally, and most significantly of all, there was for equally handy reference a brief history of the Hakkas, which was more self-assured and less grandiloquent than those purveyed by Xu Xuzeng and Lin Daquan. Wen was uncertain of the precise origin of the label 'Hakka', but he surmised that it might have originated from the census category *kehu* ('immigrant households') in use in Song times.[66]

The significance of such gazetteers as a means of mobilisation for ethnic interaction can scarcely be underestimated. Compiled by respected members of the community, they kept alive the process of categorisation, fostering group cohesiveness and maintaining the ethnic boundary, even though these were not their only purpose.

Ethnicity and Nationalism

The turn of the twentieth century witnessed an upsurge of nationalism among China's elites. That nationalism contained multiple strands that impinged on ethnic separateness in different ways. On the one hand, the stronger strands of anti-imperialism and national integration required the subordination of ethnic differences. On the other, a lesser strand stressed the racial aspect of Chinese nationalism, one which seemed particularly strong in Lingnan. Lingnan being ethnically one of the most complex of all Chinese areas, the tantalising question arises as to what connection there was between the Hakka position in Lingnan and their strong representation in the anti-Manchu revolutionary movement. At any rate, Hakka involvement in the revolution and their assertiveness of a Han racial origin unfolded side by side against the background of Punti animosity.

Thus, even as nationalism rapidly took hold among the Hakka elite, the ethnic rhetoric was kept up. In 1901 there appeared an anthology of poetry composed by poets who hailed from the Mei River valley from Song to Qing times, called *Meishui shizhuan*, there being no higher cultural credential in Chinese society than excellence in poetry. The noted poet-reformer, Huang Zunxian, lent his weight to this enterprise by furnishing a preface, in which he wrote: 'I have often said that the *keren* are an ancient race of the Zhongyuan, a fact borne out by their spoken and written language'.[67]

The year 1905 was another landmark in the development of Hakka self-consciousness. That year, the Cantonese scholar, Huang Jie, authored a school history of Guangdong, called *Guangdong xiangtu lishi*. It was issued with the approval of the provincial educational authorities for use in the new schools being set up under the imperial reforms. The offending lesson in the text dealt with the racial composition and origins of the different groups, stating: 'Among the races of Guangdong are Hakkas and Hoklos; they are not Cantonese and are not of the Han racial stock'.[68] The text provoked a storm of protests among Hakka scholars, while the Hoklos showed their sense of security by ignoring it altogether. As Campbell relates:

> A circular was sent out by some Mei-chau [i.e. Jiaying] scholars, containing an answer to the calumnious statement in the school history and also a call to all interested to attend a meeting in the Yamen to concert measures to secure its excision... In the spring of 1906...the called meeting was held. Mr Yong, editor of the Swatow daily, was Chairman. After due discussion, a 'Society for Investigation of the Origin of the Hakka People' was formed. A printed prospectus was issued, providing for the cooperation of every surname in the roster of Mei-chau clans. Each of the thirty-six townships into which the county is divided was to have a special committee to secure material for the memorial to be prepared. The provincial authorities did not await the collection of these facts before taking action. The offending statement was cut out...[69]

During this episode, the Hakka elite, numbering among them Huang Zunxian, Qiu Fengjia, and Zou Lu, threw their weight fully behind the campaign of newspapers and pamphlets to affirm Hakka racial purity.[70] In these early years of nationalism these men, many of whom like Qiu and Zhou were active members of the Tongmenghui under Sun Yat-sen's lead, saw no contradiction between their ethnic assertiveness and the broad political goals of the revolutionary movement. They were working simultaneously towards the acceptance of Hakkas by others as a rightful section of Guangdong society, and towards the establishment of a new political order in which they intended to have a place. For Hakkas these were not antithetical but interdependent goals. In this light their ethnicity may be viewed as mobilisation for the competition of power.

The strategy was transparent in the ethnic rhetoric itself. While quick to react to insults and correct misconceptions of Hakka racial origins, Hakka leaders were careful to project themselves as Chinese nationalists above all else. Thus, when Zhou Lu and Zhang Xuan co-authored the pamphlet *Hanzu Kefushi* (A history of Hakkas and Hoklos of the Han race) in reponse to the school history of Guangdong, it was with the view of promoting national unity. In a foreward, Qiu Fengjia expressed the fear that ethnic separateness, if unchecked, would destroy the Hakka group as well as the Chinese nation, at a time when China was engaged in a struggle for survival among nations.[71] Another Hakka writer, Zhong Yonghe, made the startling assertion that all three groups in Guangdong—Cantonese, Hoklos, and Hakkas—were descended from a mixture of Yue natives and Han immigrants. The fact of common racial origin was more significant than variations in speech.[72]

Hakka involvement in the republican revolution was, by all accounts, impressive. Leaving aside Sun Yat-sen—whose Hakka ancestry is still a matter of dispute[73] —of the one hundred and twelve Guangdong members of the Tongmenghui in Tokyo in 1905-1906, fifty were Hakkas from the Mei River valley. Interest in modern education had drawn many young Hakkas to Japan as private students.[74] Hakka participation in the revolutionary cause was all the more prominent by virtue of the fact that many of the early martyrs came from this cultural group: all four who perished in the uprising at Ungkung (Huanggang) near Chaozhou in 1907, and as many as one-third of the seventy-two martyrs of Huanghuagang in Guangzhou in March 1911.[75] In the years leading up to the 1911 Revolution, Hakkas were visible in journalism, in the new schools, and in the provincial assembly. In Shantou, the *New China Journal* (*Zhonghua xinbao*) was started by Hakka businessmen in 1908 and edited by the Tongmenghui member Ye Chucang, both to attack the old regime and to act as a voice for the Hakkas in eastern

Guangdong. Qiu Fengjia was vice-president of the Guangdong provincial assembly, Chen Jiongming a prominent assemblyman, and Zou Lu one of the assistant secretaries.[76]

When the revolutionaries seized Guangzhou, the Hakkas achieved a strong representation early. In the new regime, Chen Jiongming was lieutenant military governor next to the Cantonese, Hu Hanmin; Liao Zhongkai headed the ministry of finance, while Deng Geng the army ministry. Qiu Fengjia was education minister and concurrently Guangdong's representative to the Shanghai conference for the establishment of a central government. Yao Yuping was marshal of the Guangzhou troops, and Liu Yongfu commander-in-chief of the volunteer corps.[77]

In the Shantou-Chaozhou area, where the revolutionaries resisted the distant control from Guangzhou, the Hakkas had a harder time but nevertheless played a highly visible role. There the revolutionaries were divided into three ethnic groupings, Cantonese, Hoklo, and Hakka. As witnessed by the American consul, B.G. Tours, following Guangzhou's example a 'Cantonese revolutionary party', led by the American-born L.K. Goe (Liang Jin'ao), took over Chaozhou 'as representative of the Republic of China' on 10 November 1911.

> There is no actual government of any kind in Swatow at the present time. There is considerable friction between the Cantonese party who engineered the revolution in Swatow, and the Swatow revolutionary party who were at first content to follow the Cantonese lead but who now expect the lion's share of the spoil. Some open quarrelling between the two factions will be hard to avoid.[78]

In fact, the spoil seemed to be going to a Hakka party who had occupied the police headquarters in Chaozhou and seized the army. On 11 November, 'swollen greatly by new recruits and armed adherents with police rifles', the Hakka party elected Zhang Licun as 'Commander of the Chaozhou Prefecture', to the great resentment of the Cantonese and Hoklo parties.[79] But when Zhang subsequently left to fight the revolutionary cause in central China, military command was seized by Chen Hong'e, a Hoklo, who was a non-revolutionary New Army officer but had the support of the Hoklo merchants. In the elections of 1912 for the new government, Hakkas and Hoklos backed different political parties.[80]

To bring the Shantou-Chaozhou area under Guangzhou's control, acting military governor Chen Jiongming sought to replace Chen Hong'e with one of his own trusted lieutenants, the Hakka Lin Jizhen; the latter forcibly landed at Shantou and ousted Chen Hong'e. 'Lin's venture', writes Edward Friedman, 'was opposed and denounced as criminal and capricious' by the army of Colonel Chen Hong'e, the Shantou Chamber of Commerce, the Chaozhou newspaper *Illustrated News* (*Tuhua bao*), and Chaozhou military men.[81] In opposing Lin, the Hoklos called him 'the aboriginal chieftan from Taiwan', denying him Chinese racial credential. Lin, like so many Hakkas, including Qiu Fengjia, had returned from Taiwan to participate in the anti-Manchu revolution.[82] In the end, Guangzhou backed down by replacing Lin with a complete outsider, Wu Xiangda, a native of Zhejiang, to alleviate inter-ethnic tensions.[83]

Although the revolutionary regime in Guangdong ended abruptly in the summer of 1913 with Yuan Shikai's counter-revolution directed from Beijing, and Guangdong was occupied by the alien army of Long Jiguang of Guangxi, the Hakkas had demonstrated their capacity for a spectacular upward push. Individual Hakkas would continue to exploit the opportunities inherent in a modernising society, in the military, educational, and professional spheres, and as an ethnic group they would be quick to respond to ethnic insults, as shown in the Wolcott incident described below. At the same time, the realisation that the new environment permitted members of the group to forge ahead on the socio-economic ladder combined with the demands of idealistic nationalism to temper Hakka ethnicity itself.

In 1920 the Commercial Press in Shanghai published an English text book called *Geography of the World*. The author was not a Cantonese but a foreign school teacher at the Taowu Middle School in Suzhou, R.D. Wolcott by name. The Guangdong entry reads: 'In the mountains are many wild tribes and backward people, such as the Hakkas and Ikias [*She*]'. The offending passage had been taken from a nineteenth-century work by the Welsh missionary, Timothy Richard, called *Comprehensive Geography of the Chinese Empire*. For a foreigner to disseminate misinformation about the semi-barbarous racial status of the Hakkas through the nation's most prestigious publishing house was not a matter the Hakkas would take lightly. Hakka sojourners in Shanghai, students as well as leading personalities, bestirred themselves to the insult and organised the United Hakka Association (*Kexi Datonghui*), with a branch in Guangzhou. In January 1921 the association held a conference in Shanghai to discuss how to deal with the Commercial Press. Subsequently, the press issued a public statement of apology, notified the schools that had purchased the book of the error, and agreed to destroy unsold stock. That year, in Shantou, Zhou Huifu launched the newspaper *Datong ribao* (*Unity Daily*) to promote public understanding of Hakka culture and foster ethnic solidarity.[84] At the same time, the Hakkas in Hong Kong organised the Congzheng Association, which aspired to be the headquarters for all overseas Hakka organisations to be known by that name.

Significantly there was strong opposition from some Hakkas to the formation of an ethnic organisation. In particular, the Hakka student association in Japan described such a step in a declaration as 'retrogressive', 'unduly parochial', and 'out of step with the times'. It urged that the United Hakka Association be disbanded and the funds raised be spent on charity.

> At a time when the nation is faced with great difficulties and threatened by powerful neighbours, the problems of internal administration and external diplomacy, not to mention reconstruction and reform, require urgent attention. It is doubtful that these problems can be overcome even with complete unity of purpose and effort. How it is possible for us to engage in divisiveness and bring debility upon ourselves?[85]

It was probably these considerations that caused the organisation and the newspaper to go out of existence quickly.

The Hakka Position in Lingnan in 1930s

By the early 1930s the Hakkas had achieved a position in Guangdong's political and military life that was anomalous, to say the least. The view of a foreign observer looking into Guangdong in 1932 highlights this extraordinary situation. Late that year, the Japanese general consulate in Guangzhou forwarded a report to Tokyo, entitled 'The Hakka Ethnic Group, Past and Present', in which the author (unknown) spoke of 'Great Hakkaism' (*Daikyakka shugi*). He saw as quite real 'the prospect of a great Hakka leader emerging on the basis of Hakka spiritual solidarity to take national power'.[86] This may seem chiliastic in hindsight, underestimating as the author did the integrative power of Chinese nationalism, which was then gathering momentum against Japanese aggression, and he was probably unduly influenced by Hakka ethnic rhetoric or Cantonese perception of the threat. In any case, the report does capture the anomalous prominence of the Hakkas in Guangdong and the dynamic push of individual Hakkas in the military and political spheres.

The anomaly, to begin with, was that since the republican revolution, the political and military power of Guangdong was time and again in Hakka hands. The report spoke of the following Hakka eras: Chen Jiongming, 1912 to August 1913, and November 1920 to January 1923; Zhang Fakui, October 1927 to March 1928; Chen Mingshu, February 1929 to April 1931; and the current era of Chen Jitang since April 1931, which would not end until 1936.[87]

At the time of the report, Chen Jitang controlled Guangdong in virtual autonomy from the Nanjing government of Chiang Kai-shek. Along with Chen Mingshu and Zhang Fakui, he had climbed the military ladder that was wide open. All three had their initial military training at the Whampoa (Huangpu) Military Preparatory School in the early years of the republic. The school was then headed by the Hakka Deng Geng, ex-army minister of the Guangzhou revolutionary regime, and in 1918 Chen Jiongming's chief of staff. In 1921 Deng rose to become a divisional commander of the Guangdong Army organised by Sun Yat-sen.

For reasons of geography as well as political preference, all these men were tied in their fortunes to Sun and the Guomindang. In Chen Jitang's case, he enjoyed a rapid rise in the Guangdong Army: he was a brigade commander in 1923 while Li Jishen, a non-Guangdong man from Jiangsu, had overall command; in 1925 he was division commander, in 1928 a commander of one of the field armies, and in 1929 he replaced Li as chief commander of Guangdong province. With the secession from Nanjing in May 1931 he assumed both political and military power over the province until he was outmaneuvred by Chiang Kai-shek in 1936.[88]

Chen Mingshu had joined the army of another Guangdong Hakka, Yao Yuping, and participated in the siege of the Manchu garrison in Nanjing in November 1911. After military training Chen rose in the Guangdong Army: he was a regiment commander in 1920, division commander in 1925, and in 1927, after a meritorious role in the Northern Expedition, he was promoted to field army command. In 1928 he succeeded Li Jishen as chairman of the Guangdong provincial government, until his eclipse by Chen Jitang. Dissociating himself from the latter's secessionist move, Chen Mingshu was rewarded by Nanjing with garrison duty in Shanghai. There, in January 1932, he and his Nineteenth Route Army won national acclaim by stubbornly fighting the Japanese. Jealousy in Nanjing, however, caused the army's transfer to Fujian where, in November 1933, Chen launched his famous challenge to Nanjing in a bid for greater power, only to plummet into oblivion after its failure.[89]

Zhang Fakui's career was much the same as his two fellow Hakkas. He was involved early with the Guomindang and rose rapidly in the military ranks. He led a division during the Northern Expedition, which earned the name 'Ironsides' for defeating Wu Peifu's army. His command subsequently expanded over several armies, some of which became infiltrated by communists, such as Guo Moruo (a Sichuan Hakka), who served as chief of the political department of one of the armies; and Ye Jianying (a Meixian Hakka), who was chief of staff of another. In October 1927 Zhang returned to Guangzhou and ousted Li Jisen, only to find a communist coup on his hands, which he suppressed with difficulty. Subsequently, he was pushed out of Guangdong by the combined forces of Li and the two Chens. He placed his army under the temporary command of Miao Peinan (a Wuhua Hakka) which rejoined the Northern Expedition in 1928. Zhang resumed command in 1929 when, in combination with Guangxi generals, he tried in vain to retake Guangdong from Chen Jitang. He was later to rejoin Chiang Kai-shek and take on a succession of military roles during the Sino-Japanese War.[90]

As of 1932, when the Japanese report was compiled, the combined armies of Chen Jitang, Chen Mingshu (whose troops were mostly Hakka), and Zhang Fakui would have amounted to a powerful force of 150,000 to 160,000 men. This total strength, as well as the national fame of the Nineteenth Route Army, enabled the Japanese observer to anticipate the emergence of a Hakka national leader, despite the admitted rivalry among them.[91]

Examining the current regime of Chen Jitang more closely, the observer painted a picture of Hakka military, political and financial strength, which probably alarmed the Cantonese and Hoklos no end. In the army headquarters, it was 'whispered' that other than the deputy chief of staff, all the leaders from the chief of staff down to the chief medical officer were Hakka.

> To give a concrete example of the Second Army, beginning with army commander Xiang Hanping, there are seven Hakkas out of ten division commanders, and all four brigade commanders of the Independent Regiment are Hakka.

In the Third Army, beginning with commander Li Yangjing, Hakkas numbered twenty per cent of the regiment officers and above.[92]

In the political sphere, the most respected leader was Zou Lu, President of Zhongshan University, a Dapu Hakka. Those who exercised real power in the provincial administration were the provincial chairman, Lin Yungai (probably a Hakka of Xinyi county), and the department head of civil administration, Lin Yizhong, also a Hakka. The Guangdong branch of the Guomindang was headed by the Hakka, Huang Linshu. In finance, the head of the Bank of Guangdong was the Luoding Hakka by the name of Shen Daihe, the Liang-Guang salt commissioner was Chen Jitang's brother, Chen Weizhou, and the chief of Guangzhou maritime customs was yet another Hakka, Zhou Baoheng.[93]

Thus, by accident or design, the gathering of power in the hands of individuals of the Hakka ethnic group was a reality in the early 1930s. The Japanese report then took up the question of why, despite settlement of several hundred years, the Cantonese continued to treat their Hakka neighbours with contempt.

> The basic reason is said to be that the Hakkas are excessive in preserving their original customs and manners and boastful of their Central Plain origins, not conducting themselves as refugees or vagrants who had lost their

homes... There is something in the Hakka character which arouses Cantonese animosity. For example, while the Hakkas pride themselves in their habits of thrift and economy, the natives see this as greed and stinginess. And while the Hakkas take pride in their good custom of ancestral reverence and the strength of communal and group feeling, the Cantonese see superstition and obstinate parochialism. The Cantonese also hold them in contempt for their treacherous cunning.[94]

The prominence of the Hakkas in Guangdong affairs in the immediate pre-war years seemed to have produced a situation of surface calm, masking Hakka vigilance and troubled inter-ethnic tensions. Otherwise it would be difficult to explain the vehemence of the Hakka response to yet another Cantonese slight. In 1930 a Cantonese by the name of Li Zhenfang published a piece called 'Hakka Customs and Manners' (*Keijia fengsu*) in a weekly that was the organ of the department of reconstruction (*Jiansheting*) of the Guangdong government. Li, an employee of that department, wrote: 'The Hakkas are made up of two kinds, the main stock (*dazhong*) and a branch (*xiaozhong*). The former speak a bird-like chatter and are not quite civilised; the latter in recent years, after much contact with the Puntis, are quite unlike their former barbarous state (*zhenbei*, literally, 'barbarous tribes of the wilderness')'. Predictably Hakka circles rose in an uproar. The department head, Deng Yanhua, offered a public apology for lacking discrimination; the author of the article was summarily cashiered; and the editor of the weekly offered an apology which, however, did not suffice to mollify the Hakkas. As the Japanese report recounted:

> The incident led to a kind of social equality movement by the Hakkas who, after years of contempt at Cantonese hands, erupted in a fury. Hakka residents in Guangzhou huddled together in discussions, and nominated Rao Qinzhong as their representative to ask the provincial government chairman Chen Mingshu for a thorough investigation. At the same time, on 3 August, a united conference of all Hakka organizations in Guangzhou was held...and it elected eighteen representatives to deliver a

long statement of protest to the head of the Department of Reconstruction. The statement read: 'Hakkas absolutely cannot overlook the article, which incites ill-feeling among local people on the basis of communalism and sows the seeds of division among the people'. Three demands were then stated: (1) a formal apology by the head of the Department of Reconstruction; (2) the dismissal of the responsible author; (3) the apology to be widely publicised.[95]

The matter was closed only after the demands were met and the provincial chairman, Chen Mingshu, intervened personally by demoting and transferring the weekly's editor.[96]

Conclusion

This study of the Hakkas in modern times has been more suggestive than definitive in some areas. What comes across clearly is the manner in which the Hakkas at the Lingnan regional core in the nineteenth century coped with the problem of survival in the face of Cantonese animosity by means of ethnic mobilisation. In the new political environment of the twentieth century, as an ethnically aroused group, they sought to forge ahead socio-economically. During the latter phase, they were helped by the fact that their social disabilities were scarcely comparable to those of color or creed. Cultural difference, mainly linguistic, was easily overcome by the shared written language, by Hakkas acquiring another speech, and by the elevation of the 'national language' (*Guoyu*), which placed the Cantonese and the Hakkas at an equal disadvantage.

This paper has only touched on the significant roles played by the Hakkas in the nationalist movement. As a disadvantaged group, who saw their future in and directing their energies towards the larger goal of a new, integrated national order, they may have served as a check on the naturally localist tendencies of the more secure, dominant groups, Cantonese and Hoklos, but this is only speculation. Similarly suggestive is the exceptional degree of upward social mobility among members of this ethnic group and their predisposition to social change, although one should not assume that they were not socially conservative within their own community in order to preserve their social customs and organisations.

We have concentrated on the Hakkas of the Lingnan Region where they identified themselves by that ethnic label. Elsewhere members of this cultural group, particularly those in the communist soviet areas, were playing a different role. After the failed Nanchang uprising in August 1927, some communist armed units, led by Mao Zedong and Zhu De, headed for the hills in the Hunan-Jiangxi border area, while the main force moved south. The latter cut their way along the Jiangxi side of the Wuyi Mountains, then crossed over to the Fujian and continued on, through the south-western section of the Fujian, to Guangdong, sowing seeds of class warfare on the way. When the communist movement finally assumed a rural character in the early 1930s, most soviets came to be based in heavily Hakka-populated areas. Thus, when the Western Fujian Revolutionary Base Government was set up in March 1929, it held sway over ten counties. Culturally, five of them—Changting, Shanghang, Wuping, Yongding, and Ninghua—were exclusively Hakka, while the rest had a substantial Hakka population, namely, Qingliu, Guihua, Liancheng, Longyan and Jianning.[97] By the time the Central Soviet Government was proclaimed at Ruijin (a pure Hakka county) in 1931, the central soviet base area was formed by twenty counties on both sides of the Wuyi Mountains. Those on the Jiangxi side comprised the four purely Hakka counties of Ruijin, Huichang, Anyuan, and Xunwu, and the heavily Hakka-populated counties of Yudu, Xingguo, Ningdu, Shicheng and Guangchang.[98] Only Nanfeng and Liquan fell outside the Hakka linguistic boundary. On the Hunan-Jiangxi border, the numerous counties that formed the soviet base in the Jinggangshan area also had a strong Hakka presence—Ninggang, Suiquan, Yongxin, Chalin.

That these soviets came to be based in a predominantly Hakka population had to do with strategic considerations rather than any qualities inherent in the Hakka cultural group itself. But once they were established, they did owe their initial success to the Hakka tradition of female field labour, which was important for the soviet economy because the menfolk were mobilised for warfare. One problem in some of these areas for the communist revolution was to get on top of inter-ethnic conflict, as one of Mao's reports shows.[99]

Had the soviets not ultimately ended in failure, it is conceivable that members of the Hakka cultural group would have been found in even greater numbers than they were during the communist conquest and subsequent exercise of national power.[100]

NOTES

The author is indebted to the participants of the workshop, and to David Pong, Tim Wright, Jerome Ch'en, Alexander Woodside, and William Skinner for their comments. Research was supported by a grant from the Australian Research Grant Scheme.

1. Philip A. Kuhn, 'Origins of the Taiping Vision: Cross-cultural dimensions of Chinese Rebellions', *Comparative Studies in Society and History*, 19:3 (July 1977), 350-366.
2. J.A.G. Roberts, 'The Hakka-Punti War', unpublished D. Phil. thesis, Oxford University, 1969.
3. Edward J.M. Rhoads, *China's Republican Revolution: The Case of Kwangtung, 1895-1913* (Cambridge, Mass., 1975), pp. 102-103.
4. Oi-kan Yue Hashimoto, *Phonology of Cantonese* (Cambridge, 1972), pp. 1-7.
5. Yang Chengzhi, *Guangdong renmin yu wenhua* [The people of Guangdong and their culture] (Guangzhou, 1943), p. 99; C.G. Guson, 'The Peoples of Kwangtung', *Lingnan Science Journal*, 7 (1929), 9.
6. Luo Xianglin, *Keija yanjiu daolun* [An introduction to the study of the Hakkas] (Xingning, 1933).
7. S.T. Leong, 'The Hakka Chinese: Ethnicity and Migrations in Late Imperial China', presented at the 32nd Annual Meeting of the Association for Asian Studies, 21-23 March 1980, Washington, D.C., pp. 9-13.
8. *Ibid.*, pp. 14-21.
9. Wolfram Eberhard, *Social Mobility in Traditional China* (Leiden, 1962), p. 61-67.
10. Rhoads, pp. 12-13.
11. Harry J. Lamley, 'Subethnic Rivalry in the Ch'ing Period', in E.M. Ahern and H. Gates, eds., *The Anthropology of Taiwanese Society* (Stanford, 1981), pp. 282-283.
12. William L. Parish and Martin King Whyte, *Village and Family in Contemporary China* (Chicago, 1978), pp. 23-26.
13. Orlando Patterson, 'Context and Choice in Ethnic Allegiance: A Theoretical Framework and Caribbean Case Study ', in Nathan Glazer and Daniel P. Moynihan, eds., *Ethnicity: Theory and Experience* (Cambridge, Mass., 1975), pp. 309-310.
14. Abner Cohen, *Urban Ethnicity* (London, 1974), p. ix.
15. Patterson, p. 306.
16. *Ibid.*, pp. 309-310.
17. G. William Skinner, 'Urban Development in Imperial China', in Skinner, ed., *The City in Late Imperial China* (Stanford, 1977), pp. 3-31; for my use of Skinner's framework, see Leong, 'The Hakka Chinese: Ethnicity and Migration in late Imperial China'.
18. G. William Skinner, 'Chinese Peasants and the Closed Community: An Open and Shut Case', *Comparative Studies in Society and History*, 13 (1971), 270-281.
19. This is noted by Lamley, p. 286. I have examined the records of the English Presbyterian Mission, which was active on the Hakka-Hoklo isogloss

during the latter half of the nineteenth century.

20. Milton T. Stauffer, ed., *The Christian Occupation of China* (Shanghai, 1922), p. 351; D. MacIver, *A Chinese-English Dictionary: Hakka Dialect as Spoken in Kwangtung Province*, 2nd ed. (n.p., 1926), Introduction to first edition.

21. *Yuanzhou fuzhi* [Gazetteer of Yuanzhou prefecture] (1760), 13:14b-15b.

22. *Guangdong tongzhi* [Gazetteer of Guangdong province] (1822), 1934 reprint, pp. 3093-3099; Xinning xianzhi [Gazetteer of Xinning county] (1894), 1921 reprint, pp. 267-269.

23. *Guangdong tongzhi*, pp. 3094, 3098.

24. *Xin'an xianzhi* [Gazetteer of Xin'an county] (1820), 9:12a-b.

25. *Kaiping xianzhi* [Gazetteer of Kaiping county] (1823), 6:23b-24.

26. *Guangdong tongzhi*, pp. 3096, 3098.

27. E.J. Eitel, 'Ethnographical Sketches of the Hakka Chinese', *Notes and Queries on China and Japan*, 1:5 (31 May 1867), 50.

28. Myron L. Cohen, 'The Hakka or "Guest People": Dialect as a Sociocultural variable in Southeastern China', *Ethnohistory*, 15:3 (1968), 252-257.

29. See, for example, the description of Hakka settlements in *Xin'an xianzhi* (1820), juan 2; *Zengcheng xianzhi* [Gazetteer of Zencheng county] (1754), juan 3; *Xiangshan xianzhi* [Gazetteer of Xiangshan county] (1923), juan 3; *Gaoyao xianzhi* [Gazetteer of Gaoyao county] (1943), pp. 107-249; *Yangcun xianzhi* [Gazetteer of Yangcun county] (1821).

30. *Zhupi yuzhi* [Vermilion Endorsements and Edicts] (n.p., 1732), Vol. 4, p. 51b, Shiliha memorial.

31. Eitel, 'Ethnographical Sketches', p. 50.

32. Fang Junyi, 'He Tuke shuo' [Mediation between natives and Hakkas], in *Erzhixuan wencun* [Collected works of Fang Junyi] (n.p., 1878), 12:3b-4.

33. Kung-chuan Hsiao, *Rural China: Imperial Control in the Nineteenth Century* (Seattle, 1960), pp. 184-205.

34. Philip A. Kuhn, *Rebellion and Its Enemies in Late Imperial China: Militarization and Social Structure, 1796-1864* (Cambridge, Mass., 1970), pp. 64-76.

35. Fang Junyi, 12:3b.

36. *Ibid.*, 12:3.

37. Eitel, 'Ethnographical Sketches', *Notes and Queries*, 1:7 (31 July 1867), 81.

38. *Ibid.*, p. 82.

39. E.J. Eitel, 'An Outline History of the Hakkas', *The China Review*, II (July 1873-June 1874), 163.

40. Lo Wan, 'Communal Strife in Mid-Nineteenth Century Kwangtung: The Establishment of Ch'ih-ch'i', *Papers on China* (Harvard University), 19 (December 1965), 85-119.

41. Mayer's notes as incorporated in Eitel, 'An Outline History', p. 164.

42. Skinner, 'Chinese Peasants and the Closed Community', p. 280.

43. Frederik Barth, 'Introduction', in Barth, ed., *Ethnic Groups and Boundaries: The Social Organization of Cultural Difference* (Boston, 1969), pp. 98-122.

44. *Yongan sanzhi* [Three gazetteers of Yongan] (1822), 1:34b.

45. *Dongguan xianzhi* [Gazetteer of Dongguan county] (1689), 2.4:3b.

46. Eitel, 'Ethnographical Sketches', *Notes and Queries*, 1:6 (29 June 1867), p. 13b.

47. Gu Zhi, *Kerendui* [Hakka reply] (Shanghai, 1930), Pt. 2, p. 13a.

48. *Ibid.*, p. 13b.

49. George Campbell, 'Origin and Migrations of the Hakkas', *The Chinese Student Monthly*, IX:6 (April 1914), 472.

50. Luo Xianglin, *Keijia shiliao huibian* [Materials on Hakka history] (Hong Kong, 1965), pp. 297-299.
51. *Ibid.*, p. 299.
52. Luo Xianglin, *Zhongguo zupu yanjiu* [Studies on Chinese genealogies] (Hong Kong, 1971), pp. 157-70; *Pinghe xianzhi* [Gazetteer of Pinghe county] (1719), 12:37a-b, 38b-39; *Chengai xianzhi* [Gazetteer of Chengai county] (1815), 6:14.
53. Eberhard, pp. 61-63; Huang Foyi, *Zuzixiang minzu nanqianji* [Southward migration of Zuzixiang people] (Guangzhou, 1957).
54. Eberhard, pp. 66-67; Ch. Piton, 'On the Origin and History of the Hakkas', *The China Review*, II (July 1873-June 1874), 222-226; Luo Xianglin, *Kejia shiliao huibian*, pp. 377-387.
55. Qu Xuanying, *Zhongguo shehuishi congchao* [Collected works on Chinese social history] (Shanghai, 1937), I, 98-99; Li Youning and Zhang Yufa, eds., *Jindai Zhongguo nuquan yundong shiliao* [Historical materials on modern Chinese women's rights movement] (Taibei, 1975), p. 1515.
56. Luo Xianglin, *Kejia shiliao huibian*, p. 298.
57. *Ibid.*, p. 297.
58. Lo Wan, 'Communal Strife', p. 98.
59. Luo Xianglin, *Kejia yanjiu daolun*, pp. 5, 27 n. 19.
60. Lin Daquan, 'Keshuo' [Concerning the Hakkas], in Wen Tingjing, ed., *Chayang sanjia wenchao* [Literary works of three authors of Dapu county] (Taibei, 1966), pp. 131-135.
61. *Gaoyao xianzhi* [Gazetteer of Gaoyao county] (1863), 2:29b-30b; *Xinhui xianzhi* [Gazetteer of Xinhui county] (1871), 10:7, *Xinning xianshi* [Gazetteer of Xinning county] (1893), 8:6b.
62. *Xuantong Gaoyao xianzhi* [Gazetteer of Gaoyao county, compiled in the Xuantong reign], 25:39b.
63. *Yangjiang xianzhi* [Gazetteer of Yangjiang county] (1925), 7:4, 20; 21: 94b-100.
64. *Enping xianzhi* [Gazetteer of Enping county] (1934), 22:32b, 34b-35.
65. Huang Zhao, *Shigu yizen* [Gazetteer of Zhenping county] (1862), pp. 331-400.
66. Wen Zhonghe, *Jiaying zhouzhi* [Gazetteer of Jiaying independent department] (1898), 7:84b-91.
67. *Meishui shizhuan* [An anthology of poetry from the Mei Valley] (n.p., 1901), preface by Huang Zunxian.
68. Luo Xianglin, *Kejia yanjiu daolun*, pp. 5-6, 28.
69. Campbell, pp. 471-472.
70. Luo Xianglin, *Kejia yanjiu daolun*, p. 6.
71. Qiu Fenjia's foreword is preserved in Weng Huidong, comp., *Chaozhou wenkai* [Writings from Chaozhou; n.p., n.d.], 4:182-183. I have not been able to consult the pamphlet itself.
72. According to Zhong Yonghe, the Yue people were descendants of the Yue king Gou Jian, who in turn had descended from the great ruler Yu of antiquity. Zhou's essay, originally entitled *Tuke yuanliukao* [Origins of natives and Hakkas], was begun in 1900, prompted by his discovery of a racial slur on Hakkas in the county gazetteer of Sihui. It was first published in a Hong Kong newspaper, and then in 1905, on the occasion of the school text controversy, a revised version was published in Swatow and Canton newspapers. It was subsequently reissued under the new title *Yuesheng minzu kaoyuan* [Origins of the peoples of Guangdong province] in 1920 during another textbook controversy. The latter was consulted at the Zhongshan Provincial Library of Guangdong.
73. Sun Yat-sen's Hakka origin was first asserted in 1933 in Luo Xianglin,

Kejia yanjiu daolun, pp. 263-265; for a challenge to this long-accepted view, see Tan Bi'an, 'Sun Zhongshan jiashi yuanliu jiqi shangdai jingji zhuangkuang xinzeng' [New evidence on Sun Zhongshan's ancestry and his ancestors' economic situation], *Xueshu yanjiu* [Academic research], 3 (1963), 32-38.

74. Rhoads, pp. 101-104.
75. Gu Zhi, Pt. 2, p. 18b.
76. Rhoads, pp. 182, 186.
77. *Ibid.*, pp. 235-236; US Department of State, Decimal File 893.00/954, Bergholz to Minister in Peking, 15 December 1911.
78. USDS 893.00/891, Tours to Minister in Peking, 16 November, 1911.
79. *Ibid.*
80. Rhoads, pp. 237-238, 248.
81. Edward Friedman, 'Revolution or Just Another Bloody Cycle: Swatow and the 1911 Revolution', *Journal of Asian Studies*, 29:2 (Feb. 1970), 292-293.
82. Luo Xianglin, *Kejia yanjiu daolun*, p. 6.
83. Rhoads, p. 251.
84. Luo Xianglin, *Kejiayanjiu daolun*, p. 29.
85. *Ibid.*, p. 7.
86. 'Kanton Kyakka minzoku no kenkyu' [Research on the Hakkas of Guangdong], alternative title 'Kyakka minzoku konseki gaiko' [The past and present of the Hakka people], appendix to Song Wenbin, *Shina minzokushi* [A history of the Chinese people] (Tokyo, 1944), p. 357.
87. *Ibid.*, pp. 346-347.
88. For a biography of Chen Jitang, see Howard L. Boorman, ed., *Biographical Dictionary of Republican China* (New York, 1967-71), I, 160-163.
89. *Ibid.*, pp. 213-217.
90. *Ibid.*, pp. 58-61.
91. 'Kanton Kyakka minzoku no kenkyu', p. 315.
92. *Ibid.*, pp. 348-349.
93. *Ibid.*
94. *Ibid.*, p. 343.
95. *Ibid.*, p. 344.
96. Luo Xianglin, *Kejia yanjiu daolun*, pp. 10, 31. The incident was followed by another spurt of Hakka ethnic affirmation. Gu Zhi, a Meixian Hakka and professor at Zhongshan University, penned a spirited 'Hakka reply' with a view to correcting Cantonese misconceptions. It was the most complete catalogue to date of Hakka cultural and historical greatness, their impeccable ancestry, prestigious language, academic achievements, famous Hakka personalities and a proud record of patriotic anti-foreignism. In 1933, the young historian, Luo Xianglin, a Hakka of Xingning county, published his *Kejia yanjiu daolun*, which has since become the bible for the Hakka ethnic group. Methodically and with much ethnic pride, Luo examines Hakka origins and successive waves of migration, their geographical distribution, the antiquity of the Hakka language, Hakka social and cultural forms and values, concluding with a survey of leading Hakka personalities in recent decades in all walks of life.
97. Kong Yongsong and Qiu Songqing, *Minxi geming genjudi di jingji jainshe* [Economic reconstruction of the Western Fujian revolutionary base area] (Fuzhou, 1981), pp. 105-109.
98. *Ibid.*, p. 112.
99. Mao Zedong, *Mao Zedong xuanji* [Selected works of Mao Zedong] (Beijing, 1969), I, 73-74.
100. The following are some of the Hakkas, for whom biographical data is available, who made their way up from the Jiangxi Soviet period: YANG Chengwu, a native of Changting, Fujian, who participated in the western Fujian revolt of 1929, and became political commissar in the Red Army First Corps in

1932, vice-commander of the PLA Beijing-Tianjin Garrison Command in 1950, acting chief of staff in 1966, garrison commander of Beijing in 1968, and subsequently (1982) commander of Fuzhou military district. See Donald W. Klein and Anne B. Clark, *Biographic Dictionary of Chinese Communism 1921-1965* (Cambridge, Mass., 1971), pp. 968-970.

ZHANG Dingcheng, a native of Yongding, Fujian, chairman of the Western Fujian Soviet Government and member of the CCP 6th Central Committee in 1930, PLA commander of Central China Military District in 1946, chairman of Fujian in 1949-54, subsequently chief procurator. See Klein and Clark, pp. 54-58.

LIU Yongsheng, a native of Shanghang, Fujian leader of a guerilla band in western Fujian in 1931, rose to be deputy PLA commander of Fujian Military District in 1950, and chairman of Fujian Provincial Revolutionary Committee in 1968. See *Who's Who in Communist China* (Hong Kong, 1969), pp. 468-469.

LIU Yalou, a native of Wuping, Fujian, who joined the Red Army and the CCP in 1929, and became commander of the PLA air force in 1949-65. See Klein and Clark, pp. 632-634.

FU Lianzhang, a native of Changting, Fujian, who joined the Red Army as a doctor in 1927 in Fujian, and was subsequently president of the Chinese Medical Association from 1950. See Klein and Clark, pp. 285-286.

LI Qingquan, a native of Huichang, Jiangxi, political commissar in the First Front Army in 1931, chairman of Chengdu Military Control Commission and deputy political commissar of the South-West Military Region under Deng Xiaoping in 1950. See Klein and Clark, pp. 485-487.

QIU Chuangcheng, a native of Ruijin, who joined the Red Army during the Jiangxi Soviet period and became deputy commander of the PLA artillery force in 1952. See Klein and Clark, pp. 201-202.

WANG Ping, another native of Ruijin, a participant in the Long March, and subsequently chairman of Military Control Commission in Datong, Chahar, 1949-52. See Klein and Clark, pp. 917-919.

COUNTIES MENTIONED IN THE TEXT AND NOTES:

Lingnan Region
Boluo 581
Chiqi 615
Conghua 584
Donnguan 580
Enping 617
Gaoming 620
Gaoyao 607
Heping 574
Heshan 609
Hua 585
Kaiping 618
Nanhai 610
Panyu 611
Qujiang 594
Shunde 613
Xiangshan 612
Xin'an 579
Xinhui 614
Xinning 616
Xinyi 625
Xunwu 571
Yangcun 626
Yangjiang 627
Yingde 587
Yong'an 577
Zengcheng 583

Southeast Coast Region
Changting 527
Chenghai 560
Dapu 556
Fengshun 557
Guihua 517
Jianning 521
Jiaying 568
Liancheng 526
Longyan 531
Ninghua 522
Pinghe 550
Qingliu 523
Shanghang 529
Wuhua 566
Wuping 528
Yongding 530
Zhenping 569

Gan Yangzi Region
Anyuan 524
Guangchang 262
Huichang 255
Liquan 264
Nanfeng 263
Ningdu 260
Ninggang 244
Ruijin 256
Shicheng 261
Suiquan 243
Xingguo 258
Yongxin 245
Yudu 257

NOTES: Grateful acknowledgment is made to G. William Skinner who supplied the maps from which these are adapted. The county identification numbers correspond to those in his guide to regional research (forthcoming), except that the digit for one thousand in each instance has been omitted.

Sources on the distribution of the Hakkas for each relevant county are available in tabulated form but not reproduced here to save space.

THE HAKKA CHINESE

GLOSSARY

Ailiao 犵獠	Hoklo 福、河、鶴佬
Aizi 哎子	Huanggang 黃岡
Baiyue 百越	Huanghuagang 黃花岡
bendi (Punti) 本地	Huang Jie 黃節
Chen Hong'e 陳宏萼	Huang Zhao 黃釗
Chen Jiongming 陳炯明	Huang Zunxian 黃遵憲
Chen Jitang 陳濟棠	Hongtou 紅頭
Chen Mingshu 陳明樞	*Jianshe ting* 建設廳
Chen Weizhou 陳維周	*jieyuan* 解元
Chilao 犵獠	*jinshi* 進士
Congzheng 崇正	*juren* 舉人
Daikyakka shugi 大客家主義	*ke* 客
Datong ribao 大同日報	*kefei* 客匪
dazhong 大種	*kehu* 客戶
Deng Keng 鄧鏗	*keji* 客籍
Deng Yanhua 鄧彥華	*kejia* 客家
Ding Richang 丁日昌	*kejia fengsu* 客家風俗
fei 匪	*Kejia yanjiu daolun* 客家研究導論
Fenghu 豐湖	*keren* 客人
Fu Lianzhang 傅連璋	Kexi datonghui 客系大同會
Gan 贛	Li Jingquan 李井泉
Guangfuren 廣府人	Li Jishen 李濟深
Guangdong xiangtu lishi 廣東鄉土歷史	Li Yangjing 李揚敬
Guo Moruo 郭沫若	Li Zhengfang 李振芳
Guoyu 國語	Liang Jin'ao 梁金鰲
Hanzu Kefushi 漢族客福史	Liao Zhongkai 廖仲愷

325

Lin Daquan	林達泉	Wang Ping	王平
Lin Jizhen	林激真	Wen Zhonghe	溫仲和
Lin Yizhong	林冀中	Wu Peifu	吳佩孚
Lin Yungai	林蕓陔	Wu Xiangda	吳祥達
Lingnan	嶺南	Xiang Hanping	香翰屏
Liu Yalou	劉亞樓	*xiaozhong*	小種
Liu Yongfu	劉永福	*xiangyue*	鄉約
Liu Yongsheng	劉永生	Xu Xuzeng	徐旭曾
Long Jiguang	龍濟光	Yang Chengwu	楊成武
Luo Xianglin	羅香林	Yao	傜
Mei	梅	Yao Yuping	姚雨平
Meisui shizhuan		Ye Chucang	葉楚傖
Miao Peinan	繆培南	Ye Jianying	葉劍英
Qiu Chuangcheng	邱創成	*yiguan zhizu*	衣冠之族
Qiu Fengjia	邱逢甲	Yue	越
Rao Qingzhong	饒清中	Zhang Dingcheng	張鼎丞
shandao tianshao	梅水詩傳	Zhang Fakui	張發奎
She	畬	Zhang Licun	張立村
Shen Daihe	沈戴和	*zhenbei*	榛狂
Shibicun	石壁村	*Zhonghua xinbao*	中華新報
Shuiyuan	水源	Zhong Yonghe	鍾用龢
Song Xiang	宋湘	Zhongyuan	中原
Tangren	唐人	Zhou Baoheng	周寶衡
Taowu	桃塢	Zhuang	僮
Ting	汀	Zou Lu	鄒魯
Tongmenghui	同盟會	Zuzixiang	珠璣港
tu	土		
Tuhuabao	圖畫報		

11
THE CHINESE COMMUNIST PARTY'S STRATEGY FOR GALVANISING POPULAR SUPPORT, 1930-1945
K. K. Shum

It is almost universally assumed that the Chinese revolution of the twentieth century was, in essence, a peasant revolution led by the Chinese Communist Party (CCP). Therefore, in seeking an explanation for the success of this revolution, historians have largely focused their attention on how the Communists managed to win over the allegiance of the peasant masses.[1] It is seldom realised, however, that peasant support alone may not be a sufficient explanation for the success of the Chinese revolution. While the peasantry undoubtedly constituted the overwhelming majority of China's population, it does not automatically follow that a political party that directed its appeal predominantly towards the peasant masses would be assured of victory.

As in the case of traditional China, peasant rebellions would have little chance of success unless supported by a sizable number of the scholar-gentry. This is because peasants rarely contributed more than the rank-and-file to the rebel movement and had to depend on the literati for leadership, organisation and ideology. In addition, the peasants on the whole lacked a clear-cut notion of class consciousness to enable them to act as a united force. Hence, while peasants in one region fought relentlessly against the established order, peasants in other regions could be subjected to an equally, if not more, effective political, ideological and economic mobilisation by the traditional elites in support of the imperial government. (The Taiping movement is perhaps the best example of this phenomenon.) In most cases, the critical factor in deciding the outcome of such a struggle was not the participation of the peasants, but the scholar-gentry. If the rebellion received the active support of the majority of the elite, it was likely to succeed; if it alienated the majority of the elite, it was likely to fail.[2]

One may wish to point out, however, that the situation in twentieth century China was different. With the political and social disintegration following the death of Yuan Shikai, warlordism prevailed with the result that rural impoverishment and landlord exploitation had deepened and become widespread, so that the peasantry was turned into a potentially revolutionary force.[3] Moreover, the Communists had replaced the scholar-gentry as the leadership group for the peasants, and they were far more dynamic and efficient in harnessing peasant support. Yet, as this study will demonstrate, the combined strength of the Communists and peasants was still not sufficient to challenge the established order.

To begin with, peasant support for the Communists seemed contingent upon the latter's ability to offer them protection and security from attacks by the military and landlords. This can be seen by the fact that following the disastrous purge of the Communists in 1927, the peasant activities that had mushroomed during the Northern Expedition in Hunan, Guangdong and other provinces disappeared almost overnight. Moreover, when Mao began his life-long career of organising and instigating the peasants to revolutionary action in Jinggangshan shortly afterwards, he experienced the following:

> Wherever the Red Army goes, the masses are cold and aloof and only after our propaganda do they slowly move into action.[4]

Even after the Communists had slowly lured them into action by land redistribution, they still did not fully support the revolution because the Communists's strength was relatively weak. Thus Mao observed:

> In this period the poor peasants, having long been trampled down and feeling that the victory of the revolution was uncertain...dared not take vigorous action. It is taken...only when...the reactionary army has suffered several defeats and the prowess of the Red Army has been

repeatedly demonstrated.[5]

One is tempted to assume that after twenty years of revolutionary struggle and after the Communists had greatly expanded their strength vis-à-vis the Nationalists, the situation would have changed dramatically. But as late as 1948, the following was reported in a CCP organ regarding the peasant's attitude in *areas not previously controlled by the Communists*:

> In general, the peasants' political consciousness has not been raised, and their belief in the revolution is not firm. Although they are very poor, they lack a clear understanding of where their poverty comes from...they truly hate the control of the [Guomindang] and the oppression of Chiang's bandits, but they have many doubts about overthrowing his control and his basic forces.[6]

Given their low level of political consciousness, one can imagine how easily peasants who had not been 'baptised' by the Communists could fall prey to the influence of the conservative elites. Indeed, it is a well-known fact that the Nationalists relied heavily on the support of the landlords and the capitalists in suppressing communism. Although it has been suggested that the National Government's relations with them were not always harmonious and mutually beneficial,[7] it cannot be denied that they had a common interest in opposing social revolution. Besides providing the government with valuable revenues and other forms of financial support, the landlord-capitalist elite also helped to buttress its rule in various ways. In the countryside, landlords assisted in maintaining local order by such measures as the implementation of the *baojia* system,[8] the organisation of local milita and the upholding of traditional values. They could also exploit the peasants' fear of reprisals, and make use of local ties and lineage connections to secure the peasants' submission. In the cites, the capitalist elites and the more conservative elements in academic and intellectual circles, through their economic position and control of the media, educational institutions and cultural organisations, helped foster a public opinion that was hostile to communism. This, together with a vigorous Guomindang (GMD) police surveillance, made it almost impossible for the Communists to spread their influence there.

Hence, Communist attempts to mobilise the worker-peasant masses were greatly hindered by the opposition of the landlord-capitalist elites. It follows that the task of winning victory would be made much easier if the Communists had the majority of the landlord-capitalist elites on their side. This was in fact the hard lesson learnt by the CCP leaders in 1935 after their crushing defeat at the hands of the Nationalists. What they perceived as the cause of failure was not that the land revolution had failed to win the support of the peasants, but that it had alienated the entire landlord-capitalist classes. To remedy the situation, they toned down the social revolution and called for collaboration with the majority of the landlord-capitalist elites against Japan. In such a way, the Nationalists were isolated and Communist expansion was greatly facilitated.

The Experience of the Jiangxi Soviet (1930-1934)

In official Chinese Communist historiography, the Jiangxi period is known as the period of the land revolution (*tudi geming shiqi*). In order to understand how the CCP worked out its land revolutionary strategy, we must first of all achieve an understanding of how the Communists analysed the attitude of various classes towards the revolution. In Communist parlance, Chinese society could be divided into five strata. At the top were the big bourgeoisie or compradores, who had ties with the imperialist powers and served their interests. Their rural counterparts were the big landlords, staunch supporters of the feudal order, who collaborated with the imperialist powers to oppress the people. Together they constituted deadly enemies of the revolution. Below were the national bourgeoisie (native capitalists), whose interests were tied to the existing order but because they were also oppressed by the big bourgeoisie and big landlords they could be sympathetic to the revolution (naturally only when they themselves were not the targets of attack). Their rural counterparts were the rich peasants and small landlords. Underneath was a stratum of petty bourgeoisie, which was further sub-divided into an upper and a lower sector, with the former adopting an attitude similar to the national bourgeoisie and the latter favouring revolution. Their rural counterparts were the middle peasants. Then came the 'semi-proletariat' (handicraftsmen, shopkeepers and pedlars), whose rural counterparts were the poor peasants. They were the strong supporters of the revolution. Last but not least came the proletariat, the leading force of the revolution, which was made up of industrial workers. Their rural counterparts were the tenant farmers and the hired farm hands. According to Mao's estimate, there were about one million big bourgeosie (including rural counterparts), four million national bourgeoisie, fifteen million upper petty bourgeoisie, as opposed to 380 million of the rest of the population.[9]

As is well known, the CCP, under the instructions of the Comintern, entered into an alliance with the GMD in 1924 on the basis that the national bourgeoisie had a progressive role to play in the anti-feudal and anti-imperialist bourgeois-democratic revolution. Following their spilt in 1927, both the Comintern and the CCP came to the conclusion that the national bourgeoisie had joined the counter-revolutionary camp of big bourgeoisie and landlords, bringing with them the majority of the upper petty bourgeoisie. Henceforth, the CCP could reply only on the support of the workers and peasant, as well as the lower petty bourgeoisie (i.e., a united front from below). These lessons were reflected in the political resolution of the Sixth CCP National Congress held in Moscow in July 1928 under the auspices of the Comintern, which also called for the formation of workers' and peasants' soviets, the expansion of the Red Army, and the launching of the land revolution to step up the mobilisation of the peasant masses.[10]

These guidelines laid the basis of the policy orientation of the Russian Returned Students (RRS), headed by Wang Ming (Chen Shaoyu) and Bo Gu (Qing Bangxian), who dominated the central party leadership during the Jiangxi period. It is generally assumed that an acute intraparty struggle existed between Mao and the RRS. This assumption is based in part on the 'Resolution on Some Historical Problems' adopted by the Maoist party machine in 1945, which condemned the RRS for their 'leftist opportunist' mistakes. Specifically, the RRS were criticised for their excessive struggle against landlords, rich peasants and capitalists, failure to perceive the changes in class relations in the country following the Manchurian incident of September 1931 which had allowed for collaboration with the 'intermediate elements' (i.e., national bourgeoisie), and the adoption of mobile-positional warfare in the counter-offensive against the GMD's fifth encirclement campaign.[11] Some historians have been led to believe that Mao had opposed the RRS's radical orientation of the land policy, either because Mao favoured a 'united front from above' (i.e., alliance with patriotic landlords and the national bourgeoise) because it had created economic difficulties in the Soviet areas by driving away the landlords and the capitalists.[12]

While there is certain historical truth in the 1945 resolution, it should be pointed out that it was written to serve definite political purposes (see discussion below) and as such might not be an accurate reflection of the historical events. Within the parameters of the existing conditions in Jiangxi, the Party had little alternative but to rely on the land revolution in mobilising peasant support for the counter-offensive against the GMD's encirclement campaigns. An alliance with the national bourgeoisie was not only hard for the Communist to conceive after the 1927 experience, but also undesirable as it would require the Communists to relax the struggle against the rich peasants and small landlords who were their rural counterparts. At a time when the peasants were the only and most reliable source of support, a relaxation in the struggle against the landed elements might dampen the enthusiasm of the peasant masses which the Communists could hardly afford. Thus, the CCP was confronted with a dilemma which it could not resolve until driven to dire circumstances. As will be shown below, Mao and the RRS were in basic agreement on the orientation of the land policy.

At the First National Soviet Congress of November 1931 held at Ruijin, capital of the Jiangxi Soviet, a set of land and labour resolutions was adopted by Mao and his followers based on the draft proposals of the RRS. The land law called for the complete confiscation of landlords' and rich peasants' land to be redistributed among the peasant masses. In the reallotment of land, the landlords were to receive no land, while the rich peasants were to receive land of inferior quality.[13] The labour law did not call for the confiscation of the property of the capitalists, but specified a wide range of benefits to the workers at the expense of the capitalists, such as workers' supervision of the management, an eight-hour work-day, annual and sick leaves, as well as old age pensions.[14] The purpose was clearly to intensify the struggle against the landlord-capitalist elements so as to maximise support from the worker-peasant masses.

The effectiveness of the new policy was first put to test in the counter-offensive against the GMD's fourth encirclement campaign which began in May 1932. Between July and September, the Central Soviet Government under Mao's leadership ordered a full-scale political, military and economic mobilisation of the masses to support the war effort, with the expansion of the Red Army as the central objective.[15] In connection with this campaign, the Central People's Commissariat of Land issued on 28 December 1932 a directive 'On Intensifying Land Struggles and Confiscating Completely the Property of the Landlord Class', which called for a thorough search of 'all hidden or disguised landlords' whose property should be redistributed among the poor peasants in order to incite them against the landlords.[16] In early 1933, the Central Soviet Government ordered the forcible collection of contribution from the rich peasants to support the war. It decreed that efforts be made to stir up the masses to oppose the rich peasants, especially those who attempted to evade war levies by representing themselves as middle peasants.[17]

The success of the land revolution in arousing mass support for the counter-offensive is indicated by a series of reports in the CCP organs between May and June 1933, all of which declared that a large portion of the populace within the Soviet area had been activated into supporting the war mobilisation work.[18] Partly as a result of these successes, the fourth encirclement campaign was defeated. In accounting for the victory, Mao stated in July 1933:

> On the basis of the correct offensive line of the Party, the active leadership of the Soviet [government], the courageous struggle of the Red Army, and the enthusiastic support of the masses...we have smashed the enemy's fourth encirclement campaign.[19]

Thus, in so far as the mobilisation of the masses through the land revolution was concerned, it would appear that Mao was positive about its results.

In fact, in anticipation of the GMD's next military offensive, the CCP had already launched a land investigation movement in June 1933 to deepen the class struggle in the countryside. Some historians suggest that the movement was launched by the RRS to attack Mao's policy of making concessions to the rich peasants.[20] A closer examination of the documentary evidence, however, shows that Mao played the most dominant role in the movement and adhered to the line of the RRS.

The movement began with a governmental order issued by the Council of People's Commissars under the leadership of Mao on 1 June 1933. It began by noting that the land problem had not been satisfactorily solved in many areas. The purpose of the movement was to step up the class struggle among the people and to administer the last fatal blow to the feudal remnants. To this end the lower governmental units were called upon to conduct a compaign to investigate the landholdings and ferret out hidden landlords and rich peasants, whose property was to be confiscated and redistributed to the masses. The poor peasant corps and tenant farmers' union were to play the leading role in the campaign, and the Soviet Government was to absorb those active elements into its ranks to improve the Soviet organisation.[21]

Between 17 June and 1 July, Mao convened a joint conference of local Soviet officials and poor-peasants unions' representatives in eight countries to set the campaign in motion. At the conference, Mao declared:

> All past experience has proven that only through...fanning the flames of class struggle in the rural districts...can the broad masses be mobilised under the leadership of the proletariat to take part in the revolutionary war, participate in the various aspects of Soviet organisation, and build up a strong revolutionary base so that the Soviet movement can be expanded.[22]

In his 'Preliminary Conclusions on the Land Investigation Campaign' delivered in August 1933, Mao reported a general success of the movement, during which a total of more than two thousand landlords and rich peasants were identified and their property confiscated. As a result, Mao declared, the Soviet and party work had become more dynamic. The heightening of the spirit among the masses had led to other achievements such as the expansion of the Red Army, the raising of public funds, development of co-operatives, increased agricultural prodution, and the enlistment of a large number of worker-peasant activists into local Soviet organisations.[23] The same favourable assessment of the land investigation movement was presented by Mao to the Second National Soviet Congress in January 1934, in which he disclosed that a total of 6,988 landlords and rich peasants in possession of an excessive amount of land had been uncovered. Again, the success of the campaign had promoted other spheres of party work, such as consolidating the Red Army, activating mass support for the war, and achieving preliminary success in repelling the GMD's fifth encirclement campaign.[24]

Such active leadership in conducting the campaign and positive endorsement of its results hardly support the view that Mao was opposed to the land investigation movement or that the deepening of the class struggle had failed to produce favourable results in mass mobilisation.[25] Some historians argue, however, that since Mao's authority had been successively undermined by the RRS leadership he was speaking under duress and his stated views should not be taken as a reflection of his real opinion.[26] Yet this is tantamount to saying that Mao, for the sake of saving his own position, would openly support an erroneous policy which was causing great harm to the revolution. It should be realised that although Mao's position suffered a decline, he was not stripped of all vestiges of power; he still retained his position as chairman of the Central Soviet Government and had many followers in the party and military machines. If the land revolution was not producing its desired results, he would have openly voiced objection to it, as he had done in regard to the RRS's military strategy on a number of occasions, notably the Ningdu Conference of August 1932 and following the battle of Guangchang in mid-1934 (a detailed discussion of these events, however, is beyond the scope of this essay).

Nevertheless, although we can safely conclude that the land revolution had been successful in mobilising the peasants, the same cannot be said of the CCP's united front tactics. This was because the CCP was restricted by the 'united front from below' approach which rejected the national bourgeoisie in a common alliance against Japanese imperialism and Chiang Kai-shek. Thus, in response to the Japanese invasion of Manchuria in September 1931 which generated a wave of nationalistic sentiment over the country, the CCP insisted that the GMD and warlords were the 'running dogs of imperialism' who had to be overthrown before national resistance against Japan could commence.[27] In January 1933, the CCP indicated for the first time its willingness to come to an alliance with other armed forces, but on the condition that the other party should immediately grant full civil liberties and democratic rights to the people and arm them in a common struggle against the GMD and the Japanese.[28] These conditions made it extremely difficult for other parties or groups to come to a concrete agreement with the CCP.

Thus, when the Nineteenth Route Army under General Cai Tinggai in Fujian revolted against Chiang Kai-shek in November 1933 and offered to ally with the Communists in a common struggle against Japan, the CCP procrastinated since the Fujian rebels had failed to bring about a full-scale political and military mobilisation of the masses. As a result, Chiang was able to quell the rebellion with relative ease and renewed his encirclement campaign against the Communists. There is no evidence from the contemporary records to show that Mao's attitude towards the Fujian rebellion was any different from that of the RRS leadership, as Willian Dorrill's study has shown.[29]

The net result of the CCP's obscurantist policy on the issue of anti-imperialism was its failure to capitalise on the rising tide of nationalism in the country. To be sure, Communist anti-imperialist propaganda did win some support from the left-wing writers which added to the unrest among urban students and workers who were disillusioned with the Nanjing government's policy of 'internal pacification before external resistance'.[30] But to the majority of the urban populaton, the CCP's insistence on the overthrow of the GMD before national resistance was seen to be equally divisive. Most students were at a loss as to which party's policy to follow, and there was general despair and non-involvement with politics among the student population until towards the end of 1935.[31]

The failure of the CCP's united policy meant the virtual isolation of the Communists in their struggle against the GMD. Their only real strength was the support of the peasant masses within the Soviet areas, where material resources were limited. By contrast, the Nationalists had a vastly superior military machine, financial and military support from the Western powers, the firm support of the landlord and capitalist classes, collaboration from warlords against the Communists, and the acquiescence of the students and intellectuals in their 'bandit-suppression' campaigns. Under such conditions, the defeat of the

Communists seemed inevitable.

After the Communists were forced to evacuate from the Jiangxi Soviet in late 1934, Mao convened the famous Zunyi Conference in January 1935 to review the causes of defeat. Contrary to latter-day Maoist assertions, the resolution of the conference did not criticise the RRS for their leftist excesses in land and labour policies but directed the bulk of its attack on the RRS's mistaken military strategy in the counter-offensive against the GMD's fifth encirclement campaign. At the outset, it affirmed the 'correctness of the political line of the Party Central' which had 'achieved unprecedented success in mobilising the broad masses of workers and peasants in the revolutionary war'. It then criticised the RRS for their 'rightist opportunism' in underestimating the possibility of victory, implying that victory was possible provided that a correct military strategy had been adopted. Towards the end, it denounced as a grave error the Party's inability to cause a split within the counter-revolutionary forces, citing the case of the Fujian rebellion.[32] From this document, it is clear that Mao considered the mistake in military strategy, and to a lesser extent, the inability to split up the enemy camp, as primary causes for the Communists' defeat. Although Maoist historians claim that at Zunyi Mao had to concentrate on resolving the military problem first, there was apparently no attempt made to change the orientation of the Party's policy during the entire course of the Long March.[33]

In the meantime, Wang Ming, then serving as the CCP's representative to the Comintern in Moscow, offered a somewhat different assessment of the causes of defeat. Writing in November 1934, Wang attributed the strength of Chiang Kai-shek's counter-revolutionary camp to the following five factors: the support of the imperialist powers; the support of the landlord-capitalist classes; the GMD's ruthless economic exploitation of the people; the support of the warlords; and finally, the deceitful propaganda of the Nationalists, which had hoodwinked even certan sections of the petty bourgeoisie. In addition, Wang condemned the CCP's failure to come to a concrete agreement with the Fujian rebels as a 'political and military blunder'. To overcome the existing difficulties, he suggested that the Party should create a broad united front of workers, peasants, soldiers, students and merchants for the anti-imperialist and anti-Chiang Kai-shek struggles.[34]

It can be seen that to Wang, and to a lesser extent Mao, one of the main causes of the defeat in Jiangxi was the CCP's isolation and its failure to cause dissension within the Nationalist camp. The experience of the Soviet movement, therefore, showed to the Chinese Communist leaders that no matter how successful the land revolution was in generating support from the peasant masses, the Communist forces would still be unable to challenge the Nationalists. To turn the table against the GMD, the only viable alternative was to split up the enemy camp, win over a considerable section of the landlord-capitalist elites and isolate the GMD instead. This could be achieved by toning down the social revolution and directing the brunt of the CCP's attack to the external enemy, namely, Japanese imperialism. Herein lies the origins of the anti-Japanese national united front policy.

The Anti-Japanese National United Front (1935-1945)

Recent evidence indicates that the famous declaration of 1 August 1935, which marked the beginning of the anti-Japanese national united front was issued by Wang Ming unilaterally in the name of the CCP's Central Committee from Moscow, and not by the CCP itself during the Long March as Chinese Communist historians claim.[35] At the Seventh Comintern Congress of July-August 1935, Wang delivered a report stressing the importance of forming an anti-imperialist united front in the backward nations as part of the global strategy of the Comintern against fascism. In the case of China, he called for collaboration between the CCP and all anti-Japanese political and military groups in the country willing to take up arms to resist Japan and oppose Chiang Kai-shek.[36] The declaration of 1 August, which gave effect to this policy, put forward a ten-point programme which stressed the implementation of democracy and improvement in people's livelihood as a basis of common action against Japan, but it no longer insisted that the other party had to observe these recommendations before the alliance could be established.[37] There is little doubt that the declaration was as timely as it was correct, as all Communist writers agree that it has a great impact on the development of patriotic student movements at the time, leading to the December 9 Movement of student demonstrations against Japan's aggression in north China.[38]

In November 1935, Wang further expounded on the

rationale behind the new policy, which clearly reflected the lessons learnt from the failure of the Jiangxi Soviet movement. According to Wang, the anti-imperialist struggle, 'as experience shows', had a wider driving force than the land revolution. This was because, in spite of the success of the Communist forces in 'smashing' the GMD's last campaign and in establishing new Soviet regions, 'from the point of view of effective military strength the Red Army alone is still insufficient to defeat Japanese imperialism and its agents, while from the point of view of political orientation, considerable sections of the populace have not yet...support[ed] the Soviets'. To facilitate the formation of the anti-Japanese alliance, Wang proposed the following changes in the Party's policies: termination of the policy of confiscting the land and property of rich peasants and small landlords; allotment of land of equal quality instead of inferior ones to rich peasants in the event of a general redistribution as demanded by the masses; freedom of small landlords to continue to rent out their land on 'non-oppressive' conditions; non-confiscation of the land belonging to 'anti-Japanese' soldiers; and finally, confiscation only of the land but not the business enterprises of the capitalists.[39] The new policy was clearly designed to relax the struggle in the countryside against rich peasants, small landlords and capitalists (i.e., the national bourgeoisie) so as to entice them to participate in the anti-Japanese national united front.

Wang's proposals did not reach the CCP's headquarters at Wayaobao until some time in December 1935.[40] On 25 December the Politburo adopted a resolution stating that certain sections of the national bourgeoisie, numerous rich peasants, small landlords and even some warlords, confronted with the national crisis, had become sympathetic to the national revolutionary struggle against Japan and Chiang Kai-shek. Hence it was necessary to enlist their support by adopting the united front from above policy.[41]

On 27 December, Mao transmitted the new policy to a group of party activists and poured ridicule on those hardliners who might object to it:

> The forces of revolution must be pure, absolutely pure, and the road of the revolution must be straight, absolutely straight... The national bourgeoisie is entirely and eternally

counter-revolutionary. Not an inch must be conceded to the rich peasants.[42]

Instead, Mao asserted that 'the alignment of forces in the revolutionary and counter-revolutionary camps can change' under different conditions. At present, the Communist forces were still insufficient to overcome the joint forces of the Japanese imperialists and their collaborators. The united front tactics, Mao concluded, were the only correct tactics.[43]

It is clear that Mao agreed with Wang Ming's analysis of the causes of the Communist defeat. In fact, the motive behind the new policy was candidly explained by Mao to Helen Snow, who visited the Communist base areas in June 1937:

> In 1934 all provinces cooperated against the Reds, so that they had to decide to get new allies on the basis of resistance against Japan.[44]

And Bo Gu, still a top-ranking party leader, told Snow:

> For nine years we have struggled under the Soviet slogan and have had no success in the whole of China, the petty bourgeois masses and others (the peasantry with land) did not support the Soviet slogan, but they can support the nationalist and democratic slogan.[45]

From early 1936 onwards, therefore, the CCP made repeated overtures to the Nationalist and warlord armies for united resistance against Japan.[46] To facilitate the formation of the alliance, the CCP in July 1936 indirectly offered to exempt landlords who 'actively participated in the anti-Japanese enterprise' from confiscation.[47] On 25 August the CCP addressed an open letter to Chiang Kai-shek, urging an end to hostility so that they could co-operate against Japan.[48] Chiang, however, steadfastly refused to join forces with the Communists until December 1936 when he was kidnapped at Xi'an by his military subordinate, Zhang Xueliang, who had reached a secret agreement with the Communists.

The drastic turnabout in the CCP's policy from the land revolution to collaboration with the landlord-capitalist elites was not readily accepted by all members of the Party. There were those (influenced by the Trotskyists) who felt that the Party had betrayed the interests of the worker-peasant masses and capitulated to the GMD.[49] In May 1937, Mao convened the Soviet Party Representatives' Conference at Yan'an to give an official sanction to the new policy. Of particular importance was his assertion that the 'national contradiction' between China and Japan had become the principal contradiction at the present stage while the 'class contradiction' within the nation had been relegated to secondary importance.[50] This meant, in effect, that the struggle against landlord-capitalist elites was to be subordinated to the interests of united resistance against Japan.

This is not to say that the CCP was to sacrifice the interests of the worker-peasant masses in order to appease the landlord-capitalist classes. On the contrary, as the worker-peasant masses constituted the majority of the population in the anti-Japanese national united front, it was necessary to protect their basic rights and economic interests so that they could participate fully in the anti-Japanese war, for without their active participation China could not hope to win. Hence the CCP adopted the policy of rent and interest reduction (*jiangzu jiangxi*), whereby rent paid to landlords was to be lowered by a maximum of twenty-five per cent and interest rates for usury loads affixed at one-and-a-half per cent per month.[51] Similarly, workers were to enjoy certain benefits and protection (such as the eight-hour work-day which was later extended to ten-hour) but not to have control over the factories or to make excessive demands that would hinder production. The idea was to protect the basic interests of the worker-peasant masses without antagonising the landlords and capitalists, lest national unity should be undermined.

With the formal establishment of the GMD-CCP alliance following the Marco Polo Bridge incident of 7 July 1937, the question of how best to protect the Party's prerogatives and to expand its influence became an issue of overriding importance. In August 1937 Mao convened a Central Committee meeting and insisted that the Party adopt the policy of 'maintaining its independence and initiative' (*duli zizhu*) in order to have a free hand in mobilising the masses and establishing guerrilla bases.[52] In November, following the fall of Shanghai and Taiyuan, he further asserted in an internal speech to party activists that the proletariat must assume the leadership in the War of Resistance. He differentiated the united front participants into three blocs:

first, the 'left' wing composed of the proletariat, peasants and the lower petty bourgeoisie who firmly supported resistance; second, an intermediate sector comprising the national bourgeoisie and the upper petty bourgeoisie who favoured resistance but could waver at times; and third, the right-wing sector of big landlords and big capitalists who reluctantly supported the resistance but who would be prepared to capitulate to the Japanese at any time for the sake of opposing the Communists. The correct policy for the Party was to rely firmly on the left, win over the intermediate elements and isolate and oppose the ultra-rightists.[53]

Mao's analysis, however, met with strong opposition from Wang Ming, who had returned to China in late 1937 to supervise the operation of the united front. Wang put forward the slogan, 'All who oppose Japan are our friends, and all who capitulate to Japan are our enemies.'[54] This was in effect a direct rebuttal of Mao's 'three-bloc' formula.

It appeared that the principal bone of contention was that Mao was in favour of adopting a hard line towards the big bourgeoisie and big landlords, who, represented by the anti-Communist die-hards in the GMD, were bent on opposing the Communists. Wang Ming, on the other hand, wished to bring about closer collaboration with the upper stratum not only for the sake of strengthening China's resistance (and safeguarding the security of the Soviet Union from an internationalist standpoint), but also for the purpose of securing legal opportunities from the GMD for Communist expansion in both cities and countryside.

After Wang proceeded to Wuhan to establish a liaison office with the government in early 1938, therefore, he charted a course of action aimed at promoting cordial relations with the GMD. He did not neglect, however, to make use of the opportunity to expand Communist influence among the urban masses. Under the pretext of assisting the defence of the city, he established a large number of mass organisations such as the National Liberation Vanguard, the Ant Society, the Youth Salvation Corps and the Wuhan Women's Defence Corps. According to Japanese intelligence reports, by August 1938, the Communists had control over eighty thousand members in the mass organisations, which naturally alarmed the Nationalists.[55] In mid-August Chiang Kai-shek reacted by clamping down on all

Communist mass organisations in Wuhan. This incident showed that Wang's attempt to utilise the united front for an expansion of Communist influence in Nationalist areas was not at all feasible.

Hence, the Sixth Plenum of the CCP Central Committee held in October-November 1938 endorsed both the united front with the GMD and continual Communist expansion in the countryside. This explains why Mao publicly praised Chiang Kai-shek for his leadership in the resistance and reiterated the CCP's desire to collaborate closely with the Nationalists on a long-term basis.[56] Privately, he ridiculed Wang Ming's approach symbolised by the slogan 'Everything through the united front' as a 'capitulationist' line to the GMD, and further declared that the Bolshevik experience of relying on legal and parliamentary channels to expand Communist influence among the urban masses was unsuitable for China.[57] Mao's dual strategies were perfectly compatible as rural expansion was not to be achieved at the expense of openly wrecking the united front with the GMD nor undermining the co-operation with other classes.

With the defection of Wang Jingwei to the Japanese in December 1938 and the recurrence of localised clashes between Communist and Nationalist troops, Mao offered an updated analysis of the class relations within the country in December 1939. According to him, the pro-Japanese section of the big bourgeoisie and big landlords, that is, those represented by Wang Jingwei, had already turned traitors. While the pro-British and pro-American section of the big bourgeoisie and big landlords, that is, Chiang Kai-shek's faction, was still in the anti-Japanese camp, it was also vacillating because of its increasing hostility towards the Communists. Nevertheless, the entire body of the national bourgeoisie, including small landlords and rich peasants, were still *bona fide* members of the united front. The Party, therefore, must firmly ally with them to sustain the resistance and to oppose the capitulationist tendency of the big bourgeoisie and big landlords.[58]

In January 1940 Mao further elaborated on the nature and the motive forces of the Chinese revolution in his major theoretical treaties 'On New Democracy'.[59] In it, he explained that because the national bourgeoisie was weak and vacillating, it was incapable of providing revolutionary leadership, which had to be assumed by the proletariat. Nevertheless, the national bourgeoisie still had a progressive role to play not only in the War of Resistance but also in post-war construction. Hence, instead of a 'dictatorship of the proletariat', the CCP should establish a 'dictatorship of several revolutionary classes', namely, the proletariat, peasants, petty bourgeoisie and national bourgeoisie. In regard to economic policies, Mao asserted that since the Chinese economy was still backward, it was necessary to permit the existence of private property and capitalist production, so long as they did not 'dominate the livelihood of the people on a national scale'. Applied to the countryside, this meant that the holdings of big landlords would have to be taken over for redistribution to the peasants, but not those of the lesser landlords and rich peasants. It is clear that one of the principal aims of New Democracy was to consolidate the alliance with the national bourgeoisie, including small landlords and rich peasants, on a long-term basis.

As a concrete measure to institutionalise co-operation with the progressive landlord-capitalist elements, Mao inaugurated, in March 1940, the 'three-thirds system' as the appropriate structure of political power in the anti-Japanese base. The principal feature of the 'three-thirds system' was that in the governmental and legislative organs of the Communist areas the Communists formally restricted themselves to a maximum of one-third of all positions, while a second third was allocated to non-Party leftist progressives and the remaining third reserved for the intermediate elements. The basic purpose, as Mao himself put it, was to 'win over the petty bourgeoisie, the middle (i.e., national) bourgeoisie and the enlightened gentry' so as to isolate the anti-Communist diehards.[60]

There is little doubt that by instituting the 'three-thirds system' the Communists were not compromising their leading role in the government and administration of the Communist base areas, but one must not overlook the calculated appeal of the system to the landlord-capitalist elites. According to Peng Zhen's report on the administration of the Jin-Cha-Ji (Shanxi-Chaha-Hebei) Border Region in November 1941, the implementation of the 'three-thirds system' had 'enabled the landlord-capitalist classes to resist the reactionary propaganda of the Japanese bandits and the influence of anti-Communist diehards...and feel at ease in co-operating with us to support the construction of the base areas'. In describing the response of the landlords to the system, Peng said:

> They are overwhelmed with happiness, as if they have discovered all of a sudden that under the present conditions it is much more beneficial for them to support the anti-Japanese democratic government than it was to oppose it... Some of them sway their heads and sing 'The present is better than the age of Yao and Shun'.[61]

Another GMD intelligence report lamented the effectiveness of the 'policy correction meetings' (*zhengce jiuzheng hui*) held in connection with the 'three-thirds system' whereby landlords and gentry were invited to voice their views and suggest ways to improve the administration:

> These meetings are very effective. Gentry who in the past had been dissatified, after participating in such conferences, fill the skies with praise, feeling that the [CCP] government isn't so bad after all, that it can recognise its own mistakes and ask for criticism.[62]

In January 1941, one of the most tragic incidents in the War of Resistance occurred in central China, where the bulk of the Communist New Fourth Army was attacked and destroyed by Nationalist forces on the pretext that it had violated military discipline. The exact details need not concern us here but it is generally assumed that the New Fourth Army incident marked the formal rupture between the two parties, and henceforth the united front ceased to exist.[63] This interpretation, however, takes the narrow view that the united front was a bi-partisan alliance (*Guo-Gong hezuo*), neglecting that it was in fact a more broadly based 'class policy' (*jieji zhengce*). To the Communists, the incident did not mean the collapse of the united front *per se*, but merely a change in the structure or composition of the united front.

Shortly after the incident, Deng Zihui, a staunch Maoist supporter, asserted in an internally circulated article that the present situation must not be equated with the disintegration of the united front; on the contrary, with the treachery and vacillation of the wavering elements thoroughly exposed, the united front had become narrower in scope but more consolidated and homogeneous than before.[64] What he meant was that the New Fourth Army incident had thoroughly exposed the counter-revolutionary nature of the big bourgeoisie and big landlords; but the other participants remained firm supporters of the united front. In May 1941, Mao reiterated a similar position:

> In the struggle against the GMD diehards, the big comprador bourgeoisie must be distinguished from the national bourgeoisie...and the most reactionary big landlords must be distinguished from the enlightened gentry and the general run of landlords... Many of our comrades, however, still lump the different landlords and bourgeoisie groups together, as though the entire landlord class and bourgeoisie had turned traitors after the [New Fourth Army] incident; this is an oversimplification of China's complex politics. Were we to adopt this view and identify all the landlords and bourgeoisie with the GMD diehards, we would isolate ourselves.[65]

It was partly in the context of this changed composition of the united front that the CCP in the early forties launched a series of mass campaigns to generate greater support from the masses. This was because the GMD, representing the big landlords and big bourgeoisie, was making preparation for civil war which would likely ensue after the conclusion of the Sino-Japanese conflict. The inner dynamics of these compaigns have been ably analysed by Mark Selden.[66] However, his assertion that these campaigns amounted to a re-invigoration of the CCP's rural revolution at the expense of class collaboration seems lopsided.

According to Selden, the CCP's 'Decision on Land Policy in the Anti-Japanese Base Areas' issued on 28 January 1942 represented a radical reorientation of the CCP's land policy as it pointed to a more thorough-going campaign to enforce rent and interest reduction on the peasants' behalf.[67] While it is true that this would lead to more extensive mobilistion of the peasant masses, it should be noted that the basic policy of 'guaranteeing the landlords their civil liberties, political and economic rights' was still in force. There was no fundamental change in the policy of class reconciliation:

> In the rural united front, contradictions between the

landlord and the peasant...must be settled appropriately... Both sides should bow to the overall interests of national resistance. In settling disputes, the working members of the Party and government should base themselves on the above principles and follow a policy of adjusting to the interests of both sides. They should not take a one-sided stand favouring either the landlord or the peasant.[68]

This message is further elaborated in a strictly internal Party document issued shortly afterwards, which described the objective of the Party's directive as follows:

> Its basic spirit was to activate the broad peasant masses, for nothing could be achieved without the mobilisation of the masses. But after the masses have been aroused, it must be ensured that the landlords can continue to survive... Economically, the present policy of our Party is to encourage capitalist production and to preserve certain rights of the landlords... Politically, the three-thirds system is to be implemented... All these are aimed at preventing the landlord-capitalist classes from allying with the enemy and the diehards, and at winning over the majority of the landlord-capitalist classes to the anti-Japanese democratic regime... Even those who have gone over [to the side of the enemy and the diehards] can still be won over to our side.[69]

Nor has Selden given sufficient attention to the CCP as it continued to make a serious effort to promote the 'three-thirds system' in the Communist base areas. This can be seen in a series of articles published in the Party organ, *Jiefang ribao* (Liberation Daily), in the early forties.[70] Even when the Party Central was calling for the strengthening of Communist leadership in the local party, government and mass organisations under the principle of 'monolithic Party leadership' (*lingdao yiyuanhua*), it did not neglect to warn cadres that the basic principles of the three-thirds system could not be discarded, although the quality of Party members holding administrative position had to be improved.[71] To ensure that Party members understood that 'monolithic Party leadership' did not mean 'mono-Party dictatorship', the Central Committee, in May 1943, urged admission of non-aligned elements into the CCP's government.[72]

Further evidence indicating the continuation of the united front can be found in the numerous reports filed by Chinese and foreign vistors to the Communist base areas in 1944-1945. They unanimously pointed to the fact that landlords and capitalists, with the exception of traitors, were not the targets of attack in the Communist regions, that they enjoyed full civil and political rights, that there was no confiscation of the land of landlord, and that free enterprise was allowed.[73] These phenomena gave rise to the well-known misconception among American observers that the Chinese Communist were mere 'agrarian reformers' and 'democrats' rather than 'genuine communists'.[74]

It would therefore be a lopsided view to assume that, with the emergence of the 'mass-line' politics after 1941, the united front policy of class collaboration was brushed aside or played down in the interests of promoting the class struggle. On the contrary, the 'mass-line' politics actually went hand in hand with the politics of 'class collaboration', as the 'to the village', production, education and other campaigns were not directed at the landlords and capitalists. In so far as class struggle was being held in check, it can be said that the united front was the overall guiding principle of the Party's policies during the so-called Yan'an period. To the Chinese Communist, therefore, this period was known officially as the period of the anti-Japanese national united front (*kang-Ri minzu tongyi zhanxian shiqi*).

To be more specific, the anti-Japanese national united front was important to the expansion of Communist power in a number of ways. Firstly, it greatly narrowed the basis of the GMD's support from the landlord-capitalist elites and undercut its influence over the rest of the population (the petty bourgeoisie and the masses). Secondly, by neutralising the opposition of both the landlord and the national bourgeoisie, especially the former in view of China's preponderant agrarian economy, the CCP was able to expand its influence in the rural areas with relative ease. Thirdly, the progressive landlord-capitalist elites provided the CCP with the much-needed administrative skills and financial expertise to improve the administration and the rural economy, which added to the political and economic stability of the Communist base areas. Fourthly, by isolating the Nationalists and by championing national unity the CCP effectively prevented them from launching a full-scale attack on itself. This meant that the CCP was able to gain time and accumulate strength to prepare for the eventual armed confrontation with the GMD. Its equal importance to the rural strategy is perhaps best illustrated by Mao himself when he stated in 1939 (and again in 1949) that 'the united front, armed struggle and Party construction were 'the three magic weapons' with which the Communists were to win power.[75]

On the basis of the successful experience of the anti-Japanese national united front, the CCP leadership in 1945 drew up the 'Resolution on Some Historical Problems', which denounced the RRS's policies of struggle against landlords, rich peasants and capitalists in the Jiangxi period as 'leftist opportunist' error which had greatly harmed the revolution. These criticisms certainly appeared justified from hindsight, but the resolution also deliberatley absolved Mao of responsibility in executing those policies by presenting him as a consistent opponent to them. In fact, a claim was made for Mao in having discovered New Democracy as early at the late twenties:

> Comrade Mao Zedong...pointed out that after big bourgeoisie's betrayal of the revolution [in 1927] there was still...a broad stratum of people who demanded democracy and especially demanded a fight against imperialism. It was therefore necessary to treat the various intermediate classes correctly and do everything possible to make an alliance with them... In the countryside it was necessary to...provide certain economic opportunities for the rich peasants and also enable the ordinary landlords to make a living. These are all basic ideas of New Democracy, yet they were not understood and were opposed by the exponents of the 'leftist' line.[76]

Conclusion

In the light of the above discussion, the notion that the Chinese Communist revolution was a peasant revolution pure and simple and that the mobilisation of the peasants was the all-embracing factor in the Communists' success must be modified. Without the ability to win over the support or sympathy of a substantial portion of the landlord-capitalist elites, it is doubtful that they could have achieved the rapid expansion of power and influence it enjoyed during the War of Resistance.

The same strategy of obtaining a multi-class support was continued in the Civil War period (1946-1949), when the Party leadership called for the new democratic united front composed of workers, peasants, petty bourgeoisie, national bourgeoisie and 'enlightened gentry' in a common struggle against American imperialism and Chiang Kai-shek.[77] Although the CCP had now gone a step further in radicalising the land policy in the interest of greater mass mobilisation efforts (i.e., the confiscation of land not farmed by the landlords themselves), it still warned against relapsing into the 'leftist' excesses of the Jiangxi period.[78] Instead it promised that private capitalism and the rich-peasant economy would be preserved for a long period in China until the advent of socialism.[79] There is little doubt that these tactics, as implemented under the rubric of the united front and class collaboration, had caused many landlords and national and petty bourgeois elements to lose their will to resist the Communists, thus contributing greatly to the disintegration of the Nationalist camp and its eventual collapse. Small wonder that Mao, on the eve of Communist victory, denounced as a 'serious error of principle' the attempt to propagate one-sidedly the view that the workers, poor peasants and farm labourers conquered the country, without mentioning the contribution of the national bourgeosie, the intellectuals, and the 'enlightened gentry who do not oppose land reform'.[80]

NOTES

1. See Chalmers Johnson, *Peasant Nationalism and Communist Power: the Emergence of Revolutionary China, 1937-1945* (Stanford, 1962), for the view that peasant nationalism played the key role in the emergence of Communist power; and Mark Selden, *The Yenan Way in Revolutionary China* (Cambridge, Mass., 1971) for the opposite view that socio-economic factors played a more important role. Tetsuya Kataoka, *Resistance and Revolution in China: The Communist and the Second United Front* (Berkeley, 1974) offers an alternative interpretation claiming that the CCP succeeded by juxtaposing two distinct strategies, namely the land revolution and the united front with the urban bourgeoisie.

2. See Philip A. Kuhn, *Rebellion and Its Enemies in Late Imperial China* (Cambridge, Mass., 1970) for an excellent study on the subject.

3. One document that is often cited to support this view is Mao Zedong, 'Report on An Investigation of the Peasant Movement in Hunan', *Selected Works of Mao Tse-tung* (Beijing, 1967), I, 23-59. Hereafter referred to as

Selected Works.
4. See 'Struggle in the Chingkang Mountains,' *Selected Works*, I, 97.
5. *Ibid.*, p. 88.
6. Cited in Suzanne Pepper, *Civil War in China: The Political Struggle 1945-1949* (Berkely, 1978), p. 310.
7. See Lloyd E. Eastman, *The Abortive Revolution: China under Nationalist Rule, 1927-1937* (Cambridge, Mass., 1975), pp. 240-243; Parks M. Coble, Jr., *The Shanghai Capitalists and the Nationalist Government, 1927-1937* (Cambridge, Mass., 1980), *passim.*
8. The *baojia* system was a traditional device to control the rural population whereby ten families were organised into a *jia* and ten *jia* into one *bao* placed under a supervisor who would be held responsible for the conduct of the residents. The Nationalists reinstituted the system as a means of control in areas under their jurisdiction.
9. 'Zhongguo shehui ge jieji di fenxi' [An analysis of the various classes in Chinese society], in Takeuchi Minoru, ed., *Mao Zedong ji* [Collected works of Mao Zedong] (Tokyo, 1971-72), I, 161-173. Hereafter cited as *MZDJ*.
10. See 'Diliuci quanguo daibiao dahui zhengzhi wenti jueyian' [Political resolution of the Sixth National Congress], in *Gongfei woguo shiliao huibian* [A collection of historical documents on the communist bandits' crimes against the nation] (Taibei, 1964), II, 8-35.
11. 'Guanyu ruogan lishi wenti di jueyi' [Resolution on some historical problems], in *Mao Zedong xuanji* [Selected works of Mao Zedong] (Beijing, 1953), III, 955-1004.
12. See John E. Rue, *Mao Tse-tung in Opposition, 1927-1935* (Stanford, 1966); Shanti Swarup, *A Study of the Chinese Communist Movement* (Oxford, 1966).
13. See 'Zhonghua suweiai gongheguo tudifa' [Land law of the Chinese Soviet Republic], in Hsiao Tso-liang, *Power Relations within the Chinese Communist Movement, 1930-34, II, The Chinese Documents* (Seattle, 1967), pp. 435-437.
14. See 'Laodong fa' [Labour Law], in Hsiao, *Power Relations II*, pp. 440-443.
15. See [Liang] Bodai, 'Suweiai zhongyang zhengfu chengli yi zhounian yu Zhonnguo suweiai yundong' [The first anniversary of the founding of the Central Soviet Government and the Soviet movement in China], *Shihua* [True words], 9 (25 October, 1932), 9-11.
16. 'Zhongyang tudi renmin weiyuanhui xunling diyi hao—wei shenru tudi douzheng, chedi moshou dizhu jieji caichan' [Instructions No. 1 of the central people's commissariat of land—on intensifying], *Hongse Zhonghua* [Red China], 47 (14 January, 1933), 5-6.
17. 'Xiang funong muji yici zhanzheng juankuan, fadong qunchong bangzhu zhengfu gongzuo renyuan gengtian' [Collecting contributions from the rich peasants once to support the revolutionary war and mobilising the masses to help till land for government employees], cited in Hsiao Tso-liang, *The Land Revolution in China* (Seattle, 1967), p. 74.
18. See articles by Li Fuzhun, Chen Shouzhang, Zhang Wentian and 'Guanyu kuoda hongjun di jueyi' [Revolution on the expansion of the Red Army] in *Douzheng* [Struggle], 12, 14, 17 and 19 (May-July 1933).
19. Mao Zedong, 'Xin di xingshi yu xin di renwu' [New situations and new tasks], *Hongse Zhonghua*, 97 (29 July, 1933), 3.
20. Swarup, pp. 127-129, 133-135.
21. 'Zhonghua suweiai gongheguo linshi zhongyang zhengfu remin weiyuanhui xunling, di shiyi hao - zhixing guangfan shenru di chatian yundong' [Instruction No. 11 of the Council of People's Commissars of the Provisional

Central Government of the Chinese Soviet Republic—launching an extensive and intensive land investigation campaign] *Hongse Zhonghua*, 87 (20 June, 1933), 2.

22. Mao Zedong, 'Chatian yundong shi guangda quyu di zhongxin renwu' [The land investigation campaign is the central task in vast areas], *Hongse Zhonghua*, 86 (14 June, 1933), 3.

23. Mao Zedong, 'Chatian yundong di chubu zongjie', *Doucheng*, 24 (29 August 1933), 4-12.

24. Mao Zedong, 'Zhonghua suweiai gongheguo zhongyang zhixing weiyuanhui yu renmin weiyuanhui dui dierci quanguo suweiai daibiao dahui di baogao' [Report of the Central Executive Committee of the Chinese Soviet Republic and the People's Commissariat to the Second National Soviet Congress], reproduced in Hsiao, *Power Relations II*, pp. 715-716.

25. It is true that in October 1933 Mao had issued a governmental order which allowed certain landlords and rich peasants to seek re-classification, for which he was criticised. But Mao had done so probably to avoid hitting at the wrong persons, and not to change the basic policy of struggling against landlords and rich peasants.

26. Stuart Schram, *Mao Tse-tung* (London, 1967), pp. 165-166.

27. See 'Zhonghua suweiai gongheguo linshi zhongyang zhengfu xuanbu duRi zhanzheng xuanyan' [Declaration of war against Japan by the Provisional Central Government of the Chinese Soviet Republic], *Hongse Zhonghua*, 18 (21 April 1932), 2.

28. 'Zhonghua suweiai linshi zhongyang zhengfu gongnong hongjun geming junshi weiyuanhui xuanyan' [Declaration of the Chinese Soviet Provisional Central Government and the Revolutionary Military Council of the Workers' and Peasant' Red Army], *Hongse Zhonghua*, 48 (28 January 1933), 1.

29. William F. Dorrill, 'The Fukien Rebellion and the CCP: Case of Maoist Revisionism', *China Quarterly*, 37 (March 1969), 31-53.

30. See John Israel, *Student Nationalism in China, 1927-1937* (Stanford, 1966), pp. 101-3 and 157; and Gong Chu, *Wo yu hongjun* [The Red Army and I], (Hong Kong, 1954), p. 353.

31. See Helen Snow, *Notes on the Chinese Student Movement, 1935-36* (Madison, 1959), p. 20.

32. 'Zhonggong zhongyang guanyu fandui diren wuci weijiao di zongjueyi' [General resolution of the party central on the counter-offensive against the enemy's fifth 'encirclement campaign'], in *MZDJ*, IV, 379-397.

33. See Zhang Guotao, *Wo di huiyi* [Hong Kong, 1974], III, 1125, 1197-1199.

34. Wang Ming, 'Xin tiaojian yu xin celue' [New conditions and new strategy], *Wang Ming xuanji* [Selected works of Wang Ming] (Tokyo, 1971-1975), III, 356-358.

35. See Zhang Guotao, 1198-99; Guo Hualun, *Zhonggong shilun* [Analytical History of the CCP] (Taibei, 1969), III, 72-73; R.A. Ulyanousky, ed., *The Comintern and the East* (Moscow, 1979), pp. 390-391.

36. Wang Ming, *The Revolutionary Movement in the Colonial Countries* (London, 1935), *passim*.

37. Wang Ming, 'Appeal to the Whole People of China to Resist Japan and Save the Country', *International Press Correspondence*, XV, 64 (30 November, 1935), 1959-1997. It should be noted that in the 1938 Chinese version of the declaration all hostile references to Chiang Kai-shek had been deleted. See *Guo-Gong hezuo kangRi wenxian* [Documents on the GMD-CCP cooperation against Japan] (Hankow, 1938), pp. 1-7.

38. See, for example, Li Chang *et al.*, *Yierjiu huiyilu* [Recollections of the December 9 movement] (Beijing, 1961), pp. 40-41.

39. Wang Ming, 'Xin xingshi yu xin zhengce' [New situation and new

policy] *Wang Ming xuanji*, IV, 354-371.

40. Zhang Guotao, 1199; and Wang Ming, *Mao's Betrayal* (Moscow, 1979), pp. 67-68.

41. 'Zhongguo gongchandang zhongyang guanyu muqian zhengzhi xingshi yu dang di renwu jueting' [Resolution of the CCP central politburo on the present political situation and the tasks of the party], in *MZDJ* V, 19-40.

42. 'On Tactics against Japanese Imperialism', *Selected Works*, I, 164.

43. *Ibid*. p. 165.

44. Nym Wales (Helen Snow), *My Yenan Notebook* (Madison, 1961), 84.

45. *Ibid*., p. 121.

46. See 'Tingzhan yihe yizhe kangRi tongdian' [Circular telegram on cessation of civil war and unity to resist Japan], in *MZDJ*, III, 47-49.

47. 'Guanyu tudi zhengce di zhishi' [Directive on Land policy], in *MZDJ*, V, 63-65.

48. 'Zhongguo gongchandang zhi Zhongguo guomindang shu' [Letter of the CCP to the GMD], *ibid*., pp. 67-76.

49. See Wales, *My Yenan Notebook*, p. 211.

50. 'The Tasks of the Chinese Communist Party in the Period of Resistance to Japan', *Selected Works*, I, 263-265.

51. See T.A. Bisson, *Yenan in June 1937: Talks with the Communist Leaders* (Berkeley, 1973), pp. 31-32.

52. See Zhang Guotao, pp. 1295-1300; Guo Hualun, pp. 230-233; Otto Braun, *A Comintern Agent Li China* (St. Lucia, 1982), pp. 211-213, for details of the conference.

53. 'The Situation and Tasks in the Anti-Japanese War After the Fall of Shanghai and Taiyuan', *Selected Works*, II. 61-70.

54. 'Muqian kangzhan xingshi yu renwu' [The present situation and tasks of the war of resistance], reproduced in Guo Hualun, pp. 278-281.

55. See for example, Japanese Consulate-General, Shanghai, *Bukan kanraku choku-sen ni okeru koNichi sensen no doko* [Activities of the anti-Japanese front shortly before the fall of Wuhan; October 1938], pp. 3-10; and *Shina* [China] XXIX, 9 and 10 (September and October 1938), XXX, 7 (July 1939).

56. 'Lun xin jieduan' [On the new stage], *MZDJ*, VI, 163-264, esp. 166, 198, 208.

57. See 'The Question of Independence and Initiative Within the United Front' and 'Problems of War and Strategy', *Selected Works*, II, 213-232.

58. 'The Chinese Revolution and the Chinese Communist Party', *ibid*., pp. 319-321.

59. See the original version of this article 'Xin minzhu zhuyi lun' [On new domocracy], in *MZDJ*, VII, 147-205.

60. 'On the Question of Political Power in the Anti-Japanese Base Areas', *Selected Works*, II, 417-419.

61. Peng Zhen, 'Guanyu Jin-Cha-Ji bianqu dang di jianqie he gexiang juti zhengce di baogao tigang' [Outline report on the party construction and various concrete policies in the Jin-Cha-Ji border region], September 1941, reproduced in Zhongguo renmin jiefangjun zhengzhi xueyuan dangshi jiaoyan shi [Research office on party history of the political academcy of the People's Liberation Army],ed., *Zhonggong dangshi sankao ciliao* [Reference materials on the history of the Chinese Communist Party] (n.p., 1979), for internal circulation only, IX, 73-74 and 88. Yao and Shun refer to the legendary emperors in Confucius's golden age of antiquity.

62. Cited in Lyman Van Slyke, *Enemies and Friends, The United Front in Chinese Communist History* (Stanford, 1967), pp. 152-153.

63. Johnson, pp. 13-14; Selden, pp. 175, 197 and 207; and Kataoka, p. 228.

64. Deng Zihui, 'Dui Huannan shibian di jiben renshi' [Basic understanding

on the South Anhui (New Fourth Army) incident], *Dang di shenghuo* [Life in the party], 2 (February 1941), 1-8.

65. 'Conclusions on the Repulse of the Second Anti-Communist High-tide', *Selected Works*, II, 465.

66. Selden, Ch. 6.

67. *Ibid.*, pp. 232-233.

68. 'Zhonggong zhongyang guanyu kangRi genjudi di tudi zhengce di jueding', in *Gongfei woguo shiliao huibian*, III, 430-434.

69. 'Zhongyang guanyu zhixing tudi zhengce jueding di celue di zhishi' [Central directive on the strategy for the execution of the decision on land policy], in *Qunzhong gongzuo zhinan* [Guide to mass work], 'strictly confidential', (n.p., 1945), pp. 4-7.

70. 'Jiaqiang xianqu xingzheng lingdao (Editorial)' [Strengthen the administrative leadership in the counties and districts], *Jiefang ribao* (12 December 1941); Huannan (pseud.), 'Sansanzhi yu tianxia weigong' [The three-thirds system and government for the people], *ibid.*, (22 December 1941); 'Sansanzhi di yunyong (Editorial)' [The application of the three-thirds system], *ibid.*, (25 May 1942); 'Chongshi xianji sansanzhi (Editorial)' [Strengthen the three-thirds system at the district level], *ibid.*, (4 March 1942); and 'Shaan-Gan-Ning biangu zhengfu wei chongshi 'sananzhi' ji gexian shishi xin' [Directive letter of the Shaan-Gan-Ning border region government to the various districts on the strengthening of the 'three-thirds system'], *ibid.*, (9 March 1942).

71. 'Guanyu tongyi kangRi genjudi dang di lingdao ji tiaozheng ke zuzhi jian guanxi di jueting' [Directive on unifying the party leadership in the various anti-Japanese bases and adjusting the interrelations between various organisations], *Gongfei woguo shiliao huibian*, III, 160-161.

72. 'Dang di lingdao yiyuanhua he sansanzhi zhengce' [Monolithic party leadership and the policy of the three-thirds system], *Jiefang ribao* (14 May 1943).

73. See for example, Zhang Wenbo, *Shanbei quilai dake wen* [Reply to enquiry after the return from Northern Shaanxi] (Chongqing, 1945); Jin Dongping, *Yan'an guilai* [Return from Yan'an] (Chonqing, 1944); Wang Zhongming, *Shanbei zhixing* [Journey to northern Shaanxi] (Chongqing, 1944); Doak Barett, *Dixie Mission: The U.S Army Observer Group in Yenan, 1944* (Berkeley, 1970); John Service, *The Amerasia Papers: Some Problems in the History of US-China Relations* (Berkeley, 1917); Harrison Forman, *Report from Red China* (London, 1946); Stuart Gelder, *The Chinese Communist* (London, 1946); Gunther Stein, *The Challenge of Red China* (New York, 1945); Robert Payne, *Chinese Diaries: 1941-1944* (New York, 1945); and Joseph Esherick, ed., *Lost Chance in China: The World War Two Despatches of of John Service* (New York, 1974).

74. For an analysis of this episode, see K.E. Shewmaker, *Americans and Chinese Communists, 1927-1945: A Persuading Encounter* (London, 1971), esp. 238-262.

75. See *Selected Works*, II, 295; and IV, 244.

76. See 'Guanyu ruogan lishi wenti di jueyi', *Mao Zedong xuanji* (1953), III, 973-974.

77. 'Present Situation and Our Tasks' (25 December 1947), *Selected Works*, IV, 170.

78. See *ibid.*, pp. 168-169, and 174, n. 4.

79. See 'Great New High Tide of Chinese Revolution' (1 February 1947), *Selected Works*, IV, 124; and 'On the People's Democratic Dictatorship' (30 June 1949), *ibid.*, 421.

80. 'Correct the 'Left' Errors in Land Reform Propaganda' (11 February 1948), *Selected Works*, IV, 197.

12

CONCLUSIONS
David Pong and Edmund S.K. Fung

The period 1860-1949 is often viewed as one of transition. The studies in this volume, by taking us from the disintegration of the old imperial order to a reintegration under the new Communist state, confirm this view. Nevertheless, focusing as they do on the development of socio-political groups, their ideals, and the gulf between their aspirations and government policies or actions, these studies also underscore the haphazardness of this transformation. To a large extent, this disorderly transition was the function of the search for wealth and power. Having committed itself to limited reform, the Qing state had inaugurated a series of changes that it was later unable to utilise fully or incorporate into the traditional order. At the same time, 'wealth and power', often defined loosely or differently by interested parties, was unable to hold an increasingly complex society together for purposeful change.

Benefiting from hindsight, we know that the pre-1949 struggle for progress, national dignity, and independence had failed. The changes that occurred were too little and too slow. This volume, we hope, has provided some explanations.

China was not slow, as has sometimes been assumed, in responding to the challenges of the 'unprecedented situation' in which it found itself in the wake of the Opium Wars in the middle of the nineteenth century. These challenges, emanating from both internal and external sources, threatened the very existence not only of the dynasty but also of China as a civilisation and a nation-state. Scholars and officials, concerned with China's future, were eager to seek solutions in reforms, not from within the narrow confines of Qing orthodoxy, but by drawing selectively on China's intellectual and political traditions. If successfully implemented, their proposals would have significantly transformed the Qing state and prepared the ground for the realisation of a strong China. Whether such a reconstructed China could, in the face of ever intensifying imperialism, preserve its territorial and administrative integrity remains a moot point. The significance of the reformist 'programme' of the 1860s and 1870s lies in the fact that it represented a 'great leap' in the exploration of new ideas. Though partly disguised in traditional garb, these ideas foreshadowed many later attempts to build a modern nation. But in the context of the late Qing, they had set goals to which the Manchu court was unwilling to commit itself. Hence the progressive breakdown of the imperial order and the increasing cynicism both from within and outside the government.

The Qing court's half-hearted support for change, combined with the influence that came with international commerce and the foreign presence at the treaty ports, did bring into existence new ideas and social forces. Population growth, demographic changes, and large-scale rebellions, which have received only passing references in this volume, also broke up the now much larger scholar-gentry body into several interest groups.[1] Each of these groups cherished its own goals and aspirations. For as long as there was hope that the ruling dynasty would pursue policies that would satisfy the quest for wealth and power on the one hand and their particularistic needs on the other, they supported it. The throne recognised this phenomenon, and when the earlier game of playing one group against the other, notably the reformers against the conservative die hards, failed, it introduced in 1901 its own reforms that were as sweeping as any proposed in the preceding decades. The strategy worked, at least temporarily. Until the last years of the Qing, the Lingnan Hakka leaders sought gratification through traditional service to the state, as did the new breed of diplomat-officials from the treaty-port commercial community. Even the movement for women emancipation, which had no direct political objectives at the time, tried to advance its cause within the established order. It was not until the insincerity of the Manchu court became apparent, and high-sounding reformist rhetorics were not backed up by genuine change, that numerous groups, old and new, deserted the dynasty.

The chaos that followed has often been attributed to the existence of an ideological vacuum. Confucianism as the state orthodoxy was banished for ever. This, however, must be seen in a proper perspective, for it was the emergent socio-political groups and their espousal of new ideals—itself a reaction against Qing manipulation of Confucian orthodoxy—that led to that ideological void, and not *vice versa*. The Revolution of 1911, despite its avowed desire to establish a republic, was therefore largely the work of these interest groups against a common enemy. Once that enemy was disposed of, they went their different ways. Unfortunately, the bulk of these groups was not as yet powerful enough to impose their own pet solutions on the rest of China. At the same time, the new leaders of the Republic made only token efforts to satisfy their competing demands. If anything, the out-moded Yuan Shikai and his warlord successors had created an environment that proved inviting for these groups to compete for political influence if not for power. Thus, hitherto marginal elements—militarists, ex-Qing reformers and nationalistic diplomats, treaty-port leaders, and intellectuals, newly reinforced by a feminine component—now moved to centre stage. Competition, and chaos, once ushered in, remained.

During the 1910s and the 1920s nationalism—the modern form of the wealth and power formula—became the main integrating force. It was largely the claim that it could fulfil the new nationalistic aspirations that brought the GMD to power in 1928. The Nationalist government promised economic and social change as well. Hopes were high and there was considerable popular support for the government at first. The Nanjing decade, marked by a period of relative peace and stability, did see some social reforms in education and women emancipation, steps towards fostering economic development, and a diplomatic offensive through peaceful means. But most of the internal developments owed little to direct government efforts, and none was significant enough to win them long-term support: the vested interests of those who had an input into GMD policy made sure that these changes were restricted. Being militarily impotent, except against some of its internal enemies, Nanjing's diplomacy also brought limited results. Recourse to the fascist model did little for Chiang Kai-shek and his party; the Italian connection was as short-lived as it was tenuous. The Japanese seizure of the North-east and, finally, all-out invasion brutally exposed the widening gap between the GMD's stated goals and the harsh reality of its helplessness. In the end, the government was brought down by a majority of those socio-political groups whose common nationalistic aspirations and particular interests it had promised but failed to satisfy.

It is difficult to weigh the relative importance of the various factors causing the wide gap between ideal and reality, goals and implementation, in the period 1860-1949. The studies in this volume do offer some answers. In Chapters 2-4 we see a persistent call from concerned officials and others for a stronger central government and leadership. The absence of a resolute and enlightened leadership, and one politically astute enough to make sacrifices, even temporarily, in order to effect the necessary changes was certainly critical. There were physical and ideological constraints as well, as conservatism grew with every advance made by the reformists. A resolute central government could keep conservatism in check,[2] but as the legitimacy of the throne came under a cloud after the succession crisis of 1874, firm leadership became a rarity. Even the adept Empress-Dowager Cixi was unable to manoeuvre successfully among the rising demands for change from the growing number of active socio-political groups.[3] Force had to be used in 1898 to get rid of the reformers, and intrigues in 1907 and 1908 to neutralise Yuan Shikai and his associates. The uninhibited resurgence of Manchu interests and power just before and after her death in 1908, resulting in the removal of the new diplomat-officials, practitioners of the new diplomacy of nationalism, further alienated the treaty-port commercial community and the gentry groups that had been looking forward to genuine constitutional government. Post-1911 leadership, substituting individual or class interests for 'greater Manchuism', could do no better.

There is no question that Chinese society in the twentieth century was more pluralistic than before. But because changes under the Qing were modest in scale, the emergent socio-political groups were weak. The lack of a resolute leadership, which compelled these groups to jockey for influence, also resulted in much division within themselves. No single group or coalition was thus in a position to gain nation-wide predominance after 1911, yet they were strong enough to survive and to be reckoned with. No one could remain in power for long without making concessions to the majority of them.

The weakness of the state in the twentieth century had therefore become increasingly a product of the government's inability to galvanise broadly-based support. In our context, this suggests serious shortfalls between policies and achievements. The unsuccessful attempts to regulate the coal industry and to create a modern educational system are cases in point. Administrative incompetence, corruption, intra-government rivalry, defiant regional forces and an inherited weak economy further exacerbated the government's impotence.

Despite the weaknesses of the emergent socio-political groups, one can still see, from time to time, group or even class interests at work. These interests, when successfully exerted, had dictated policies largely beneficial to the already socially advantaged. Of the reform measures introduced in the last decade of the Qing, the necessity to abolish the traditional civil service examinations to make way for a modern educational system was certainly one that many had come to accept. Nevertheless, scholar-gentry opposition could be neutralised only because they had been able to seek gratification elsewhere, first, through the self-government movement and provincial and national assemblies, and second, through their commercial interests and managerial skills, which had been fast developing and which had enabled them to take advantage of the new reforms. But perhaps the most blatant expression of class interests studied in this volume was education under the Nationalists. Its elitism succeeded only in widening the gap between the rich and the poor and between the city and the countryside. The failure to deal with rural problems was directly related to the rise of opposition groups, primarily the peasants, many of whom found the Communist alternative more attractive.

Practically all Chinese leaders throughout the period paid lip service to self-strengthening. But when it came to specific proposals for or against change, one can hardly dissociate them from the vested interests of their proponents.

'Convervatism', when taken to mean the preservation of the old order and opposition to sweeping innovation, was a powerful force throughout the period 1860-1949. In a country such as China where there was a strong belief that the established order was founded on a glorious past, convervatism was appealing. In order to appreciate the overall thrust of conservatism, however, we must take note of another dimension of its manifestation. Because all the socio-political groups examined in this volume had in varying degrees adopted policies favourable to their own interests and at others' expense, all of them could be viewed as partly progressive and partly conservative. And because none of the groups, especially since 1911, was able to dominate the politial scene for long, all could blame 'widespread conservatism' for their frustrated goals. When so qualified, we can speak of conservatism as a major obstacle to change. The women's movement is a case in point. From the very start, it was subordinated to the quest for wealth and power, and the vast majority of its spokesmen were men, 'progressive' men whose main object was to build a stronger China. The interests of the state were also very much behind the limited legal rights and opportunities granted women during the Nanjing period. But the emancipation of women also struck at the heart of deeply-ingrained social attitudes cherished by the male half of the population, attitudes that could not be easily removed. In short, women liberation came up against two kinds of conservatism, that of the die-hards and that of the 'progressives'. It is therefore not surprising that, even today, after decades of socialist revolution, sexual equality is still something to be achieved.[4]

Last but certainly not least, imperialism played an important role in China's modern transformation. The impact of imperialism on the country's economy still awaits further study. Even if the overall effect had been minor, as some scholars argue,[5] it should be borne in mind that foreign economic activities had been concentrated in specific areas, especially in and around treaty ports, and in certain coal-mining regions. That these areas bore the brunt of imperialism, and therefore its influence, is demonstrated by the birth of a Western-oriented Chinese community, whose scions began to make an inroad into the political arena at the beginning of the present century.

Politically, however, the adverse effect of imperialism is irrefutable. It stood directly in the way of China's quest for national independence and international equality. Chinese nationalistic aspirations were realised only when the powers, guided by their broader interests, were prepared to accommodate China's specific wishes. This happened rarely, in the 1900s when Yuan Shikai's diplomat-officials thwarted Russian and German advances, and again in the first years of the Nanjing decade when China regained tariff autonomy and some of the treaty-port concessions. (The same can be said of the renunciation of extraterritorial rights by Britain and the United States in 1943, which is beyond the scope of the studies in this volume.) Military weakness insured that China could get only what the powers were willing to give.

As noted earlier, there had been a persistent call for a stronger central government since the 1860s. A strong government would surely be in a better position to regulate or satisfy the diverse demands from competing socio-political groups. In the twentieth century, a powerful government could also enjoy the support of patriotic elements. It could thus begin to narrow the gulf between ideal and reality and become an effective integrating agent.

As the history of the 1930s reveals, it was the relentless Japanese aggression that proved fatal to the Chinese government. The invasion halted the Nationalist drive towards treaty revision as well as exposing their military weakness. In fact, such weakness may well explain, at least in part, the government's lack of will to fight, which, in the end, cost it a great deal of popular support and, thereby, the mandate to rule.

Of all the socio-political groups examined in this volume, only two attained their goals, namely the Hakkas of Lingnan and the Communists. The Hakkas' success can be attributed partly to their sustained efforts made over two centuries, partly to the rising tide of nationalism with which they identified, and partly to the political instability after 1911 which afforded fresh opportunities for ethnic assertiveness. The ultimate triumph of the Communists was due in large measure to their realisation that peasant support, however important, was insufficient to win power. They were astute enough to modify, albeit temporarily, their long-term class interests and adopted a national united front strategy in 1935. This strategy eventually won them the support of the national bourgeoisie and progressive elements in the landlord-capitalist classes who had become disillusioned and bitter with the Nationalist leadership.

If there are morals in the successes of the Hakkas and the Communists, these may be that, firstly, minority communities in China will have a better chance of gaining political influence by integrating into the larger national polity and by identifying with the national interest rather than by promoting separatist or particularistic ones. Secondly, any political party seeking to win power and consolidate it must enjoy the support of the modern and educated elite, as well as of the rural masses. Neither the domination of the landlords, militarists, or the capitalists nor the dictatorship of the proletariat has shown to date that it could best serve China's interests.

With the onset of dynastic decline at the end of the eighteenth century and the encounter with the West in the nineteenth, the discrepency between ideal and reality in the traditional state was starkly revealed. In hindsight, the initial attempts to close that gap had been patriotic and visionary but were doomed to fail for lack of imperial support. Frustration soon led to alienation. By the time the imperial obstacle had been removed, however, Chinese society had become too complex to be manageable, certainly not by the mediocre leadership that was China's fate to experience. The prolonged political disintegration that ensued had allowed powerful interest groups to emerge, each seeking its own ways to narrow that gap. The reintegration under the Nanjing government was all too brief and superficial. Early support for the regime also ended in alienation, repeating, on a smaller scale, the late-Qing scenario.

In any developing nation, the discrepancy between ideal and reality will always be present, but it must not be allowed to loom so large as to become disruptive. By all acounts, present-day China has reduced that gap to within tolerable levels. Success thus far is no guarantee against future alienation. Mass mobilisation, political campaigns, socialist education, and real material progress may well produce salutary results in the long run. But the present government would do well by managing the still divergent group aspirations realistically and flexibly. Let it not be forgotten that it was an alliance of many groups that brought about the successful establishment of the People's Republic in 1949.

NOTES

1. Chang Chung-li, *The Chinese Gentry* (Seattle, 1962), pp. 149-195; see also references in Chapter 9 in this volume. For a general analysis of the changing character and the fragmentation of the gentry, see Marianne Bastid-Bruguiere, 'Currents of Social Change', in *The Cambridge History of China, Volume 11: Late Ch'ing, 1800-1911, Part 2*, John K. Fairbank and Kwang-ching

Liu, eds. (Cambridge, 1980), pp. 536-539.

2. Kwang-ching Liu, 'Politics, Intellectual Outlook, and Reform: The T'ung-wen Kuan Controversy of 1867', in Paul A. Cohen and John E. Schrecker, eds., *Reform in Nineteenth-century China* (Cambridge, Mass., 1976), 87-100.

3. For an example of how Cixi tried to balance between two rival bureaucratic camps, see Lloyd E. Eastman, *Throne and Mandarins: China's Search for a Policy during the Sino-French Controversy, 1880-1885* (Cambridge, Mass., 1967).

4. Phyllis Andors, *The Unfinished Liberation of Chinese Women, 1949-1980* (Bloomington, Indiana, 1983).

5. See, for example, Rhoads Murphey's *The Outsiders: The Western Experience in India and China* (Ann Arbor, 1977).

SUGGESTED READINGS

This list is not intended to be a complete listings of relevant scholarship, but a short one that contains a few selected titles in the English language for each of the topics covered in this book.

Pong: *The Vocabulary of Change*

Brown, Shannon R. 'The Ewo Filature: A Study in the Transfer of Technology to China in the 19th Century', *Technology and Culture*, XX, 3 (July 1979), 550-568.

Chang Hao. 'On the *Ching-shih* ideal in Neo- Confucianism', *Ch'ing-shih wen-t'i*, 3, 1(November 1974), 36-61.

Hou, Yen-p'ing and Wang Erh-min. 'Changing Chinese Views of Western Relations, 1840-95, in John K. Fairbank and Kwang-ching Liu, eds., *The Cambridge History of China*, Vol. 11, *Late Ch'ing, 1800-1911*, Part 2, pp. 142-201. Cambridge: Cambridge University Press, 1980.

Levenson, Joseph R. *Confucian China and Its Modern Fate: A Trilogy*. Berkeley: University of California Press, 1968.

Liu Kwang-ching. 'Nineteenth-century China: The Disintegration of the Old Order and the Impact of the West', in Ping-ti Ho and Tang Tsou, eds., *China in Crisis*, Vol. 1, book 1, pp. 93-178. Chicago: University of Chicago Press, 1968.

———. 'Li Hung-chang in Chihli: The Emergence of a Policy, 1870-1875', in Albert Feuerwerker, Rhoads Murphey, and Mary C. Wright, eds., *Approaches to Modern Chinese History*, pp. 68-104. Berkeley: University of California Press, 1967.

———. 'Politics, Intellectual Outlook and Reform: T'ung-wen Kuan Controversy of 1867', in Paul A. Cohen and John E. Schrecker, eds., *Reform in Nineteenth-century China*, pp. 87-100. Cambridge, Mass.: East Asian Research Center, Harvard University, 1976.

Metzger, Thomas A. *The Internal Organization of Ch'ing Bureaucracy: Legal, Normative, and Communication Aspects*. Cambridge, Mass.: Harvard University Press, 1973.

Metzger, Thomas A. *Escape from Predicament: Neo-Confucianism and China's*

SUGGESTED READINGS

Evolving Political Culture. New York: Columbia University Press, 1977.

Mitchell, Peter M. 'The Limits of Reformism: Wei Yuan's Reaction to Western Intrusion', *Modern Asian Studies*, 6, 2 (April 1972), 175-204.

Pong, David. 'Confucian Patriotism and the Destruction of the Woosung Railway, 1877', *Modern Asian Studies*, 7, 4 (October 1973), 647-676.

Sturdevant, Sandra. 'Imperialism, Sovereignty, and Self- strengthening: A Reassessment of the 1870's', in Paul A. Cohen and John E. Schrecker, eds., *Reform in Nineteenth-century China*, pp. 63-70. Cambridge, Mass.: East Asian Research Center, Harvard University, 1976.

Whitbeck, Judith. 'From K'ao-cheng to Ching-shih: Kung Tzu-chen and the Redirection of Literati Commitment in Early Nineteenth Century China', in *Jinshi Zhongguo jingshi sixiang yantaohui lunwenji* ['Proceedings of the Conference on the Theory of State craft of Modern China'], pp. 323-340. Taipei: Institute of Modern History, Academia Sinica, 1984. (This volume contains many articles pertaining to the subject at hand. With few exceptions, they are all in Chinese).

Wright, Mary C. *The Last Stand of Chinese Conservatism: The T'ung-chih Restoration, 1862-1874*. Stanford: Stanford University Press, 1962; rev. edn. with new preface, New York, Atheneum, 1966.

Godley: Lessons from an Italian Connection

Chang, Maria J. 'Fascism and Modern China', *China Quarterly*, 70 (September 1979), 553-567.

Eastman, Lloyd E. 'Fascism and Modern China: A Rejoinder', *China Quarterly*, 80 (December 1979), 838-842.

———. 'Fascism and Modern China: A Rejoinder', *China Quarterly*, 80 (December 1979), 838-842.

———. *The Abortive Revolution: China under Nationalist Rule, 1927-1937*. Cambridge, Mass.: Harvard University Press, 1974.

———. 'The Kuomintang in the 1930's', in Charlotte Furth, ed., *The Limits of Change: Essays on Conservative Alternatives in Republican China*. Cambridge, Mass.: Harvard University Press, 1976, pp. 191-210.

Grieder, Jerome B. *Intellectuals and the State in Modern China: A Narrative History*. New York: Free Press, 1981.

Kirby, William C. *Germany and Republican China*. Stanford: Stanford University Press, 1984, particularly chapter 6: 'Frugality, Fascism and New Life', pp. 145-185.

Tamagna, Frank M. *Italy's Interests and Policies in the Far East*. New York: Institute of Pacific Relations, 1941.

Tien Hung-mao. *Government and Politics in Kuomintang China 1927-1937*. Stanford: Stanford University Press, 1972.

Borthwick: *Changing Concepts of the Role of Women from the Late Qing to the May Fourth Period*

Borthwick, Sally. *Education and Social Change in China: The Beginnings of the Modern Era*. Stanford: Hoover Institution Press, 1983.

Holmgren, Jennifer. 'Myth, Fantasy or Scholarship: Images of the Status of Women in Traditional China', *Australian Journal of Chinese Affairs*, 6

(July 1981), 147-170.

———. 'The Economic Foundation of Virtue: Widow Remarriage in Early and Modern China', *Australian Journal of Chinese Affairs*, 13 (January 1985), in press.

Lang, Olga. *Chinese Family and Society*, first ed. New Haven: Columbia University Press, 1946, repr. Archon Books, 1968.

Witke, Roxane. 'Transformation of Attitudes Towards Women During the May Fourth Era of Modern China', Ph.D. thesis, University of California, Berkeley, 1970.

Wolf, Margery and Witke, Roxane, eds. *Women in Chinese Society*. Stanford: Stanford University Press, 1975.

Young, Marilyn B, ed. *Women in China: Studies in Social Change and Feminism*. Ann Arbor: Michigan University Press, 1973.

Wright: The Nationalist State and the Regulation of Chinese Industry during the Nanjing Decade

Bush, Richard. *The Politics of Cotton Textiles in Kuomintang China, 1927-1937*. New York: Garland Publishing Inc, 1982.

Coble, Parks M. Jr. *The Shanghai Capitalists and the Nationalist Government, 1927-1937*. Cambridge, Mass.: Council on East Asian Studies, Harvard University, 1980.

Eastman, Lloyd E. *The Abortive Revolution: China Under Nationalist Rule, 1927-1937*. Cambridge, Mass.: Harvard University Press, 1974.

———. 'New Insights into the Nature of the Nationalist Regime', *Republican China* 9, 2 (February 1984), 8-18; plus two responses to Eastman's article by Joseph Fewsmith and Bradley Geisert, *ibid.*, 19-39.

Paauw, Douglas, 'The Kuomintang and Economic Stagnation 1928-1937', *Journal of Asian Studies* 16, 2 (February 1957), 213-220.

Sih, Paul K.T, ed. *The Strenuous Decade: China's Nation- Building Efforts, 1927-1937*.

Wright, Tim. *Coal Mining in China's Economy and Society, 1895-1937* Cambridge: Cambridge University Press, 1984.

Mackerras: Education in the Guomindang Period, 1928-1949

Becker, C.H., M. Falski, P. Langevin, and R.H. Tawney. *The Reorganisation of Education in China*. Paris : League of Nations' Institute of Intellectual Cooperation, 1932.

Buck, Pearl S. *Tell the People: Talks with James Yen about the Mass Education Movement*. New York: John Day, 1945.

Chen, Theodore H. E. 'Education in China 1927-1937' , in Paul K. T. Sih, ed., *The Strenuous Decade: China's Nation-Building Efforts, 1927-1937*. New York: St John's University Press, 1970, pp. 289-314.

Djung, Lu-dzai. *A History of Democratic Education in Modern China*. Shanghai: Commercial Press, 1934.

Fenn, William Purviance. *Christian Higher Education in Changing China 1880-1950*. Grand Rapids: W. B. Eerdmans, 1976.

Israel, John. *Student Nationalism in China, 1927- 1937*. Stanford: Stanford

SUGGESTED READINGS

University Press, 1966.

Lewis, Ida Bell. *The Education of Girls in China*, New York: AMS Press, 1919.

Liao, T'ai-ch'u. 'Rural Education in Transition, a Study of the Old-fashioned Chinese Schools (Szu Shu) in Shantung and Szechuan', *Yenching Journal of Social Studies*, 1V (February 1949), 19-67.

Peake, Cyrus H. *Nationalism and Education in Modern China*. New York: Columbia University Press, 1932.

Wang Shih-chieh. 'Education', in Kwei Chungshu, ed., *The Chinese Year Book 1935-36 Premier Issue*, Kraus Reprint, Nendeln, 1968, pp. 456-532. All issues of *The Chinese Year Book* contain valuable material on education. *The Chinese Year Book* was a regular and entirely English-language publication. It is distinct from the mainly British *The China Year Book*, which began publication in 1912 edited by H.T. Montague Bell and H.G.W. Woodhead. All issues of *The China Year Book* also contain chapters on education. Both yearbooks have been reprinted by the Kraus Reprints in Nendeln , Liechtenstein.

Fung: Nationalist Foreign Policy, 1928-1937

Borg, Dorothy. *The United States and the Far Eastern Crisis of 1933-1938*. Cambridge, Mass.: Cambridge University Press, 1964.

Chan, F. Gilbert. *China at the Crossroads: Nationalists and Communists, 1927-1949*. Boulder: Westview Press, 1980.

Clubb, O. Edmund. *Twentieth Century China*. New York: Columbia University Press, 1964.

Coox, Alvin D. and Conroy, Hilary. eds. *China and Japan: Search for Balance Since World War 1*. Santa Barbara: ABC-Clio Books , 1978.

Endicott, S. L. *Diplomacy and Enterprise: British China Policy 1933-1937*. Manchester: manchester University Press, 1975.

Fung, Edmund S. K. 'Anti-imperialism and the Left Guomindang', *Modern China*, 11, 1 (January 1985), 39-76.

———. 'The Sino-British Rapprochment', *Modern Asian Studies*, 17, 1 (1983), 79-106.

Iriye, Akira. *After Imperialism: The Search for a New Order in the Far East 1921-1931*. Cambridge, Mass.: Harvard University Press, 1965.

Kirby, William C. *Germany and Republican China*. Stanford: Stanford University Press, 1984.

Levi, Werner. *Modern China's Foreign Policy*. Minneapolis: University of Minnesota Press, 1953.

Mancall, M. *China at the Center: 300 Years of Foreign Policy*. New York: The Free Press, 1984.

Wright, Stanley F. *China's Struggle for Tariff Autonomy, 1843- 1938*. Shanghai: Kelly and Walsh, 1938.

Sigel: The Diplomacy of Nationalism, 1900-1911

Bays, Daniel H. *China Enters the Twentieth Century*. Ann Arbor: University of Michigan Press, 1978.

SUGGESTED READINGS

Carlson, Ellsworth C. *The Kaiping Mines (1877-1912)*. Second Edition. Cambridge, Mass.: Harvard University Press, 1971.

Fairbank, John K. and Kwang-ching Liu, eds. *The Cambridge History of China Volume 11. Late Ch'ing, 1800-1911, Part 2*. Cambridge: Cambridge University Press, 1980.

Feuerwerker, Albert. *China's Early Industrialization*. Cambridge, Mass.: Harvard University Press, 1958.

Hao Yen-p'ing. *The Comprador in Nineteenth Century China*. Cambridge, Mass.: Harvard University Press, 1970.

Hunt, Michael H. *Frontier Defense and the Open Door*. New Haven: Yale University Press, 1973.

Lee En-han. *China's Quest for Railway Autonomy*. Singapore: Singapore University Press, 1977.

MacKinnon, Stephen R. *Power and Politics in Late Imperial China*. Berkeley: University of California Press, 1980.

Schrecker, John E. *Imperialism and Chinese Nationalism*. Cambridge, Mass.: Harvard University Press, 1971.

Teng Ssu-yu and Fairbank, John K. eds. *China's Response to the West*. Cambridge, Mass.: Harvard University Press, 1961.

Wright, Mary C. ed. *China in Revolution: The First Phase, 1900-1913*. New Haven: Yale University Press, 1968.

Liew: Some Reflections on Political Change, 1895-1916

Ch'en, Jerome. *Yuan Shih-k'ai*. Second edition. Stanford: Stanford University Press, 1972.

Esherick, Joseph W. *Reform and Revolution in China: The 1911 Revolution in Hunan and Hubei*. Berkeley: University of California Press, 1976.

Fincher, John. *Chinese Democracy: The Self-Government Movement in Local, Provincial and National Politics, 1905-1914*. Canberra: Australian National University Press, 1981.

Fung, Edmund S. K. *The Military Dimension of the Chinese Revolution: The New Army and Its Role in the Revolution of 1911*. Vancouver: University of British Columbia Press, 1980.

Gasster, M. *Chinese Intellectuals and the Revolution of 1911: The Birth of Modern Chinese Radicalism*. Seattle: University of Washington Press, 1969.

Lewis, C. M. *Prologue to the Chinese Revolution: The Transformation of Ideas and Institutions in Hunan Province, 1891-1907*. Cambridge, Mass.: Harvard University Press, 1976.

Liew, K. S. *Struggle for Democracy: Sung Chiao-jen and the 1911 Chinese Revolution*. Berkeley: University of California Press, 1971.

MacKinnon, Stephen R. *Power and Politics in Late Imperial China: Yuan Shih-kai in Beijing and Tianjin, 1901-1908*. Berkeley: University of California Press, 1980.

Rankin, M. B. *Early Chinese Revolutionaries: Radical Intellectuals in Shanghai and Chekiang, 1902-1911*. Cambridge, Mass.: Harvard University Press,

SUGGESTED READINGS

1971.

Rhoads, E. J. M. *China's Republican Revolution: The Case of Kwangtung, 1895-1963*. Cambridge, Mass.: Harvard University Press, 1975.

Schiffrin, Harold Z. *Sun Yat-sen and the Origins of the Chinese Revolution*. Berkeley: University of California Press, 1968.

The Cambridge History of China, XI: Late Ch'ing 1800-1911, Part 2, eds., J. K. and K. C. Liu. Cambridge: Cambridge University Press, 1980.

Wright, Mary C. ed. *China in Revolution: The First Phase, 1900-1913*. New Haven: Yale University Press, 1968.

Young, Ernest. *The Presidency of Yuan Shih-k'ai: Liberalism and Dictatorship in Early Republican China*. Ann Arbor: University of Michigan Press, 1977.

Leong: The Hakka Chinese of Lingnan

Cohen, Myron L. 'The Hakka or Guest People; Dialect as a Socio-cultural Variable in Southeastern China', *Ethnohistory*, 15, 3 (1968), 237-297.

Kuhn, Philip A. 'Origins of the Taiping Vision: Cross-cultural Dimensions of Chinese Rebellions', *Comparative Studies in Society and History*, 19, 3 (July 1977), 350-366.

Lamley, Harry J. 'Subethnic Rivalry in the Qing Period', in E. M. Ahern and H. Gates, eds., *The Anthropology of Taiwanese Society*. Stanford: Stanford University Press, 1968, pp. 282-318.

Shum: *The Chinese Communist Party's Strategy in Galvanising Popular Support, 1930-1945*

Bianco, L. *Origins of the Chinese Revolution, 1915-1949*. Stanford: Stanford University Press, 1967.

Kim, I. *The Politics of Chinese Communism: Kiangsi Under the Soviets*. Berkeley: University of California Press, 1973.

Johnson, C. A. *Peasant Nationalism and Communist Power: The Emergence of Revolutionary China, 1937-45*. Stanford: Stanford University Press, 1962.

Schram, S. R. *Mao Tse-tung*. Harmondsworth: Penguin Books, 1967.

Selden, M. *The Yenan Way in Revolutionary China*. Cambridge, Mass.: Harvard University Press, 1971.

Other general works of interest

Crowley, James B., ed. *Modern East Asia: Essays in Interpretation*. New York: Harcourt, Brace and World, 1970.

Feuerwerker, Albert, ed. *Modern China*. Englewood Cliffs, N.J.: Prentice-Hall, 1964.

Feuerwerker, Albert, Rhoads Murphey, and Mary C. Wright, eds. *Approaches to Modern Chinese History*. Berkeley: University of California Press, 1967.

Fogel, Joshua A. and William T. Rowe. *Perspectives on a Changing China*. Boulder: Westview Press, 1979.

Hsü, Immanuel C.Y. *The Rise of Modern China*. Third edition. New York:

SUGGESTED READINGS

Oxford University Press, 1983.

Levenson, Joseph R. ed. *Modern China: An Interpretive Anthology*. New York: Macmillan, 1970.

Rozman, Gilbert, ed. *The Modernization of China*. New York : The Free Press, 1981.

Sheridan, James E. *China in Disintegration: The Republican Era in Chinese History 1912-1949*. New York: The Free Press, 1975.

NOTES ON THE CONTRIBUTORS

Sally Borthwick is a research fellow in the Department of Political and Social Change, Research School of Pacific Studies, Australian National University, and the author of *Education and Social Change in China: The Beginnings of the Modern Era* (Stanford: Hoover Institution Press, 1983).

Edmund S. K. Fung is senior lecturer in Chinese history in the School of Modern Asian Studies, Griffith University, author of *The Military Dimension of the Chinese Revolution: The New Army and its Role in the Revolution of 1911* (Vancouver: University of British Columbia Press, 1980), and co-author of *From Fear to Friendship: Australia's Policies Towards the People's Republic of China, 1966-1982* (St. Lucia: University of Queensland Press, 1985).

Michael R. Godley is lecturer in South-east Asian history, Monash University, and the author of *The Mandarin-capitalists from Nanyang: Overseas Chinese Enterprise in the Modernization of China 1893-1911* (Cambridge: Cambridge University Press, 1981). He is currently working on a study of Jiang Baili.

S. T. Leong is professor of Chinese studies in the School of Human Communication, Murdoch University, and the author of *Sino-Soviet Diplomatic Relations, 1917-1926* (Canberra: Australian National University Press, 1976).

K. S. Liew is senior lecturer in history, University of

Tasmania, and the author of *Struggle for Democracy: Sung Chiao-yen and the 1911 Chinese Revolution* (Berkeley: University of California Press, 1971).

Colin Mackerras is foundation professor in the School of Modern Asian Studies, Griffith University, and the author of several books on China, the most recent being *The Performing Arts in Contemporary China* (London: Routledge and Kegan Paul, 1981), *Modern China: A Chronology* (London: Thames and Hudson, 1982), and as editor and contributor, *Chinese Theatre from Its Origins to the Present Day* (Honolulu: University of Hawaii Press, 1983).

David Pong is associate professor in East Asian history, University of Delaware, and the author of *A Critical Guide to the Kwangtung Provincial Archives Deposited at the Public Record Office of London* (East Asian Research Center: Harvard University, 1975). He is currently completing a two-volume study on the late Qing official and reformer, Shen Baozhen.

K. K. Shum is lecturer in Chinese history, University of New South Wales. He is currently working on China's special economic zones, among other things.

Louis T. Sigel is senior lecturer in economic history, University of New South Wales. He is presently doing research on China's special economic zones.

Tim Wright is lecturer in Chinese studies in the School of Human Communication, Murdoch University, and the author of *Coal Mining in China's Economy and Society, 1895-1937* (Cambridge: Cambridge University Press, 1984). He is currently working on the politics of the Great Depression in China.

INDEX

Allen, Young J, 69, 74, 81, 83, 88n
Amau Eiji, 206
America (see United States)
American Boxer Indemnity Fund, 170
Analects, 33
Andowa, 106
Anhui, 137, 141-42
Anglo-Oriental Society for the Suppression of the Opium Trade, 231
Annam, 29, 189
annei, 203
Anti-Comintern Pact, 93, 116
Ant Society, 342
Arrow War, 3

badao, 189
Bahbo Italo, 96
Baiyue, 289
Baker, Edward, 241
Bank of China, 97
bao, 175
baojia, 329
Barnes, J.S., 101
Barth, Frederik, 301
Bays, David, 261
Beijing Adhesion Convention (1906), 241
Beijing-Hankou Line, 134
Beijing Language School, 36, 45
Beijing Tariff Conference, 192
Beijing Women's Normal School, 82, 85
Beiping-Shenyang Railway, 198
Beiyang Army, 275; and loyalty to Yuan Shikai, 255, 277
Beiyang Navy, 253
Belgium, 192

'bendi', 294
Berlin, 94, 98, 102, 103, 115-16, 118
bianfa, 38-39
biantong, 39
Bismarck, Otto Eduard L. von, 278
Black Shirts, 97
Blue Shirts, 102, 104-05, 113, 116
Board of Revenue, 44
Bodong Company, 143
Bo Gu, 331, 340
Book of Change, 39
Book of Poetry, 64
Book of Rites, 32, 66
Boscarelli, Raffaele, 98, 99
Boshan coal guild, 141, 146
Boxer indemnity, 98, 193
Boxer Rebellion, 257, 261
Brazil, 114
Bredon, Robert, 242
Britain, 18, 73, 117-18; opens embassy in Nanjing, 98; decline of economic interest in China, 142-43; viewed as major imperialist power, 186; recognition of the National Government, 192; and Chinese foreign policy, 193-94; role of in world economic system, 223; decline of in world economic system, 233; position in China, 243-44
bureaucracy, 243, 245, 255, 261; reform of, 44, 53, 226
Bureau of Commerce (1901), 238
Bureau of Railways and Mines (1902), 238
Bureau of Mine Supervision (1906), 238

Cai Tingkai, 202, 204, 336

INDEX

Cai Yuanpei, 188
Calboli, Paulucci de, 117
Campbell, George, 302
Canton (see Guangzhou)
Carnegie, Lancelot, 241
Cavour, 107-08
Central People's Commissariat of Land, 333
Central Political Council, 188; report of, 200
Central Soviet Government, 318, 333
Central Supervisory Council, 188
Chang, Carson (Zhang Jiasen), 106, 108, 112
Chang Peng-yuan, 274
Changsha, 176
Changsha Rice Riot, 261
Chaozhou, 289, 291, 311
Chao Yuenren, (Zhao Yuanren), 80
Chen Baozhen, 256
Chen Bijun, 77, 80
Chen Duxiu, 83, 84, 90n
Chen Gongbo, 117-18, 128, 138
Chen Hong'e, 310-11
Ch'en Jerome, 259, 275
Chen Jiongming, 310-11, 313
Chen Jitang, 313-15
Chen Lifu, 112-13
Chen Mingshu, 204, 313-14, 317
Chen Sanli, 256
Chen Weizhou, 315
Chen Yi, 277
Cheng Tianfang, 103, 118
chi, 31
Chiang Kai-shek (Jiang Jieshi), 20, 22, 93, 97, 102, 104, 110, 114, 190; view of fascism, 105, 113; view of the military's role, 105; religious ideas of, 119; anti-Sovietism of, 195-96; anti-communist campaigns of, 199, 203; opposition to, 201, 204, 210 Germany, 205; 'Enemy or Friend?', 207; on territorial infringement, 209; and the student movement, 210; rejects alliance with CCP, 340; conflict with CCP, 343, and the Italian solution, 9; comparison with Mussolini, 101; on Chinese society, 111; on spiritual values, their importance, 113; on the Italian connection, 115-116; heads National Government, 155; education under, 159-60, 173; heads Military Affairs Committee, 202 (see also Guomindang, Yuan Shikai, Sun Yat-sen and National Government)
China Development Finance Corporation, 143
China Foundation for Education and Culture, 170
China Merchants' Steam Navigation Company (CMSN Co.), 42, 232
China Vegetable Oil Corporation, 131
Chinese Anti-foot-binding Society, 72
Chinese Chamber of Commerce (Shanghai), 202
Chinese Coal Relief Association, 137, 139
Chinese Communist Party (CCP), 6, 167, 169, 186, 210, 212, 252; relations with Nationalists, 329; and the Jiangxi Soviet, 330; alliance with GMD, 331-32, 335-36, 340-41, 348-49; Sixth National Congress of, 331; First National Soviet Congress of, 332; relations with landlords, 332, 350; on class struggle in rural areas, 333; Second National Soviet Congress of, 335; reaction to Japanese invasion, 335; anti-imperialist sentiments of, 336; policy on rent, interest reduction, 341; 'Decision on Land Policy in the Anti-Japanese Base Areas', 346 and the 'three-thirds' system, 347; 'Resolution on some Historical Problems', 349; analysis of Chinese society, 330-31; Six Plenum of CEC of, 343; role of peasant support of, 20, 257, 327-28; united front with GMD, 21, 155, 338-49
Chinese Eastern Railway, 15, 195
Chinese Educational Mission, 233, 237
Chinese People's Convention, 194, 198
Chow Tse-tsung, 85, 90n
Christianity (see missionaries)
Chuzo Ichiko, 256, 260, 276
Ciano, Edda Mussolini, 97, 120n
Ciano, Galeazzo, 93, 95-96, 99, 101, 104, 114-17
Cixi, Empress Dowager, 236, 256, 258; violates dynastic rule, 50; and ban on opium, 241; supports

INDEX

Yuan Shikai, 236; death of, 244
Clubb, Edmund, 186
Coal industry, position under Nationalist government, 11, 137; foreign control of, 133-34, 142; cartels within, 133-148 *passim*; Japanese penetration of, 134-35, 148; the effects of the depression on, 135-36; and the 1933 conferences, 138
Cohen, Myron, 298
Comintern, 193, 331, 337; seventh congress of 338 comprador-merchants, 230-31; and western education, 232
Comprehensive Geography of the Chinese Empire, 311
Confucianism, 31, 227, 244, 252, 259; role of in family, 8; role in decline of Qing, 25-26, 226, and the 'three submissions', 64, 76; on government-people relations, 46; attitude to women of, 63-67 *passim*; gradual decline of, 83
Congzheng Association, 312
constitutionalism, Manchu support of, 262
constitutionalist, 271, 278; social support for, 269; and parliamentary government, 262; support for revolutionaries, 264
Conte Biancamano, 96
Conte Rosso, 96, 98, 115
Conte Verde, 96, 119
Cora, Julio, 114
Council of People's Commissars, 334
Curzon, Lord, 240

Da Zhonghua Match Company, 132
Dai Jitao, 199
Daikyakka shugi, 312
Dalian, 198
Dante, 107
Datong Mines, 145
Datong ribao, 312
Datong shu, 75, 83
dazhong, 316
De, Prince, 210
December Ninth Movement (1935), 179, 238
Deng Geng, 310, 313
Deng Yanhua, 316
Deng Zihui, 345
Denmark, 192
Depression, Great, 135-36

Dewey, John (1859-1952), 154
Ding Richang, 33, 43, 51-53, 57n, 58n, 225, 228, 230, 306; position of, 30, 38; and changes to the examination system, 35, 45; and the self-strengthening movement 37-38, 41; view of reforms, 39; and the foundation of Chinese newspapers, 47; and the abolition of sinecures, 48; on economic development, 226
Ding Wenjiang, 103
Dingxian, 170
Dong Huai, 32
Dongfong zazhi, 83
Dorrill, William, 336
Douhet, Guilio, 98
duli zizhu, 341

Eastman, Lloyd E., 94, 105, 111, 119n
education, role of education under GMD, 12-13, 153-54; reforms in, 35, 255; social role of, 153-54; 176-77; social basis of, 169-70; and the position of women, 77, 79, 82, 170-73 *passim*; role of bureaucracy in, 180; Japan and Germany role models for, 73; and the curriculum for women, 74, 78 examination system, and bureaucracy reform, 45; abolition of, 159, 258, 260 (see also women, examination system)
Eitel, E.J., 299-300
Emanuel, Victor, 114
Emperor Protection Society, 259
Ernü yingxiong zhuan, 66
Esherick, Joseph, 270, 272
Executive Yuan, 202
extraterritoriality, 188, 191 193-94, 196, 199, 224, 230

Fairbank, John King, 278
Far Eastern Cultural Association, 116
fascism, 94-95, 100-05, 108, 110-11, 116
fei, 306
feiyue, 191
Feng Guifen, 7, 27, 31, 33, 40-41, 48, 56n, 58n;
Feng Yuxiang, 82, 196, 204
Fenghu Academy, 302
Fifth Congress of the National

INDEX

Federation of Educational Associations, 154
Fincher, John, 273-75, 278
FitzGerald, C.P., 251
foot-binding, 8, 68-70 *passim*, 72; extent of, 79
Four Modernisations, 4
France, 98, 106, 118, 148, 192-93, 232, 234, 277
Franco-Prussian War, 110
French Revolution, 87, 107
Friedman, Edward, 311
Fu Zuoyi, 210
fuguo qiangbing, 223
Fujian, 204
Fung, Edmund, 276-78
Funü zazhi, 83, 84
fuqiang, 41
Fuzhou Navy Yard, 36, 38, 45
Fuzhou, 289

Galimberti, Cesare, 100, 108
Gansu, 210
Garibaldi, 107-08
General Bureau of Foreign Affairs (1901), 238
gengzhan, 43
Gentile, 116
gentry, 262; reaction to 1911 Revolution, 260; conservatism of, 260; divisions within, 260, 263; influence on the masses, 261; relations with bourgeoisie, 261; and creation of reform movement, 253
Geothe (initials unknown), 111
Gerarchia, 108
Germany, 18, 73, 94, 95, 97, 98, 102, 103, 112, 115-18, 192, 193, 234, 243; colonialisation of Shangdong, 238-39
Gong Zizhen, 30; attitude to reform, 28
Gong, Prince, 28, 29, 32, 36, 55n, 222
Grandi Dino, 96
Great Harmony on Earth, 155, 187, 189
Great Proletarian Cultural Revolution, 113
Grey, Edward, 242
Gu WeiJun (Wellington Koo), 118
guandu shangban, 51, 222, 226
Guangxi, 176
Guangxu, Emperor, 256, 259
Guangzhou, 2, 3, 30, 166, 176, 186, 228, 254, 289
guanshang yiti, 51
Guiliang, 28, 32, 33, 55n
Guomindang (GMD), 109, 111, 117, 139, 336, 338; influence of Italy on, 9-10; programme of the, 11; and lack of control over industry, 12; educational aims of, 12; reaction to Japan's invasion of Manchuria, 15; in alliance with CCP, 21, 331; problems of, 93-94; Sun Yat-sen's view of, 104; divisions within, 142; Third National Congress of, 155; and educational aims, 166, 175, 177-78; extent of education under, 169, 171-72; First National Congress of, 171; Extraordinary National Congress of, 174; Programme of Armed Resistance and National Reconstruction, 174; Second National Congress, 189; Fifth National Congress, 209; and mass movements, 185; anti-imperialism of 186-87; fourth encirclement campaign, 333; and the unequal treaties, 190-198 *passim*; fifth encirclement campaign, 331, 335; Fourth Plenum of CEC of, 178, 186; Fifth Plenum of CEC of, 187
Guo Taiqi, 118
guoji minsheng, 42

Hague, The, 207
Hainan Island, 290
Hakka, 356, 361; rise of as ethnic group, 19, 289, 300-1; conflict with Punti, 19, 287, 290, 295, 299-300, 305, 307; position under Qing dynasty, 20; response to 1911 revolution, 20; and the Taiping Rebellion, 287; influence of, 288; relations with CCP, 288; relations with GMD, 288; differences from neighbours, 289; and perfectural spread, 295, 298-99; 318; and the Cantonese, 287-300 *passim*; anti-foreign sentiments of, 303; on foot-binding, 305; on the role of women, 305; and the gazetteers, 306; and language, 307, 317; and a rise in self-consciousness, 308; students in Japan, 309, 312; political participation of, 309-11; and the Wolcott

INDEX

incident, 311; and the Japanese report on, 312-13, 315-16; position in Guangdong, 315-16; and military representation, 315; and the establishment of Soviets, 288, 318
Hammond (initials unknown), 142
Hankou, 81, 193
Hanzu kefushi, 309
Harbin, 195
Hart, Robert, 29, 243
Hart-Wade Memoranda, 37, 49
He Qi, 224
He Xiangning, 80
He-Umezu, 207
Hirota Kōki, 207-08
Hitler, 97 98, 101, 103, 106, 109, 115
'Hoklos', 288-91, 309, 315
Holmgren, Jennifer, 66
Hong Kong, 80, 119, 176, 312
Hotta (initial unknown), 116
Hu Hanmin, 195, 201, 310
Hu Shi, 102, 204-05
Hua Mulan, 66
Huabei Coal Company, 145
Huainan mine, 142, 144
Huanan Rice Company, 140
Huang Fu, 203; and the unequal treaties, 190
Huang Jie, 308
Huang Junzai, 28
Huang Linshu, 315
Huang Xing, 278
Huang Zhao, 307
Huang Zunxian, 255, 307-8
Huangchao Rebellion, 304
Huangpu (Whampoa) Military Academy, 105, 313
Huangzhou, 188, 206, 302
Huazhong Coal Industry Company, 144
Huludao, 198
Hunan, 131, 270, 328
Hundred Days' Reform, 259

Ikias (*She*), 311
Imperialism, 212, 236, 244, 338; Japanese, 5, 15, 154, 197, 208, 335; view of under Nationalists, 187
Imperial Maritime Customs Service 241-42
India, 240

Institute of Banking, 139
Italy, 93, 94, 95, 102, 107-09, 114-15; model for China, 9-10, 95, 99, 100, 106, 118; relations with Japan, 10, 99, 113, 115, 117-18; and the Boxer indemnity, 98, 206; and Shanghai invasion, 118; and conflict with China over Japan, 115; signs trade agreement with Japan, 117; signs tariff agreement with China, 192

Japan, 18, 21, 38, 77-78, 80, 97, 118, 139, 146, 173, 175, 177-80 *passim*, 186, 211-12, 232, 273; imperialism of, 5, 15, 26, 154, 197, 208; defeat of China in 1895, 8; relations with Italy, 10, 99, 113, 115, 117-18; contrast with China, 11, 15; control of Shandong mines, 11, 197; war with China (1937-1945), 12; rivalry with China, 15; invasion of Taiwan by, 39, 49; invasion of Manchuria by, 96, 133, 186; control of Chinese coal industry, 134-35, 148; and the attack on Shanghai, 135, 202; views on treaties with China, 191-92; recognition of Nationalist Government, 192; relations with Nationalist Government, 186, 191-210 *passim*; and Shandong (1928), 197; withdraws from League of Nations, 202; creates Manchukuo, 202; conflict with China over Korea, 246-47; defeats China (1895), 253-54; and the 1911 Revolution, 267-68; and the Hakkas, 309, 312-13, 315-16; school system seen as model, 73; opens embassy in Nanjing, 98; and rise of militarism, 99; signs tripartite agreement, 116; on the Chinese coal cartel, 143; criticism of Japanese model of education, 154; and internal Chinese politics, 193; and control over North-east, 244; and Chinese nationalism, 252; united front against, 338-349 *passim*
Japanese Guandong Army, 198, 201, 207, 210
Ji'nan incident, 197.
Jiang Baili, 93-94, 98, 99, 102, 106-19 *passim*

INDEX

Jiang Guangnai, 202
Jiang Menglin, 167
Jiang Tingfu, 103-4, 118
Jiang Weiguo, 102
Jiang Zuobin, 201, 208
Jiangnan Arsenal, 36, 38
Jiangsu province, 224-25; education within 167-69
Jiangxi, 131, 199
Jiangxi Soviet period (1930-1934), 20, 22, 330, 337, 339
jiangzu jiangxi, 341
Jiaozhou, 239
Jiefang ribao, 347
jieji zhengce, 345
Jilin-Changchun Railway, 247
Jin Ling, 82
Jin Yi, 75
Jincheng Bank, 145
Jincheng Banking Corporation, 144
Jinggangshan, 328
Jinghua yuan, 67
jingshi shuyuan, 46
jingshi, 36, 48, 305
Jingxing Mines, 139, 145
Jinzhou, 198, 200-1
jiro fuqing, 189
Jiujiang, 193
Jordan, John, 243
Jouett, John Hamilton, 206
Ju Jiahua, 105
Judicial Yuan, 207
juzhong juwai yixin, 46

kai fengqi, 51
kai liyuan, 42
Kailuan, 141
Kailuan Mining administration, 133-37, 139, 141, 143-46, 246
Kaiping Slack, 145
kaiyuan jieliu, 226
Kang Youwei, 70, 75, 83, 84, 253, 256, 259, 264
Kangxi emperor, 68
Kefei, 306
'Keji', 294
Keijia fengsu, 316
Khabarovsk Protocol, 196
Komura Jutaro, 246
Kong Xiangxi (H.H. Kung), 97, 98, 99, 114, 128
Koo, Wellington (Mrs), 96
Korea, 38, 189, 232, 246
Kossuth (initials unknown), 109
Krupps, 97

Kuhn, Philip, 299
Kunming, 176

Lampson, Miles, 202
League of Nations, 114, 199-200-02, 204
Legislative Yuan, 195
Leizhou peninsula, 290, 300
Lenin, 113
Lhasa Convention, 240
Li Fan, 43
Li Hongzhang, 31, 43, 51-52, 56n, 222-23, 225, 256-57; governor-general of Zhil, 30; on foreign intrusion, 34-35; and the establishment of Chinese arsenal, 36; role in self-strengthening movement, 39; on the role of Western Learning, 45; on programme of economic growth, 226, 228; and the decline of self-strengthening movement, 253; and regional army, 275
Li Jishen, 204, 313-14
Li Shoutang, 45, 47-48
Li Yangjing, 315
Li Zhenfang, 316
Liang Qichao, 75, 83, 84, 87, 106, 108-09, 112, 228, 253, 256; view on education for women, 71-74 *passim*; and the Italian revival, 107; founds Emperor Protection Society, 259
Liang Shanbo and Zhu Yingtai, 67
Lianzhou mine, 246
Liao T'ai-ch'u, 162-63, 174, 178
Liao Zhongkai, 310
Lienu zhuan, 64-65
lijin, 41, 192
Lin Daquan, 306-7
Lin Sen, 108, 114
Lin Yizhong, 315
Lin Yungai, 315
Lin Zexu, 28
lingdao yiyuanhua, 347
liquan, 34
Little, Mrs., 69
Liu Hongsheng, 132
Liu Kunyi, 31, 35, 37, 257, 268
Liu Wenduo, 93- 98-101, 114-15, 117
Liu Yongfu, 310
Lloyd-triestino Line, 96
Lojacono, Vincente, 98-99, 113
London Missionary Society, 224, 299
Long Jiguang, 311

INDEX

Long March, 21, 210, 337-38
Lordi Roberto, 98, 206
Luda Company, 138, 143-45
Luo Wen'gan, 202-03
Luo Yingliu, 46
Luoyang, 202
Lytton Commission, 202; report of, 205

Ma Jianzhong, 224
Ma Ling, 224
Machiavelli (initials unknown), 101
MacKinnon, Stephen, 272
Malaya, 80
Manchukuo (see Manchuria)
Manchuria, 76, 117, 135, 143, 195-98, 200-3, 207-8, 212; invasion of by Japan, 15, 133, 186; Ministry of Foreign Affairs, 104; position within National Government, 15
Mao Zedong, 20-21, 318, 328-29, 336, 339, 343, 346, 350; conflict with RRS, 332, 335, 337; on mass mobilisation, 333; 'Preliminary Conclusions on the Land Investigation Campaign', 334; position within party, 335; view at Zuni Conference, 337; on Wang's analysis of CCP defeat, 240; on contradictions within China, 341; on united front groups, 341-42; conflict with Wang Ming, 342-43; on class relations with China, 343; 'On New Democracy', 343-44; 'three-thirds system', 21, 344; 'On Theory', 110; 'On Practice', 110
Marco Polo Bridge incident, 93, 211, 241
Marco Polo, 99
Marxism, 87, 113, 155, 261
Match Sales Union, 132
May Fourth era, 12, 63, 72, 74, 85, 87, 107, 112, 154; results of, 9
Mayer, W.F., 300
Mazzini, 106-9, 112
McTyeire School The, 69
Mei River, 289, 292, 294, 307, 309
Meiji Restoration, 268
Meishu shizhuan, 307
Mencius, 65
Miao Peinan, 314
Military Affairs Commission, 202
Milne, William, C., 68
Ministry of Education, 78, 153, 156-57, 159; reforms in, 160; introduces compulsory education, 166; Second National Education Conference, 167; and female education, 170
Ministry of Industry, 131, 141-44, 147
Missionaries, 164-65, 230; attitude to foot-binding, 68-69; and child-slavery, 68; and the education of females, 68-69, 74, 78, 82, 171
Mongolia, 159
Morrison, George, 239-40, 245
Mortecuccoli, 118
Moscow (see Soviet Union)
mufu, 228
Mussolini, Benito, 9, 10, 93, 95, 96, 97, 98, 100, 104, 106, 108-09, 110, 112, 114-15, 117, 206; attitude to China, 99-100; view of Japanese militarism, 99, 113; and concept of fascism, 101, 111
Myrdal, Gunnar, 127

Nanjing, 2, 10, 81, 98, 99, 104, 115, 140, 147, 188, 190, 196-99, 203-04; Treaty of, 2-3
Naples, 96
Nathan, Andrew, 262
Nathan, E.J., 145
National Bank of Shanghai, 144
National Coal Conference, 140
National Commercial Bank, 145
National Economic Council, 131, 138
National Economic Reconstruction, 100
National Education Conference, 153, 155, 170
National Government (1928-1949), 6; response to Japanese Imperialism, 5; relations with Italy, 10
National Liberation Vanguard, 342
National Mining Association, 135
National Peking University, 176
National Reconstruction Commission, 142
National South-west Associated University, 176
National Tea Company, 131
Nationalism, 12, 13, 157-58, 164, 176, 179, 187, 230, 252, 257, 276, 307; and foreign policy objectives, 187; economic programme of, 127-28; twelve educational points of, 155; Law on Primary

381

Schools, 156; Law on Secondary Schools, 157; and tertiary education, 158; and technical schools, 158; and foreign nationals, 194; and tariff treaties, 192; relations with Soviet Union, 186, 194, 202; relations with Japan, 110 *passim*; relations with CCP, 329-49 *passim*
Nazi (see Germany)
Negotiation Bureau (1900), 238
neiluan waihuan, 37
Netherlands, 192
new armies, 269, 276; political stance of, 262
New Fourth Army, 345-46
New Life Movement, 100, 102, 105, 111, 113, 175, 178
Nine-Power Treaty, 200
Nineteenth Route Army, 202, 314, 336
Ningbo, 144, 200
Ningdu Conference (1932), 335
North China Union College for Women, 78
North River, 289, 295
North-west Bandit-Suppression Forces, 210
Northern Expedition, 155, 190, 314, 328
Norway, 192
Nu jie zhong, 75, 81

opium, 16, 231, 234, 241, 292
Opium War (1839-1842), 1, 2, 234, 273
Ouxhou wenyi fuxing shi, 107

Paris, 96, 118
Parks, Coble, 147
Patterson, Orlando, 291, 301
peasants, as revolutionary force, 257, 327; divisions within, 334; role of in mass movements, 333; place in communist ideology, 328, 331-32, 337
Peng Zhen, 344-45
People's Federated Anti-Japanese Army, 204
People's Liberation Army, 105
People's Republic of China, founding of, 3; programmes of, 4; continuity with pre-revolution China, 4
People's Tribune, The, 102
Perovskaya, Sophia, 76

Pokotilov, 240
Political Studies Clique, 110, 139
Portsmouth Conference (1965), 269
'practical statecraft', 26, 35
Protestants, 235; educational institutions of, 13, 164-65, 171
Punti, 19, 287, 290, 295, 299-300, 305, 307, 316

qi quan zai wo, 34
Qian Yongming, 139
Qin Liangyu, 66
Qin-Doihara Agreement (1935), 207
Qing dynasty, 1, 5, 6, 187; reforms under, 7-8; reaction to Wade-Hart memoranda, 39; and efforts at modernisation, 127; revised criminal code of, 81
Qing Prince, 236, 245
Qingdai xueshu gailun, 107
Qingdao, 200, 239
Qinghua University, 176
Qiu Fengjia, 308-11
Qiu Jin, 76, 80
qunce qunli, 49

Rajchman, Ludwig, 200
Rassengna di politica internazionale, 108
Reconstruction Finance Corporation, 205
Red Army, 331, 335, 339
Red Guards, 113
reformers, social background, 253; relations with dynasty, 47, 254; differences with revolutionaries, 254; gain support of Empress Dowager, 258; attempt reform of education system, 46, 258; interest in Western learning, 258-59; role of bourgeoisie in, 262; and the Hundred Days, 254; divisions within, 261; opposition to Yuan Shikai, 266; and the bureaucracy, 44, 46-8; on the influence of the West, 45; relations with foreign powers, 222 (see also Ding Richang, Li Hongzhang, Shen Baozhen, Zuo Zongtang and Tang Caichang)
Rehe province, 203
Reichswehr, 205
Revolution of, 1911, 18, 19, 252, 257, 259, 264-65; different views of, 266-278 *passim*

382

INDEX

revolutionaries, 271; social backgrounds of, 253; relations with dynasty, 254; and the Guangzhou revolt, 254; opposition to Yuan Shikai, 266; and anti-Manchu sentiment, 268
Rhoads, Edward, 272-74
Ribbentrop, 116-118
Ricci, Matteo, 224
Richard, Timothy, 74, 311
Risorgimento, 106-107, 109
Roland, Madame, 76
Rome, 94-95, 98, 101, 106, 108, 110, 114, 116-117
Rome-Berlin alliance, 115
Rome-Tokyo axis, 113
Rong Hong, 228, 230, 232
Rozman, Gilbert, 2
Ruilin, 30
Russia (see Soviet Union)
Russian Returned Students, domination of CCP, 331; rivalry with Mao, 331, 334-35; conflict in party, 337, 349; agreement with Mao over land policy, 20; criticism of united front, 21
Russo-Japanese War, 240

Salt Bank, 145
Schram, Stuart R, 269-70
Second Sino-foreign War (1856-1860), results of, 3
Seeckt, von General, 98, 205
Selden, Mark, 346
'self-strengthening', 25, 54, 70, 253; definition of, 32; basic principles of, 33-35; objectives of, 41-42, 226; and relations to foreign powers, 187, 222, 225
Shaanxi, 210
shanduo tianshao, 295
Shang Yang, 43
Shanghai, 95-96, 97, 98, 109, 117-118, 128, 133, 135-136, 140-141, 143, 144, 147, 170, 200, 338
Shanghai International Settlement, 193
Shanghai Power Company, 145
shangwu, 154
shangxia yixin, 46
shangzhan, 43, 226
Shanxi, 139, 166-167, 170, 210
shehui jiaoyu, 170
Shen Baozhen, 35, 37, 38, 39, 41, 44-48 *passim*, 52-53

Shen Daihe, 315
Sheng Xuanhuai, 225, 245, 247
Shenyang (Mukden) incident, 198-99, 201
Shenzhou nü zi xinshi, 81
shi yü neng, 110
Shijiazhuang, 139
shiwu, 53
shixue, 35
shiyong zhi cai, 35
shou liquan, 35
shouhui liquan, 35, 43
Shuiwuchu, 242
Shumu dawen, 228
Siam, 189
Sih, Paul (Xue Guangqian), 100, 110
Sima Guang, 47
Sino-Japanese Commercial Treaty (1896), 197, 211
Sino-Japanese Conflict (1932), 96, 115, 135, 314, 346
Sino-Japanese War (1894-1895), 63, 70, 106, 288
Sino-Soviet Agreement (1924), 195-196
sishu, 162-165 *passim*, 168, 174, 178
Skinner, William, 19, 292
Smiles, Samuel, 110
Snow, Helen, 340
Society for Strengthening Learning, 256
Society for Women's Participation in Government, 81
Song Jiaoren, 278; leads Nationalist Party, 265; assassinated, 265
Song Xiang, 304
Song Ziwen (T.V. Soong), 98, 99, 140, 143, 199-200, 203, 205
Sony Zheyuan, 201, 203
South Manchurian Railway Company, 133, 196, 198
South-west Political Council, 147
Soviet Union, 18, 98, 103, 118-119, 186, 193-194, 205, 212, 244, 252, 342; and the Chinese Eastern Railway, 195; resumes relations with China, 203
Soviet Party Representatives' Conference (1937), 341
Spain, 192
Special Foreign Affairs Committee, 199-200
Stefani News Agency, 100
Stefani, Alberto de, 93, 100, 114-115, 119

INDEX

Stimson, Henry, 200
Sugimura, 115
Suiyuan, 210
Sun Jia'nai, 256
Sun Yat-sen, 105, 177, 187, 278; and post-1911 programme, 11; and Hakka support, 303, 308-309, 313; on widening party base, 267; and path to modernisation, 127; supports Yuan as president, 265; seeks support against dynasty, 264; on foreign policy, 187; Principle of People's Livelihood, 128; Fundamentals of National Reconstruction, 128; Three Principles of the People, 104, 189; 'General Theory of Knowledge and Action', 104; and the first Chinese revolutionary group, 253-254
Suzhou University, 101, 104
Sweden, 192

Taipings, 3, 29, 39, 263, 287, 303, 327
Taiwan, 3, 39, 49, 226, 311
Tan Sitong, 74-75, 84, 89
Tan Yankai, 167
Tanaka, Kukuei, 197-98
Tang Caichang, 256
Tang Hualong, 166
Tang Liangli, 102-03
Tang Qunying, 81
Tang Ronghao, 239
Tang Shaoyi, 231, 237-39; governor of Fengtian, 246; reforms of the railways, 243; on foreign intrusion, 240; on opium, 241-42; becomes Premier of Republic, 243
Tang Tingshu, 224, 228, 231-32, 237
Tang Xiangming, 277
Tanggu Truce (1933), 203-04
tariffs, 188, 191-92, 199, 210, 223, 230, 233
Three Principles of the People (*sanmin zhuyi*), 104, 155, 177, 189
Tianjin Customs daotai, 239
Tianjin massacre, 230
Tianjin, 3, 139, 193, 200
tianxia weigong, 189
Tianzu Hui, 69
Tibet, 29, 159, 240
Tieliang, 242
Ting River, 289, 292, 294
Tokyo, 114, 115-17, 186, 196, 198, 200-01, 207-08, 246

tongchou quanju, 34
tongji quanju, 34
Tongmenghui, 80, 267-68, 308-9
tongpan chouhua, 44
Tongzhi Restoration (1862-1874), 94
tongzi jun, 157
Tours, B.G., 310
Trautman, Oskar, 115
treaties, 185-86, 196-98, 211, 222, 234; unequal, 187, 189, 190-198 *passim*
Treaty of Shimoneseki (1895), 229
Turkey, 102, 103
Twenty-ninth Army, 201, 203

United Hakka Associations, 312
United States, 17, 43, 46, 73, 84, 98, 118, 131, 142, 146, 148, 186, 193-94, 200-1, 205, 212, 230, 252; signs treaty with Nanking, 192
United States Reserve Corps, 206

Versailles, Treaty of, effect on Italy, 106; Chinese delegation to, 106
Vietnam, 176, 232
Volpe, Gioacchino, 106
Volunteer Corps to Resist Russia, 76

Wade, Thomas, 29
waiwu, 32
Waiwubu, 240, 245-46
Wang Anshi, 38
Wang Chonghui, 207
Wang Jingwei, 80, 102, 117, 202-3, 343; on Tanggu True, 204; criticism of Japana, 206
Wang Ming 21, 331; and 1st August declaration, 338-39; opposition to Mao, 342; on CCP defeat, 337-38
Wang Tao, 224, 228
Wang Tao, 27
Wang Zhengting, view on treaties, 190-92; on relations with West, 193; on relations with Japan, 193; on relations with Britain, 193; on relations with Soviet Union, 195; 'revolutionary diplomacy' of, 197
wangdao, 189
Wanguo gongbao, 69
War of Resistance, 13, 173, 211, 345 349
warlordism, 277-78, 328
Watatsuki, 201
Wayaobao, 339
Wei Yuan, 28, 32, 36

INDEX

Weihaiwei, 193
weimin xingli, 227
weiyu choumou, 33
Wen Kang, 66
Wen Yiduo, 176
Wen Zhonghe, 306-07
Weng Tonghe, 256
Wenxiang, 28, 32, 33, 55n
Western Fujian Revolutionary Base Government, 318
White Lotus Rebellion (1793-1802), 263
Wolcott, R.D., 311
women, position in traditional China, 8, 63-64; changes in May Fourth era, 9; view of in Qing period, 63, 65, 67, 77, 79; role of in Confucian society, 64, 66; and levels of education, 77-78; as seen by Western missionaries, 68, 69; and educational curriculum, 78; and anti-foot-binding campaigns, 69, 82; male support for rights of, 74-75; and education, 69-72 *passim*, 77-78, 79, 82, 170-73; positions of, outside family, 73; position of, within family, 73; percentage of school population, 79; and the role model Qiu Jin, 76-77; and the role of journals, 79-80; and employment, 80, 83; under the Republic, 81-85; contrast in rural-urban women's role, 75
Women's Society of Comrades to Resist Russia, 76
World Economic Conference, 205
Wright, Mary, 94, 269, 274
Wu Dingchang, 139
Wu Peifu, 314
Wu Qingshu, 81
Wu Rulun, 87n; attitude to women's education, 77
Wu Tingfang, 240
Wu, Empress, 67
Wuchang uprising, 264, 276; results of 265
Wuhan Women's Defence Corps, 342
Wuhan, 200
Wuxi, 225

Xi'an, 116, 178, 210, 340
Xiamen, 193
Xianfeng emperor, 3
Xiang Jingyu, 87

xiangyue, 299
xiaozhong, 316
Xin qingnian, 83, 84
xinfa, 37
Xinyangwupai, 268
xiuyue, 191
Xu Jiyu, 32
Xu Run, 224, 232
Xue Fucheng, 225, 227
Xue Nanming, 225
Xue Shaouxuan, 225
Xue Xuzeng, 302-3; on Hakka origins, 304-7
Xuehaitang, 228

Yan Xishan, 82, 105
Yang Buwei, 80
Yang Jie, 99
Yang Shixiang, 238
Yangmen nü jiang, 66
yangwai, 203
yangwu, 36, 37, 53
Yangzi, 49, 139, 142
Yanji border dispute, 246
Yao Yuping, 310, 314
Yao, 290
Ye Chucang, 309
Ye Jianying, 314
Yen, James Y.C., 170
Yidali jianguo sangjie zhuan, 109-10
yiguan zhi zu, 290
Yingkou, 198
Yokoyama Suguru, 275; view of 1911 Revolution, 268-69, 271
Yongzheng emperor, 47
Young China, 237-47 *passim*
Young Husband expedition (1904), 240
Young, Ernest, 272
Youth Salvation Corps, 342
Yuan Shikai, 18, 270, 268, 357; extent of opposition to, 266; seeks to establish monarchy, 266; first cabinet collapses, 265; gains presidency, 265, 276; trains new army, 255, 265; as Governor-General of Zhili, 239, 275; as Governor of Ji'nan, 238; rise of, 236; fall of, 17, 227; role of women under, 81; view on education, 154; Governor of Shandong, 257; and faction within bureaucracy, 245; criticism of, 273; and the Manchus, 275; and the counter-revolution (1913), 311; death

of, 328
Yuesheng mine, 142
Yunnan province, 170; education within 168-69

Zhang Fakui, 313-14
Zhang Jian, 256, 278
Zhang Licun, 310
Zhang Qun, 209
Zhang Xuan, 309
Zhang Xueliang ('Young Marshal'), 95-96, 97, 98, 111; support for Mussolini, 101-103; role in Manchuria, 196; refuses to fight communists, 116; kidnaps Chiang, 210, 340
Zhang Yintang, 241
Zhang Zhidong, 39, 72, 74, 77, 80, 228, 255-57, 268, 277
Zhang Zhujun, 81
Zhao Fengchang, 276
Zhao Shuji, 33
Zhejiang, 144
Zhen Lanbin, 43
Zhen Zuolin, 53, 195, 198
zhenbei, 316
Zheng Guanying, 224, 228, 231, 237
Zheng Guanying, 27
Zheng Guofan, 39, 222, 225, 228; on Chinese society, 28-29; on foreign help, 34; and the founding of arsenal, 36; on self-strengthening, 37; on economic development, 43; sends students overseas, 46; death of, 110; and regional armies, 275
Zhengfeng Company, 139
Zhenjiang, 193
Zhili, 30, 245
Zhong Yonghe, 309
Zhongfu Bank, 145
Zhongguo xin nü jie, 68, 69, 75, 82
Zhonghua Industrial Company, 145
Zhongshan University, 315
zhongwai yixin, 46
Zhongxing, 137, 139, 141, 143-44
Zhongxue wei ti, Xixue wei yong, 40
Zhou Baoheng, 315
Zhou Fohai, 167
Zhou Fu, 238
Zhou Huifu, 312
Zhou Shenxuan, 304
Zhou Zuomin, 139
Zhu De, 318
Zhu Xi, 47
Zhuge Liang, 101
Zichuan mines, 193
ziqiang zhi duo, 37
zizhi, 37
zizhu zhi quan, 34
Zonghi Yamen, 28, 29, 36, 37, 39, 44, 45, 222
Zou Lu, 308-10, 315
Zou Rong, 111
Zunyi Conference (1935), 237
Zuo Qiuming, 47
Zuo Zongtang, 37, 48-49, 52, 275